P

GENERAL EDITOR: CHRISTOPHER RICKS

POEMS AND BALLADS & ATALANTA IN CALYDON

ALGERNON CHARLES SWINBURNE was born in 1837 of an aristocratic family. He was educated for a time at Eton (where he may have developed his fascination with flagellation) and later matriculated at Balliol College, Oxford. There he met and formed lasting friendships with Pre-Raphaelite artists and writers, including William Morris, Edward Burne-Jones and Dante Gabriel Rossetti. Over the next few years, he travelled in France and Italy, wrote many poems and led a Bohemian life in London. He lived for a time in Tudor House, with Rossetti. Under the influence of the death of his sister, the end of his romantic attachment to his cousin Mary Gordon, and the collapse of the Tudor House ménage, Swinburne wrote *Atalanta in Calydon*, published in 1865, the work that first brought him critical notice; Tennyson praised it highly. *Poems and Ballads* appeared in the next year and brought sensational success and the angry attention of critics who were outraged by its choice of topics (sado-masochism, lesbianism, necrophilia and the rejection of Christianity). His behaviour and bouts of drinking became worse, and he was often rescued by his family. Eventually, in 1879, he was taken to live with his friend Theodore Watts (later Watts-Dunton) in Putney, under whose watchful eye Swinburne's health improved and drinking ceased. Many more volumes of poetry followed, including the second and third series of *Poems and Ballads* (1878 and 1889) and *Tristram of Lyonesse* (1882). In addition, he published many dramas and works of literary criticism. He wrote in a wide variety of literary forms, from classical verse styles to medieval and Renaissance genres, from burlesques to ballads and roundels, and had a large influence on early Modern poets. Swinburne lived in comparative seclusion with Watts-Dunton at The Pines, Putney, until his death in 1909.

KENNETH HAYNES has written on German and British Hellenism and edited *Horace in English* (with D. S. Carne-Ross) for Penguin Classics. He is a member of the Department of Classical Studies at Boston University and the Assistant Director of the Editorial Institute at Boston University.

ALGERNON CHARLES
SWINBURNE

POEMS AND BALLADS &
ATALANTA IN CALYDON

Edited by **KENNETH HAYNES**

PENGUIN BOOKS

PENGUIN BOOKS

Published by the Penguin Group
Penguin Books Ltd, 27 Wrights Lane, London w8 5TZ, England
Penguin Putnam Inc., 375 Hudson Street, New York, New York 10014, USA
Penguin Books Australia Ltd, Ringwood, Victoria, Australia
Penguin Books Canada Ltd, 10 Alcorn Avenue, Toronto, Ontario, Canada M4V 3B2
Penguin Books India (P) Ltd, 11, Community Centre, Panchsheel Park, New Delhi – 110 017, India
Penguin Books (NZ) Ltd, Private Bag 102902, NSMC, Auckland, New Zealand
Penguin Books (South Africa) (Pty) Ltd, 5 Watkins Street, Denver Ext 4, Johannesburg 2094, South Africa

Penguin Books Ltd, Registered Offices: Harmondsworth, Middlesex, England

Poems and Ballads first published 1866
Atalanta in Calydon first published 1865
Published together in Penguin Classics 2000
1

Set in 10/11.5 pt PostScript Monotype Ehrhardt
Typeset by Rowland Phototypesetting Ltd, Bury St Edmunds, Suffolk
Printed in England by Clays Ltd, St Ives plc

CONTENTS

ACKNOWLEDGEMENTS

I am grateful to friends for their generous help: Rosalie Anders, Ron Bush, Donald Carne-Ross, David Ferry, Jeff Henderson, Ellen O'Reilly, Bruce Redford, Christopher Ricks, Lisa Rodensky, Roger Shattuck, and Rosanna Warren. I am also grateful to the Interlibrary Loan Department of Mugar Library at Boston University, the Arnold Arboretum, and the Fitzwilliam Museum of Cambridge University.

ACKNOWLEDGMENTS

PREFACE

Selection

The present volume contains *Poems and Ballads* (1866) and *Atalanta in Calydon* (1865). Although it was published later, *Poems and Ballads* is here printed first. Many of the poems in it were written before *Atalanta*, and it is, perhaps, the better introduction to Swinburne. The two works are the most famous and influential of Swinburne's writings, and they also contain much of his best poetry.

Dates

Poems and Ballads was published in mid-July 1866 (Lang, *Letters* Vol. 1, p. 167) by Edward Moxon & Co. The volume inspired violent criticism, and Moxon withdrew the book. John Camden Hotten bought the approximately 700 remaining copies from Moxon and reissued it with his own title-page. Later in the same year, Hotten reprinted it.

In 'Dedication, 1865' Swinburne describes the earliest poems of the collection as written seven years previously, that is, in 1858. A convenient summary of what is known about the dates of the composition may be found in Ann Walder, *Swinburne's Flowers of Evil* (Uppsala, 1976) pp. 64–7; she relies mainly on Georges Lafourcade, *La Jeunesse de Swinburne* (Paris, 1928). In 1876, Swinburne assembled a list of seventeen poems that he planned to have transferred to a projected volume of specifically early verse: 'The Leper', 'Rondel ['Kissing her hair']', 'A Song in Time of Order', 'A Song in Time of Revolution', 'Before Parting', 'The Sundew', 'At Eleusis', 'August', 'A Christmas Carol', 'The Masque of Queen Bersabe', 'St. Dorothy', 'The Two Dreams', 'Aholibah', 'After Death', 'May Janet', 'The Sea-Swallows', and 'The Year of Love' (Lang, 3, 200).

Atalanta in Calydon was published in March 1865 by Edward Moxon & Co., Swinburne's father having paid 'considerably more than £100' for it (Lang, 2, 213). Moxon brought out a second edition in 1865, and Hotten took it over in 1866. For more details, see the notes to *Atalanta in Calydon*.

Text

The text of this selection relies on the 1904 *Poems*, which differs only slightly from the 1865 *Atalanta in Calydon* and the 1866 *Poems and Ballads*. Uncertainties about stanza breaks at the foot of the page in the irregular choral odes of *Atalanta* have been resolved by consulting the two editions of 1865. The few minor errors in the first dedicatory Greek epigraph have been silently corrected and the correct 1865 text restored. Four errors apparently reintroduced into the 1904 *Poems* from an uncorrected *Poems and Ballads* have been corrected (see Thomas James Wise, *A Bibliography of the Writings in Prose and Verse of Algernon Charles Swinburne*, 1925, p. 52). Several poems in *Poems and Ballads* had been published previously, sometimes with significant variations; bibliographical citations to these earlier versions have been included in the notes to individual poems.

Manuscripts

References to facsimiles, reproductions and descriptions of manuscripts have been included when known to me.

Life

In the Table of Dates and elsewhere, I have freely drawn on Rikky Rooksby, *A. C. Swinburne: A Poet's Life* (Scolar Press, 1997), the best-researched and most accurate of the biographies of Swinburne. In those cases where biographies offer conflicting accounts, I have followed Rooksby.

Annotation

The explanatory notes at the end of this volume are metrical, textual
and contextual. I have specified the metre of each lyric, occasionally
offering parallels or discussing its history. Difficult passages have
been glossed, and I have tried to identify sources, explain allusions,
and provide parallels. In addition, I have drawn on the large scholarly
literature about the French and Victorian contexts of many of
Swinburne's themes. I have tried to give credit to previous readers
for their discoveries but in general have corrected occasional errors
in silence.

Scholarly reception

See Clyde K. Hyder, 'Algernon Charles Swinburne' in *The Victorian
Poets: A Guide to Research* (ed. F. E. Faverty, Harvard, 1968) and
Rikky Rooksby, 'A Century of Swinburne' in *The Whole Music of
Passion* (Scolar Press, 1993).

Currently, the only complete edition of Swinburne's works is
The Complete Works of Algernon Charles Swinburne, edited by Sir
Edmund Gosse and Thomas James Wise (known as the Bonchurch
edition, published 1925–7 and reprinted in 1968); however, the text
of this edition is unreliable. This collection includes the only full
bibliography, which is likewise untrustworthy.

In the second volume of *La Jeunesse de Swinburne* (Paris, 1928),
Georges Lafourcade attempted the only comprehensive criticism of
all Swinburne's early works. Critics who have subsequently
examined particular manuscripts in greater detail (among them,
Randolph Hughes in his edition of Swinburne's *Lucretia Borgia*,
1942, or Edward Philip Schuldt in his dissertation, *Four Early
Unpublished Plays of Algernon Charles Swinburne*, 1976) have found
many inaccuracies in Lafourcade's account. Nonetheless,
Lafourcade provided much information still not available elsewhere.

Several careful studies of Swinburne's style exist in German,
including H. W. F. Wollaeger, *Studien über Swinburne's Poetischen
Stil* (Heidelberg, 1899), Bruno Herlet, *Versuch eines Kommentars zu
Swinburnes 'Atalanta'* (Bamberg, 1909–10), and Alfred Eidenbenz,

Das Starre Wortmuster und die Zeit in Swinburne's 'Poems and Ballads' (Zürich, 1944).

Cecil Y. Lang published six volumes of Swinburne's letters in 1959–62, with comprehensive annotations and index. Terry L. Meyers has published (and is publishing) additional letters by Swinburne.

Clyde K. Hyder has edited *Swinburne Replies* (Syracuse, 1966), a collection of three of Swinburne's responses to his critics; *Swinburne: The Critical Heritage* (New York, 1970), a representative sample of the critical responses to Swinburne; and *Swinburne as Critic* (Routledge & Kegan Paul, 1972), an annotated and indexed anthology of Swinburne's literary and artistic criticism.

Kirk H. Beertz published a bibliography of secondary works about Swinburne in 1982.

The most pressing need in the Swinburne scholarship is a critical edition of his works, based on a careful study of the manuscripts and the establishment of the dates of composition. Timothy A. J. Burnett gives an example of such work in his study of the first manuscript page of 'Anactoria', and he and Nicholas Shrimpton offer another example in their editing of an early version of 'The Two Dreams' (both printed in *The Whole Music of Passion*, 1993).

Critical reception

Swinburne's poetry has inspired conflicting critical reactions. For the contemporary uproar over the immorality of Swinburne's *Poems and Ballads*, see Clyde K. Hyder, *Swinburne: The Critical Heritage* (1970). In the following paragraphs, when bibliographical information is not given, it can be found in Further Reading.

His poems have sometimes been found too long or too diffuse. Robert Browning objects to his verses because they combine 'the *minimum* of thought and idea in the *maximum* of word and phraseology' (*Critical Heritage*, p. 115). Swinburne's mother 'constantly deplores' the fact that he spoils his writing by not knowing when to stop (Lang, 4, 214). Matthew Arnold is offended by 'Swinburne's fatal habit of using one hundred words where one would suffice' (*Critical Heritage*, p. 117). A. E. Housman finds that even in Swinburne's best work 'there is no reason why they should begin where they do or end where they do; there is no reason why the middle should be in the middle; there is hardly a reason why, having once begun, they should ever end at all'. T. S. Eliot finds that Swinburne is diffuse but believes that his 'diffuseness is one of his glories'. Other critics, including Jerome J. McGann, have found that Swinburne's diffuseness is a way of creating effects through echoing and enhancing suggestions rather than through the concentration of a *mot juste*.

He has been found vague or meaningless. Tennyson's praise, 'He is a reed through which all things blow into music', is equivocal (*Critical Heritage*, p. 113). Housman believes that Swinburne almost totally lacked the ability to write descriptive poetry; instead of rendering nature, he 'picks up the sausage-machine into which he crammed anything and everything; round goes the handle, and out the other end comes . . . noise'. Ezra Pound writes that Swinburne 'neglected the value of words as words, and was intent on their value as sound', though he also finds that Swinburne's 'inaccurate writing' is 'by no means ubiquitous'. W. H. Auden generalizes that nineteenth-century poets typically have much greater prosodic skill but much less control of diction than twentieth-century poets (*19th Century British Minor Poets*, 1966), and perhaps the generalization applies with particular force to Swinburne. Lang disputes the charge of vagueness and finds in the poetry and the letters 'literal accuracy of the natural scenes' (Lang, 1, xxi).

His metrical accomplishments have been variously judged. Of the major Victorian poets, he employed the largest number of verse forms, according to Robert Huntington Fletcher: Browning wrote in about 200 verse forms; Tennyson, in about 240; Swinburne, in about 420 (*Journal of English and Germanic Philology*, 8, 1908). Pound admires his rhythm-building faculty, and in particular his ability to perceive and recreate Greek melopoeia. Housman enumerates his achievements: he made the anapest fit for serious poetry, dignifying and strengthening it so that it yielded a combination of speed and magnificence new to English poetry; he revitalized the heroic couplet; he had an unexampled control of rhyme and in particular a pre-eminent mastery of feminine rhyme. Nonetheless, Housman finds that his metres, like Pope's, appeal only to the 'external ear'. T. S. Eliot finds that the technical novelty of the metres wears off and their effect is diminished ('Reflections on "Vers Libre"', 1917).

Swinburne has been thought to be writing about literature rather than life. William Morris confesses that he could never really sympathize with Swinburne's poetry because he thought it 'founded on literature, not on nature' (*Critical Heritage*, p. 123). Housman agrees that the only theme Swinburne 'thoroughly loved and understood' was literature, and disputes Swinburne's insistence that literature is as valid a subject for poetry as any living thing. Eliot has been influential in his insistence that in Swinburne the object has ceased to exist and we are left with a complete, self-sufficient world of words. On the other hand, 'The Triumph of Time' has been called a *cri de coeur*. William Rossetti notes a paradox in many of the poems in *Poems and Ballads*: Swinburne is simultaneously exceedingly imitative and distinctly original (*Critical Heritage*, p. 70).

He has been found monotonous or narrow, especially in his later poetry. Gerard Hopkins writes that 'Swinburne's genius is astonishing, but it will, I think, only do one thing' (letter to Bridges, 1879). Housman contrasts the 'great and even overpowering richness' of *Poems and Ballads* with the threadbare style in the poems of his later life. Empson writes that Swinburne 'normally . . . only wrote well about his appalling ideas about sex' (*The Modern Poet*, ed. Ian Hamilton, 1968, p. 184). Rikky Rooksby provides a discriminating defence of some of the later poetry in 'Swinburne without Tears: A Guide to the Later Poetry', *Victorian Poetry* 26:4 (Winter 1988), 413–30.

A contemporary reviewer complained about the difficulty of his syntax and the 'wild prodigal way' he heaped images, metaphors, and allusions (*Critical Heritage*, p. 11). Some later critics have argued that this difficulty is intrinsic to the meaning of his verse, that the tension between the onward-rushing metre and a complex grammar requiring patient glossing is related to the experience of living a torn and divided life.

Influence

Despite the various and often unfavourable critical judgements of his verse, it had a marked influence on later poets.

Thomas Hardy's early and abiding high estimate of Swinburne, and indeed his identification with Swinburne, are briefly sketched in Lennart A. Björk, *The Literary Notes of Thomas Hardy*, Volume 1, 1974, Notes, 373–4. 'A Singer Asleep' is Hardy's most eloquent testimony to Swinburne.

A. E. Housman's translations from Greek are written in Swinburne's style. For his influence on Housman's poetry, see Archie Burnett's Oxford English Text edition of Housman and P. G. Naiditch, *An Index to Archie Burnett's Commentary on 'The Poems of A. E. Housman'* (Housman Society, 1998).

D'Annunzio drew on Swinburne extensively. See Paul Falzon, 'Reminiscences of Swinburne in d'Annunzio', *Notes and Queries*, 11th series, 5:201–3; 'Fonti d'Annunziane' in *La Critica*, 8:22–31, 10:257–63, 11:431–40, and 12:15–25; and Calvin S. Brown, Jr., 'More Swinburne–d'Annunzio Parallels', *Publications of the Modern Language Association*, 55:559–67.

W. B. Yeats endorsed Swinburne as a candidate for Poet Laureate upon the death of Tennyson, and he declared himself 'King of the Cats' upon Swinburne's death.

Stefan George translated several poems from *Poems and Ballads* into German, the first in 1896 and the remainder in 1905. The translations are studied by Karen Paul and William H. McClain in *Modern Language Notes*, 86:706–14.

Ezra Pound's early poems 'Salve O Pontifex!' and 'Swinburne: A Critique' are evidence of Swinburne's importance to him. The falling rhythms of Canto 17, it has been argued, recall Swinburne's adaptations of classical metres (Peter Nicholls, *Ezra Pound: Politics, Economics, and Writing*, 1984, pp. 34–5). Swinburne's paganism was always important to Pound; in 1942, for example, he wrote that Swinburne was a member of his church.

Despite T. S. Eliot's declaration that 'Swinburne and the poets of the nineties were entirely missed out of my personal history', some lines suited him well enough to adapt; compare memory mixed with desire in 'To Victor Hugo', l. 31, and *The Waste Land*, ll. 2–3.

TABLE OF DATES

1837   5 April: Algernon Charles Swinburne born to Captain Charles Henry Swinburne, later Admiral, the second son of Sir John Edward Swinburne (the baronetcy went back to the seventeenth century) and Lady Jane Henrietta Swinburne, daughter of the third Earl of Ashburnham; he was the first of six surviving children.

1837–49   Much of Swinburne's childhood spent on the Isle of Wight (East Dene, Bonchurch) and at his paternal grandfather's estate, Capheaton in Northumberland, with visits to Ashburnham Place in Sussex. His religious formation was Anglo-Catholic. Riding, swimming and reading in the libraries at Capheaton and Ashburnham were principal pastimes.

      Browning's *Sordello* published in 1840.

1849–54   Educated at Eton. Suffered bullying; was probably flogged and a witness of floggings, a recurrent interest throughout his creative life. It is not known why he left Eton. He read Shakespeare unexpurgated, Lamb's *Specimens of the English Dramatic Poets*, and steeped himself in Elizabethan and Jacobean drama; wrote at least three imitations of Elizabethan drama. Also read Sappho, Hugo and Landor, lifelong idols. Presented to Wordsworth in 1849, and later to Samuel Rogers.

      Arnold's *The Strayed Reveller* in 1849 and *Empedocles on Etna* in 1852. Théophile Gautier's *Émaux et camées* in 1852. Dickens's *Bleak House* in serial publication 1852–3. Hugo's *Châtiments* in 1853.

      In France, the *coup d'état* of 1851 and the formation of the Second Empire under Napoleon III, Swinburne's *bête noire*, in 1852; Hugo in exile.

1854–6   Prepared for Oxford by two private tutors, the first near Capheaton and the second near Bristol. While in Northumberland he was befriended and encouraged by Lady

Pauline Trevelyan, who lived nearby and exercised a stabilizing influence on Swinburne until she died in 1866. Visited France and Germany in 1855.

Tennyson's *Maud* in 1855; first edition of Whitman's *Leaves of Grass* in 1855.

1856–60 Matriculated at Balliol College, Oxford, where at first he studied in the School of Classical Greats (Benjamin Jowett was his tutor) but later decided to read for Honours in Law and Modern History. He was an original member of the Old Mortality Society, a radical group which discussed literary and political topics; he wrote essays for its magazine *Undergraduate Papers*. In 1857 he met William Morris, Edward Burne Jones (later Burne-Jones) and Dante Gabriel Rossetti, who were painting Arthurian murals for the Union debating hall. Rejected Christianity and became an enthusiastic republican. Continued his intensive study of French literature and Elizabethan drama; also read and imitated medieval and Pre-Raphaelite poetry. Rusticated in November 1859, he returned to Oxford in April 1860, but failed to take a degree. Wrote the earliest of the poems in *Poems and Ballads*.

William Morris's *The Defence of Guenevere* published in 1856; in 1857 Baudelaire's *Les Fleurs du mal* published; he is prosecuted, found guilty of obscenity and blasphemy, and fined. First part of Hugo's *La Légende des siècles* published in 1859. Tennyson's *Idylls of the King* also published in 1859.

1860 The Admiral gave Swinburne an allowance to live in London, where he visited Rossetti, Burne-Jones, Morris and Ford Madox Brown. *The Queen-Mother and Rosamond* attracted little attention. Death of Swinburne's paternal grandfather, Sir John Edward Swinburne, whom he had greatly admired.

1861 Travelled to Mentone and several Italian cities. Back in London he developed friendship with Richard Monckton Milnes (Lord Houghton from 1863). Met Simeon Solomon, and met Richard Burton at Milnes'.

The Risorgimento culminated in the establishment of the Kingdom of Italy; Venetia would be annexed in 1866 and Papal Rome in 1870. Mazzini, however, true to his republican principles, opposed the new Italian state.

1862   Travelled to Paris and then to the Pyrenees. Published poems
        in *Once a Week* and *Spectator*; reviewed Baudelaire's *Les Fleurs
        du mal* and Hugo's *Les Misérables*. He wrote an epistolary
        novel, *A Year's Letters*. After the death of Rossetti's wife,
        Elizabeth Siddal, he moved with him into Tudor House in
        Cheyne Walk in Chelsea. Besides Morris and Burne-Jones,
        visitors included James McNeill Whistler and Simeon
        Solomon.

        Swinburne defended George Meredith's *Modern Love*, the
        morality of which had been attacked in the *Spectator*.

1863   Travelled to Paris with Whistler, and met the painters
        Édouard Manet and Henri Fantin-Latour. Back in London,
        Swinburne's drinking and behaviour became immoderate.
        His favourite sister Edith died in September of tuberculosis.
        The family travelled to Italy after her death, except for
        Swinburne, who stayed for four months with relatives. He
        developed a romantic interest in his cousin Mary Gordon;
        they collaborated on stories, rode; he worked on *Atalanta in
        Calydon*.

1864   Travelled to Paris with Houghton and then to Italy where he
        visited Landor. Break-up of Tudor House; friendship with
        Rossetti was strained. Mary Gordon announced her marriage
        to Colonel Disney-Leith, probably the greatest romantic
        disappointment of Swinburne's life. Perhaps began work on
        the novel *Lesbia Brandon*, never finished. Completed *Atalanta
        in Calydon* while staying three months in Cornwall with the
        painter John William Inchbold.

        Browning's *Dramatis Personae*.

1865   Published *Atalanta in Calydon* in March, which brought him
        fame. His father sold East Dene and the family soon moved to
        Holmwold, Shiplake, Henley-on-Thames. Swinburne found
        new lodgings in London and in November published
        Chastelard, a verse drama based on an episode in the life of
        Mary Stuart, the first in a trilogy of plays about her; an early
        draft of the drama was nearly complete in 1861. The reviews
        were not favourable. Close friendship with George Powell,
        with whom he shared an interest in flagellation.

        Death of Landor, to whom Swinburne dedicated *Atalanta
        in Calydon*.

1866 Published *Poems and Ballads* in July, which brought him notoriety and much angry critical abuse. Fearing litigation, the publisher Moxon & Co. withdrew the book in early August; by mid-September it was on sale again, reissued by John Camden Hotten, one of whose specialties was erotic literature. At Hotten's request, Swinburne responded to his critics with *Notes on Poems and Reviews* (see Appendix 1).

First volume of the anthology *Le Parnasse contemporain* (later volumes in 1871 and 1876).

1867 Met his idol Mazzini, who encouraged him to write political poetry. His convulsive fits, followed by fainting, to which he had been subject since the early 1860s, became more serious in July; he stayed with his family until September. This became a pattern: dissolute life in London threatening his health followed by recuperation in Holmwood. Late in the year he began an affair with Adah Isaacs Menken, a famous American actress and performer; it lasted about six months. Published *William Blake: A Critical Study*, begun in the early 1860s; included a statement of art for art's sake.

Baudelaire died in August; a premature rumour of his death in May inspired Swinburne to write 'Ave atque Vale'. William Morris's *Life and Death of Jason* appeared, for which Swinburne published an appreciation.

1868 Frequented a flagellation brothel (as he had perhaps done earlier). In September he stayed with Powell at a cottage in Normandy; rumours of the irregular domestic ménage circulated. Further fits followed by recovery upon his removal from London. Read a French translation of the *Mahabharata*, with excessive enthusiasm according to William Rossetti.

First part of Browning's *The Ring and the Book*.

1869 Travelled with Burton through France, stayed again with Powell in Normandy. Back in London, then in Holmwood.

Tennyson's *Holy Grail*, in reaction to which Swinburne started an overture to the story of Tristram and Iseult (published in 1871).

1870 Finished 'Hertha' and 'The Eve of Revolution'. Battle with Hotten, who threatened Swinburne with an injunction if another publisher brought out his work. The other publisher, Ellis, meanwhile delayed nervously about *Songs before Sunrise*.

Drunken bouts in London again threatened his health; the Admiral brought him to Holmwood.

Publication of Dante Gabriel Rossetti's *Poems* (retrieved from the grave of his wife), which Swinburne reviewed with great enthusiasm. Declaration of the French Republic.

1871   Ellis published *Songs before Sunrise*. Reviewed Simeon Solomon's *A Vision of Love* and worked on *Bothwell*, the second and longest part of the trilogy about Mary Stuart. Dissolute living injured his health, and he was again retrieved by the Admiral. In October, Robert Buchanan launched a polemical attack on Rossetti and Swinburne, 'The Fleshly School of Poetry'.

1872   Published *Under the Microscope*, his response to Buchanan, in which he also mocked Tennyson's Arthurian poems. Dante Gabriel Rossetti, under the stress of the controversy, collapsed and broke permanently with Swinburne. Theodore Watts (later Watts-Dunton) intervened on Swinburne's behalf with Hotten.

Death of Théophile Gautier; Swinburne wrote elegies for him in Greek, Latin, French and English; they were published the next year.

1873   Simeon Solomon arrested for soliciting at a men's toilet; Swinburne expressed his loathing and they did not meet again.

1874   *Bothwell* published in May by Chatto and Windus, who had bought Hotten's press.

1875   *Songs of Two Nations* (i.e., France and Italy). Discussed with Jowett the plan of *Erectheus*, his more rigorous imitation of a Greek tragedy. Wrote 'A Forsaken Garden' and 'By the North Sea'. Mocked Buchanan in print, who then sued Swinburne for libel, and who won in court the next year.

1876   *Erechtheus* published; began controversy with F. J. Furnivall and mocked the new Shakespeare Society; their quarrel would be revived in the early 1880s.

1877   Serial publication of *A Year's Letters*; translated Villon. Published 'The Sailing of the Swallow', which would form the first canto of *Tristram of Lyonesse*. Father died; inherited £5,000; more dissipation.

1878   *Poems and Ballads, Second Series* published, the earliest poems

of which dated from 1867; 'inscribed to Richard F. Burton'.
Very seriously ill.

1879 Watts moved Swinburne temporarily into the house Watts
shared with his sister; from there he went again to Holmwood,
where Lady Jane Swinburne and Watts agreed that he must
not live in London. Holiday on the coast in September, after
which Watts and Swinburne moved into The Pines, Putney.
Composed 'On the Cliffs' and 'Thalassius', which appeared
in the next year in *Songs of the Springtides*.

1880 *Songs of the Springtides*, *Studies in Song* (including 'By the
North Sea' and a skilful translation from Aristophanes), and
Heptalogia, a collection of seven parodies of contemporary
poets, himself included.

1881 Bertie Mason, Watts's nephew, left The Pines for several
months; Swinburne despondent.

1882 *Mary Stuart*, the final instalment of the trilogy, published and
coldly received. Death of Dante Gabriel Rossetti; Watts,
though not Swinburne, attended the funeral. *Tristram of
Lyonesse* dedicated 'to my best friend Theodore Watts'. At
the end of November, travelled to Paris to see *Le Roi s'amuse*;
met Hugo and Leconte de Lisle, 'the Frenchman I most
wanted to see outside of the master's own peculiar circle'.

1883 *A Century of Roundels*, dedicated to Christina Rossetti.

1884 *A Midsummer Holiday*.

1885 Death of Hugo. Death of Lord Houghton.

1886 Met Thomas J. Wise, who later produced several forged 'first
editions' of Swinburne's poems.

1887 *Loctrine*; essay and attack on 'Whitmania'.

1888 Quarrel with Whistler, 'Mr Whistler's Lectures on Art'.

1889 *Poems and Ballads, Third Series*. Swinburne visited by writers
of the 'Nineties. Max Beerbohm recounts his 1899 visit in the
essay 'No. 2. The Pines'. Arthur Symons's visits over a decade
recorded in his *Memoirs*.

1890 Death of Richard Burton.

1891 Renewed correspondence with Mary Disney-Leith (formerly
Mary Gordon).

1892 *The Sisters*.
        Death of Tennyson; some writers (including Yeats) sought
to have Swinburne made Poet Laureate.

FURTHER READING

T. S. Eliot, 'Swinburne as Poet' (1920) in *Selected Essays* (Faber, 1932, 3rd ed. 1951)

A. E. Housman, 'Swinburne' (1910) in Christopher Ricks (ed.), *Collected Poems and Selected Prose* (Penguin, 1988)

Clyde K. Hyder, *Swinburne: The Critical Heritage* (Barnes & Noble, 1970)

Clyde K. Hyder (ed.), *Swinburne as Critic* (Routledge and Kegan Paul, 1972)

Georges Lafourcade, *La Jeunesse de Swinburne* (Paris, 1928)

Cecil Y. Lang (ed.), *Letters of Algernon Charles Swinburne* (Yale, 1959–62)

Jerome J. McGann, *Swinburne: An Experiment in Criticism* (University of Chicago Press, 1972)

Ezra Pound, 'Swinburne Versus His Biographers' (1918) in *Literary Essays* (New Directions, 1954)

Rikky Rooksby, *A. C. Swinburne: A Poet's Life* (Scolar Press, 1997)

Rikky Rooksby and Nicholas Shrimpton (eds.), *The Whole Music of Passion* (Scolar Press, 1993)

The following abbreviations have been used in the Preface and Notes:

Lafourcade	Georges Lafourcade, *La Jeunesse de Swinburne* (Paris, 1928)
Lang	Cecil Y. Lang (ed.), *Letters of Algernon Charles Swinburne* (Yale, 1959–62) (volume and page number given in brackets)
OED	*Oxford English Dictionary*
Rooksby	Rikky Rooksby, *A. C. Swinburne: A Poet's Life* (Scolar Press, 1997)

William Rossetti   William Michael Rossetti, *Swinburne's Poems and Ballads: A Criticism* (reprinted in Hyder, *Critical Heritage*)

POEMS AND BALLADS

TO

MY FRIEND

EDWARD BURNE JONES

THESE POEMS

ARE AFFECTIONATELY AND ADMIRINGLY

DEDICATED

A Ballad of Life

I found in dreams a place of wind and flowers,
   Full of sweet trees and colour of glad grass,
   In midst whereof there was
A lady clothed like summer with sweet hours.
Her beauty, fervent as a fiery moon,
   Made my blood burn and swoon
      Like a flame rained upon.
Sorrow had filled her shaken eyelids' blue,
And her mouth's sad red heavy rose all through
10   Seemed sad with glad things gone.

She held a little cithern by the strings,
   Shaped heartwise, strung with subtle-coloured hair
   Of some dead lute-player
That in dead years had done delicious things.
The seven strings were named accordingly;
   The first string charity,
      The second tenderness,
The rest were pleasure, sorrow, sleep, and sin,
And loving-kindness, that is pity's kin
20   And is most pitiless.

There were three men with her, each garmented
   With gold and shod with gold upon the feet;
   And with plucked ears of wheat
The first man's hair was wound upon his head:
His face was red, and his mouth curled and sad;
   All his gold garment had
      Pale stains of dust and rust.
A riven hood was pulled across his eyes;
The token of him being upon this wise
30   Made for a sign of Lust.

The next was Shame, with hollow heavy face
 Coloured like green wood when flame kindles it.
 He hath such feeble feet
They may not well endure in any place.
His face was full of grey old miseries,
 And all his blood's increase
  Was even increase of pain.
The last was Fear, that is akin to Death;
He is Shame's friend, and always as Shame saith
  Fear answers him again.

My soul said in me; This is marvellous,
 Seeing the air's face is not so delicate
 Nor the sun's grace so great,
If sin and she be kin or amorous.
And seeing where maidens served her on their knees,
 I bade one crave of these
  To know the cause thereof.
Then Fear said: I am Pity that was dead.
And Shame said: I am Sorrow comforted.
  And Lust said: I am Love.

Thereat her hands began a lute-playing
 And her sweet mouth a song in a strange tongue;
 And all the while she sung
There was no sound but long tears following
Long tears upon men's faces, waxen white
 With extreme sad delight.
  But those three following men
Became as men raised upon among the dead;
Great glad mouths open and fair cheeks made red
  With child's blood come again.

Then I said: Now assuredly I see
 My lady is perfect, and transfigureth
 All sin and sorrow and death,
Making them fair as her own eyelids be,
Or lips wherein my whole soul's life abides;
 Or as her sweet white sides

And bosom carved to kiss.
Now therefore, if her pity further me,
Doubtless for her sake all my days shall be
70   As righteous as she is.

Forth, ballad, and take roses in both arms,
    Even till the top rose touch thee in the throat
Where the least thornprick harms;
    And girdled in thy golden singing-coat,
Come thou before my lady and say this;
    Borgia, thy gold hair's colour burns in me,
        Thy mouth makes beat my blood in feverish rhymes;
    Therefore so many as these roses be,
        Kiss me so many times.
80 Then it may be, seeing how sweet she is,
    That she will stoop herself none otherwise
        Than a blown vine-branch doth,
    And kiss thee with soft laughter on thine eyes,
        Ballad, and on thy mouth.

A Ballad of Death

Kneel down, fair Love, and fill thyself with tears,
Girdle thyself with sighing for a girth
Upon the sides of mirth,
Cover thy lips and eyelids, let thine ears
Be filled with rumour of people sorrowing;
Make thee soft raiment out of woven sighs
Upon the flesh to cleave,
Set pains therein and many a grievous thing,
And many sorrows after each his wise
10 For armlet and for gorget and for sleeve.

O Love's lute heard about the lands of death,
Left hanged upon the trees that were therein;
O Love and Time and Sin,
Three singing mouths that mourn now underbreath,

Three lovers, each one evil spoken of;
O smitten lips wherethrough this voice of mine
Came softer with her praise;
Abide a little for our lady's love.
The kisses of her mouth were more than wine,
20   And more than peace the passage of her days.

O Love, thou knowest if she were good to see.
O Time, thou shalt not find in any land
Till, cast out of thine hand,
The sunlight and the moonlight fail from thee,
Another woman fashioned like as this.
O Sin, thou knowest that all thy shame in her
Was made a goodly thing;
Yea, she caught Shame and shamed him with her kiss,
With her fair kiss, and lips much lovelier
30   Than lips of amorous roses in late spring.

By night there stood over against my bed
Queen Venus with a hood striped gold and black,
Both sides drawn fully back
From brows wherein the sad blood failed of red,
And temples drained of purple and full of death.
Her curled hair had the wave of sea-water
And the sea's gold in it.
Her eyes were as a dove's that sickeneth.
Strewn dust of gold she had shed over her,
40   And pearl and purple and amber on her feet.

Upon her raiment of dyed sendaline
Were painted all the secret ways of love
And covered things thereof,
That hold delight as grape-flowers hold their wine;
Red mouths of maidens and red feet of doves,
And brides that kept within the bride-chamber
Their garment of soft shame,
And weeping faces of the wearied loves
That swoon in sleep and awake wearier,
50   With heat of lips and hair shed out like flame.

The tears that through her eyelids fell on me
Made mine own bitter where they ran between
As blood had fallen therein,
She saying; Arise, lift up thine eyes and see
If any glad thing be or any good
Now the best thing is taken forth of us;
Even she to whom all praise
Was as one flower in a great multitude,
One glorious flower of many and glorious,
60 One day found gracious among many days:

Even she whose handmaiden was Love – to whom
At kissing times across her stateliest bed
Kings bowed themselves and shed
Pale wine, and honey with the honeycomb,
And spikenard bruised for a burnt-offering;
Even she between whose lips the kiss became
As fire and frankincense;
Whose hair was as gold raiment on a king,
Whose eyes were as the morning purged with flame,
70 Whose eyelids as sweet savour issuing thence.

Then I beheld, and lo on the other side
My lady's likeness crowned and robed and dead.
Sweet still, but now not red,
Was the shut mouth whereby men lived and died.
And sweet, but emptied of the blood's blue shade,
The great curled eyelids that withheld her eyes.
And sweet, but like spoilt gold,
The weight of colour in her tresses weighed.
And sweet, but as a vesture with new dyes,
80 The body that was clothed with love of old.

Ah! that my tears filled all her woven hair
And all the hollow bosom of her gown –
Ah! that my tears ran down
Even to the place where many kisses were,

Even where her parted breast-flowers have place,
Even where they are cloven apart – who knows not this?
Ah! the flowers cleave apart
And their sweet fills the tender interspace;
Ah! the leaves grown thereof were things to kiss
90   Ere their fine gold was tarnished at the heart.

Ah! in the days when God did good to me,
Each part about her was a righteous thing;
Her mouth an almsgiving,
The glory of her garments charity,
The beauty of her bosom a good deed,
In the good days when God kept sight of us;
Love lay upon her eyes,
And on that hair whereof the world takes heed;
And all her body was more virtuous
100   Than souls of women fashioned otherwise.

Now, ballad, gather poppies in thine hands
And sheaves of brier and many rusted sheaves
Rain-rotten in rank lands,
Waste marigold and late unhappy leaves
And grass that fades ere any of it be mown;
And when thy bosom is filled full thereof
Seek out Death's face ere the light altereth,
And say 'My master that was thrall to Love
Is become thrall to Death.'
110   Bow down before him, ballad, sigh and groan,
But make no sojourn in thy outgoing;
For haply it may be
That when thy feet return at evening
Death shall come in with thee.

Laus Veneris

Lors dit en plourant; Hélas trop malheureux homme et mauldict
pescheur, oncques ne verrai-je clémence et miséricorde de Dieu.
Ores m'en irai-je d'icy et me cacherai dedans le mont Horsel, en
requérant de faveur et d'amoureuse merci ma doulce dame Vénus,
car pour son amour serai-je bien à tout jamais damné en enfer. Voicy
la fin de tous mes faicts d'armes et de toutes mes belles chansons.
Hélas, trop belle estoyt la face de ma dame et ses yeulx, et en mauvais
jour je vis ces chouses-là. Lors s'en alla tout en gémissant et se
retourna chez elle, et là vescut tristement en grand amour près de sa
dame. Puis après advint que le pape vit un jour esclater sur son
baston force belles fleurs rouges et blanches et maints boutons de
feuilles, et ainsi vit-il reverdir toute l'escorce. Ce dont il eut grande
crainte et moult s'en esmut, et grande pitié lui prit de ce chevalier
qui s'en estoyt départi sans espoir comme un homme misérable et
damné. Doncques envoya force messaigers devers luy pour le
ramener, disant qu'il aurait de Dieu grace et bonne absolution de
son grand pesché d'amour. Mais oncques plus ne le virent; car
toujours demeura ce pauvre chevalier auprès de Vénus la haulte et
forte déesse ès flancs de la montagne amoureuse.

> *Livre des grandes merveilles d'amour, escript en latin et en*
> *françoys par Maistre Antoine Gaget.* 1530.

Asleep or waking is it? for her neck,
Kissed over close, wears yet a purple speck
   Wherein the pained blood falters and goes out;
Soft, and stung softly – fairer for a fleck.

But though my lips shut sucking on the place,
There is no vein at work upon her face;
   Her eyelids are so peaceable, no doubt
Deep sleep has warmed her blood through all its ways.

Lo, this is she that was the world's delight;
The old grey years were parcels of her might;
   The strewings of the ways wherein she trod
Were the twain seasons of the day and night.

Lo, she was thus when her clear limbs enticed
All lips that now grow sad with kissing Christ,
    Stained with blood fallen from the feet of God,
The feet and hands whereat our souls were priced.

Alas, Lord, surely thou art great and fair.
But lo her wonderfully woven hair!
    And thou didst heal us with thy piteous kiss;
20   But see now, Lord; her mouth is lovelier.

She is right fair; what hath she done to thee?
Nay, fair Lord Christ, lift up thine eyes and see;
    Had now thy mother such a lip – like this?
Thou knowest how sweet a thing it is to me.

Inside the Horsel here the air is hot;
Right little peace one hath for it, God wot;
    The scented dusty daylight burns the air,
And my heart chokes me till I hear it not.

Behold, my Venus, my soul's body, lies
30   With my love laid upon her garment-wise,
    Feeling my love in all her limbs and hair
And shed between her eyelids through her eyes.

She holds my heart in her sweet open hands
Hanging asleep; hard by her head there stands,
    Crowned with gilt thorns and clothed with flesh like fire,
Love, wan as foam blown up the salt burnt sands –

Hot as the brackish waifs of yellow spume
That shift and steam – loose clots of arid fume
    From the sea's panting mouth of dry desire;
40   There stands he, like one labouring at a loom.

The warp holds fast across; and every thread
That makes the woof up has dry specks of red;
    Always the shuttle cleaves clean through, and he
Weaves with the hair of many a ruined head.

Love is not glad nor sorry, as I deem;
Labouring he dreams, and labours in the dream,
　　Till when the spool is finished, lo I see
His web, reeled off, curls and goes out like steam.

Night falls like fire; the heavy lights run low,
50　And as they drop, my blood and body so
　　Shake as the flame shakes, full of days and hours
That sleep not neither weep they as they go.

Ah yet would God this flesh of mine might be
Where air might wash and long leaves cover me,
　　Where tides of grass break into foam of flowers,
Or where the wind's feet shine along the sea.

Ah yet would God that stems and roots were bred
Out of my weary body and my head,
　　That sleep were sealed upon me with a seal,
60　And I were as the least of all his dead.

Would God my blood were dew to feed the grass,
Mine ears made deaf and mine eyes blind as glass,
　　My body broken as a turning wheel,
And my mouth stricken ere it saith Alas!

Ah God, that love were as a flower or flame,
That life were as the naming of a name,
　　That death were not more pitiful than desire,
That these things were not one thing and the same!

Behold now, surely somewhere there is death:
70　For each man hath some space of years, he saith,
　　A little space of time ere time expire,
A little day, a little way of breath.

And lo, between the sundawn and the sun,
His day's work and his night's work are undone;
　　And lo, between the nightfall and the light,
He is not, and none knoweth of such an one.

Ah God, that I were as all souls that be,
As any herb or leaf of any tree,
　　As men that toil through hours of labouring night,
80　As bones of men under the deep sharp sea.

Outside it must be winter among men;
For at the gold bars of the gates again
　　I heard all night and all the hours of it
The wind's wet wings and fingers drip with rain.

Knights gather, riding sharp for cold; I know
The ways and woods are strangled with the snow;
　　And with short song the maidens spin and sit
Until Christ's birthnight, lily-like, arow.

The scent and shadow shed about me make
90　The very soul in all my senses ache;
　　The hot hard night is fed upon my breath,
And sleep beholds me from afar awake.

Alas, but surely where the hills grow deep,
Or where the wild ways of the sea are steep,
　　Or in strange places somewhere there is death,
And on death's face the scattered hair of sleep.

There lover-like with lips and limbs that meet
They lie, they pluck sweet fruit of life and eat;
　　But me the hot and hungry days devour,
100　And in my mouth no fruit of theirs is sweet.

No fruit of theirs, but fruit of my desire,
For her love's sake whose lips through mine respire;
　　Her eyelids on her eyes like flower on flower,
Mine eyelids on mine eyes like fire on fire.

So lie we, not as sleep that lies by death,
With heavy kisses and with happy breath;
　　Not as man lies by woman, when the bride
Laughs low for love's sake and the words he saith.

For she lies, laughing low with love; she lies
110 And turns his kisses on her lips to sighs,
 To sighing sound of lips unsatisfied,
And the sweet tears are tender with her eyes.

Ah, not as they, but as the souls that were
Slain in the old time, having found her fair;
 Who, sleeping with her lips upon their eyes,
Heard sudden serpents hiss across her hair.

Their blood runs round the roots of time like rain:
She casts them forth and gathers them again;
 With nerve and bone she weaves and multiplies
120 Exceeding pleasure out of extreme pain.

Her little chambers drip with flower-like red,
Her girdles, and the chaplets of her head,
 Her armlets and her anklets; with her feet
She tramples all that winepress of the dead.

Her gateways smoke with fume of flowers and fires,
With loves burnt out and unassuaged desires;
 Between her lips the steam of them is sweet,
The languor in her ears of many lyres.

Her beds are full of perfume and sad sound,
130 Her doors are made with music, and barred round
 With sighing and with laughter and with tears,
With tears whereby strong souls of men are bound.

There is the knight Adonis that was slain;
With flesh and blood she chains him for a chain;
 The body and the spirit in her ears
Cry, for her lips divide him vein by vein.

Yea, all she slayeth; yea, every man save me;
Me, love, thy lover that must cleave to thee
 Till the ending of the days and ways of earth,
140 The shaking of the sources of the sea.

Me, most forsaken of all souls that fell;
Me, satiated with things insatiable;
    Me, for whose sake the extreme hell makes mirth,
Yea, laughter kindles at the heart of hell.

Alas thy beauty! for thy mouth's sweet sake
My soul is bitter to me, my limbs quake
    As water, as the flesh of men that weep,
As their heart's vein whose heart goes nigh to break.

Ah God, that sleep with flower-sweet finger-tips
150 Would crush the fruit of death upon my lips;
    Ah God, that death would tread the grapes of sleep
And wring their juice upon me as it drips.

There is no change of cheer for many days,
But change of chimes high up in the air, that sways
    Rung by the running fingers of the wind;
And singing sorrows heard on hidden ways.

Day smiteth day in twain, night sundereth night,
And on mine eyes the dark sits as the light;
    Yea, Lord, thou knowest I know not, having sinned,
160 If heaven be clean or unclean in thy sight.

Yea, as if earth were sprinkled over me,
Such chafed harsh earth as chokes a sandy sea,
    Each pore doth yearn, and the dried blood thereof
Gasps by sick fits, my heart swims heavily,

There is a feverish famine in my veins;
Below her bosom, where a crushed grape stains
    The white and blue, there my lips caught and clove
An hour since, and what mark of me remains?

I dare not always touch her, lest the kiss
170 Leave my lips charred. Yea, Lord, a little bliss,
    Brief bitter bliss, one hath for a great sin;
Nathless thou knowest how sweet a thing it is.

Sin, is it sin whereby men's souls are thrust
Into the pit? yet had I a good trust
    To save my soul before it slipped therein,
Trod under by the fire-shod feet of lust.

For if mine eyes fail and my soul takes breath,
I look between the iron sides of death
    Into sad hell where all sweet love hath end,
180 All but the pain that never finisheth.

There are the naked faces of great kings,
The singing folk with all their lute-playings;
    There when one cometh he shall have to friend
The grave that covets and the worm that clings.

There sit the knights that were so great of hand,
The ladies that were queens of fair green land,
    Grown grey and black now, brought unto the dust,
Soiled, without raiment, clad about with sand.

There is one end for all of them; they sit
190 Naked and sad, they drink the dregs of it,
    Trodden as grapes in the wine-press of lust,
Trampled and trodden by the fiery feet.

I see the marvellous mouth whereby there fell
Cities and people whom the gods loved well,
    Yet for her sake on them the fire gat hold,
And for their sakes on her the fire of hell.

And softer than the Egyptian lote-leaf is,
The queen whose face was worth the world to kiss,
    Wearing at breast a suckling snake of gold;
200 And large pale lips of strong Semiramis,

Curled like a tiger's that curl back to feed;
Red only where the last kiss made them bleed;
    Her hair most thick with many a carven gem,
Deep in the mane, great-chested, like a steed.

Yea, with red sin the faces of them shine;
But in all these there was no sin like mine;
    No, not in all the strange great sins of them
That made the wine-press froth and foam with wine.

For I was of Christ's choosing, I God's knight,
No blinkard heathen stumbling for scant light;
    I can well see, for all the dusty days
Gone past, the clean great time of goodly fight.

I smell the breathing battle sharp with blows,
With shriek of shafts and snapping short of bows;
    The fair pure sword smites out in subtle ways,
Sounds and long lights are shed between the rows

Of beautiful mailed men; the edged light slips,
Most like a snake that takes short breath and dips
    Sharp from the beautifully bending head,
With all its gracious body lithe as lips

That curl in touching you; right in this wise
My sword doth, seeming fire in mine own eyes,
    Leaving all colours in them brown and red
And flecked with death; then the keen breaths like sighs,

The caught-up choked dry laughters following them,
When all the fighting face is grown a flame
    For pleasure, and the pulse that stuns the ears,
And the heart's gladness of the goodly game.

Let me think yet a little; I do know
These things were sweet, but sweet such years ago,
    Their savour is all turned now into tears;
Yea, ten years since, where the blue ripples blow,

The blue curled eddies of the blowing Rhine,
I felt the sharp wind shaking grass and vine
    Touch my blood too, and sting me with delight
Through all this waste and weary body of mine

That never feels clear air; right gladly then
I rode alone, a great way off my men,
   And heard the chiming bridle smite and smite,
240 And gave each rhyme thereof some rhyme again,

Till my song shifted to that iron one;
Seeing there rode up between me and the sun
   Some certain of my foe's men, for his three
White wolves across their painted coats did run.

The first red-bearded, with square cheeks – alack,
I made my knave's blood turn his beard to black;
   The slaying of him was a joy to see:
Perchance too, when at night he came not back,

Some woman fell a-weeping, whom this thief
250 Would beat when he had drunken; yet small grief
   Hath any for the ridding of such knaves;
Yea, if one wept, I doubt her teen was brief.

This bitter love is sorrow in all lands,
Draining of eyelids, wringing of drenched hands,
   Sighing of hearts and filling up of graves;
A sign across the head of the world he stands,

An one that hath a plague-mark on his brows;
Dust and spilt blood do track him to his house
   Down under earth; sweet smells of lip and cheek,
260 Like a sweet snake's breath made more poisonous

With chewing of some perfumed deadly grass,
Are shed all round his passage if he pass,
   And their quenched savour leaves the whole soul weak,
Sick with keen guessing whence the perfume was.

As one who hidden in deep sedge and reeds
Smells the rare scent made where a panther feeds,
   And tracking ever slotwise the warm smell
Is snapped upon by the sweet mouth and bleeds,

His head far down the hot sweet throat of her —
So one tracks love, whose breath is deadlier,
   And lo, one springe and you are fast in hell,
Fast as the gin's grip of a wayfarer.

I think now, as the heavy hours decease
One after one, and bitter thoughts increase
   One upon one, of all sweet finished things;
The breaking of the battle; the long peace

Wherein we sat clothed softly, each man's hair
Crowned with green leaves beneath white hoods of vair;
   The sounds of sharp spears at great tourneyings,
And noise of singing in the late sweet air.

I sang of love too, knowing nought thereof;
'Sweeter,' I said, 'the little laugh of love
   Than tears out of the eyes of Magdalen,
Or any fallen feather of the Dove.

'The broken little laugh that spoils a kiss,
The ache of purple pulses, and the bliss
   Of blinded eyelids that expand again —
Love draws them open with those lips of his,

'Lips that cling hard till the kissed face has grown
Of one same fire and colour with their own;
   Then ere one sleep, appeased with sacrifice,
Where his lips wounded, there his lips atone.'

I sang these things long since and knew them not;
'Lo, here is love, or there is love, God wot,
   This man and that finds favour in his eyes,'
I said, 'but I, what guerdon have I got?

'The dust of praise that is blown everywhere
In all men's faces with the common air;
   The bay-leaf that wants chafing to be sweet
Before they wind it in a singer's hair.'

So that one dawn I rode forth sorrowing;
I had no hope but of some evil thing,
   And so rode slowly past the windy wheat
And past the vineyard and the water-spring,

Up to the Horsel. A great elder-tree
Held back its heaps of flowers to let me see
   The ripe tall grass, and one that walked therein,
Naked, with hair shed over to the knee.

She walked between the blossom and the grass;
310   I knew the beauty of her, what she was,
   The beauty of her body and her sin,
And in my flesh the sin of hers, alas!

Alas! for sorrow is all the end of this.
O sad kissed mouth, how sorrowful it is!
   O breast whereat some suckling sorrow clings,
Red with the bitter blossom of a kiss!

Ah, with blind lips I felt for you, and found
About my neck your hands and hair enwound,
   The hands that stifle and the hair that stings,
320   I felt them fasten sharply without sound.

Yea, for my sin I had great store of bliss:
Rise up, make answer for me, let thy kiss
   Seal my lips hard from speaking of my sin,
Lest one go mad to hear how sweet it is.

Yet I waxed faint with fume of barren bowers,
And murmuring of the heavy-headed hours;
   And let the dove's beak fret and peck within
My lips in vain, and Love shed fruitless flowers.

So that God looked upon me when your hands
330   Were hot about me; yea, God brake my bands
   To save my soul alive, and I came forth
Like a man blind and naked in strange lands

That hears men laugh and weep, and knows not whence
Nor wherefore, but is broken in his sense;
  Howbeit I met folk riding from the north
Towards Rome, to purge them of their souls' offence,

And rode with them, and spake to none; the day
Stunned me like lights upon some wizard way,
  And ate like fire mine eyes and mine eyesight;
340 So rode I, hearing all these chant and pray,

And marvelled; till before us rose and fell
White cursed hills, like outer skirts of hell
  Seen where men's eyes look through the day to night,
Like a jagged shell's lips, harsh, untunable,

Blown in between by devil's wrangling breath;
Nathless we won well past that hell and death,
  Down to the sweet land where all airs are good,
Even unto Rome where God's grace tarrieth.

Then came each man and worshipped at his knees
350 Who in the Lord God's likeness bears the keys
  To bind or loose, and called on Christ's shed blood,
And so the sweet-souled father gave him ease.

But when I came I fell down at his feet,
Saying, 'Father, though the Lord's blood be right sweet,
  The spot it takes not off the panther's skin,
Nor shall an Ethiop's stain be bleached with it.

'Lo, I have sinned and have spat out at God,
Wherefore his hand is heavier and his rod
  More sharp because of mine exceeding sin,
360 And all his raiment redder than bright blood

'Before mine eyes; yea, for my sake I wot
The heat of hell is waxen seven times hot
  Through my great sin.' Then spake he some sweet word,
Giving me cheer; which thing availed me not;

Yea, scarce I wist if such indeed were said;
For when I ceased – lo, as one newly dead
   Who hears a great cry out of hell, I heard
The crying of his voice across my head.

'Until this dry shred staff, that hath no whit
370 Of leaf nor bark, bear blossom and smell sweet,
   Seek thou not any mercy in God's sight,
For so long shalt thou be cast out from it.'

Yea, what if dried-up stems wax red and green,
Shall that thing be which is not nor has been?
   Yea, what if sapless bark wax green and white,
Shall any good fruit grow upon my sin?

Nay, though sweet fruit were plucked of a dry tree,
And though men drew sweet waters of the sea,
   There should not grow sweet leaves on this dead stem,
380 This waste wan body and shaken soul of me.

Yea, though God search it warily enough,
There is not one sound thing in all thereof;
   Though he search all my veins through, searching them
He shall find nothing whole therein but love.

For I came home right heavy, with small cheer,
And lo my love, mine own soul's heart, more dear
   Than mine own soul, more beautiful than God,
Who hath my being between the hands of her –

Fair still, but fair for no man saving me,
390 As when she came out of the naked sea
   Making the foam as fire whereon she trod,
And as the inner flower of fire was she.

Yea, she laid hold upon me, and her mouth
Clove unto mine as soul to body doth,
   And, laughing, made her lips luxurious;
Her hair had smells of all the sunburnt south,

Strange spice and flower, strange savour of crushed fruit,
And perfume the swart kings tread underfoot
   For pleasure when their minds wax amorous,
400 Charred frankincense and grated sandal-root.

And I forgot fear and all weary things,
All ended prayers and perished thanksgivings,
   Feeling her face with all her eager hair
Cleave to me, clinging as a fire that clings

To the body and to the raiment, burning them;
As after death I know that such-like flame
   Shall cleave to me for ever; yea, what care,
Albeit I burn then, having felt the same?

Ah love, there is no better life than this;
410 To have known love, how bitter a thing it is,
   And afterward be cast out of God's sight;
Yea, these that know not, shall they have such bliss

High up in barren heaven before his face
As we twain in the heavy-hearted place,
   Remembering love and all the dead delight,
And all that time was sweet with for a space?

For till the thunder in the trumpet be,
Soul may divide from body, but not we
   One from another; I hold thee with my hand,
420 I let mine eyes have all their will of thee,

I seal myself upon thee with my might,
Abiding alway out of all men's sight
   Until God loosen over sea and land
The thunder of the trumpets of the night.

EXPLICIT LAUS VENERIS.

Phædra

HIPPOLYTUS; PHÆDRA; CHORUS OF TRŒZENIAN WOMEN

HIPPOLYTUS.
Lay not thine hand upon me; let me go;
Take off thine eyes that put the gods to shame;
What, wilt thou turn my loathing to thy death?

PHÆDRA.
Nay, I will never loosen hold nor breathe
Till thou have slain me; godlike for great brows
Thou art, and thewed as gods are, with clear hair:
Draw now thy sword and smite me as thou art god,
For verily I am smitten of other gods,
Why not of thee?

CHORUS.
                                    O queen, take heed of words;
10   Why wilt thou eat the husk of evil speech?
Wear wisdom for that veil about thy head
And goodness for the binding of thy brows.

PHÆDRA.
Nay, but this god hath cause enow to smite;
If he will slay me, baring breast and throat,
I lean toward the stroke with silent mouth
And a great heart. Come, take thy sword and slay;
Let me not starve between desire and death,
But send me on my way with glad wet lips;
For in the vein-drawn ashen-coloured palm
20   Death's hollow hand holds water of sweet draught
To tip and slake dried mouths at, as a deer
Specked red from thorns laps deep and loses pain.
Yea, if mine own blood ran upon my mouth,
I would drink that. Nay, but be swift with me;
Set thy sword here between the girdle and breast,
For I shall grow a poison if I live.

Are not my cheeks as grass, my body pale,
And my breath like a dying poisoned man's?
O whatsoever of godlike names thou be,
30   By thy chief name I charge thee, thou strong god,
And bid thee slay me. Strike, up to the gold,
Up to the hand-grip of the hilt; strike here;
For I am Cretan of my birth; strike now;
For I am Theseus' wife; stab up to the rims,
I am born daughter to Pasiphae.
See thou spare not for greatness of my blood,
Nor for the shining letters of my name:
Make thy sword sure inside thine hand and smite,
For the bright writing of my name is black,
40   And I am sick with hating the sweet sun.

HIPPOLYTUS.
Let not this woman wail and cleave to me,
That am no part of the gods' wrath with her;
Loose ye her hands from me lest she take hurt.

CHORUS.
Lady, this speech and majesty are twain;
Pure shame is of one counsel with the gods.

HIPPOLYTUS.
Man is as beast when shame stands off from him.

PHÆDRA.
Man, what have I to do with shame or thee?
I am not of one counsel with the gods.
I am their kin, I have strange blood in me,
50   I am not of their likeness nor of thine:
My veins are mixed, and therefore am I mad,
Yea therefore chafe and turn on mine own flesh,
Half of a woman made with half a god.
But thou wast hewn out of an iron womb
And fed with molten mother-snow for milk.
A sword was nurse of thine; Hippolyta,

That had the spear to father, and the axe
To bridesman, and wet blood of sword-slain men
For wedding-water out of a noble well,
60   Even she did bear thee, thinking of a sword,
And thou wast made a man mistakingly.
Nay, for I love thee, I will have thy hands,
Nay, for I will not loose thee, thou art sweet,
Thou art my son, I am thy father's wife,
I ache toward thee with a bridal blood,
The pulse is heavy in all my married veins,
My whole face beats, I will feed full of thee,
My body is empty of ease, I will be fed,
I am burnt to the bone with love, thou shalt not go,
70   I am heartsick, and mine eyelids prick mine eyes,
Thou shalt not sleep nor eat nor say a word
Till thou hast slain me. I am not good to live.

CHORUS.
This is an evil born with all its teeth,
When love is cast out of the bound of love.

HIPPOLYTUS.
There is no hate that is so hateworthy.

PHÆDRA.
I pray thee turn that hate of thine my way,
I hate not it nor anything of thine.
Lo, maidens, how he burns about the brow,
And draws the chafing sword-strap down his hand.
80   What wilt thou do? wilt thou be worse than death?
Be but as sweet as is the bitterest,
The most dispiteous out of all the gods,
I am well pleased. Lo, do I crave so much?
I do but bid thee be unmerciful,
Even the one thing thou art. Pity me not:
Thou wert not quick to pity. Think of me
As of a thing thy hounds are keen upon
In the wet woods between the windy ways,

And slay me for a spoil. This body of mine
90   Is worth a wild beast's fell or hide of hair,
And spotted deeper than a panther's grain.
I were but dead if thou wert pure indeed;
I pray thee by thy cold green holy crown
And by the fillet-leaves of Artemis.
Nay, but thou wilt not. Death is not like thee,
Albeit men hold him worst of all the gods.
For of all gods Death only loves not gifts,[1]
Nor with burnt-offering nor blood-sacrifice
Shalt thou do aught to get thee grace of him;
100   He will have nought of altar and altar-song,
And from him only of all the lords in heaven
Persuasion turns a sweet averted mouth.
But thou art worse: from thee with baffled breath
Back on my lips my prayer falls like a blow,
And beats upon them, dumb. What shall I say?
There is no word I can compel thee with
To do me good and slay me. But take heed;
I say, be wary; look between thy feet,
Lest a snare take them though the ground be good.

HIPPOLYTUS.

110   Shame may do most where fear is found most weak;
That which for shame's sake yet I have not done,
Shall it be done for fear's? Take thine own way;
Better the foot slip than the whole soul swerve.

PHÆDRA.

The man is choice and exquisite of mouth;
Yet in the end a curse shall curdle it.

CHORUS.

He goes with cloak upgathered to the lip,
Holding his eye as with some ill in sight.

---

[1] Æsch. Fr. Niobe:–
μόνος θεῶν γὰρ Θάνατος οὐ δώρων ἐρᾷ, κ.τ.λ.

PHÆDRA.

A bitter ill he hath i' the way thereof,
And it shall burn the sight out as with fire.

CHORUS.

120   Speak no such word whereto mischance is kin.

PHÆDRA.

Out of my heart and by fate's leave I speak.

CHORUS.

Set not thy heart to follow after fate.

PHÆDRA.

O women, O sweet people of this land,
O goodly city and pleasant ways thereof,
And woods with pasturing grass and great well-heads,
And hills with light and night between your leaves,
And winds with sound and silence in your lips,
And earth and water and all immortal things,
I take you to my witness what I am.
130   There is a god about me like as fire,
Sprung whence, who knoweth, or who hath heart to say?
A god more strong than whom slain beasts can soothe,
Or honey, or any spilth of blood-like wine,
Nor shall one please him with a whitened brow
Nor wheat nor wool nor aught of plaited leaf.
For like my mother am I stung and slain,
And round my cheeks have such red malady
And on my lips such fire and foam as hers.
That is that Ate out of Amathus
140   That breeds up death and gives it one for love.
She hath slain mercy, and for dead mercy's sake
(Being frighted with this sister that was slain)
Flees from before her fearful-footed shame,
And will not bear the bending of her brows
And long soft arrows flown from under them
As from bows bent. Desire flows out of her
As out of lips doth speech: and over her

Shines fire, and round her and beneath her fire.
She hath sown pain and plague in all our house,
150 Love loathed of love, and mates unmatchable,
Wild wedlock, and the lusts that bleat or low,
And marriage-fodder snuffed about of kine.
Lo how the heifer runs with leaping flank
Sleek under shaggy and speckled lies of hair,
And chews a horrible lip, and with harsh tongue
Laps alien froth and licks a loathlier mouth.
Alas, a foul first steam of trodden tares,
And fouler of these late grapes underfoot.
A bitter way of waves and clean-cut foam
160 Over the sad road of sonorous sea
The high gods gave king Theseus for no love,
Nay, but for love, yet to no loving end.
Alas the long thwarts and the fervent oars,
And blown hard sails that straightened the scant rope!
There were no strong pools in the hollow sea
To drag at them and suck down side and beak,
No wind to catch them in the teeth and hair,
No shoal, no shallow among the roaring reefs,
No gulf whereout the straining tides throw spars,
170 No surf where white bones twist like whirled white fire.
But like to death he came with death, and sought
And slew and spoiled and gat him that he would.
For death, for marriage, and for child-getting,
I set my curse against him as a sword;
Yea, and the severed half thereof I leave
Pittheus, because he slew not (when that face
Was tender, and the life still soft in it)
The small swathed child, but bred him for my fate.
I would I had been the first that took her death
180 Out from between wet hoofs and reddened teeth,
Splashed horns, fierce fetlocks of the brother bull!
For now shall I take death a deadlier way,
Gathering it up between the feet of love
Or off the knees of murder reaching it.

The Triumph of Time

Before our lives divide for ever,
    While time is with us and hands are free,
(Time, swift to hasten and swift to sever
    Hand from hand, as we stand by the sea)
I will say no word that a man might say
Whose whole life's love goes down in a day;
For this could never have been; and never,
    Though the gods and the years relent, shall be.

Is it worth a tear, is it worth an hour,
10   To think of things that are well outworn?
Of fruitless husk and fugitive flower,
    The dream foregone and the deed forborne?
Though joy be done with and grief be vain,
Time shall not sever us wholly in twain;
Earth is not spoilt for a single shower;
    But the rain has ruined the ungrown corn.

It will grow not again, this fruit of my heart,
    Smitten with sunbeams, ruined with rain.
The singing seasons divide and depart,
20   Winter and summer depart in twain.
It will grow not again, it is ruined at root,
The bloodlike blossom, the dull red fruit;
Though the heart yet sickens, the lips yet smart,
    With sullen savour of poisonous pain.

I have given no man of my fruit to eat;
    I trod the grapes, I have drunken the wine.
Had you eaten and drunken and found it sweet,
    This wild new growth of the corn and vine,
This wine and bread without lees or leaven,
30   We had grown as gods, as the gods in heaven,
Souls fair to look upon, goodly to greet,
    One splendid spirit, your soul and mine.

In the change of years, in the coil of things,
   In the clamour and rumour of life to be,
We, drinking love at the furthest springs,
   Covered with love as a covering tree,
We had grown as gods, as the gods above,
Filled from the heart to the lips with love,
Held fast in his hands, clothed warm with his wings,
40   O love, my love, had you loved but me!

We had stood as the sure stars stand, and moved
   As the moon moves, loving the world; and seen
Grief collapse as a thing disproved,
   Death consume as a thing unclean.
Twain halves of a perfect heart, made fast
Soul to soul while the years fell past;
Had you loved me once, as you have not loved;
   Had the chance been with us that has not been.

I have put my days and dreams out of mind,
50   Days that are over, dreams that are done.
Though we seek life through, we shall surely find
   There is none of them clear to us now, not one.
But clear are these things; the grass and the sand,
Where, sure as the eyes reach, ever at hand,
With lips wide open and face burnt blind,
   The strong sea-daisies feast on the sun.

The low downs lean to the sea; the stream,
   One loose thin pulseless tremulous vein,
Rapid and vivid and dumb as a dream,
60   Works downward, sick of the sun and the rain;
No wind is rough with the rank rare flowers;
The sweet sea, mother of loves and hours,
Shudders and shines as the grey winds gleam,
   Turning her smile to a fugitive pain.

Mother of loves that are swift to fade,
   Mother of mutable winds and hours.
A barren mother, a mother-maid,
   Cold and clean as her faint salt flowers.
I would we twain were even as she,
70   Lost in the night and the light of the sea,
Where faint sounds falter and wan beams wade,
   Break, and are broken, and shed into showers.

The loves and hours of the life of a man,
   They are swift and sad, being born of the sea.
Hours that rejoice and regret for a span,
   Born with a man's breath, mortal as he;
Loves that are lost ere they come to birth,
Weeds of the wave, without fruit upon earth.
I lose what I long for, save what I can,
80   My love, my love, and no love for me!

It is not much that a man can save
   On the sands of life, in the straits of time,
Who swims in sight of the great third wave
   That never a swimmer shall cross or climb.
Some waif washed up with the strays and spars
That ebb-tide shows to the shore and the stars;
Weed from the water, grass from a grave,
   A broken blossom, a ruined rhyme.

There will no man do for your sake, I think,
90   What I would have done for the least word said.
I had wrung life dry for your lips to drink,
   Broken it up for your daily bread:
Body for body and blood for blood,
As the flow of the full sea risen to flood
That yearns and trembles before it sink,
   I had given, and lain down for you, glad and dead.

Yea, hope at highest and all her fruit,
    And time at fullest and all his dower,
I had given you surely, and life to boot,
100   Were we once made one for a single hour.
But now, you are twain, you are cloven apart,
Flesh of his flesh, but heart of my heart;
And deep in one is the bitter root,
    And sweet for one is the lifelong flower.

To have died if you cared I should die for you, clung
    To my life if you bade me, played my part
As it pleased you – these were the thoughts that stung,
    The dreams that smote with a keener dart
Than shafts of love or arrows of death;
110   These were but as fire is, dust, or breath,
Or poisonous foam on the tender tongue
    Of the little snakes that eat my heart.

I wish we were dead together to–day,
    Lost sight of, hidden away out of sight,
Clasped and clothed in the cloven clay,
    Out of the world's way, out of the light,
Out of the ages of worldly weather,
Forgotten of all men altogether,
As the world's first dead, taken wholly away,
120   Made one with death, filled full of the night.

How we should slumber, how we should sleep,
    Far in the dark with the dreams and the dews!
And dreaming, grow to each other, and weep,
    Laugh low, live softly, murmur and muse;
Yea, and it may be, struck through by the dream,
Feel the dust quicken and quiver, and seem
Alive as of old to the lips, and leap
    Spirit to spirit as lovers use.

Sick dreams and sad of a dull delight;
For what shall it profit when men are dead
To have dreamed, to have loved with the whole soul's
      might,
      To have looked for day when the day was fled?
Let come what will, there is one thing worth,
To have had fair love in the life upon earth:
To have held love safe till the day grew night,
      While skies had colour and lips were red.

Would I lose you now? would I take you then,
      If I lose you now that my heart has need?
And come what may after death to men,
      What thing worth this will the dead years breed?
Lose life, lose all; but at least I know,
O sweet life's love, having loved you so,
Had I reached you on earth, I should lose not again,
      In death nor life, nor in dream or deed.

Yea, I know this well: were you once sealed mine,
      Mine in the blood's beat, mine in the breath,
Mixed into me as honey in wine,
      Not time, that sayeth and gainsayeth,
Nor all strong things had severed us then;
Not wrath of gods, nor wisdom of men,
Nor all things earthly, nor all divine,
      Nor joy nor sorrow, nor life nor death.

I had grown pure as the dawn and the dew,
      You had grown strong as the sun or the sea.
But none shall triumph a whole life through:
      For death is one, and the fates are three.
At the door of life, by the gate of breath,
There are worse things waiting for men than death;
Death could not sever my soul and you,
      As these have severed your soul from me.

You have chosen and clung to the chance they sent you,
    Life sweet as perfume and pure as prayer.
But will it not one day in heaven repent you?
    Will they solace you wholly, the days that were?
Will you lift up your eyes between sadness and bliss,
Meet mine, and see where the great love is,
And tremble and turn and be changed? Content you;
    The gate is strait; I shall not be there.

But you, had you chosen, had you stretched hand,
170   Had you seen good such a thing were done,
I too might have stood with the souls that stand
    In the sun's sight, clothed with the light of the sun;
But who now on earth need care how I live?
Have the high gods anything left to give,
Save dust and laurels and gold and sand?
    Which gifts are goodly; but I will none.

O all fair lovers about the world,
    There is none of you, none, that shall comfort me.
My thoughts are as dead things, wrecked and whirled
180   Round and round in a gulf of the sea;
And still, through the sound and the straining stream,
Through the coil and chafe, they gleam in a dream,
The bright fine lips so cruelly curled,
    And strange swift eyes where the soul sits free.

Free, without pity, withheld from woe,
    Ignorant; fair as the eyes are fair.
Would I have you change now, change at a blow,
    Startled and stricken, awake and aware?
Yea, if I could, would I have you see
190   My very love of you filling me,
And know my soul to the quick, as I know
    The likeness and look of your throat and hair?

I shall not change you. Nay, though I might,
    Would I change my sweet one love with a word?
I had rather your hair should change in a night,
    Clear now as the plume of a black bright bird;
Your face fail suddenly, cease, turn grey,
Die as a leaf that dies in a day.
I will keep my soul in a place out of sight,
200   Far off, where the pulse of it is not heard.

Far off it walks, in a bleak blown space,
    Full of the sound of the sorrow of years.
I have woven a veil for the weeping face,
    Whose lips have drunken the wine of tears;
I have found a way for the failing feet,
A place for slumber and sorrow to meet;
There is no rumour about the place,
    Nor light, nor any that sees or hears.

I have hidden my soul out of sight, and said
210   'Let none take pity upon thee, none
Comfort thy crying: for lo, thou art dead,
    Lie still now, safe out of sight of the sun.
Have I not built thee a grave, and wrought
Thy grave-clothes on thee of grievous thought,
With soft spun verses and tears unshed,
    And sweet light visions of things undone?

'I have given thee garments and balm and myrrh,
    And gold, and beautiful burial things.
But thou, be at peace now, make no stir;
220   Is not thy grave as a royal king's?
Fret not thyself though the end were sore;
Sleep, be patient, vex me no more.
Sleep; what hast thou to do with her?
    The eyes that weep, with the mouth that sings?'

Where the dead red leaves of the years lie rotten,
　　The cold old crimes and the deeds thrown by,
The misconceived and the misbegotten,
　　I would find a sin to do ere I die,
Sure to dissolve and destroy me all through,
230　That would set you higher in heaven, serve you
And leave you happy, when clean forgotten,
　　As a dead man out of mind, am I.

Your lithe hands draw me, your face burns through me,
　　I am swift to follow you, keen to see;
But love lacks might to redeem or undo me;
　　As I have been, I know I shall surely be;
'What should such fellows as I do?' Nay,
My part were worse if I chose to play;
For the worst is this after all; if they knew me,
240　　Not a soul upon earth would pity me.

And I play not for pity of these; but you,
　　If you saw with your soul what man am I,
You would praise me at least that my soul all through
　　Clove to you, loathing the lives that lie;
The souls and lips that are bought and sold,
The smiles of silver and kisses of gold,
The lapdog loves that whine as they chew,
　　The little lovers that curse and cry.

There are fairer women, I hear; that may be;
250　　But I, that I love you and find you fair,
Who are more than fair in my eyes if they be,
　　Do the high gods know or the great gods care?
Though the swords in my heart for one were seven,
Should the iron hollow of doubtful heaven,
That knows not itself whether night-time or day be,
　　Reverberate words and a foolish prayer?

I will go back to the great sweet mother,
    Mother and lover of men, the sea.
I will go down to her, I and none other,
260   Close with her, kiss her and mix her with me;
Cling to her, strive with her, hold her fast:
O fair white mother, in days long past
Born without sister, born without brother,
    Set free my soul as thy soul is free.

O fair green-girdled mother of mine,
    Sea, that art clothed with the sun and the rain,
Thy sweet hard kisses are strong like wine,
    Thy large embraces are keen like pain.
Save me and hide me with all thy waves,
270 Find me one grave of thy thousand graves,
Those pure cold populous graves of thine
    Wrought without hand in a world without stain.

I shall sleep, and move with the moving ships,
    Change as the winds change, veer in the tide;
My lips will feast on the foam of thy lips,
    I shall rise with thy rising, with thee subside;
Sleep, and not know if she be, if she were,
Filled full with life to the eyes and hair,
As a rose is fulfilled to the roseleaf tips
280 With splendid summer and perfume and pride.

This woven raiment of nights and days,
    Were it once cast off and unwound from me,
Naked and glad would I walk in thy ways,
    Alive and aware of thy ways and thee;
Clear of the whole world, hidden at home,
Clothed with the green and crowned with the foam,
A pulse of the life of thy straits and bays,
    A vein in the heart of the streams of the sea.

Fair mother, fed with the lives of men,
290   Thou art subtle and cruel of heart, men say.
Thou hast taken, and shalt not render again;
    Thou art full of thy dead, and cold as they.
But death is the worst that comes of thee;
Thou art fed with our dead, O mother, O sea,
But when hast thou fed on our hearts? or when,
    Having given us love, hast thou taken away?

O tender-hearted, O perfect lover,
    Thy lips are bitter, and sweet thine heart.
The hopes that hurt and the dreams that hover,
300   Shall they not vanish away and apart?
But thou, thou art sure, thou art older than earth;
Thou art strong for death and fruitful of birth;
Thy depths conceal and thy gulfs discover;
    From the first thou wert; in the end thou art.

And grief shall endure not for ever, I know.
    As things that are not shall these things be;
We shall live through seasons of sun and of snow,
    And none be grievous as this to me.
We shall hear, as one in a trance that hears,
310   The sound of time, the rhyme of the years;
Wrecked hope and passionate pain will grow
    As tender things of a spring-tide sea.

Sea-fruit that swings in the waves that hiss,
    Drowned gold and purple and royal rings.
And all time past, was it all for this?
    Times unforgotten, and treasures of things?
Swift years of liking and sweet long laughter,
That wist not well of the years thereafter
Till love woke, smitten at heart by a kiss,
320   With lips that trembled and trailing wings?

There lived a singer in France of old
    By the tideless dolorous midland sea.
In a land of sand and ruin and gold
    There shone one woman, and none but she.
And finding life for her love's sake fail,
Being fain to see her, he bade set sail,
Touched land, and saw her as life grew cold,
    And praised God, seeing; and so died he.

Died, praising God for his gift and grace:
330   For she bowed down to him weeping, and said
'Live;' and her tears were shed on his face
    Or ever the life in his face was shed.
The sharp tears fell through her hair, and stung
Once, and her close lips touched him and clung
Once, and grew one with his lips for a space;
    And so drew back, and the man was dead.

O brother, the gods were good to you.
    Sleep, and be glad while the world endures.
Be well content as the years wear through;
340   Give thanks for life, and the loves and lures;
Give thanks for life, O brother, and death,
For the sweet last sound of her feet, her breath,
For gifts she gave you, gracious and few,
    Tears and kisses, that lady of yours.

Rest, and be glad of the gods; but I,
    How shall I praise them, or how take rest?
There is not room under all the sky
    For me that know not of worst or best,
Dream or desire of the days before,
350 Sweet things or bitterness, any more.
Love will not come to me now though I die,
    As love came close to you, breast to breast.

I shall never be friends again with roses;
    I shall loathe sweet tunes, where a note grown strong
Relents and recoils, and climbs and closes,
    As a wave of the sea turned back by song.
There are sounds where the soul's delight takes fire,
Face to face with its own desire;
A delight that rebels, a desire that reposes;
360   I shall hate sweet music my whole life long.

The pulse of war and passion of wonder,
    The heavens that murmur, the sounds that shine,
The stars that sing and the loves that thunder,
    The music burning at heart like wine,
An armed archangel whose hands raise up
All senses mixed in the spirit's cup
Till flesh and spirit are molten in sunder –
    These things are over, and no more mine.

These were a part of the playing I heard
370   Once, ere my love and my heart were at strife;
Love that sings and hath wings as a bird,
    Balm of the wound and heft of the knife.
Fairer than earth is the sea, and sleep
Than overwatching of eyes that weep,
Now time has done with his one sweet word,
    The wine and leaven of lovely life.

I shall go my ways, tread out my measure,
    Fill the days of my daily breath
With fugitive things not good to treasure,
380   Do as the world doth, say as it saith;
But if we had loved each other – O sweet,
Had you felt, lying under the palms of your feet,
The heart of my heart, beating harder with pleasure
    To feel you tread it to dust and death –

Ah, had I not taken my life up and given
    All that life gives and the years let go,
The wine and honey, the balm and leaven,
    The dreams reared high and the hopes brought low?
Come life, come death, not a word be said;
390 Should I lose you living, and vex you dead?
I never shall tell you on earth; and in heaven,
    If I cry to you then, will you hear or know?

Les Noyades

Whatever a man of the sons of men
    Shall say to his heart of the lords above,
They have shown man verily, once and again,
    Marvellous mercies and infinite love.

In the wild fifth year of the change of things,
    When France was glorious and blood-red, fair
With dust of battle and deaths of kings,
    A queen of men, with helmeted hair,

Carrier came down to the Loire and slew,
10   Till all the ways and the waves waxed red:
Bound and drowned, slaying two by two,
    Maidens and young men, naked and wed.

They brought on a day to his judgment-place
    One rough with labour and red with fight,
And a lady noble by name and face,
    Faultless, a maiden, wonderful, white.

She knew not, being for shame's sake blind,
    If his eyes were hot on her face hard by.
And the judge bade strip and ship them, and bind
20   Bosom to bosom, to drown and die.

The white girl winced and whitened; but he
   Caught fire, waxed bright as a great bright flame
Seen with thunder far out on the sea,
   Laughed hard as the glad blood went and came.

Twice his lips quailed with delight, then said,
   'I have but a word to you all, one word;
Bear with me; surely I am but dead;'
   And all they laughed and mocked him and heard.

'Judge, when they open the judgment-roll,
30   I will stand upright before God and pray:
"Lord God, have mercy on one man's soul,
   For his mercy was great upon earth, I say.

'"Lord, if I loved thee – Lord, if I served –
   If these who darkened thy fair Son's face
I fought with, sparing not one, nor swerved
   A hand's-breadth, Lord, in the perilous place –

'"I pray thee say to this man, O Lord,
   Sit thou for him at my feet on a throne.
I will face thy wrath, though it bite as a sword,
40   And my soul shall burn for his soul, and atone.

'"For, Lord, thou knowest, O God most wise,
   How gracious on earth were his deeds towards me.
Shall this be a small thing in thine eyes,
   That is greater in mine than the whole great sea?"

'I have loved this woman my whole life long,
   And even for love's sake when have I said
"I love you"? when have I done you wrong,
   Living? but now I shall have you dead.

'Yea, now, do I bid you love me, love?
50   Love me or loathe, we are one not twain.
But God be praised in his heaven above
   For this my pleasure and that my pain!

'For never a man, being mean like me,
    Shall die like me till the whole world dies.
I shall drown with her, laughing for love; and she
    Mix with me, touching me, lips and eyes.

'Shall she not know me and see me all through,
    Me, on whose heart as a worm she trod?
You have given me, God requite it you,
60   What man yet never was given of God.'

O sweet one love, O my life's delight,
    Dear, though the days have divided us,
Lost beyond hope, taken far out of sight,
    Not twice in the world shall the gods do thus.

Had it been so hard for my love? but I,
    Though the gods gave all that a god can give,
I had chosen rather the gift to die,
    Cease, and be glad above all that live.

For the Loire would have driven us down to the sea,
70   And the sea would have pitched us from shoal to shoal;
And I should have held you, and you held me,
    As flesh holds flesh, and the soul the soul.

Could I change you, help you to love me, sweet,
    Could I give you the love that would sweeten death,
We should yield, go down, locked hands and feet,
    Die, drown together, and breath catch breath;

But you would have felt my soul in a kiss,
    And known that once if I loved you well;
And I would have given my soul for this
80   To burn for ever in burning hell.

A Leave-Taking

Let us go hence, my songs; she will not hear.
Let us go hence together without fear;
Keep silence now, for singing-time is over,
And over all old things and all things dear.
She loves not you nor me as all we love her.
Yea, though we sang as angels in her ear,
    She would not hear.

Let us rise up and part; she will not know.
Let us go seaward as the great winds go,
Full of blown sand and foam; what help is here?
There is no help, for all these things are so,
And all the world is bitter as a tear.
And how these things are, though ye strove to show,
    She would not know.

Let us go home and hence; she will not weep.
We gave love many dreams and days to keep,
Flowers without scent, and fruits that would not grow,
Saying 'If thou wilt, thrust in thy sickle and reap.'
All is reaped now; no grass is left to mow;
And we that sowed, though all we fell on sleep,
    She would not weep.

Let us go hence and rest; she will not love.
She shall not hear us if we sing hereof,
Nor see love's ways, how sore they are and steep.
Come hence, let be, lie still; it is enough.
Love is a barren sea, bitter and deep;
And though she saw all heaven in flower above,
    She would not love.

Let us give up, go down; she will not care.
Though all the stars made gold of all the air,
And the sea moving saw before it move
One moon-flower making all the foam-flowers fair;

Though all those waves went over us, and drove
Deep down the stifling lips and drowning hair,
    She would not care.

Let us go hence, go hence; she will not see.
Sing all once more together; surely she,
She too, remembering days and words that were,
Will turn a little toward us, sighing; but we,
40 We are hence, we are gone, as though we had not been
        there.
Nay, and though all men seeing had pity on me,
    She would not see.

Itylus

Swallow, my sister, O sister swallow,
   How can thine heart be full of the spring?
      A thousand summers are over and dead.
What hast thou found in the spring to follow?
   What hast thou found in thine heart to sing?
      What wilt thou do when the summer is shed?

O swallow, sister, O fair swift swallow,
   Why wilt thou fly after spring to the south,
      The soft south whither thine heart is set?
10 Shall not the grief of the old time follow?
   Shall not the song thereof cleave to thy mouth?
      Hast thou forgotten ere I forget?

Sister, my sister, O fleet sweet swallow,
   Thy way is long to the sun and the south;
      But I, fulfilled of my heart's desire,
Shedding my song upon height, upon hollow,
   From tawny body and sweet small mouth
      Feed the heart of the night with fire.

I the nightingale all spring through,
20   O swallow, sister, O changing swallow,
All spring through till the spring be done,
Clothed with the light of the night on the dew,
Sing, while the hours and the wild birds follow,
Take flight and follow and find the sun.

Sister, my sister, O soft light swallow,
Though all things feast in the spring's guest-chamber,
How hast thou heart to be glad thereof yet?
For where thou fliest I shall not follow,
Till life forget and death remember,
30   Till thou remember and I forget.

Swallow, my sister, O singing swallow,
I know not how thou hast heart to sing.
Hast thou the heart? is it all past over?
Thy lord the summer is good to follow,
And fair the feet of thy lover the spring:
But what wilt thou say to the spring thy lover?

O swallow, sister, O fleeting swallow,
My heart in me is a molten ember
And over my head the waves have met.
40   But thou wouldst tarry or I would follow,
Could I forget or thou remember,
Couldst thou remember and I forget.

O sweet stray sister, O shifting swallow,
The heart's division divideth us.
Thy heart is light as a leaf of a tree;
But mine goes forth among sea-gulfs hollow
To the place of the slaying of Itylus,
The feast of Daulis, the Thracian sea.

O swallow, sister, O rapid swallow,
50   I pray thee sing not a little space.
        Are not the roofs and the lintels wet?
The woven web that was plain to follow,
    The small slain body, the flowerlike face,
        Can I remember if thou forget?

O sister, sister, thy first-begotten!
    The hands that cling and the feet that follow,
    The voice of the child's blood crying yet
Who hath remembered me? who hath forgotten?
    Thou hast forgotten, O summer swallow,
60   But the world shall end when I forget.

Anactoria

τίνος αὖ τὺ πειθοῖ
μὰψ σαγηνεύσας φιλότατα;
            SAPPHO.

My life is bitter with thy love; thine eyes
Blind me, thy tresses burn me, thy sharp sighs
Divide my flesh and spirit with soft sound,
And my blood strengthens, and my veins abound.
I pray thee sigh not, speak not, draw not breath;
Let life burn down, and dream it is not death.
I would the sea had hidden us, the fire
(Wilt thou fear that, and fear not my desire?)
Severed the bones that bleach, the flesh that cleaves,
10 And let our sifted ashes drop like leaves.
I feel thy blood against my blood: my pain
Pains thee, and lips bruise lips, and vein stings vein.
Let fruit be crushed on fruit, let flower on flower,
Breast kindle breast, and either burn one hour.
Why wilt thou follow lesser loves? are thine
Too weak to bear these hands and lips of mine?

I charge thee for my life's sake, O too sweet
To crush love with thy cruel faultless feet,
I charge thee keep thy lips from hers or his,
20   Sweetest, till theirs be sweeter than my kiss:
Lest I too lure, a swallow for a dove,
Erotion or Erinna to my love.
I would my love could kill thee; I am satiated
With seeing thee live, and fain would have thee dead.
I would earth had thy body as fruit to eat,
And no mouth but some serpent's found thee sweet.
I would find grievous ways to have thee slain,
Intense device, and superflux of pain;
Vex thee with amorous agonies, and shake
30   Life at thy lips, and leave it there to ache;
Strain out thy soul with pangs too soft to kill,
Intolerable interludes, and infinite ill;
Relapse and reluctation of the breath,
Dumb tunes and shuddering semitones of death.
I am weary of all thy words and soft strange ways,
Of all love's fiery nights and all his days,
And all the broken kisses salt as brine
That shuddering lips make moist with waterish wine,
And eyes the bluer for all those hidden hours
40   That pleasure fills with tears and feeds from flowers,
Fierce at the heart with fire that half comes through,
But all the flowerlike white stained round with blue;
The fervent underlid, and that above
Lifted with laughter or abashed with love;
Thine amorous girdle, full of thee and fair,
And leavings of the lilies in thine hair.
Yea, all sweet words of thine and all thy ways,
And all the fruit of nights and flower of days,
And stinging lips wherein the hot sweet brine
50   That Love was born of burns and foams like wine,
And eyes insatiable of amorous hours,
Fervent as fire and delicate as flowers,
Coloured like night at heart, but cloven through
Like night with flame, dyed round like night with blue,

Clothed with deep eyelids under and above –
Yea, all thy beauty sickens me with love;
Thy girdle empty of thee and now not fair,
And ruinous lilies in thy languid hair.
Ah, take no thought for Love's sake; shall this be,
60   And she who loves thy lover not love thee?
Sweet soul, sweet mouth of all that laughs and lives,
Mine is she, very mine; and she forgives.
For I beheld in sleep the light that is
In her high place in Paphos, heard the kiss
Of body and soul that mix with eager tears
And laughter stinging through the eyes and ears;
Saw Love, as burning flame from crown to feet,
Imperishable, upon her storied seat;
Clear eyelids lifted toward the north and south,
70   A mind of many colours, and a mouth
Of many tunes and kisses; and she bowed,
With all her subtle face laughing aloud,
Bowed down upon me, saying, 'Who doth thee wrong,
Sappho?' but thou – thy body is the song,
Thy mouth the music; thou art more than I,
Though my voice die not till the whole world die;
Though men that hear it madden; though love weep,
Though nature change, though shame be charmed to sleep.
Ah, wilt thou slay me lest I kiss thee dead?
80   Yet the queen laughed from her sweet heart and said:
'Even she that flies shall follow for thy sake,
And she shall give thee gifts that would not take,
Shall kiss that would not kiss thee' (yea, kiss me)
'When thou wouldst not' – when I would not kiss thee!
Ah, more to me than all men as thou art,
Shall not my songs assuage her at the heart?
Ah, sweet to me as life seems sweet to death,
Why should her wrath fill thee with fearful breath?
Nay, sweet, for is she God alone? hath she
90   Made earth and all the centuries of the sea,
Taught the sun ways to travel, woven most fine
The moonbeams, shed the starbeams forth as wine,

Bound with her myrtles, beaten with her rods,
The young men and the maidens and the gods?
Have we not lips to love with, eyes for tears,
And summer and flower of women and of years?
Stars for the foot of morning, and for noon
Sunlight, and exaltation of the moon;
Waters that answer waters, fields that wear
100 Lilies, and languor of the Lesbian air?
Beyond those flying feet of fluttered doves,
Are there not other gods for other loves?
Yea, though she scourge thee, sweetest, for my sake,
Blossom not thorns and flowers not blood should break.
Ah that my lips were tuneless lips, but pressed
To the bruised blossom of thy scourged white breast!
Ah that my mouth for Muses' milk were fed
On the sweet blood thy sweet small wounds had bled!
That with my tongue I felt them, and could taste
110 The faint flakes from thy bosom to the waist!
That I could drink thy veins as wine, and eat
Thy breasts like honey! that from face to feet
Thy body were abolished and consumed,
And in my flesh thy very flesh entombed!
Ah, ah, thy beauty! like a beast it bites,
Stings like an adder, like an arrow smites.
Ah sweet, and sweet again, and seven times sweet,
The paces and the pauses of thy feet!
Ah sweeter than all sleep or summer air
120 The fallen fillets fragrant from thine hair!
Yea, though their alien kisses do me wrong,
Sweeter thy lips than mine with all their song;
Thy shoulders whiter than a fleece of white,
And flower-sweet fingers, good to bruise or bite
As honeycomb of the inmost honey-cells,
With almond-shaped and roseleaf-coloured shells
And blood like purple blossom at the tips
Quivering; and pain made perfect in thy lips
For my sake when I hurt thee; O that I
130 Durst crush thee out of life with love, and die,

Die of thy pain and my delight, and be
Mixed with thy blood and molten into thee!
Would I not plague thee dying overmuch?
Would I not hurt thee perfectly? not touch
Thy pores of sense with torture, and make bright
Thine eyes with bloodlike tears and grievous light?
Strike pang from pang as note is struck from note,
Catch the sob's middle music in thy throat,
Take thy limbs living, and new-mould with these
140   A lyre of many faultless agonies?
Feed thee with fever and famine and fine drouth,
With perfect pangs convulse thy perfect mouth,
Make thy life shudder in thee and burn afresh,
And wring thy very spirit through the flesh?
Cruel? but love makes all that love him well
As wise as heaven and crueller than hell.
Me hath love made more bitter toward thee
Than death toward man; but were I made as he
Who hath made all things to break them one by one,
150   If my feet trod upon the stars and sun
And souls of men as his have alway trod,
God knows I might be crueller than God.
For who shall change with prayers or thanksgivings
The mystery of the cruelty of things?
Or say what God above all gods and years
With offering and blood-sacrifice of tears,
With lamentation from strange lands, from graves
Where the snake pastures, from scarred mouths of slaves,
From prison, and from plunging prows of ships
160   Through flamelike foam of the sea's closing lips –
With thwartings of strange signs, and wind-blown hair
Of comets, desolating the dim air,
When darkness is made fast with seals and bars,
And fierce reluctance of disastrous stars,
Eclipse, and sound of shaken hills, and wings
Darkening, and blind inexpiable things –
With sorrow of labouring moons, and altering light
And travail of the planets of the night,

And weeping of the weary Pleiads seven,
170   Feeds the mute melancholy lust of heaven?
Is not his incense bitterness, his meat
Murder? his hidden face and iron feet
Hath not man known, and felt them on their way
Threaten and trample all things and every day?
Hath he not sent us hunger? who hath cursed
Spirit and flesh with longing? filled with thirst
Their lips who cried unto him? who bade exceed
The fervid will, fall short the feeble deed,
Bade sink the spirit and the flesh aspire,
180   Pain animate the dust of dead desire,
And life yield up her flower to violent fate?
Him would I reach, him smite, him desecrate,
Pierce the cold lips of God with human breath,
And mix his immortality with death.
Why hath he made us? what had all we done
That we should live and loathe the sterile sun,
And with the moon wax paler as she wanes,
And pulse by pulse feel time grow through our veins?
Thee too the years shall cover; thou shalt be
190   As the rose born of one same blood with thee,
As a song sung, as a word said, and fall
Flower-wise, and be not any more at all,
Nor any memory of thee anywhere;
For never Muse has bound above thine hair
The high Pierian flower whose graft outgrows
All summer kinship of the mortal rose
And colour of deciduous days, nor shed
Reflex and flush of heaven about thine head,
Nor reddened brows made pale by floral grief
200   With splendid shadow from that lordlier leaf.
Yea, thou shalt be forgotten like spilt wine,
Except these kisses of my lips on thine
Brand them with immortality; but me –
Men shall not see bright fire nor hear the sea,
Nor mix their hearts with music, nor behold
Cast forth of heaven, with feet of awful gold

And plumeless wings that make the bright air blind,
Lightning, with thunder for a hound behind
Hunting through fields unfurrowed and unsown,
210   But in the light and laughter, in the moan
And music, and in grasp of lip and hand
And shudder of water that makes felt on land
The immeasurable tremor of all the sea,
Memories shall mix and metaphors of me.
Like me shall be the shuddering calm of night,
When all the winds of the world for pure delight
Close lips that quiver and fold up wings that ache;
When nightingales are louder for love's sake,
And leaves tremble like lute-strings or like fire;
220   Like me the one star swooning with desire
Even at the cold lips of the sleepless moon,
As I at thine; like me the waste white noon,
Burnt through with barren sunlight; and like me
The land-stream and the tide-stream in the sea.
I am sick with time as these with ebb and flow,
And by the yearning in my veins I know
The yearning sound of waters; and mine eyes
Burn as that beamless fire which fills the skies
With troubled stars and travailing things of flame;
230   And in my heart the grief consuming them
Labours, and in my veins the thirst of these,
And all the summer travail of the trees
And all the winter sickness; and the earth,
Filled full with deadly works of death and birth,
Sore spent with hungry lusts of birth and death,
Has pain like mine in her divided breath;
Her spring of leaves is barren, and her fruit
Ashes; her boughs are burdened, and her root
Fibrous and gnarled with poison; underneath
240   Serpents have gnawn it through with tortuous teeth
Made sharp upon the bones of all the dead,
And wild birds rend her branches overhead.
These, woven as raiment for his word and thought,
These hath God made, and me as these, and wrought

Song, and hath lit it at my lips; and me
Earth shall not gather though she feed on thee.
As a shed tear shalt thou be shed; but I –
Lo, earth may labour, men live long and die,
Years change and stars, and the high God devise
250   New things, and old things wane before his eyes
Who wields and wrecks them, being more strong than
      they –
But, having made me, me he shall not slay.
Nor slay nor satiate, like those herds of his
Who laugh and live a little, and their kiss
Contents them, and their loves are swift and sweet,
And sure death grasps and gains them with slow feet,
Love they or hate they, strive or bow their knees –
And all these end; he hath his will of these.
Yea, but albeit he slay me, hating me –
260   Albeit he hide me in the deep dear sea
And cover me with cool wan foam, and ease
This soul of mine as any soul of these,
And give me water and great sweet waves, and make
The very sea's name lordlier for my sake,
The whole sea sweeter – albeit I die indeed
And hide myself and sleep and no man heed,
Of me the high God hath not all his will.
Blossom of branches, and on each high hill
Clean air and wind, and under in clamorous vales
270   Fierce noises of the fiery nightingales,
Buds burning in the sudden spring like fire,
The wan washed sand and the waves' vain desire,
Sails seen like blown white flowers at sea, and words
That bring tears swiftest, and long notes of birds
Violently singing till the whole world sings –
I Sappho shall be one with all these things,
With all high things for ever; and my face
Seen once, my songs once heard in a strange place,
Cleave to men's lives, and waste the days thereof
280   With gladness and much sadness and long love.
Yea, they shall say, earth's womb has borne in vain
New things, and never this best thing again;

Borne days and men, borne fruits and wars and wine,
Seasons and songs, but no song more like mine.
And they shall know me as ye who have known me here,
Last year when I loved Atthis, and this year
When I love thee; and they shall praise me, and say
'She hath all time as all we have our day,
Shall she not live and have her will' – even I?
290 Yea, though thou diest, I say I shall not die.
For these shall give me of their souls, shall give
Life, and the days and loves wherewith I live,
Shall quicken me with loving, fill with breath,
Save me and serve me, strive for me with death.
Alas, that neither moon nor snow nor dew
Nor all cold things can purge me wholly through,
Assuage me nor allay me nor appease,
Till supreme sleep shall bring me bloodless ease;
Till time wax faint in all his periods;
300 Till fate undo the bondage of the gods,
And lay, to slake and satiate me all through,
Lotus and Lethe on my lips like dew,
And shed around and over and under me
Thick darkness and the insuperable sea.

Hymn to Proserpine
(AFTER THE PROCLAMATION IN ROME OF THE
CHRISTIAN FAITH)

Vicisti, Galilæe.

I have lived long enough, having seen one thing, that love
        hath an end;
Goddess and maiden and queen, be near me now and
        befriend.
Thou art more than the day or the morrow, the seasons that
        laugh or that weep;
For these give joy and sorrow; but thou, Proserpina, sleep.
Sweet is the treading of wine, and sweet the feet of the dove;

But a goodlier gift is thine than foam of the grapes or love.
Yea, is not even Apollo, with hair and harpstring of gold,
A bitter God to follow, a beautiful God to behold?
I am sick of singing: the bays burn deep and chafe: I am
    fain
10   To rest a little from praise and grievous pleasure and pain.
For the Gods we know not of, who give us our daily breath,
We know they are cruel as love or life, and lovely as death.
O Gods dethroned and deceased, cast forth, wiped out in a
    day!
From your wrath is the world released, redeemed from your
    chains, men say.
New Gods are crowned in the city; their flowers have
    broken your rods;
They are merciful, clothed with pity, the young
    compassionate Gods.
But for me their new device is barren, the days are bare;
Things long past over suffice, and men forgotten that were.
Time and the Gods are at strife; ye dwell in the midst
    thereof,
20   Draining a little life from the barren breasts of love.
I say to you, cease, take rest; yea, I say to you all, be at
    peace,
Till the bitter milk of her breast and the barren bosom shall
    cease.
Wilt thou yet take all, Galilean? but these thou shalt not
    take,
The laurel, the palms and the pæan, the breasts of the
    nymphs in the brake;
Breasts more soft than a dove's, that tremble with tenderer
    breath;
And all the wings of the Loves, and all the joy before death;
All the feet of the hours that sound as a single lyre,
Dropped and deep in the flowers, with strings that flicker
    like fire.
More than these wilt thou give, things fairer than all these
    things?

30   Nay, for a little we live, and life hath mutable wings.
     A little while and we die; shall life not thrive as it may?
     For no man under the sky lives twice, outliving his day.
     And grief is a grievous thing, and a man hath enough of his
         tears:
     Why should he labour, and bring fresh grief to blacken his
         years?
     Thou hast conquered, O pale Galilean; the world has grown
         grey from thy breath;
     We have drunken of things Lethean, and fed on the fullness
         of death.
     Laurel is green for a season, and love is sweet for a day;
     But love grows bitter with treason, and laurel outlives not
         May.
     Sleep, shall we sleep after all? for the world is not sweet in
         the end;
40   For the old faiths loosen and fall, the new years ruin and
         rend.
     Fate is a sea without shore, and the soul is a rock that
         abides;
     But her ears are vexed with the roar and her face with the
         foam of the tides.
     O lips that the live blood faints in, the leavings of racks and
         rods!
     O ghastly glories of saints, dead limbs of gibbeted Gods!
     Though all men abase them before you in spirit, and all
         knees bend,
     I kneel not neither adore you, but standing, look to the
         end.
     All delicate days and pleasant, all spirits and sorrows are
         cast
     Far out with the foam of the present that sweeps to the surf
         of the past:
     Where beyond the extreme sea-wall, and between the
         remote sea-gates,
50   Waste water washes, and tall ships founder, and deep death
         waits:

Where, mighty with deepening sides, clad about with the
    seas as with wings,
And impelled of invisible tides, and fulfilled of unspeakable
    things,
White-eyed and poisonous-finned, shark-toothed and
    serpentine-curled,
Rolls, under the whitening wind of the future, the wave of
    the world.
The depths stand naked in sunder behind it, the storms flee
    away;
In the hollow before it the thunder is taken and snared as a
    prey;
In its sides is the north-wind bound; and its salt is of all
    men's tears;
With light of ruin, and sound of changes, and pulse of
    years:
With travail of day after day, and with trouble of hour upon
    hour;
60 And bitter as blood is the spray; and the crests are as fangs
    that devour:
And its vapour and storm of its steam as the sighing of
    spirits to be;
And its noise as the noise in a dream; and its depth as the
    roots of the sea:
And the height of its heads as the height of the utmost stars
    of the air:
And the ends of the earth at the might thereof tremble, and
    time is made bare.
Will ye bridle the deep sea with reins, will ye chasten the
    high sea with rods?
Will ye take her to chain her with chains, who is older than
    all ye Gods?
All ye as a wind shall go by, as a fire shall ye pass and be
    past;
Ye are Gods, and behold, ye shall die, and the waves be
    upon you at last.

In the darkness of time, in the deeps of the years, in the
    changes of things,
70 Ye shall sleep as a slain man sleeps, and the world shall
    forget you for kings.
Though the feet of thine high priests tread where thy lords
    and our forefathers trod,
Though these that were Gods are dead, and thou being dead
    art a God,
Though before thee the throned Cytherean be fallen, and
    hidden her head,
Yet thy kingdom shall pass, Galilean, thy dead shall go
    down to thee dead.
Of the maiden thy mother men sing as a goddess with grace
    clad around;
Thou art throned where another was king; where another
    was queen she is crowned.
Yea, once we had sight of another: but now she is queen, say
    these.
Not as thine, not as thine was our mother, a blossom of
    flowering seas,
Clothed round with the world's desire as with raiment, and
    fair as the foam,
80 And fleeter than kindled fire, and a goddess, and mother of
    Rome.
For thine came pale and a maiden, and sister to sorrow; but
    ours,
Her deep hair heavily laden with odour and colour of
    flowers,
White rose of the rose-white water, a silver splendour, a
    flame,
Bent down unto us that besought her, and earth grew sweet
    with her name.
For thine came weeping, a slave among slaves, and rejected;
    but she
Came flushed from the full-flushed wave, and imperial, her
    foot on the sea.

And the wonderful waters knew her, the winds and the
    viewless ways,
And the roses grew rosier, and bluer the sea-blue stream of
    the bays.
Ye are fallen, our lords, by what token? we wist that ye
    should not fall.
90   Ye were all so fair that are broken; and one more fair than ye
    all.
But I turn to her still, having seen she shall surely abide in
    the end;
Goddess and maiden and queen, be near me now and
    befriend.
O daughter of earth, of my mother, her crown and blossom
    of birth,
I am also, I also, thy brother; I go as I came unto earth.
In the night where thine eyes are as moons are in heaven,
    the night where thou art,
Where the silence is more than all tunes, where sleep
    overflows from the heart,
Where the poppies are sweet as the rose in our world, and
    the red rose is white,
And the wind falls faint as it blows with the fume of the
    flowers of the night,
And the murmur of spirits that sleep in the shadow of Gods
    from afar
100   Grows dim in thine ears and deep as the deep dim soul of a
    star,
In the sweet low light of thy face, under heavens untrod by
    the sun,
Let my soul with their souls find place, and forget what is
    done and undone.
Thou art more than the Gods who number the days of our
    temporal breath;
For these give labour and slumber; but thou, Proserpina,
    death.
Therefore now at thy feet I abide for a season in silence. I
    know
I shall die as my fathers died, and sleep as they sleep; even
    so.

For the glass of the years is brittle wherein we gaze for a
      span;
A little soul for a little bears up this corpse which is man.[1]
So long I endure, no longer; and laugh not again, neither
      weep.
110 For there is no God found stronger than death; and death is
      a sleep.

Ilicet

There is an end of joy and sorrow;
Peace all day long, all night, all morrow,
    But never a time to laugh or weep.
The end is come of pleasant places,
The end of tender words and faces,
    The end of all, the poppied sleep.

No place for sound within their hearing,
No room to hope, no time for fearing,
    No lips to laugh, no lids for tears.
10 The old years have run out all their measure;
No chance of pain, no chance of pleasure,
    No fragment of the broken years.

Outside of all the worlds and ages,
There where the fool is as the sage is,
    There where the slayer is clean of blood,
No end, no passage, no beginning,
There where the sinner leaves off sinning,
    There where the good man is not good.

There is not one thing with another,
20 But Evil saith to Good: My brother,
    My brother, I am one with thee:

[1] ψυχάριον εἶ βαστάζον νεκρόν.   EPICTETUS.

They shall not strive nor cry for ever:
No man shall choose between them: never
   Shall this thing end and that thing be.

Wind wherein seas and stars are shaken
Shall shake them, and they shall not waken;
   None that has lain down shall arise;
The stones are sealed across their places;
One shadow is shed on all their faces,
30   One blindness cast on all their eyes.

Sleep, is it sleep perchance that covers
Each face, as each face were his lover's?
   Farewell; as men that sleep fare well.
The grave's mouth laughs unto derision
Desire and dread and dream and vision,
   Delight of heaven and sorrow of hell.

No soul shall tell nor lip shall number
The names and tribes of you that slumber;
   No memory, no memorial.
40   'Thou knowest' – who shall say thou knowest?
There is none highest and none lowest:
   An end, an end, an end of all.

Good night, good sleep, good rest from sorrow
To these that shall not have good morrow;
   The gods be gentle to all these.
Nay, if death be not, how shall they be?
Nay, is there help in heaven? it may be
   All things and lords of things shall cease.

The stooped urn, filling, dips and flashes;
50   The bronzèd brims are deep in ashes;
   The pale old lips of death are fed.
Shall this dust gather flesh hereafter?
Shall one shed tears or fall to laughter,
   At sight of all these poor old dead?

Nay, as thou wilt; these know not of it;
Thine eyes' strong weeping shall not profit,
   Thy laughter shall not give thee ease;
Cry aloud, spare not, cease not crying,
Sigh, till thou cleave thy sides with sighing,
60   Thou shalt not raise up one of these.

Burnt spices flash, and burnt wine hisses,
The breathing flame's mouth curls and kisses
   The small dried rows of frankincense;
All round the sad red blossoms smoulder,
Flowers coloured like the fire, but colder,
   In sign of sweet things taken hence;

Yea, for their sake and in death's favour
Things of sweet shape and of sweet savour
   We yield them, spice and flower and wine;
70   Yea, costlier things than wine or spices,
Whereof none knoweth how great the price is,
   And fruit that comes not of the vine.

From boy's pierced throat and girl's pierced bosom
Drips, reddening round the blood-red blossom,
   The slow delicious bright soft blood,
Bathing the spices and the pyre,
Bathing the flowers and fallen fire,
   Bathing the blossom by the bud.

Roses whose lips the flame has deadened
80   Drink till the lapping leaves are reddened
   And warm wet inner petals weep;
The flower whereof sick sleep gets leisure,
Barren of balm and purple pleasure,
   Fumes with no native steam of sleep.

Why will ye weep? what do ye weeping?
For waking folk and people sleeping,
   And sands that fill and sands that fall,

The days rose-red, the poppied hours,
Blood, wine, and spice and fire and flowers,
    There is one end of one and all.

Shall such an one lend love or borrow?
Shall these be sorry for thy sorrow?
    Shall these give thanks for words or breath?
Their hate is as their loving-kindness;
The frontlet of their brows is blindness,
    The armlet of their arms is death.

Lo, for no noise or light of thunder
Shall these grave-clothes be rent in sunder;
    He that hath taken, shall he give?
He hath rent them: shall he bind together?
He hath bound them: shall he break the tether?
    He hath slain them: shall he bid them live?

A little sorrow, a little pleasure,
Fate metes us from the dusty measure
    That holds the date of all of us;
We are born with travail and strong crying,
And from the birth-day to the dying
    The likeness of our life is thus.

One girds himself to serve another,
Whose father was the dust, whose mother
    The little dead red worm therein;
They find no fruit of things they cherish;
The goodness of a man shall perish,
    It shall be one thing with his sin.

In deep wet ways by grey old gardens
Fed with sharp spring the sweet fruit hardens;
    They know not what fruits wane or grow;
Red summer burns to the utmost ember;
They know not, neither can remember,
    The old years and flowers they used to know.

Ah, for their sakes, so trapped and taken,
For theirs, forgotten and forsaken,
   Watch, sleep not, gird thyself with prayer.
Nay, where the heart of wrath is broken,
Where long love ends as a thing spoken,
   How shall thy crying enter there?

Though the iron sides of the old world falter,
The likeness of them shall not alter
   For all the rumour of periods,
130 The stars and seasons that come after,
The tears of latter men, the laughter
   Of the old unalterable gods.

Far up above the years and nations,
The high gods, clothed and crowned with patience,
   Endure through days of deathlike date;
They bear the witness of things hidden;
Before their eyes all life stands chidden,
   As they before the eyes of Fate.

Not for their love shall Fate retire,
140 Nor they relent for our desire,
   Nor the graves open for their call.
The end is more than joy and anguish,
Than lives that laugh and lives that languish,
   The poppied sleep, the end of all.

Hermaphroditus

I

Lift up thy lips, turn round, look back for love,
   Blind love that comes by night and casts out rest;
   Of all things tired thy lips look weariest,
Save the long smile that they are wearied of.
Ah sweet, albeit no love be sweet enough,
   Choose of two loves and cleave unto the best;

Two loves at either blossom of thy breast
Strive until one be under and one above.
Their breath is fire upon the amorous air,
10   Fire in thine eyes and where thy lips suspire:
And whosoever hath seen thee, being so fair,
    Two things turn all his life and blood to fire;
A strong desire begot on great despair,
    A great despair cast out by strong desire.

II

Where between sleep and life some brief space is,
    With love like gold bound round about the head,
    Sex to sweet sex with lips and limbs is wed,
Turning the fruitful feud of hers and his
To the waste wedlock of a sterile kiss;
20   Yet from them something like as fire is shed
    That shall not be assuaged till death be dead,
Though neither life nor sleep can find out this.
Love made himself of flesh that perisheth
    A pleasure-house for all the loves his kin;
But on the one side sat a man like death,
    And on the other a woman sat like sin.
So with veiled eyes and sobs between his breath
    Love turned himself and would not enter in.

III

Love, is it love or sleep or shadow or light
30   That lies between thine eyelids and thine eyes?
    Like a flower laid upon a flower it lies,
Or like the night's dew laid upon the night.
Love stands upon thy left hand and thy right,
    Yet by no sunset and by no moonrise
    Shall make thee man and ease a woman's sighs,
Or make thee woman for a man's delight.
To what strange end hath some strange god made fair
    The double blossom of two fruitless flowers?
Hid love in all the folds of all thy hair,

40   Fed thee on summers, watered thee with showers,
        Given all the gold that all the seasons wear
            To thee that art a thing of barren hours?

IV

        Yea, love, I see; it is not love but fear.
            Nay, sweet, it is not fear but love, I know;
            Or wherefore should thy body's blossom blow
        So sweetly, or thine eyelids leave so clear
        Thy gracious eyes that never made a tear –
            Though for their love our tears like blood should flow,
            Though love and life and death should come and go,
50   So dreadful, so desirable, so dear?
        Yea, sweet, I know; I saw in what swift wise
            Beneath the woman's and the water's kiss
            Thy moist limbs melted into Salmacis,
        And the large light turned tender in thine eyes,
        And all thy boy's breath softened into sighs;
            But Love being blind, how should he know of this?

Au Musée du Louvre, Mars 1863.

Fragoletta

        O Love! what shall be said of thee?
        The son of grief begot by joy?
        Being sightless, wilt thou see?
        Being sexless, wilt thou be
        Maiden or boy?

        I dreamed of strange lips yesterday
        And cheeks wherein the ambiguous blood
        Was like a rose's – yea,
        A rose's when it lay
10   Within the bud.

What fields have bred thee, or what groves
Concealed thee, O mysterious flower,
O double rose of Love's,
With leaves that lure the doves
From bud to bower?

I dare not kiss it, lest my lip
Press harder than an indrawn breath,
And all the sweet life slip
Forth, and the sweet leaves drip,
20   Bloodlike, in death.

O sole desire of my delight!
O sole delight of my desire!
Mine eyelids and eyesight
Feed on thee day and night
Like lips of fire.

Lean back thy throat of carven pearl,
Let thy mouth murmur like the dove's;
Say, Venus hath no girl,
No front of female curl,
30   Among her Loves.

Thy sweet low bosom, thy close hair,
Thy strait soft flanks and slenderer feet,
Thy virginal strange air,
Are these not over fair
For Love to greet?

How should he greet thee? what new name,
Fit to move all men's hearts, could move
Thee, deaf to love or shame,
Love's sister, by the same
40   Mother as Love?

Ah sweet, the maiden's mouth is cold,
Her breast-blossoms are simply red,
Her hair mere brown or gold,
Fold over simple fold
Binding her head.

Thy mouth is made of fire and wine,
Thy barren bosom takes my kiss
And turns my soul to thine
And turns thy lip to mine,
50   And mine it is.

Thou hast a serpent in thine hair,
In all the curls that close and cling;
And ah, thy breast-flower!
Ah love, thy mouth too fair
To kiss and sting!

Cleave to me, love me, kiss mine eyes.
Satiate thy lips with loving me;
Nay, for thou shalt not rise;
Lie still as Love that dies
60   For love of thee.

Mine arms are close about thine head,
My lips are fervent on thy face,
And where my kiss hath fed
Thy flower-like blood leaps red
To the kissed place.

O bitterness of things too sweet!
O broken singing of the dove!
Love's wings are over fleet,
And like the panther's feet
70   The feet of Love.

Rondel

These many years since we began to be,
What have the gods done with us? what with me,
What with my love? they have shown me fates and fears,
Harsh springs, and fountains bitterer than the sea,
Grief a fixed star, and joy a vane that veers,
    These many years.

With her, my love, with her have they done well?
But who shall answer for her? who shall tell
Sweet things or sad, such things as no man hears?
10 May no tears fall, if no tears ever fell,
From eyes more dear to me than starriest spheres
    These many years!

But if tears ever touched, for any grief,
Those eyelids folded like a white-rose leaf,
Deep double shells wherethrough the eye–flower peers,
Let them weep once more only, sweet and brief,
Brief tears and bright, for one who gave her tears
    These many years.

Satia Te Sanguine

If you loved me ever so little,
    I could bear the bonds that gall,
I could dream the bonds were brittle;
    You do not love me at all.

O beautiful lips, O bosom
    More white than the moon's and warm,
A sterile, a ruinous blossom
    Is blown your way in a storm.

As the lost white feverish limbs
    Of the Lesbian Sappho, adrift
In foam where the sea-weed swims,
    Swam loose for the streams to lift,

My heart swims blind in a sea
    That stuns me; swims to and fro,
And gathers to windward and lee
    Lamentation, and mourning, and woe.

A broken, an emptied boat,
    Sea saps it, winds blow apart,
Sick and adrift and afloat,
    The barren waif of a heart.

Where, when the gods would be cruel,
    Do they go for a torture? where
Plant thorns, set pain like a jewel?
    Ah, not in the flesh, not there!

The racks of earth and the rods
    Are weak as foam on the sands;
In the heart is the prey for gods,
    Who crucify hearts, not hands.

Mere pangs corrode and consume,
    Dead when life dies in the brain;
In the infinite spirit is room
    For the pulse of an infinite pain.

I wish you were dead, my dear;
    I would give you, had I to give,
Some death too bitter to fear;
    It is better to die than live.

I wish you were stricken of thunder
    And burnt with a bright flame through,
Consumed and cloven in sunder,
    I dead at your feet like you.

If I could but know after all,
    I might cease to hunger and ache,
Though your heart were ever so small,
    If it were not a stone or a snake.

You are crueller, you that we love,
    Than hatred, hunger, or death;
You have eyes and breasts like a dove,
    And you kill men's hearts with a breath.

As plague in a poisonous city
50   Insults and exults on her dead,
So you, when pallid for pity
    Comes love, and fawns to be fed.

As a tame beast writhes and wheedles,
    He fawns to be fed with wiles;
You carve him a cross of needles,
    And whet them sharp as your smiles.

He is patient of thorn and whip,
    He is dumb under axe or dart;
You suck with a sleepy red lip
60   The wet red wounds in his heart.

You thrill as his pulses dwindle,
    You brighten and warm as he bleeds,
With insatiable eyes that kindle
    And insatiable mouth that feeds.

Your hands nailed love to the tree,
    You stript him, scourged him with rods,
And drowned him deep in the sea
    That hides the dead and their gods.

And for all this, die will he not;
70   There is no man sees him but I;
You came and went and forgot;
    I hope he will some day die.

A Litany

ἐν οὐρανῷ φαεννὰς
κρύψω παρ' ὑμὶν αὐγὰς,
μίας πρὸ νυκτὸς ἑπτὰ νύκτας ἕξετε, κ.τ.λ.

Anth. Sac.

FIRST ANTIPHONE

All the bright lights of heaven
 I will make dark over thee;
One night shall be as seven
 That its skirts may cover thee;
I will send on thy strong men a sword,
 On thy remnant a rod;
Ye shall know that I am the Lord,
 Saith the Lord God.

SECOND ANTIPHONE

All the bright lights of heaven
10 Thou hast made dark over us;
One night has been as seven
 That its skirt might cover us;
Thou hast sent on our strong men a sword,
 On our remnant a rod;
We know that thou art the Lord,
 O Lord our God.

THIRD ANTIPHONE

As the tresses and wings of the wind
 Are scattered and shaken,
I will scatter all them that have sinned,
20 There shall none be taken;
As a sower that scattereth seed,
 So will I scatter them;
As one breaketh and shattereth a reed,
 I will break and shatter them.

FOURTH ANTIPHONE

As the wings and the locks of the wind
    Are scattered and shaken,
Thou hast scattered all them that have sinned,
    There was no man taken;
As a sower that scattereth seed,
30   So hast thou scattered us;
As one breaketh and shattereth a reed,
    Thou hast broken and shattered us.

FIFTH ANTIPHONE

From all thy lovers that love thee
    I God will sunder thee;
I will make darkness above thee,
    And thick darkness under thee;
Before me goeth a light,
    Behind me a sword;
Shall a remnant find grace in my sight?
40   I am the Lord.

SIXTH ANTIPHONE

From all our lovers that love us
    Thou God didst sunder us;
Thou madest darkness above us,
    And thick darkness under us;
Thou hast kindled thy wrath for a light,
    And made ready thy sword;
Let a remnant find grace in thy sight,
    We beseech thee, O Lord.

SEVENTH ANTIPHONE

Wilt thou bring fine gold for a payment
50   For sins on this wise?
For the glittering of raiment
    And the shining of eyes,
For the painting of faces
    And the sundering of trust,
For the sins of thine high places
    And delight of thy lust?

For your high things ye shall have lowly,
    Lamentation for song;
For, behold, I God am holy,
60   I the Lord am strong;
Ye shall seek me and shall not reach me
    Till the wine-press be trod;
In that hour ye shall turn and beseech me,
    Saith the Lord God.

EIGHTH ANTIPHONE
Not with fine gold for a payment,
    But with coin of sighs,
But with rending of raiment
    And with weeping of eyes,
But with shame of stricken faces
70   And with strewing of dust,
For the sin of stately places
    And lordship of lust;

With voices of men made lowly,
    Made empty of song,
O Lord God most holy,
    O God most strong,
We reach out hands to reach thee
    Ere the wine-press be trod;
We beseech thee, O Lord, we beseech thee,
80   O Lord our God.

NINTH ANTIPHONE
In that hour thou shalt say to the night,
    Come down and cover us;
To the cloud on thy left and thy right,
    Be thou spread over us;
A snare shall be as thy mother,
    And a curse thy bride;
Thou shalt put her away, and another
    Shall lie by thy side.

Thou shalt neither rise up by day
90   Nor lie down by night;
Would God it were dark! thou shalt say;
    Would God it were light!
And the sight of thine eyes shall be made
    As the burning of fire;
And thy soul shall be sorely afraid
    For thy soul's desire.

Ye whom your lords loved well,
    Putting silver and gold on you,
The inevitable hell
100   Shall surely take hold on you;
Your gold shall be for a token,
    Your staff for a rod;
With the breaking of bands ye are broken,
    Saith the Lord God.

TENTH ANTIPHONE
In our sorrow we said to the night,
    Fall down and cover us;
To the darkness at left and at right,
    Be thou shed over us;
We had breaking of spirit to mother
110   And cursing to bride;
And one was slain, and another
    Stood up at our side.

We could not arise by day,
    Nor lie down by night;
Thy sword was sharp in our way,
    Thy word in our sight;
The delight of our eyelids was made
    As the burning of fire;
And our souls became sorely afraid
120   For our soul's desire.

We whom the world loved well,
    Laying silver and gold on us,
The kingdom of death and of hell
    Riseth up to take hold on us;
Our gold is turned to a token,
    Our staff to a rod;
Yet shalt thou bind them up that were broken,
    O Lord our God.

A Lamentation

I

Who hath known the ways of time
    Or trodden behind his feet?
        There is no such man among men.
For chance overcomes him, or crime
    Changes; for all things sweet
        In time wax bitter again.
Who shall give sorrow enough,
    Or who the abundance of tears?
Mine eyes are heavy with love
10   And a sword gone thorough mine ears,
        A sound like a sword and fire,
        For pity, for great desire;
Who shall ensure me thereof,
    Lest I die, being full of my fears?

Who hath known the ways and the wrath,
    The sleepless spirit, the root
        And blossom of evil will,
            The divine device of a god?
Who shall behold it or hath?
20   The twice-tongued prophets are mute,
        The many speakers are still;
            No foot has travelled or trod,

No hand has meted, his path.
   Man's fate is a blood-red fruit,
     And the mighty gods have their fill
       And relax not the rein, or the rod.

Ye were mighty in heart from of old,
   Ye slew with the spear, and are slain.
Keen after heat is the cold,
30   Sore after summer is rain,
And melteth man to the bone.
   As water he weareth away,
   As a flower, as an hour in a day,
Fallen from laughter to moan.
But my spirit is shaken with fear
   Lest an evil thing begin,
New-born, a spear for a spear,
   And one for another sin.
Or ever our tears began,
40   It was known from of old and said;
One law for a living man,
   And another law for the dead.
For these are fearful and sad,
   Vain, and things without breath;
     While he lives let a man be glad,
       For none hath joy of his death.

II

Who hath known the pain, the old pain of earth,
   Or all the travail of the sea,
The many ways and waves, the birth
50 Fruitless, the labour nothing worth?
   Who hath known, who knoweth, O gods? not we.

There is none shall say he hath seen,
   There is none he hath known.
Though he saith, Lo, a lord have I been,
   I have reaped and sown;

I have seen the desire of mine eyes,
    The beginning of love,
The season of kisses and sighs
    And the end thereof.
60   I have known the ways of the sea,
    All the perilous ways,
Strange winds have spoken with me,
    And the tongues of strange days.
I have hewn the pine for ships;
    Where steeds run arow,
I have seen from their bridled lips
    Foam blown as the snow.
With snapping of chariot-poles
    And with straining of oars
70   I have grazed in the race the goals,
    In the storm the shores;
As a greave is cleft with an arrow
    At the joint of the knee,
I have cleft through the sea-straits narrow
    To the heart of the sea.
When air was smitten in sunder
    I have watched on high
The ways of the stars and the thunder
    In the night of the sky;
80   Where the dark brings forth light as a flower,
    As from lips that dissever;
One abideth the space of an hour,
    One endureth for ever.
Lo, what hath he seen or known,
    Of the way and the wave
Unbeholden, unsailed on, unsown,
    From the breast to the grave?

Or ever the stars were made, or skies,
    Grief was born, and the kinless night,
90   Mother of gods without form or name.

And light is born out of heaven and dies,
　　And one day knows not another's light,
　　　But night is one, and her shape the same.

But dumb the goddesses underground
　　Wait, and we hear not on earth if their feet
　　　Rise, and the night wax loud with their wings;
Dumb, without word or shadow of sound;
　　And sift in scales and winnow as wheat
　　　Men's souls, and sorrow of manifold things.

III

100　Nor less of grief than ours
　　　The gods wrought long ago
　　　　To bruise men one by one;
　　But with the incessant hours
　　　Fresh grief and greener woe
　　　　Spring, as the sudden sun
　　Year after year makes flowers;
　　　And these die down and grow,
　　　　And the next year lacks none.

　　As these men sleep, have slept
110　　The old heroes in time fled,
　　　　No dream-divided sleep;
　　And holier eyes have wept
　　　Than ours, when on her dead
　　　　Gods have seen Thetis weep,
　　With heavenly hair far-swept
　　　Back, heavenly hands outspread
　　　　Round what she could not keep,

　　Could not one day withhold,
　　　One night; and like as these
120　　　White ashes of no weight,
　　Held not his urn the cold

Ashes of Heracles?
    For all things born one gate
Opens, no gate of gold;
    Opens; and no man sees
        Beyond the gods and fate.

Anima Anceps

Till death have broken
Sweet life's love-token,
Till all be spoken
    That shall be said,
What dost thou praying,
O soul, and playing
With song and saying,
    Things flown and fled?
For this we know not —
10 That fresh springs flow not
And fresh griefs grow not
    When men are dead;
When strange years cover
Lover and lover,
And joys are over
    And tears are shed.

If one day's sorrow
Mar the day's morrow —
If man's life borrow
20   And man's death pay —
If souls once taken,
If lives once shaken,
Arise, awaken,
    By night, by day —
Why with strong crying
And years of sighing,
Living and dying,
    Fast ye and pray?

For all your weeping,
30   Waking and sleeping,
Death comes to reaping
    And takes away.

Though time rend after
Roof-tree from rafter,
A little laughter
    Is much more worth
Than thus to measure
The hour, the treasure,
The pain, the pleasure,
40   The death, the birth;
Grief, when days alter,
Like joy shall falter;
Song-book and psalter,
    Mourning and mirth.
Live like the swallow;
Seek not to follow
Where earth is hollow
    Under the earth.

In the Orchard
(PROVENÇAL BURDEN)

Leave go my hands, let me catch breath and see;
Let the dew-fall drench either side of me;
    Clear apple-leaves are soft upon that moon
Seen sidelong like a blossom in the tree;
    Ah God, ah God, that day should be so soon.

The grass is thick and cool, it lets us lie.
Kissed upon either cheek and either eye,
    I turn to thee as some green afternoon
Turns toward sunset, and is loth to die;
10   Ah God, ah God, that day should be so soon.

Lie closer, lean your face upon my side,
Feel where the dew fell that has hardly dried,
  Hear how the blood beats that went nigh to swoon;
The pleasure lives there when the sense has died;
  Ah God, ah God, that day should be so soon.

O my fair lord, I charge you leave me this:
Is it not sweeter than a foolish kiss?
  Nay take it then, my flower, my first in June,
My rose, so like a tender mouth it is:
20 Ah God, ah God, that day should be so soon.

Love, till dawn sunder night from day with fire,
Dividing my delight and my desire,
  The crescent life and love the plenilune,
Love me though dusk begin and dark retire;
  Ah God, ah God, that day should be so soon.

Ah, my heart fails, my blood draws back; I know,
When life runs over, life is near to go;
  And with the slain of love love's ways are strewn,
And with their blood, if love will have it so;
30 Ah God, ah God, that day should be so soon.

Ah, do thy will now; slay me if thou wilt;
There is no building now the walls are built,
  No quarrying now the corner-stone is hewn,
No drinking now the vine's whole blood is spilt;
  Ah God, ah God, that day should be so soon.

Nay, slay me now; nay, for I will be slain;
Pluck thy red pleasure from the teeth of pain,
  Break down thy vine ere yet grape-gatherers prune,
Slay me ere day can slay desire again;
40 Ah God, ah God, that day should be so soon.

Yea, with thy sweet lips, with thy sweet sword; yea,
Take life and all, for I will die, I say;
    Love, I gave love, is life a better boon?
For sweet night's sake I will not live till day;
    Ah God, ah God, that day should be so soon.

Nay, I will sleep then only; nay, but go.
Ah sweet, too sweet to me, my sweet, I know
    Love, sleep, and death go to the sweet same tune;
Hold my hair fast, and kiss me through it so.
50   Ah God, ah God, that day should be so soon.

A Match

If love were what the rose is,
    And I were like the leaf,
Our lives would grow together
In sad or singing weather,
Blown fields or flowerful closes,
    Green pleasure or grey grief;
If love were what the rose is,
    And I were like the leaf.

If I were what the words are,
10   And love were like the tune,
With double sound and single
Delight our lips would mingle,
With kisses glad as birds are
    That get sweet rain at noon;
If I were what the words are,
    And love were like the tune.

If you were life, my darling,
    And I your love were death,
We'd shine and snow together
20 Ere March made sweet the weather
With daffodil and starling

And hours of fruitful breath;
If you were life, my darling,
   And I your love were death.

If you were thrall to sorrow,
   And I were page to joy,
We'd play for lives and seasons
With loving looks and treasons
And tears of night and morrow
30   And laughs of maid and boy;
If you were thrall to sorrow,
   And I were page to joy.

If you were April's lady,
   And I were lord in May,
We'd throw with leaves for hours
And draw for days with flowers,
Till day like night were shady
   And night were bright like day;
If you were April's lady,
40   And I were lord in May.

If you were queen of pleasure,
   And I were king of pain,
We'd hunt down love together,
Pluck out his flying-feather,
And teach his feet a measure,
   And find his mouth a rein;
If you were queen of pleasure,
   And I were king of pain.

Faustine

Ave Faustina Imperatrix, morituri te salutant.

Lean back, and get some minutes' peace;
    Let your head lean
Back to the shoulder with its fleece
    Of locks, Faustine.

The shapely silver shoulder stoops,
    Weighed over clean
With state of splendid hair that droops
    Each side, Faustine.

Let me go over your good gifts
10   That crown you queen;
A queen whose kingdom ebbs and shifts
    Each week, Faustine.

Bright heavy brows well gathered up:
    White gloss and sheen;
Carved lips that make my lips a cup
    To drink, Faustine,

Wine and rank poison, milk and blood,
    Being mixed therein
Since first the devil threw dice with God
20   For you, Faustine.

Your naked new-born soul, their stake,
    Stood blind between;
God said 'let him that wins her take
    And keep Faustine.'

But this time Satan throve, no doubt;
    Long since, I ween,
God's part in you was battered out;
    Long since, Faustine.

The die rang sideways as it fell,
    Rang cracked and thin,
Like a man's laughter heard in hell
    Far down, Faustine,

A shadow of laughter like a sigh,
    Dead sorrow's kin;
So rang, thrown down, the devil's die
    That won Faustine.

A suckling of his breed you were,
    One hard to wean;
But God, who lost you, left you fair,
    We see, Faustine.

You have the face that suits a woman
    For her soul's screen –
The sort of beauty that's called human
    In hell, Faustine.

You could do all things but be good
    Or chaste of mien;
And that you would not if you could,
    We know, Faustine.

Even he who cast seven devils out
    Of Magdalene
Could hardly do as much, I doubt,
    For you, Faustine.

Did Satan make you to spite God?
    Or did God mean
To scourge with scorpions for a rod
    Our sins, Faustine?

I know what queen at first you were,
    As though I had seen
Red gold and black imperious hair
    Twice crown Faustine.

As if your fed sarcophagus
    Spared flesh and skin,
You come back face to face with us,
    The same Faustine.

She loved the games men played with death,
    Where death must win;
As though the slain man's blood and breath
    Revived Faustine.

Nets caught the pike, pikes tore the net;
    Lithe limbs and lean
70 From drained-out pores dripped thick red sweat
    To soothe Faustine.

She drank the steaming drift and dust
    Blown off the scene;
Blood could not ease the bitter lust
    That galled Faustine.

All round the foul fat furrows reeked,
    Where blood sank in;
The circus splashed and seethed and shrieked
80   All round Faustine.

But these are gone now: years entomb
    The dust and din;
Yea, even the bath's fierce reek and fume
    That slew Faustine.

Was life worth living then? and now
    Is life worth sin?
Where are the imperial years? and how
    Are you Faustine?

Your soul forgot her joys, forgot
90   Her times of teen;
Yea, this life likewise will you not
    Forget, Faustine?

For in the time we know not of
    Did fate begin
Weaving the web of days that wove
    Your doom, Faustine.

The threads were wet with wine, and all
    Were smooth to spin;
They wove you like a Bacchanal,
100   The first Faustine.

And Bacchus cast your mates and you
    Wild grapes to glean;
Your flower-like lips were dashed with dew
    From his, Faustine.

Your drenched loose hands were stretched to hold
    The vine's wet green,
Long ere they coined in Roman gold
    Your face, Faustine.

Then after change of soaring feather
110   And winnowing fin,
You woke in weeks of feverish weather,
    A new Faustine.

A star upon your birthday burned,
    Whose fierce serene
Red pulseless planet never yearned
    In heaven, Faustine.

Stray breaths of Sapphic song that blew
    Through Mitylene
Shook the fierce quivering blood in you
120   By night, Faustine.

The shameless nameless love that makes
    Hell's iron gin
Shut on you like a trap that breaks
    The soul, Faustine.

And when your veins were void and dead,
  What ghosts unclean
Swarmed round the straitened barren bed
  That hid Faustine?

What sterile growths of sexless root
130   Or epicene?
What flower of kisses without fruit
  Of love, Faustine?

What adders came to shed their coats?
  What coiled obscene
Small serpents with soft stretching throats
  Caressed Faustine?

But the time came of famished hours,
  Maimed loves and mean,
This ghastly thin-faced time of ours,
140   To spoil Faustine.

You seem a thing that hinges hold,
  A love-machine
With clockwork joints of supple gold –
  No more, Faustine.

Not godless, for you serve one God,
  The Lampsacene,
Who metes the gardens with his rod;
  Your lord, Faustine.

If one should love you with real love
150   (Such things have been,
Things your fair face knows nothing of,
  It seems, Faustine);

That clear hair heavily bound back,
  The lights wherein
Shift from dead blue to burnt-up black;
  Your throat, Faustine,

Strong, heavy, throwing out the face
   And hard bright chin
And shameful scornful lips that grace
160   Their shame, Faustine,

Curled lips, long since half kissed away,
   Still sweet and keen;
You'd give him – poison shall we say?
   Or what, Faustine?

A Cameo

There was a graven image of Desire
   Painted with red blood on a ground of gold
   Passing between the young men and the old,
And by him Pain, whose body shone like fire,
And Pleasure with gaunt hands that grasped their hire.
   Of his left wrist, with fingers clenched and cold,
   The insatiable Satiety kept hold,
Walking with feet unshod that pashed the mire.
The senses and the sorrows and the sins,
10   And the strange loves that suck the breasts of Hate
Till lips and teeth bite in their sharp indenture,
Followed like beasts with flap of wings and fins.
   Death stood aloof behind a gaping grate,
Upon whose lock was written *Peradventure*.

Song before Death
(FROM THE FRENCH)
1795

Sweet mother, in a minute's span
   Death parts thee and my love of thee;
Sweet love, that yet art living man,

Come back, true love, to comfort me.
Back, ah, come back! ah wellaway!
But my love comes not any day.

As roses, when the warm West blows,
    Break to full flower and sweeten spring,
My soul would break to a glorious rose
10   In such wise at his whispering.
In vain I listen; wellaway!
My love says nothing any day.

You that will weep for pity of love
    On the low place where I am lain,
I pray you, having wept enough,
    Tell him for whom I bore such pain
That he was yet, ah! wellaway!
My true love to my dying day.

Rococo

Take hands and part with laughter;
    Touch lips and part with tears;
Once more and no more after,
    Whatever comes with years.
We twain shall not remeasure
    The ways that left us twain;
Nor crush the lees of pleasure
    From sanguine grapes of pain.

We twain once well in sunder,
10   What will the mad gods do
For hate with me, I wonder,
    Or what for love with you?
Forget them till November,
    And dream there's April yet;
Forget that I remember,
    And dream that I forget.

Time found our tired love sleeping,
    And kissed away his breath;
But what should we do weeping,
20   Though light love sleep to death?
We have drained his lips at leisure,
    Till there's not left to drain
A single sob of pleasure,
    A single pulse of pain.

Dream that the lips once breathless
    Might quicken if they would;
Say that the soul is deathless;
    Dream that the gods are good;
Say March may wed September,
30   And time divorce regret;
But not that you remember,
    And not that I forget.

We have heard from hidden places
    What love scarce lives and hears:
We have seen on fervent faces
    The pallor of strange tears:
We have trod the wine-vat's treasure,
    Whence, ripe to steam and stain,
Foams round the feet of pleasure
40   The blood-red must of pain.

Remembrance may recover
    And time bring back to time
The name of your first lover,
    The ring of my first rhyme;
But rose-leaves of December
    The frosts of June shall fret,
The day that you remember,
    The day that I forget.

The snake that hides and hisses
50   In heaven we twain have known;
The grief of cruel kisses,

The joy whose mouth makes moan;
The pulse's pause and measure,
    Where in one furtive vein
Throbs through the heart of pleasure
    The purpler blood of pain.

We have done with tears and treasons
    And love for treason's sake;
Room for the swift new seasons,
60   The years that burn and break,
Dismantle and dismember
    Men's days and dreams, Juliette;
For love may not remember,
    But time will not forget.

Life treads down love in flying,
    Time withers him at root;
Bring all dead things and dying,
    Reaped sheaf and ruined fruit,
Where, crushed by three days' pressure,
70   Our three days' love lies slain;
And earlier leaf of pleasure,
    And latter flower of pain.

Breathe close upon the ashes,
    It may be flame will leap;
Unclose the soft close lashes,
    Lift up the lids, and weep.
Light love's extinguished ember,
    Let one tear leave it wet
For one that you remember
80   And ten that you forget.

Stage Love

When the game began between them for a jest,
He played king and she played queen to match the best;
Laughter soft as tears, and tears that turned to laughter,
These were things she sought for years and sorrowed after.

Pleasure with dry lips, and pain that walks by night;
All the sting and all the stain of long delight;
These were things she knew not of, that knew not of her,
When she played at half a love with half a lover.

Time was chorus, gave them cues to laugh or cry;
They would kill, befool, amuse him, let him die;
Set him webs to weave to-day and break to-morrow,
Till he died for good in play, and rose in sorrow.

What the years mean; how time dies and is not slain;
How love grows and laughs and cries and wanes again;
These were things she came to know, and take their
        measure,
When the play was played out so for one man's pleasure.

The Leper

Nothing is better, I well think,
    Than love; the hidden well-water
Is not so delicate to drink:
    This was well seen of me and her.

I served her in a royal house;
    I served her wine and curious meat.
For will to kiss between her brows,
    I had no heart to sleep or eat.

Mere scorn God knows she had of me,
    A poor scribe, nowise great or fair,
Who plucked his clerk's hood back to see
    Her curled-up lips and amorous hair.

I vex my head with thinking this.
    Yea, though God always hated me,
And hates me now that I can kiss
    Her eyes, plait up her hair to see

How she then wore it on the brows,
    Yet am I glad to have her dead
Here in this wretched wattled house
    Where I can kiss her eyes and head.

Nothing is better, I well know,
    Than love; no amber in cold sea
Or gathered berries under snow:
    That is well seen of her and me.

Three thoughts I make my pleasure of:
    First I take heart and think of this:
That knight's gold hair she chose to love,
    His mouth she had such will to kiss.

Then I remember that sundawn
    I brought him by a privy way
Out at her lattice, and thereon
    What gracious words she found to say.

(Cold rushes for such little feet –
    Both feet could lie into my hand.
A marvel was it of my sweet
    Her upright body could so stand.)

'Sweet friend, God give you thank and grace;
    Now am I clean and whole of shame,
Nor shall men burn me in the face
    For my sweet fault that scandals them.'

I tell you over word by word.
   She, sitting edgewise on her bed,
Holding her feet, said thus. The third,
   A sweeter thing than these, I said.

God, that makes time and ruins it
   And alters not, abiding God,
Changed with disease her body sweet,
   The body of love wherein she abode.

Love is more sweet and comelier
50   Than a dove's throat strained out to sing.
All they spat out and cursed at her
   And cast her forth for a base thing.

They cursed her, seeing how God had wrought
   This curse to plague her, a curse of his.
Fools were they surely, seeing not
   How sweeter than all sweet she is.

He that had held her by the hair,
   With kissing lips blinding her eyes,
Felt her bright bosom, strained and bare,
60   Sigh under him, with short mad cries

Out of her throat and sobbing mouth
   And body broken up with love,
With sweet hot tears his lips were loth
   Her own should taste the savour of,

Yea, he inside whose grasp all night
   Her fervent body leapt or lay,
Stained with sharp kisses red and white,
   Found her a plague to spurn away.

I hid her in this wattled house,
70   I served her water and poor bread.
For joy to kiss between her brows
   Time upon time I was nigh dead.

Bread failed; we got but well-water
    And gathered grass with dropping seed.
I had such joy of kissing her,
    I had small care to sleep or feed.

Sometimes when service made me glad
    The sharp tears leapt between my lids,
Falling on her, such joy I had
80   To do the service God forbids.

'I pray you let me be at peace,
    Get hence, make room for me to die.'
She said that: her poor lip would cease,
    Put up to mine, and turn to cry.

I said, 'Bethink yourself how love
    Fared in us twain, what either did;
Shall I unclothe my soul thereof?
    That I should do this, God forbid.'

Yea, though God hateth us, he knows
90   That hardly in a little thing
Love faileth of the work it does
    Till it grow ripe for gathering.

Six months, and now my sweet is dead
    A trouble takes me; I know not
If all were done well, all well said,
    No word or tender deed forgot.

Too sweet, for the least part in her,
    To have shed life out by fragments; yet,
Could the close mouth catch breath and stir,
100   I might see something I forget.

Six months, and I sit still and hold
    In two cold palms her cold two feet.
Her hair, half grey half ruined gold,
    Thrills me and burns me in kissing it.

Love bites and stings me through, to see
  Her keen face made of sunken bones.
Her worn-off eyelids madden me,
  That were shot through with purple once.

She said, 'Be good with me; I grow
110 So tired for shame's sake, I shall die
If you say nothing:' even so.
  And she is dead now, and shame put by.

Yea, and the scorn she had of me
  In the old time, doubtless vexed her then.
I never should have kissed her. See
  What fools God's anger makes of men!

She might have loved me a little too,
  Had I been humbler for her sake.
But that new shame could make love new
120 She saw not – yet her shame did make.

I took too much upon my love,
  Having for such mean service done
Her beauty and all the way thereof,
  Her face and all the sweet thereon.

Yea, all this while I tended her,
  I know the old love held fast his part:
I know the old scorn waxed heavier,
  Mixed with sad wonder, in her heart.

It may be all my love went wrong –
130 A scribe's work writ awry and blurred,
Scrawled after the blind evensong –
  Spoilt music with no perfect word.

But surely I would fain have done
  All things the best I could. Perchance
Because I failed, came short of one,
  She kept at heart that other man's.

I am grown blind with all these things:
    It may be now she hath in sight
Some better knowledge; still there clings
140   The old question. Will not God do right?*

A Ballad of Burdens

The burden of fair women. Vain delight,
    And love self-slain in some sweet shameful way,
And sorrowful old age that comes by night
    As a thief comes that has no heart by day,
    And change that finds fair cheeks and leaves them grey,
And weariness that keeps awake for hire,
    And grief that says what pleasure used to say;
This is the end of every man's desire.

---

* En ce temps-là estoyt dans ce pays grand nombre de ladres et de meseaulx, ce dont le roy eut grand desplaisir, veu que Dieu dust en estre moult griefvement courroucé. Ores il advint qu'une noble damoyselle appelée Yolande de Sallières estant atteincte et touste guastée de ce vilain mal, tous ses amys et ses parens ayant devant leurs yeux la paour de Dieu la firent issir fors de leurs maisons et oncques ne voulurent recepvoir ni reconforter chose mauldicte de Dieu et à tous les hommes puante et abhominable. Ceste dame avoyt esté moult belle et gracieuse de formes, et de son corps elle estoyt large et de vie lascive. Pourtant nul des amans qui l'avoyent souventesfois accollée et baisée moult tendrement ne voulust plus héberger si laide femme et si détestable pescheresse. Ung seul clerc qui feut premièrement son lacquays et son entremetteur en matière d'amour la reçut chez luy et la récéla dans une petite cabane. Là mourut la meschinette de grande misère et de male mort: et après elle décéda ledist clerc qui pour grand amour l'avoyt six mois durant soignée, lavée, habillée et deshabillée tous les jours de ses mains propres. Mesme dist-on que ce meschant homme et mauldict clerc se remémourant de la grande beauté passée et guastée de ceste femme se délectoyt maintesfois à la baiser sur sa bouche orde et lépreuse et l'accoller doulcement de ses mains amoureuses. Aussy est-il mort de ceste mesme maladie abhominable. Cecy advint près Fontainebellant en Gastinois. Et quand ouyt le roy Philippe ceste adventure moult en estoyt esmerveillé.
    Grandes Chroniques de France, 1505.

The burden of bought kisses. This is sore,
A burden without fruit in childbearing;
Between the nightfall and the dawn threescore,
Threescore between the dawn and evening.
The shuddering in thy lips, the shuddering
In thy sad eyelids tremulous like fire,
Makes love seem shameful and a wretched thing.
This is the end of every man's desire.

The burden of sweet speeches. Nay, kneel down,
Cover thy head, and weep; for verily
These market-men that buy thy white and brown
In the last days shall take no thought for thee.
In the last days like earth thy face shall be,
Yea, like sea-marsh made thick with brine and mire,
Sad with sick leavings of the sterile sea.
This is the end of every man's desire.

The burden of long living. Thou shalt fear
Waking, and sleeping mourn upon thy bed;
And say at night 'Would God the day were here,'
And say at dawn 'Would God the day were dead.'
With weary days thou shalt be clothed and fed,
And wear remorse of heart for thine attire,
Pain for thy girdle and sorrow upon thine head;
This is the end of every man's desire.

The burden of bright colours. Thou shalt see
Gold tarnished, and the grey above the green;
And as the thing thou seest thy face shall be,
And no more as the thing beforetime seen.
And thou shalt say of mercy 'It hath been,'
And living, watch the old lips and loves expire,
And talking, tears shall take thy breath between;
This is the end of every man's desire.

The burden of sad sayings. In that day
   Thou shalt tell all thy days and hours, and tell
Thy times and ways and words of love, and say
   How one was dear and one desirable,
   And sweet was life to hear and sweet to smell,
But now with lights reverse the old hours retire
   And the last hour is shod with fire from hell;
This is the end of every man's desire.

The burden of four seasons. Rain in spring,
50   White rain and wind among the tender trees;
A summer of green sorrows gathering,
   Rank autumn in a mist of miseries,
   With sad face set towards the year, that sees
The charred ash drop out of the dropping pyre,
   And winter wan with many maladies;
This is the end of every man's desire.

The burden of dead faces. Out of sight
   And out of love, beyond the reach of hands,
Changed in the changing of the dark and light,
60   They walk and weep about the barren lands
   Where no seed is nor any garner stands,
Where in short breaths the doubtful days respire,
   And time's turned glass lets through the sighing sands;
This is the end of every man's desire.

The burden of much gladness. Life and lust
   Forsake thee, and the face of thy delight;
And underfoot the heavy hour strews dust,
   And overhead strange weathers burn and bite;
   And where the red was, lo the bloodless white,
70 And where truth was, the likeness of a liar,
   And where day was, the likeness of the night;
This is the end of every man's desire.

L'ENVOY

Princes, and ye whom pleasure quickeneth,
    Heed well this rhyme before your pleasure tire;
For life is sweet, but after life is death.
    This is the end of every man's desire.

Rondel

Kissing her hair I sat against her feet,
Wove and unwove it, wound and found it sweet;
Made fast therewith her hands, drew down her eyes,
Deep as deep flowers and dreamy like dim skies;
With her own tresses bound and found her fair,
    Kissing her hair.

Sleep were no sweeter than her face to me,
Sleep of cold sea-bloom under the cold sea;
What pain could get between my face and hers?
What new sweet thing would love not relish worse?
Unless, perhaps, white death had kissed me there,
    Kissing her hair?

Before the Mirror
(VERSES WRITTEN UNDER A PICTURE)

Inscribed to J. A. Whistler

I

White rose in red rose-garden
    Is not so white;
Snowdrops that plead for pardon
    And pine for fright

Because the hard East blows
Over their maiden rows
     Grow not as this face grows from pale to bright.

Behind the veil, forbidden,
     Shut up from sight,
Love, is there sorrow hidden,
     Is there delight?
Is joy thy dower or grief,
White rose of weary leaf,
     Late rose whose life is brief, whose loves are light?

Soft snows that hard winds harden
     Till each flake bite
Fill all the flowerless garden
     Whose flowers took flight
Long since when summer ceased,
And men rose up from feast,
     And warm west wind grew east, and warm day night.

II

'Come snow, come wind or thunder
     High up in air,
I watch my face, and wonder
     At my bright hair;
Nought else exalts or grieves
The rose at heart, that heaves
     With love of her own leaves and lips that pair.

'She knows not loves that kissed her
     She knows not where.
Art thou the ghost, my sister,
     White sister there,
Am I the ghost, who knows?
My hand, a fallen rose,
     Lies snow-white on white snows, and takes no care.

'I cannot see what pleasures
   Or what pains were;
What pale new loves and treasures
   New years will bear;
40   What beam will fall, what shower,
What grief or joy for dower;
     But one thing knows the flower; the flower is fair.'

III

Glad, but not flushed with gladness,
   Since joys go by;
Sad, but not bent with sadness,
   Since sorrows die;
Deep in the gleaming glass
She sees all past things pass,
     And all sweet life that was lie down and lie.

50   There glowing ghosts of flowers
   Draw down, draw nigh;
And wings of swift spent hours
   Take flight and fly;
She sees by formless gleams,
She hears across cold streams,
     Dead mouths of many dreams that sing and sigh.

Face fallen and white throat lifted,
   With sleepless eye
She sees old loves that drifted,
60   She knew not why,
Old loves and faded fears
Float down a stream that hears
     The flowing of all men's tears beneath the sky.

Erotion

Sweet for a little even to fear, and sweet,
O love, to lay down fear at love's fair feet;
Shall not some fiery memory of his breath
Lie sweet on lips that touch the lips of death?
Yet leave me not; yet, if thou wilt, be free;
Love me no more, but love my love of thee.
Love where thou wilt, and live thy life; and I,
One thing I can, and one love cannot – die.
Pass from me; yet thine arms, thine eyes, thine hair,
Feed my desire and deaden my despair.
Yet once more ere time change us, ere my cheek
Whiten, ere hope be dumb or sorrow speak,
Yet once more ere thou hate me, one full kiss;
Keep other hours for others, save me this.
Yea, and I will not (if it please thee) weep,
Lest thou be sad; I will but sigh, and sleep.
Sweet, does death hurt? thou canst not do me wrong:
I shall not lack thee, as I loved thee, long.
Hast thou not given me above all that live
Joy, and a little sorrow shalt not give?
What even though fairer fingers of strange girls
Pass nestling through thy beautiful boy's curls
As mine did, or those curled lithe lips of thine
Meet theirs as these, all theirs come after mine;
And though I were not, though I be not, best,
I have loved and love thee more than all the rest.
O love, O lover, loose or hold me fast,
I had thee first, whoever have thee last;
Fairer or not, what need I know, what care?
To thy fair bud my blossom once seemed fair.
Why am I fair at all before thee, why
At all desired? seeing thou art fair, not I.
I shall be glad of thee, O fairest head,
Alive, alone, without thee, with thee, dead;
I shall remember while the light lives yet,
And in the night-time I shall not forget.

Though (as thou wilt) thou leave me ere life leave,
I will not, for thy love I will not, grieve;
Not as they use who love not more than I,
40   Who love not as I love thee though I die;
And though thy lips, once mine, be oftener prest
To many another brow and balmier breast,
And sweeter arms, or sweeter to thy mind,
Lull thee or lure, more fond thou wilt not find.

In Memory of Walter Savage Landor

Back to the flower-town, side by side,
   The bright months bring,
New-born, the bridegroom and the bride,
   Freedom and spring.

The sweet land laughs from sea to sea,
   Filled full of sun;
All things come back to her, being free;
   All things but one.

In many a tender wheaten plot
10   Flowers that were dead
Live, and old suns revive; but not
   That holier head.

By this white wandering waste of sea,
   Far north, I hear
One face shall never turn to me
   As once this year.

Shall never smile and turn and rest
   On mine as there,
Nor one most sacred hand be prest
20   Upon my hair.

I came as one whose thoughts half linger,
    Half run before;
The youngest to the oldest singer
    That England bore.

I found him whom I shall not find
    Till all grief end,
In holiest age our mightiest mind,
    Father and friend.

But thou, if anything endure,
30   If hope there be,
O spirit that man's life left pure,
    Man's death set free,

Not with disdain of days that were
    Look earthward now;
Let dreams revive the reverend hair,
    The imperial brow;

Come back in sleep, for in the life
    Where thou art not
We find none like thee. Time and strife
40   And the world's lot

Move thee no more; but love at least
    And reverent heart
May move thee, royal and released,
    Soul, as thou art.

And thou, his Florence, to thy trust
    Receive and keep,
Keep safe his dedicated dust,
    His sacred sleep.

So shall thy lovers, come from far,
50   Mix with thy name
As morning-star with evening-star
    His faultless fame.

A Song in Time of Order. 1852

Push hard across the sand,
    For the salt wind gathers breath;
Shoulder and wrist and hand,
    Push hard as the push of death.

The wind is as iron that rings,
    The foam-heads loosen and flee;
It swells and welters and swings,
    The pulse of the tide of the sea.

And up on the yellow cliff
10   The long corn flickers and shakes;
Push, for the wind holds stiff,
    And the gunwale dips and rakes.

Good hap to the fresh fierce weather,
    The quiver and beat of the sea!
While three men hold together,
    The kingdoms are less by three.

Out to the sea with her there,
    Out with her over the sand;
Let the kings keep the earth for their share!
20   We have done with the sharers of land.

They have tied the world in a tether,
    They have bought over God with a fee;
While three men hold together,
    The kingdoms are less by three.

We have done with the kisses that sting,
    The thief's mouth red from the feast,
The blood on the hands of the king
    And the lie at the lips of the priest.

Will they tie the winds in a tether,
30 Put a bit in the jaws of the sea?
While three men hold together,
  The kingdoms are less by three.

Let our flag run out straight in the wind!
  The old red shall be floated again
When the ranks that are thin shall be thinned,
  When the names that were twenty are ten;

When the devil's riddle is mastered
  And the galley-bench creaks with a Pope,
We shall see Buonaparte the bastard
40 Kick heels with his throat in a rope.

While the shepherd sets wolves on his sheep
  And the emperor halters his kine,
While Shame is a watchman asleep
  And Faith is a keeper of swine,

Let the wind shake our flag like a feather,
  Like the plumes of the foam of the sea!
While three men hold together,
  The kingdoms are less by three.

All the world has its burdens to bear,
50 From Cayenne to the Austrian whips;
Forth, with the rain in our hair
  And the salt sweet foam in our lips;

In the teeth of the hard glad weather,
  In the blown wet face of the sea;
While three men hold together,
  The kingdoms are less by three.

A Song in Time of Revolution. 1860

The heart of the rulers is sick, and the high-priest covers his
    head:
For this is the song of the quick that is heard in the ears of
    the dead.

The poor and the halt and the blind are keen and mighty
    and fleet:
Like the noise of the blowing of wind is the sound of the
    noise of their feet.

The wind has the sound of a laugh in the clamour of days
    and of deeds:
The priests are scattered like chaff, and the rulers broken
    like reeds.

The high-priest sick from qualms, with his raiment bloodily
    dashed;
The thief with branded palms, and the liar with cheeks
    abashed.

They are smitten, they tremble greatly, they are pained for
    their pleasant things:
10 For the house of the priests made stately, and the might in
    the mouth of the kings.

They are grieved and greatly afraid; they are taken, they
    shall not flee:
For the heart of the nations is made as the strength of the
    springs of the sea.

They were fair in the grace of gold, they walked with
    delicate feet:
They were clothed with the cunning of old, and the smell of
    their garments was sweet.

For the breaking of gold in their hair they halt as a man
    made lame:
They are utterly naked and bare; their mouths are bitter
    with shame.

Wilt thou judge thy people now, O king that wast found
    most wise?
Wilt thou lie any more, O thou whose mouth is emptied of
    lies?

Shall God make a pact with thee, till his hook be found in
    thy sides?
20 Wilt thou put back the time of the sea, or the place of the
    season of tides?

Set a word in thy lips, to stand before God with a word in
    thy mouth:
That 'the rain shall return in the land, and the tender dew
    after drouth.'

But the arm of the elders is broken, their strength is
    unbound and undone:
They wait for a sign of a token; they cry, and there cometh
    none.

Their moan is in every place, the cry of them filleth the
    land:
There is shame in the sight of their face, there is fear in the
    thews of their hand.

They are girdled about the reins with a curse for the girdle
    thereon:
For the noise of the rending of chains the face of their
    colour is gone.

For the sound of the shouting of men they are grievously
    stricken at heart:
30 They are smitten asunder with pain, their bones are smitten
    apart.

There is none of them all that is whole; their lips gape open
    for breath;
They are clothed with sickness of soul, and the shape of the
    shadow of death.

The wind is thwart in their feet; it is full of the shouting of
    mirth;
As one shaketh the sides of a sheet, so it shaketh the ends of
    the earth.

The sword, the sword is made keen; the iron has opened its
    mouth;
The corn is red that was green; it is bound for the sheaves of
    the south.

The sound of a word was shed, the sound of the wind as a
    breath,
In the ears of the souls that were dead, in the dust of the
    deepness of death;

Where the face of the moon is taken, the ways of the stars
    undone,
40 The light of the whole sky shaken, the light of the face of
    the sun:

Where the waters are emptied and broken, the waves of the
    waters are stayed;
Where God has bound for a token the darkness that maketh
    afraid;

Where the sword was covered and hidden, and dust had
    grown in its side,
A word came forth which was bidden, the crying of one that
    cried:

The sides of the two-edged sword shall be bare, and its
    mouth shall be red,
For the breath of the face of the Lord that is felt in the
    bones of the dead.

To Victor Hugo

In the fair days when God
    By man as godlike trod,
And each alike was Greek, alike was free,
    God's lightning spared, they said,
    Alone the happier head
Whose laurels screened it; fruitless grace for thee,
    To whom the high gods gave of right
Their thunders and their laurels and their light.

    Sunbeams and bays before
10   Our master's servants wore,
For these Apollo left in all men's lands;
    But far from these ere now
    And watched with jealous brow
Lay the blind lightnings shut between God's hands,
    And only loosed on slaves and kings
The terror of the tempest of their wings.

    Born in those younger years
    That shone with storms of spears
And shook in the wind blown from a dead world's pyre,
20   When by her back-blown hair
    Napoleon caught the fair
And fierce Republic with her feet of fire,
    And stayed with iron words and hands
Her flight, and freedom in a thousand lands:

    Thou sawest the tides of things
    Close over heads of kings,
And thine hand felt the thunder, and to thee
    Laurels and lightnings were
    As sunbeams and soft air
30 Mixed each in other, or as mist with sea
    Mixed, or as memory with desire,
Or the lute's pulses with the louder lyre.

For thee man's spirit stood
Disrobed of flesh and blood,
And bare the heart of the most secret hours;
    And to thine hand more tame
    Than birds in winter came
High hopes and unknown flying forms of powers,
    And from thy table fed, and sang
40 Till with the tune men's ears took fire and rang.

    Even all men's eyes and ears
    With fiery sound and tears
Waxed hot, and cheeks caught flame and eyelid light,
    At those high songs of thine
    That stung the sense like wine,
Or fell more soft than dew or snow by night,
    Or wailed as in some flooded cave
Sobs the strong broken spirit of a wave.

    But we, our master, we
50   Whose hearts uplift to thee,
Ache with the pulse of thy remembered song,
    We ask not nor await
    From the clenched hands of fate,
As thou, remission of the world's old wrong;
    Respite we ask not, nor release;
Freedom a man may have, he shall not peace.

    Though thy most fiery hope
    Storm heaven, to set wide ope
The all-sought-for gate whence God or Chance debars
60   All feet of men, all eyes –
    The old night resumes her skies,
Her hollow hiding-place of clouds and stars,
    Where nought save these is sure in sight;
And, paven with death, our days are roofed with night.

One thing we can; to be
    Awhile, as men may, free;
But not by hope or pleasure the most stern
    Goddess, most awful-eyed,
    Sits, but on either side
70 Sit sorrow and the wrath of hearts that burn,
    Sad faith that cannot hope or fear,
And memory grey with many a flowerless year.

    Not that in stranger's wise
    I lift not loving eyes
To the fair foster-mother France, that gave
    Beyond the pale fleet foam
    Help to my sires and home,
Whose great sweet breast could shelter those and save
    Whom from her nursing breasts and hands
80 Their land cast forth of old on gentler lands.

    Not without thoughts that ache
    For theirs and for thy sake,
I, born of exiles, hail thy banished head;
    I whose young song took flight
    Toward the great heat and light
On me a child from thy far splendour shed,
    From thine high place of soul and song,
Which, fallen on eyes yet feeble, made them strong.

    Ah, not with lessening love
    For memories born hereof,
90 I look to that sweet mother-land, and see
    The old fields and fair full streams,
    And skies, but fled like dreams
The feet of freedom and the thought of thee;
    And all between the skies and graves
The mirth of mockers and the shame of slaves.

She, killed with noisome air,
Even she! and still so fair,
Who said 'Let there be freedom,' and there was
100   Freedom; and as a lance
The fiery eyes of France
Touched the world's sleep and as a sleep made pass
Forth of men's heavier ears and eyes
Smitten with fire and thunder from new skies.

Are they men's friends indeed
Who watch them weep and bleed?
Because thou hast loved us, shall the gods love thee?
Thou, first of men and friend,
Seest thou, even thou, the end?
110 Thou knowest what hath been, knowest thou what shall be?
Evils may pass and hopes endure;
But fate is dim, and all the gods obscure.

O nursed in airs apart,
O poet highest of heart,
Hast thou seen time, who hast seen so many things?
Are not the years more wise,
More sad than keenest eyes,
The years with soundless feet and sounding wings?
Passing we hear them not, but past
120 The clamour of them thrills us, and their blast.

Thou art chief of us, and lord;
Thy song is as a sword
Keen-edged and scented in the blade from flowers;
Thou art lord and king; but we
Lift younger eyes, and see
Less of high hope, less light on wandering hours;
Hours that have borne men down so long,
Seen the right fail, and watched uplift the wrong.

But thine imperial soul,
130   As years and ruins roll
To the same end, and all things and all dreams
        With the same wreck and roar
        Drift on the dim same shore,
Still in the bitter foam and brackish streams
        Tracks the fresh water-spring to be
And sudden sweeter fountains in the sea.

        As once the high God bound
        With many a rivet round
Man's saviour, and with iron nailed him through,
140   At the wild end of things,
        Where even his own bird's wings
Flagged, whence the sea shone like a drop of dew,
        From Caucasus beheld below
Past fathoms of unfathomable snow;

        So the strong God, the chance
        Central of circumstance,
Still shows him exile who will not be slave;
        All thy great fame and thee
        Girt by the dim strait sea
150 With multitudinous walls of wandering wave;
        Shows us our greatest from his throne
Fate-stricken, and rejected of his own.

        Yea, he is strong, thou say'st,
        A mystery many-faced,
The wild beasts know him and the wild birds flee;
        The blind night sees him, death
        Shrinks beaten at his breath,
And his right hand is heavy on the sea:
        We know he hath made us, and is king;
160 We know not if he care for anything.

Thus much, no more, we know;
 He bade what is be so,
Bade light be and bade night be, one by one;
 Bade hope and fear, bade ill
 And good redeem and kill,
Till all men be aweary of the sun
 And his world burn in its own flame
And bear no witness longer of his name.

 Yet though all this be thus,
170 Be those men praised of us
Who have loved and wrought and sorrowed and not sinned
 For fame or fear or gold,
 Nor waxed for winter cold,
Nor changed for changes of the worldly wind;
 Praised above men of men be these,
Till this one world and work we know shall cease.

 Yea, one thing more than this,
 We know that one thing is,
The splendour of a spirit without blame,
180 That not the labouring years
 Blind-born, nor any fears,
Nor men nor any gods can tire or tame;
 But purer power with fiery breath
Fills, and exalts above the gulfs of death.

 Praised above men be thou,
 Whose laurel-laden brow,
Made for the morning, droops not in the night;
 Praised and beloved, that none
 Of all thy great things done
190 Flies higher than thy most equal spirit's flight;
 Praised, that nor doubt nor hope could bend
Earth's loftiest head, found upright to the end.

Before Dawn

Sweet life, if life were stronger,
Earth clear of years that wrong her,
Then two things might live longer,
   Two sweeter things than they;
Delight, the rootless flower,
And love, the bloomless bower;
Delight that lives an hour,
   And love that lives a day.

From evensong to daytime,
10 When April melts in Maytime,
Love lengthens out his playtime,
   Love lessens breath by breath,
And kiss by kiss grows older
On listless throat or shoulder
Turned sideways now, turned colder
   Than life that dreams of death.

This one thing once worth giving
Life gave, and seemed worth living;
Sin sweet beyond forgiving
20   And brief beyond regret:
To laugh and love together
And weave with foam and feather
And wind and words the tether
   Our memories play with yet.

Ah, one thing worth beginning,
One thread in life worth spinning,
Ah sweet, one sin worth sinning
   With all the whole soul's will;
To lull you till one stilled you,
30 To kiss you till one killed you,
To feel you till one filled you,
   Sweet lips, if love could fill;

To hunt sweet Love and lose him
Between white arms and bosom,
Between the bud and blossom,
   Between your throat and chin;
To say of shame — what is it?
Of virtue — we can miss it,
Of sin — we can but kiss it,
40   And it's no longer sin;

To feel the strong soul, stricken
Through fleshly pulses, quicken
Beneath swift sighs that thicken,
   Soft hands and lips that smite;
Lips that no love can tire,
With hands that sting like fire,
Weaving the web Desire
   To snare the bird Delight.

But love so lightly plighted,
50 Our love with torch unlighted,
Paused near us unaffrighted,
   Who found and left him free;
None, seeing us cloven in sunder,
Will weep or laugh or wonder;
Light love stands clear of thunder,
   And safe from winds at sea.

As, when late larks give warning
Of dying lights and dawning,
Night murmurs to the morning,
60   'Lie still, O love, lie still;'
And half her dark limbs cover
The white limbs of her lover,
With amorous plumes that hover
   And fervent lips that chill;

As scornful day represses
Night's void and vain caresses,
And from her cloudier tresses

Unwinds the gold of his,
With limbs from limbs dividing
70   And breath by breath subsiding;
For love has no abiding,
    But dies before the kiss;

So hath it been, so be it;
For who shall live and flee it?
But look that no man see it
    Or hear it unaware;
Lest all who love and choose him
See Love, and so refuse him;
For all who find him lose him,
80   But all have found him fair.

Dolores
(NOTRE–DAME DES SEPT DOULEURS)

Cold eyelids that hide like a jewel
    Hard eyes that grow soft for an hour;
The heavy white limbs, and the cruel
    Red mouth like a venomous flower;
When these are gone by with their glories,
    What shall rest of thee then, what remain,
O mystic and sombre Dolores,
    Our Lady of Pain?

Seven sorrows the priests give their Virgin;
10   But thy sins, which are seventy times seven,
Seven ages would fail thee to purge in,
    And then they would haunt thee in heaven:
Fierce midnights and famishing morrows,
    And the loves that complete and control
All the joys of the flesh, all the sorrows
    That wear out the soul.

O garment not golden but gilded,
　　O garden where all men may dwell,
O tower not of ivory, but builded
20　　By hands that reach heaven from hell;
O mystical rose of the mire,
　　O house not of gold but of gain,
O house of unquenchable fire,
　　Our Lady of Pain!

O lips full of lust and of laughter,
　　Curled snakes that are fed from my breast,
Bite hard, lest remembrance come after
　　And press with new lips where you pressed.
For my heart too springs up at the pressure,
30　　Mine eyelids too moisten and burn;
Ah, feed me and fill me with pleasure,
　　Ere pain come in turn.

In yesterday's reach and to-morrow's,
　　Out of sight though they lie of to-day,
There have been and there yet shall be sorrows
　　That smite not and bite not in play.
The life and the love thou despisest,
　　These hurt us indeed, and in vain,
O wise among women, and wisest,
40　　Our Lady of Pain.

Who gave thee thy wisdom? what stories
　　That stung thee, what visions that smote?
Wert thou pure and a maiden, Dolores,
　　When desire took thee first by the throat?
What bud was the shell of a blossom
　　That all men may smell to and pluck?
What milk fed thee first at what bosom?
　　What sins gave thee suck?

We shift and bedeck and bedrape us,
    Thou art noble and nude and antique;
Libitina thy mother, Priapus
    Thy father, a Tuscan and Greek.
We play with light loves in the portal,
    And wince and relent and refrain;
Loves die, and we know thee immortal,
    Our Lady of Pain.

Fruits fail and love dies and time ranges;
    Thou art fed with perpetual breath,
And alive after infinite changes,
    And fresh from the kisses of death;
Of languors rekindled and rallied,
    Of barren delights and unclean,
Things monstrous and fruitless, a pallid
    And poisonous queen.

Could you hurt me, sweet lips, though I hurt you?
    Men touch them, and change in a trice
The lilies and languors of virtue
    For the raptures and roses of vice;
Those lie where thy foot on the floor is,
    These crown and caress thee and chain,
O splendid and sterile Dolores,
    Our Lady of Pain.

There are sins it may be to discover,
    There are deeds it may be to delight.
What new work wilt thou find for thy lover,
    What new passions for daytime or night?
What spells that they know not a word of
    Whose lives are as leaves overblown?
What tortures undreamt of, unheard of,
    Unwritten, unknown?

Ah beautiful passionate body
    That never has ached with a heart!
On thy mouth though the kisses are bloody,
    Though they sting till it shudder and smart,
More kind than the love we adore is,
    They hurt not the heart or the brain,
O bitter and tender Dolores,
    Our Lady of Pain.

As our kisses relax and redouble,
90   From the lips and the foam and the fangs
Shall no new sin be born for men's trouble,
    No dream of impossible pangs?
With the sweet of the sins of old ages
    Wilt thou satiate thy soul as of yore?
Too sweet is the rind, say the sages,
    Too bitter the core.

Hast thou told all thy secrets the last time,
    And bared all thy beauties to one?
Ah, where shall we go then for pastime,
100   If the worst that can be has been done?
But sweet as the rind was the core is;
    We are fain of thee still, we are fain,
O sanguine and subtle Dolores,
    Our Lady of Pain.

By the hunger of change and emotion,
    By the thirst of unbearable things,
By despair, the twin-born of devotion,
    By the pleasure that winces and stings,
The delight that consumes the desire,
110   The desire that outruns the delight,
By the cruelty deaf as a fire
    And blind as the night,

By the ravenous teeth that have smitten
　　Through the kisses that blossom and bud,
By the lips intertwisted and bitten
　　Till the foam has a savour of blood,
By the pulse as it rises and falters,
　　By the hands as they slacken and strain,
I adjure thee, respond from thine altars,
120　　Our Lady of Pain.

Wilt thou smile as a woman disdaining
　　The light fire in the veins of a boy?
But he comes to thee sad, without feigning,
　　Who has wearied of sorrow and joy;
Less careful of labour and glory
　　Than the elders whose hair has uncurled;
And young, but with fancies as hoary
　　And grey as the world.

I have passed from the outermost portal
130　　To the shrine where a sin is a prayer;
What care though the service be mortal?
　　O our Lady of Torture, what care?
All thine the last wine that I pour is,
　　The last in the chalice we drain,
O fierce and luxurious Dolores,
　　Our Lady of Pain.

All thine the new wine of desire,
　　The fruit of four lips as they clung
Till the hair and the eyelids took fire,
140　　The foam of a serpentine tongue,
The froth of the serpents of pleasure,
　　More salt than the foam of the sea,
Now felt as a flame, now at leisure
　　As wine shed for me.

Ah thy people, thy children, thy chosen,
   Marked cross from the womb and perverse!
They have found out the secret to cozen
   The gods that constrain us and curse;
They alone, they are wise, and none other;
150   Give me place, even me, in their train,
O my sister, my spouse, and my mother,
   Our Lady of Pain.

For the crown of our life as it closes
   Is darkness, the fruit thereof dust;
No thorns go as deep as a rose's,
   And love is more cruel than lust.
Time turns the old days to derision,
   Our loves into corpses or wives;
And marriage and death and division
160   Make barren our lives.

And pale from the past we draw nigh thee,
   And satiate with comfortless hours;
And we know thee, how all men belie thee,
   And we gather the fruit of thy flowers;
The passion that slays and recovers,
   The pangs and the kisses that rain
On the lips and the limbs of thy lovers,
   Our Lady of Pain.

The desire of thy furious embraces
170   Is more than the wisdom of years,
On the blossom though blood lie in traces,
   Though the foliage be sodden with tears.
For the lords in whose keeping the door is
   That opens on all who draw breath
Gave the cypress to love, my Dolores,
   The myrtle to death.

And they laughed, changing hands in the measure,
    And they mixed and made peace after strife;
Pain melted in tears, and was pleasure;
180   Death tingled with blood, and was life.
Like lovers they melted and tingled,
    In the dusk of thine innermost fane;
In the darkness they murmured and mingled,
    Our Lady of Pain.

In a twilight where virtues are vices,
    In thy chapels, unknown of the sun,
To a tune that enthralls and entices,
    They were wed, and the twain were as one.
For the tune from thine altar hath sounded
190   Since God bade the world's work begin,
And the fume of thine incense abounded,
    To sweeten the sin.

Love listens, and paler than ashes,
    Through his curls as the crown on them slips,
Lifts languid wet eyelids and lashes,
    And laughs with insatiable lips.
Thou shalt hush him with heavy caresses,
    With music that scares the profane;
Thou shalt darken his eyes with thy tresses,
200   Our Lady of Pain.

Thou shalt blind his bright eyes though he wrestle,
    Thou shalt chain his light limbs though he strive;
In his lips all thy serpents shall nestle,
    In his hands all thy cruelties thrive.
In the daytime thy voice shall go through him,
    In his dreams he shall feel thee and ache;
Thou shalt kindle by night and subdue him
    Asleep and awake.

Thou shalt touch and make redder his roses
   With juice not of fruit nor of bud;
When the sense in the spirit reposes,
   Thou shalt quicken the soul through the blood.
Thine, thine the one grace we implore is,
   Who would live and not languish or feign,
O sleepless and deadly Dolores,
   Our Lady of Pain.

Dost thou dream, in a respite of slumber,
   In a lull of the fires of thy life,
Of the days without name, without number,
   When thy will stung the world into strife;
When, a goddess, the pulse of thy passion
   Smote kings as they revelled in Rome;
And they hailed thee re-risen, O Thalassian,
   Foam-white, from the foam?

When thy lips had such lovers to flatter;
   When the city lay red from thy rods,
And thine hands were as arrows to scatter
   The children of change and their gods;
When the blood of thy foemen made fervent
   A sand never moist from the main,
As one smote them, their lord and thy servant,
   Our Lady of Pain.

On sands by the storm never shaken,
   Nor wet from the washing of tides;
Nor by foam of the waves overtaken,
   Nor winds that the thunder bestrides;
But red from the print of thy paces,
   Made smooth for the world and its lords,
Ringed round with a flame of fair faces,
   And splendid with swords.

There the gladiator, pale for thy pleasure,
   Drew bitter and perilous breath;
There torments laid hold on the treasure
   Of limbs too delicious for death;
When thy gardens were lit with live torches;
   When the world was a steed for thy rein;
When the nations lay prone in thy porches,
   Our Lady of Pain.

When, with flame all around him aspirant,
250   Stood flushed, as a harp-player stands,
The implacable beautiful tyrant,
   Rose-crowned, having death in his hands;
And a sound as the sound of loud water
   Smote far through the flight of the fires,
And mixed with the lightning of slaughter
   A thunder of lyres.

Dost thou dream of what was and no more is,
   The old kingdoms of earth and the kings?
Dost thou hunger for these things, Dolores,
260   For these, in a world of new things?
But thy bosom no fasts could emaciate,
   No hunger compel to complain
Those lips that no bloodshed could satiate,
   Our Lady of Pain.

As of old when the world's heart was lighter,
   Through thy garments the grace of thee glows,
The white wealth of thy body made whiter
   By the blushes of amorous blows,
And seamed with sharp lips and fierce fingers,
270   And branded by kisses that bruise;
When all shall be gone that now lingers,
   Ah, what shall we lose?

Thou wert fair in the fearless old fashion,
    And thy limbs are as melodies yet,
And move to the music of passion
    With lithe and lascivious regret.
What ailed us, O gods, to desert you
    For creeds that refuse and restrain?
Come down and redeem us from virtue,
280   Our Lady of Pain.

All shrines that were Vestal are flameless,
    But the flame has not fallen from this;
Though obscure be the god, and though nameless
    The eyes and the hair that we kiss;
Low fires that love sits by and forges
    Fresh heads for his arrows and thine;
Hair loosened and soiled in mid orgies
    With kisses and wine.

Thy skin changes country and colour,
290   And shrivels or swells to a snake's.
Let it brighten and bloat and grow duller,
    We know it, the flames and the flakes,
Red brands on it smitten and bitten,
    Round skies where a star is a stain,
And the leaves with thy litanies written,
    Our Lady of Pain.

On thy bosom though many a kiss be,
    There are none such as knew it of old.
Was it Alciphron once or Arisbe,
300   Male ringlets or feminine gold,
That thy lips met with under the statue,
    Whence a look shot out sharp after thieves
From the eyes of the garden-god at you
    Across the fig-leaves?

Then still, through dry seasons and moister,
    One god had a wreath to his shrine;
Then love was the pearl of his oyster,[1]
    And Venus rose red out of wine.
We have all done amiss, choosing rather
310   Such loves as the wise gods disdain;
Intercede for us thou with thy father,
    Our Lady of Pain.

In spring he had crowns of his garden,
    Red corn in the heat of the year,
Then hoary green olives that harden
    When the grape-blossom freezes with fear;
And milk-budded myrtles with Venus
    And vine-leaves with Bacchus he trod;
And ye said, 'We have seen, he hath seen us,
320   A visible God.'

What broke off the garlands that girt you?
    What sundered you spirit and clay?
Weak sins yet alive are as virtue
    To the strength of the sins of that day.
For dried is the blood of thy lover,
    Ipsithilla, contracted the vein;
Cry aloud, 'Will he rise and recover,
    Our Lady of Pain?'

Cry aloud; for the old world is broken:
330   Cry out; for the Phrygian is priest,
And rears not the bountiful token
    And spreads not the fatherly feast.
From the midmost of Ida, from shady
    Recesses that murmur at morn,
They have brought and baptized her, Our Lady,
    A goddess new-born.

---

[1] Nam te præcipuè in suis urbibus colit ora
Hellespontia, cæteris ostreosior oris.
                    CATULL. *Carm*. xviii.

And the chaplets of old are above us,
    And the oyster-bed teems out of reach;
Old poets outsing and outlove us,
340   And Catullus makes mouths at our speech.
Who shall kiss, in thy father's own city,
    With such lips as he sang with, again?
Intercede for us all of thy pity,
    Our Lady of Pain.

Out of Dindymus heavily laden
    Her lions draw bound and unfed
A mother, a mortal, a maiden,
    A queen over death and the dead.
She is cold, and her habit is lowly,
350   Her temple of branches and sods;
Most fruitful and virginal, holy,
    A mother of gods.

She hath wasted with fire thine high places,
    She hath hidden and marred and made sad
The fair limbs of the Loves, the fair faces
    Of gods that were goodly and glad.
She slays, and her hands are not bloody;
    She moves as a moon in the wane,
White-robed, and thy raiment is ruddy,
360   Our Lady of Pain.

They shall pass and their places be taken,
    The gods and the priests that are pure.
They shall pass, and shalt thou not be shaken?
    They shall perish, and shalt thou endure?
Death laughs, breathing close and relentless
    In the nostrils and eyelids of lust,
With a pinch in his fingers of scentless
    And delicate dust.

But the worm shall revive thee with kisses;
370   Thou shalt change and transmute as a god,
As the rod to a serpent that hisses,
    As the serpent again to a rod.
Thy life shall not cease though thou doff it;
    Thou shalt live until evil be slain,
And good shall die first, said thy prophet,
    Our Lady of Pain.

Did he lie? did he laugh? does he know it,
    Now he lies out of reach, out of breath,
Thy prophet, thy preacher, thy poet,
380   Sin's child by incestuous Death?
Did he find out in fire at his waking,
    Or discern as his eyelids lost light,
When the bands of the body were breaking
    And all came in sight?

Who has known all the evil before us,
    Or the tyrannous secrets of time?
Though we match not the dead men that bore us
    At a song, at a kiss, at a crime –
Though the heathen outface and outlive us,
390   And our lives and our longings are twain –
Ah, forgive us our virtues, forgive us,
    Our Lady of Pain.

Who are we that embalm and embrace thee
    With spices and savours of song?
What is time, that his children should face thee?
    What am I, that my lips do thee wrong?
I could hurt thee – but pain would delight thee;
    Or caress thee – but love would repel;
And the lovers whose lips would excite thee
400   Are serpents in hell.

Who now shall content thee as they did,
    Thy lovers, when temples were built
And the hair of the sacrifice braided
    And the blood of the sacrifice spilt,
In Lampsacus fervent with faces,
    In Aphaca red from thy reign,
Who embraced thee with awful embraces,
    Our Lady of Pain?

Where are they, Cotytto or Venus,
410   Astarte or Ashtaroth, where?
Do their hands as we touch come between us?
    Is the breath of them hot in thy hair?
From their lips have thy lips taken fever,
    With the blood of their bodies grown red?
Hast thou left upon earth a believer
    If these men are dead?

They were purple of raiment and golden,
    Filled full of thee, fiery with wine,
Thy lovers, in haunts unbeholden,
420   In marvellous chambers of thine.
They are fled, and their footprints escape us,
    Who appraise thee, adore, and abstain,
O daughter of Death and Priapus,
    Our Lady of Pain.

What ails us to fear overmeasure,
    To praise thee with timorous breath,
O mistress and mother of pleasure,
    The one thing as certain as death?
We shall change as the things that we cherish,
430   Shall fade as they faded before,
As foam upon water shall perish,
    As sand upon shore.

We shall know what the darkness discovers,
    If the grave-pit be shallow or deep;
And our fathers of old, and our lovers,
    We shall know if they sleep not or sleep.
We shall see whether hell be not heaven,
    Find out whether tares be not grain,
And the joys of thee seventy times seven,
440   Our Lady of Pain.

The Garden of Proserpine

Here, where the world is quiet;
    Here, where all trouble seems
Dead winds' and spent waves' riot
    In doubtful dreams of dreams;
I watch the green field growing
For reaping folk and sowing,
For harvest-time and mowing,
    A sleepy world of streams.

I am tired of tears and laughter,
10   And men that laugh and weep;
Of what may come hereafter
    For men that sow to reap:
I am weary of days and hours,
Blown buds of barren flowers,
Desires and dreams and powers
    And everything but sleep.

Here life has death for neighbour,
    And far from eye or ear
Wan waves and wet winds labour,
20   Weak ships and spirits steer;
They drive adrift, and whither
They wot not who make thither;
But no such winds blow hither,
    And no such things grow here.

No growth of moor or coppice,
   No heather-flower or vine,
But bloomless buds of poppies,
   Green grapes of Proserpine,
Pale beds of blowing rushes
30 Where no leaf blooms or blushes
Save this whereout she crushes
   For dead men deadly wine.

Pale, without name or number,
   In fruitless fields of corn,
They bow themselves and slumber
   All night till light is born;
And like a soul belated,
In hell and heaven unmated,
By cloud and mist abated
40   Comes out of darkness morn.

Though one were strong as seven,
   He too with death shall dwell,
Nor wake with wings in heaven,
   Nor weep for pains in hell;
Though one were fair as roses,
His beauty clouds and closes;
And well though love reposes,
   In the end it is not well.

Pale, beyond porch and portal,
50 Crowned with calm leaves, she stands
Who gathers all things mortal
   With cold immortal hands;
Her languid lips are sweeter
Than love's who fears to greet her
To men that mix and meet her
   From many times and lands.

She waits for each and other,
    She waits for all men born;
Forgets the earth her mother,
60   The life of fruits and corn;
And spring and seed and swallow
Take wing for her and follow
Where summer song rings hollow
    And flowers are put to scorn.

There go the loves that wither,
    The old loves with wearier wings;
And all dead years draw thither,
    And all disastrous things;
Dead dreams of days forsaken,
70   Blind buds that snows have shaken,
Wild leaves that winds have taken,
    Red strays of ruined springs.

We are not sure of sorrow,
    And joy was never sure;
To-day will die to-morrow;
    Time stoops to no man's lure;
And love, grown faint and fretful,
With lips but half regretful
Sighs, and with eyes forgetful
80   Weeps that no loves endure.

From too much love of living,
    From hope and fear set free,
We thank with brief thanksgiving
    Whatever gods may be
That no life lives for ever;
That dead men rise up never;
That even the weariest river
    Winds somewhere safe to sea.

Then star nor sun shall waken,
90   Nor any change of light:
Nor sound of waters shaken,
        Nor any sound or sight:
Nor wintry leaves nor vernal,
Nor days nor things diurnal;
Only the sleep eternal
        In an eternal night.

Hesperia

Out of the golden remote wild west where the sea without
        shore is,
    Full of the sunset, and sad, if at all, with the fulness of
        joy,
As a wind sets in with the autumn that blows from the
        region of stories,
    Blows with a perfume of songs and of memories beloved
        from a boy,
Blows from the capes of the past oversea to the bays of the
        present,
    Filled as with shadow of sound with the pulse of invisible
        feet,
Far out to the shallows and straits of the future, by rough
        ways or pleasant,
    Is it thither the wind's wings beat? is it hither to me, O
        my sweet?
For thee, in the stream of the deep tide-wind blowing in
        with the water,
10   Thee I behold as a bird borne in with the wind from the
        west,
    Straight from the sunset, across white waves whence rose as
        a daughter
        Venus thy mother, in years when the world was a water at
        rest.

Out of the distance of dreams, as a dream that abides after
    slumber,
  Strayed from the fugitive flock of the night, when the
    moon overhead
Wanes in the wan waste heights of the heaven, and stars
    without number
  Die without sound, and are spent like lamps that are
    burnt by the dead,
Comes back to me, stays by me, lulls me with touch of
    forgotten caresses,
  One warm dream clad about with a fire as of life that
    endures;
The delight of thy face, and the sound of thy feet, and the
    wind of thy tresses,
20   And all of a man that regrets, and all of a maid that
    allures.
But thy bosom is warm for my face and profound as a
    manifold flower,
  Thy silence as music, thy voice as an odour that fades in a
    flame;
Not a dream, not a dream is the kiss of thy mouth, and the
    bountiful hour
  That makes me forget what was sin, and would make me
    forget were it shame.
Thine eyes that are quiet, thine hands that are tender, thy
    lips that are loving,
  Comfort and cool me as dew in the dawn of a moon like a
    dream;
And my heart yearns baffled and blind, moved vainly toward
    thee, and moving
  As the refluent seaweed moves in the languid exuberant
    stream,
Fair as a rose is on earth, as a rose under water in prison,
30   That stretches and swings to the slow passionate pulse of
    the sea,
Closed up from the air and the sun, but alive, as a ghost
    rearisen,

Pale as the love that revives as a ghost rearisen in me.
From the bountiful infinite west, from the happy memorial
    places
Full of the stately repose and the lordly delight of the dead,
Where the fortunate islands are lit with the light of ineffable
    faces,
And the sound of a sea without wind is about them, and
    sunset is red,
Come back to redeem and release me from love that recalls
    and represses,
That cleaves to my flesh as a flame, till the serpent has
    eaten his fill;
From the bitter delights of the dark, and the feverish, the
    furtive caresses
40 That murder the youth in a man or ever his heart have its
    will.
Thy lips cannot laugh and thine eyes cannot weep; thou art
    pale as a rose is,
Paler and sweeter than leaves that cover the blush of the bud;
And the heart of the flower is compassion, and pity the core
    it encloses,
Pity, not love, that is born of the breath and decays with
    the blood.
As the cross that a wild nun clasps till the edge of it bruises
    her bosom,
So love wounds as we grasp it, and blackens and burns as
    a flame;
I have loved overmuch in my life; when the live bud bursts
    with the blossom,
Bitter as ashes or tears is the fruit, and the wine thereof
    shame.
As a heart that its anguish divides is the green bud cloven
    asunder;
50 As the blood of a man self-slain is the flush of the leaves
    that allure;
And the perfume as poison and wine to the brain, a delight
    and a wonder;
And the thorns are too sharp for a boy, too slight for a
    man, to endure.

Too soon did I love it, and lost love's rose; and I cared not
  for glory's:
  Only the blossoms of sleep and of pleasure were mixed in
    my hair.
Was it myrtle or poppy thy garland was woven with, O my
  Dolores?
  Was it pallor of slumber, or blush as of blood, that I
    found in thee fair?
For desire is a respite from love, and the flesh not the heart
  is her fuel;
  She was sweet to me once, who am fled and escaped from
    the rage of her reign;
Who behold as of old time at hand as I turn, with her mouth
  growing cruel,
60   And flushed as with wine with the blood of her lovers,
      Our Lady of Pain.

Low down where the thicket is thicker with thorns than
  with leaves in the summer,
  In the brake is a gleaming of eyes and a hissing of tongues
    that I knew;
And the lithe long throats of her snakes reach round her,
  their mouths overcome her,
  And her lips grow cool with their foam, made moist as a
    desert with dew.
With the thirst and the hunger of lust though her beautiful
  lips be so bitter,
  With the cold foul foam of the snakes they soften and
    redden and smile;
And her fierce mouth sweetens, her eyes wax wide and her
  eyelashes glitter,
  And she laughs with a savour of blood in her face, and a
    savour of guile.
She laughs, and her hands reach hither, her hair blows
  hither and hisses,
70   As a low-lit flame in a wind, back-blown till it shudder
      and leap;

Let her lips not again lay hold on my soul, nor her
      poisonous kisses,
  To consume it alive and divide from thy bosom, Our
      Lady of Sleep.
Ah daughter of sunset and slumber, if now it return into
      prison,
  Who shall redeem it anew? but we, if thou wilt, let us fly;
Let us take to us, now that the white skies thrill with a moon
      unarisen,
  Swift horses of fear or of love, take flight and depart and
      not die.
They are swifter than dreams, they are stronger than death;
      there is none that hath ridden,
  None that shall ride in the dim strange ways of his life as
      we ride;
By the meadows of memory, the highlands of hope, and the
      shore that is hidden,
80   Where life breaks loud and unseen, a sonorous invisible
      tide;
By the sands where sorrow has trodden, the salt pools bitter
      and sterile,
  By the thundering reef and the low sea-wall and the
      channel of years,
Our wild steeds press on the night, strain hard through
      pleasure and peril,
  Labour and listen and pant not or pause for the peril that
      nears;
And the sound of them trampling the way cleaves night as
      an arrow asunder,
  And slow by the sand-hill and swift by the down with its
      glimpses of grass,
Sudden and steady the music, as eight hoofs trample and
      thunder,
  Rings in the ear of the low blind wind of the night as we
      pass;

Shrill shrieks in our faces the blind bland air that was mute
    as a maiden,
90   Stung into storm by the speed of our passage, and deaf
    where we past;
And our spirits too burn as we bound, thine holy but mine
    heavy-laden,
    As we burn with the fire of our flight; ah love, shall we
    win at the last?

Love at Sea

We are in love's land to-day;
    Where shall we go?
Love, shall we start or stay,
    Or sail or row?
There's many a wind and way,
And never a May but May;
We are in love's hand to-day;
    Where shall we go?

Our landwind is the breath
10 Of sorrows kissed to death
    And joys that were;
Our ballast is a rose;
Our way lies where God knows
    And love knows where
        We are in love's hand to-day –

Our seamen are fledged Loves,
Our masts are bills of doves,
    Our decks fine gold;
Our ropes are dead maids' hair,
20 Our stores are love-shafts fair
    And manifold.
        We are in love's land to-day –

Where shall we land you, sweet?
On fields of strange men's feet,
   Or fields near home?
Or where the fire-flowers blow,
Or where the flowers of snow
   Or flowers of foam?
      We are in love's hand to-day –

30 Land me, she says, where love
Shows but one shaft, one dove,
   One heart, one hand.
– A shore like that, my dear,
Lies where no man will steer,
   No maiden land.

Imitated from Théophile Gautier.

April

FROM THE FRENCH OF THE VIDAME DE CHARTRES
12— ?

When the field catch flower
   And the underwood is green,
And from bower unto bower
   The songs of the birds begin,
    I sing with sighing between.
When I laugh and sing,
   I am heavy at heart for my sin;
I am sad in the spring
   For my love that I shall not win,
10   For a foolish thing.

This profit I have of my woe,
   That I know, as I sing,
I know he will needs have it so
   Who is master and king,

Who is lord of the spirit of spring.
I will serve her and will not spare
   Till her pity awake
Who is good, who is pure, who is fair,
   Even her for whose sake
20   Love hath ta'en me and slain unaware.

O my lord, O Love,
   I have laid my life at thy feet;
Have thy will thereof,
   Do as it please thee with it,
   For what shall please thee is sweet.
I am come unto thee
   To do thee service, O Love;
Yet cannot I see
   Thou wilt take any pity thereof,
30   Any mercy on me.

But the grace I have long time sought
   Comes never in sight,
If in her it abideth not,
   Through thy mercy and might,
   Whose heart is the world's delight.
Thou hast sworn without fail I shall die,
   For my heart is set
On what hurts me, I wot not why,
   But cannot forget
40   What I love, what I sing for and sigh.

She is worthy of praise,
   For this grief of her giving is worth
All the joy of my days
   That lie between death's day and birth,
   All the lordship of things upon earth.
Nay, what have I said?
   I would not be glad if I could;
My dream and my dread
   Are of her, and for her sake I would
50   That my life were fled.

Lo, sweet, if I durst not pray to you,
    Then were I dead;
If I sang not a little to say to you,
    (Could it be said)
    O my love, how my heart would be fed;
Ah sweet who hast hold of my heart,
    For thy love's sake I live,
Do but tell me, ere either depart,
    What a lover may give
60 For a woman so fair as thou art.

The lovers that disbelieve,
    False rumours shall grieve
And evil-speaking shall part.

Before Parting

A month or twain to live on honeycomb
Is pleasant; but one tires of scented time,
Cold sweet recurrence of accepted rhyme,
And that strong purple under juice and foam
Where the wine's heart has burst;
Nor feel the latter kisses like the first.

Once yet, this poor one time; I will not pray
Even to change the bitterness of it,
The bitter taste ensuing on the sweet,
10 To make your tears fall where your soft hair lay
All blurred and heavy in some perfumed wise
Over my face and eyes.

And yet who knows what end the scythèd wheat
Makes of its foolish poppies' mouths of red?
These were not sown, these are not harvested,
They grow a month and are cast under feet
And none has care thereof,
As none has care of a divided love.

I know each shadow of your lips by rote,
20   Each change of love in eyelids and eyebrows;
The fashion of fair temples tremulous
With tender blood, and colour of your throat;
I know not how love is gone out of this,
Seeing that all was his.

Love's likeness there endures upon all these:
But out of these one shall not gather love.
Day hath not strength nor the night shade enough
To make love whole and fill his lips with ease,
As some bee-builded cell
30   Feels at filled lips the heavy honey swell.

I know not how this last month leaves your hair
Less full of purple colour and hid spice,
And that luxurious trouble of closed eyes
Is mixed with meaner shadow and waste care;
And love, kissed out by pleasure, seems not yet
Worth patience to regret.

The Sundew

A little marsh-plant, yellow green,
And pricked at lip with tender red.
Tread close, and either way you tread
Some faint black water jets between
Lest you should bruise the curious head.

A live thing maybe; who shall know?
The summer knows and suffers it;
For the cool moss is thick and sweet
Each side, and saves the blossom so
10   That it lives out the long June heat.

The deep scent of the heather burns
About it; breathless though it be,
Bow down and worship; more than we
Is the least flower whose life returns,
Least weed renascent in the sea.

We are vexed and cumbered in earth's sight
With wants, with many memories;
These see their mother what she is,
Glad-growing, till August leave more bright
20 The apple-coloured cranberries.

Wind blows and bleaches the strong grass,
Blown all one way to shelter it
From trample of strayed kine, with feet
Felt heavier than the moorhen was,
Strayed up past patches of wild wheat.

You call it sundew: how it grows,
If with its colour it have breath,
If life taste sweet to it, if death
Pain its soft petal, no man knows:
30 Man has no sight or sense that saith.

My sundew, grown of gentle days,
In these green miles the spring begun
Thy growth ere April had half done
With the soft secret of her ways
Or June made ready for the sun.

O red-lipped mouth of marsh-flower,
I have a secret halved with thee.
The name that is love's name to me
Thou knowest, and the face of her
40 Who is my festival to see.

The hard sun, as thy petals knew,
Coloured the heavy moss-water:
Thou wert not worth green midsummer
Nor fit to live to August blue,
O sundew, not remembering her.

Félise

Mais où sont les neiges d'antan?

What shall be said between us here
    Among the downs, between the trees,
In fields that knew our feet last year,
    In sight of quiet sands and seas,
      This year, Félise?

Who knows what word were best to say?
    For last year's leaves lie dead and red
On this sweet day, in this green May,
    And barren corn makes bitter bread.
10   What shall be said?

Here as last year the fields begin,
    A fire of flowers and glowing grass;
The old fields we laughed and lingered in,
    Seeing each our souls in last year's glass,
      Félise, alas!

Shall we not laugh, shall we not weep,
    Not we, though this be as it is?
For love awake or love asleep
    Ends in a laugh, a dream, a kiss,
20   A song like this.

I that have slept awake, and you
   Sleep, who last year were well awake.
Though love do all that love can do,
   My heart will never ache or break
     For your heart's sake.

The great sea, faultless as a flower,
   Throbs, trembling under beam and breeze,
And laughs with love of the amorous hour.
   I found you fairer once, Félise,
30   Than flowers or seas.

We played at bondsman and at queen;
   But as the days change men change too;
I find the grey sea's notes of green,
   The green sea's fervent flakes of blue,
     More fair than you.

Your beauty is not over fair
   Now in mine eyes, who am grown up wise.
The smell of flowers in all your hair
   Allures not now; no sigh replies
40   If your heart sighs.

But you sigh seldom, you sleep sound,
   You find love's new name good enough.
Less sweet I find it than I found
   The sweetest name that ever love
     Grew weary of.

My snake with bright bland eyes, my snake
   Grown tame and glad to be caressed,
With lips athirst for mine to slake
   Their tender fever! who had guessed
50   You loved me best?

I had died for this last year, to know
  You loved me. Who shall turn on fate?
I care not if love come or go
  Now, though your love seek mine for mate.
  It is too late.

The dust of many strange desires
  Lies deep between us; in our eyes
Dead smoke of perishable fires
  Flickers, a fume in air and skies,
60   A steam of sighs.

You loved me and you loved me not;
  A little, much, and overmuch.
Will you forget as I forgot?
  Let all dead things lie dead; none such
  Are soft to touch.

I love you and I do not love,
  Too much, a little, not at all;
Too much, and never yet enough.
  Birds quick to fledge and fly at call
70   Are quick to fall.

And these love longer now than men,
  And larger loves than ours are these.
No diver brings up love again
  Dropped once, my beautiful Félise,
  In such cold seas.

Gone deeper than all plummets sound,
  Where in the dim green dayless day
The life of such dead things lies bound
  As the sea feeds on, wreck and stray
80   And castaway.

Can I forget? yea, that can I,
 And that can all men; so will you,
Alive, or later, when you die.
 Ah, but the love you plead was true?
 Was mine not too?

I loved you for that name of yours
 Long ere we met, and long enough.
Now that one thing of all endures –
 The sweetest name that ever love
90 Waxed weary of.

Like colours in the sea, like flowers,
 Like a cat's splendid circled eyes
That wax and wane with love for hours,
 Green as green flame, blue-grey like skies,
 And soft like sighs –

And all these only like your name,
 And your name full of all of these.
I say it, and it sounds the same –
 Save that I say it now at ease,
100 Your name, Félise.

I said 'she must be swift and white,
 And subtly warm, and half perverse,
And sweet like sharp soft fruit to bite,
 And like a snake's love lithe and fierce.'
 Men have guessed worse.

What was the song I made of you
 Here where the grass forgets our feet
As afternoon forgets the dew?
 Ah that such sweet things should be fleet,
110 Such fleet things sweet!

As afternoon forgets the dew,
   As time in time forgets all men,
As our old place forgets us two,
   Who might have turned to one thing then,
   But not again.

    O lips that mine have grown into
      Like April's kissing May,
    O fervent eyelids letting through
    Those eyes the greenest of things blue,
120   The bluest of things grey,

    If you were I and I were you,
      How could I love you, say?
    How could the roseleaf love the rue,
    The day love nightfall and her dew,
      Though night may love the day?

You loved it may be more than I;
   We know not; love is hard to seize,
And all things are not good to try;
   And lifelong loves the worst of these
130   For us, Félise.

Ah, take the season and have done,
   Love well the hour and let it go:
Two souls may sleep and wake up one,
   Or dream they wake and find it so,
   And then – you know.

Kiss me once hard as though a flame
   Lay on my lips and made them fire;
The same lips now, and not the same;
   What breath shall fill and re-inspire
140   A dead desire?

The old song sounds hollower in mine ear
    Than thin keen sounds of dead men's speech –
A noise one hears and would not hear;
    Too strong to die, too weak to reach
    From wave to beach.

We stand on either side the sea,
    Stretch hands, blow kisses, laugh and lean
I toward you, you toward me;
    But what hears either save the keen
150   Grey sea between?

A year divides us, love from love,
    Though you love now, though I loved then.
The gulf is strait, but deep enough;
    Who shall recross, who among men
    Shall cross again?

Love was a jest last year, you said,
    And what lives surely, surely dies.
Even so; but now that love is dead,
    Shall love rekindle from wet eyes,
160   From subtle sighs?

For many loves are good to see;
    Mutable loves, and loves perverse;
But there is nothing, nor shall be,
    So sweet, so wicked, but my verse
    Can dream of worse.

For we that sing and you that love
    Know that which man may, only we.
The rest live under us; above,
    Live the great gods in heaven, and see
170   What things shall be.

So this thing is and must be so;
    For man dies, and love also dies.
Though yet love's ghost moves to and fro
    The sea-green mirrors of your eyes,
    And laughs, and lies.

Eyes coloured like a water-flower,
    And deeper than the green sea's glass;
Eyes that remember one sweet hour –
    In vain, we swore it should not pass;
180   In vain, alas!

Ah my Félise, if love or sin,
    If shame or fear could hold it fast,
Should we not hold it? Love wears thin,
    And they laugh well who laugh the last.
    Is it not past?

The gods, the gods are stronger; time
    Falls down before them, all men's knees
Bow, all men's prayers and sorrows climb
    Like incense towards them; yea, for these
190   Are gods, Félise.

Immortal are they, clothed with powers,
    Not to be comforted at all;
Lords over all the fruitless hours;
    Too great to appease, too high to appal,
    Too far to call.

For none shall move the most high gods,
    Who are most sad, being cruel; none
Shall break or take away the rods
    Wherewith they scourge us, not as one
200   That smites a son.

By many a name of many a creed
  We have called upon them, since the sands
Fell through time's hour-glass first, a seed
  Of life; and out of many lands
  Have we stretched hands.

When have they heard us? who hath known
  Their faces, climbed unto their feet,
Felt them and found them? Laugh or groan,
  Doth heaven remurmur and repeat
210 Sad sounds or sweet?

Do the stars answer? in the night
  Have ye found comfort? or by day
Have ye seen gods? What hope, what light,
  Falls from the farthest starriest way
  On you that pray?

Are the skies wet because we weep,
  Or fair because of any mirth?
Cry out; they are gods; perchance they sleep;
  Cry; thou shalt know what prayers are worth,
220 Thou dust and earth.

O earth, thou art fair; O dust, thou art great;
  O laughing lips and lips that mourn,
Pray, till ye feel the exceeding weight
  Of God's intolerable scorn,
  Not to be borne.

Behold, there is no grief like this;
  The barren blossom of thy prayer,
Thou shalt find out how sweet it is.
  O fools and blind, what seek ye there,
230 High up in the air?

Ye must have gods, the friends of men,
   Merciful gods, compassionate,
And these shall answer you again.
   Will ye beat always at the gate,
   Ye fools of fate?

Ye fools and blind; for this is sure,
   That all ye shall not live, but die.
Lo, what thing have ye found endure?
   Or what thing have ye found on high
240   Past the blind sky?

The ghosts of words and dusty dreams,
   Old memories, faiths infirm and dead.
Ye fools; for which among you deems
   His prayer can alter green to red
   Or stones to bread?

Why should ye bear with hopes and fears
   Till all these things be drawn in one,
The sound of iron-footed years,
   And all the oppression that is done
250   Under the sun?

Ye might end surely, surely pass
   Out of the multitude of things,
Under the dust, beneath the grass,
   Deep in dim death, where no thought stings,
   No record clings.

No memory more of love or hate,
   No trouble, nothing that aspires,
No sleepless labour thwarting fate,
   And thwarted; where no travail tires,
260   Where no faith fires.

All passes, nought that has been is,
    Things good and evil have one end.
Can anything be otherwise
    Though all men swear all things would mend
    With God to friend?

Can ye beat off one wave with prayer,
    Can ye move mountains? bid the flower
Take flight and turn to a bird in the air?
    Can ye hold fast for shine or shower
270   One wingless hour?

Ah sweet, and we too, can we bring
    One sigh back, bid one smile revive?
Can God restore one ruined thing,
    Or he who slays our souls alive
    Make dead things thrive?

Two gifts perforce he has given us yet,
    Though sad things stay and glad things fly;
Two gifts he has given us, to forget
    All glad and sad things that go by,
280   And then to die.

We know not whether death be good,
    But life at least it will not be:
Men will stand saddening as we stood,
    Watch the same fields and skies as we
    And the same sea.

Let this be said between us here,
    One love grows green when one turns grey;
This year knows nothing of last year;
    To-morrow has no more to say
290   To yesterday.

Live and let live, as I will do,
    Love and let love, and so will I.
But, sweet, for me no more with you:
    Not while I live, not though I die.
    Goodnight, goodbye.

An Interlude

In the greenest growth of the Maytime,
    I rode where the woods were wet,
Between the dawn and the daytime;
    The spring was glad that we met.

There was something the season wanted,
    Though the ways and the woods smelt sweet;
The breath at your lips that panted,
    The pulse of the grass at your feet.

You came, and the sun came after,
10   And the green grew golden above;
And the flag-flowers lightened with laughter,
    And the meadow-sweet shook with love.

Your feet in the full-grown grasses
    Moved soft as a weak wind blows;
You passed me as April passes,
    With face made out of a rose.

By the stream where the stems were slender,
    Your bright foot paused at the sedge;
It might be to watch the tender
20   Light leaves in the springtime hedge,

On boughs that the sweet month blanches
    With flowery frost of May:
It might be a bird in the branches,
    It might be a thorn in the way.

I waited to watch you linger
　　With foot drawn back from the dew,
Till a sunbeam straight like a finger
　　Struck sharp through the leaves at you.

And a bird overhead sang *Follow*,
30　　And a bird to the right sang *Here*;
And the arch of the leaves was hollow,
　　And the meaning of May was clear.

I saw where the sun's hand pointed,
　　I knew what the bird's note said;
By the dawn and the dewfall anointed,
　　You were queen by the gold on your head.

As the glimpse of a burnt-out ember
　　Recalls a regret of the sun,
I remember, forget, and remember
40　　What Love saw done and undone.

I remember the way we parted,
　　The day and the way we met;
You hoped we were both broken-hearted,
　　And knew we should both forget.

And May with her world in flower
　　Seemed still to murmur and smile
As you murmured and smiled for an hour;
　　I saw you turn at the stile.

A hand like a white wood-blossom
50　　You lifted, and waved, and passed,
With head hung down to the bosom,
　　And pale, as it seemed, at last.

And the best and the worst of this is
　　That neither is most to blame
If you've forgotten my kisses
　　And I've forgotten your name.

Hendecasyllabics

In the month of the long decline of roses
I, beholding the summer dead before me,
Set my face to the sea and journeyed silent,
Gazing eagerly where above the sea-mark
Flame as fierce as the fervid eyes of lions
Half divided the eyelids of the sunset;
Till I heard as it were a noise of waters
Moving tremulous under feet of angels
Multitudinous, out of all the heavens;
Knew the fluttering wind, the fluttered foliage,
Shaken fitfully, full of sound and shadow;
And saw, trodden upon by noiseless angels,
Long mysterious reaches fed with moonlight,
Sweet sad straits in a soft subsiding channel,
Blown about by the lips of winds I knew not,
Winds not born in the north nor any quarter,
Winds not warm with the south nor any sunshine;
Heard between them a voice of exultation,
'Lo, the summer is dead, the sun is faded,
Even like as a leaf the year is withered,
All the fruits of the day from all her branches
Gathered, neither is any left to gather.
All the flowers are dead, the tender blossoms,
All are taken away; the season wasted,
Like an ember among the fallen ashes.
Now with light of the winter days, with moonlight,
Light of snow, and the bitter light of hoarfrost,
We bring flowers that fade not after autumn,
Pale white chaplets and crowns of latter seasons,
Fair false leaves (but the summer leaves were falser),
Woven under the eyes of stars and planets
When low light was upon the windy reaches
Where the flower of foam was blown, a lily
Dropt among the sonorous fruitless furrows
And green fields of the sea that make no pasture:

Since the winter begins, the weeping winter,
All whose flowers are tears, and round his temples
Iron blossom of frost is bound for ever.'

Sapphics

All the night sleep came not upon my eyelids,
Shed not dew, nor shook nor unclosed a feather,
Yet with lips shut close and with eyes of iron
   Stood and beheld me.

Then to me so lying awake a vision
Came without sleep over the seas and touched me,
Softly touched mine eyelids and lips; and I too,
   Full of the vision,

Saw the white implacable Aphrodite,
10 Saw the hair unbound and the feet unsandalled
Shine as fire of sunset on western waters;
   Saw the reluctant

Feet, the straining plumes of the doves that drew her,
Looking always, looking with necks reverted,
Back to Lesbos, back to the hills whereunder
   Shone Mitylene;

Heard the flying feet of the Loves behind her
Make a sudden thunder upon the waters,
As the thunder flung from the strong unclosing
20   Wings of a great wind.

So the goddess fled from her place, with awful
Sound of feet and thunder of wings around her;
While behind a clamour of singing women
   Severed the twilight.

Ah the singing, ah the delight, the passion!
All the Loves wept, listening; sick with anguish,
Stood the crowned nine Muses about Apollo;
    Fear was upon them,

While the tenth sang wonderful things they knew not.
30 Ah the tenth, the Lesbian! the nine were silent,
None endured the sound of her song for weeping;
    Laurel by laurel,

Faded all their crowns; but about her forehead,
Round her woven tresses and ashen temples
White as dead snow, paler than grass in summer,
    Ravaged with kisses,

Shone a light of fire as a crown for ever.
Yea, almost the implacable Aphrodite
Paused, and almost wept; such a song was that song.
40   Yea, by her name too

Called her, saying, 'Turn to me, O my Sappho;'
Yet she turned her face from the Loves, she saw not
Tears for laughter darken immortal eyelids,
    Heard not about her

Fearful fitful wings of the doves departing,
Saw not how the bosom of Aphrodite
Shook with weeping, saw not her shaken raiment,
    Saw not her hands wrung;

Saw the Lesbians kissing across their smitten
50 Lutes with lips more sweet than the sound of lute-strings,
Mouth to mouth and hand upon hand, her chosen,
    Fairer than all men;

Only saw the beautiful lips and fingers,
Full of songs and kisses and little whispers,
Full of music; only beheld among them
    Soar, as a bird soars

Newly fledged, her visible song, a marvel,
Made of perfect sound and exceeding passion,
Sweetly shapen, terrible, full of thunders,
60   Clothed with the wind's wings.

Then rejoiced she, laughing with love, and scattered
Roses, awful roses of holy blossom;
Then the Loves thronged sadly with hidden faces
      Round Aphrodite,

Then the Muses, stricken at heart, were silent;
Yea, the gods waxed pale; such a song was that song.
All reluctant, all with a fresh repulsion,
      Fled from before her.

All withdrew long since, and the land was barren,
70   Full of fruitless women and music only.
Now perchance, when winds are assuaged at sunset,
      Lulled at the dewfall,

By the grey sea-side, unassuaged, unheard of,
Unbeloved, unseen in the ebb of twilight,
Ghosts of outcast women return lamenting,
      Purged not in Lethe,

Clothed about with flame and with tears, and singing
Songs that move the heart of the shaken heaven,
Songs that break the heart of the earth with pity,
80   Hearing, to hear them.

At Eleusis

Men of Eleusis, ye that with long staves
Sit in the market-houses, and speak words
Made sweet with wisdom as the rare wine is
Thickened with honey; and ye sons of these
Who in the glad thick streets go up and down

For pastime or grave traffic or mere chance;
And all fair women having rings of gold
On hands or hair; and chiefest over these
I name you, daughters of this man the king,
10 Who dipping deep smooth pitchers of pure brass
Under the bubbled wells, till each round lip
Stooped with loose gurgle of waters incoming,
Found me an old sick woman, lamed and lean,
Beside a growth of builded olive-boughs
Whence multiplied thick song of thick-plumed throats –
Also wet tears filled up my hollow hands
By reason of my crying into them –
And pitied me; for as cold water ran
And washed the pitchers full from lip to lip,
20 So washed both eyes full the strong salt of tears.
And ye put water to my mouth, made sweet
With brown hill-berries; so in time I spoke
And gathered my loose knees from under me.
Moreover in the broad fair halls this month
Have I found space and bountiful abode
To please me. I Demeter speak of this,
Who am the mother and the mate of things:
For as ill men by drugs or singing words
Shut the doors inward of the narrowed womb
30 Like a lock bolted with round iron through,
Thus I shut up the body and sweet mouth
Of all soft pasture and the tender land,
So that no seed can enter in by it
Though one sow thickly, nor some grain get out
Past the hard clods men cleave and bite with steel
To widen the sealed lips of them for use.
None of you is there in the peopled street
But knows how all the dry-drawn furrows ache
With no green spot made count of in the black:
40 How the wind finds no comfortable grass
Nor is assuaged with bud nor breath of herbs;
And in hot autumn when ye house the stacks,
All fields are helpless in the sun, all trees
Stand as a man stripped out of all but skin.

Nevertheless ye sick have help to get
By means and stablished ordinance of God;
For God is wiser than a good man is.
But never shall new grass be sweet in earth
Till I get righted of my wound and wrong
50   By changing counsel of ill-minded Zeus.
For of all other gods is none save me
Clothed with like power to build and break the year.
I make the lesser green begin, when spring
Touches not earth but with one fearful foot;
And as a careful gilder with grave art
Soberly colours and completes the face,
Mouth, chin and all, of some sweet work in stone,
I carve the shapes of grass and tender corn
And colour the ripe edges and long spikes
60   With the red increase and the grace of gold.
No tradesman in soft wools is cunninger
To kill the secret of the fat white fleece
With stains of blue and purple wrought in it.
Three moons were made and three moons burnt away
While I held journey hither out of Crete
Comfortless, tended by grave Hecate
Whom my wound stung with double iron point;
For all my face was like a cloth wrung out
With close and weeping wrinkles, and both lids
70   Sodden with salt continuance of tears.
For Hades and the sidelong will of Zeus
And that lame wisdom that has writhen feet,
Cunning, begotten in the bed of Shame,
These three took evil will at me, and made
Such counsel that when time got wing to fly
This Hades out of summer and low fields
Forced the bright body of Persephone:
Out of pure grass, where she lying down, red flowers
Made their sharp little shadows on her sides,
80   Pale heat, pale colour on pale maiden flesh –
And chill water slid over her reddening feet,
Killing the throbs in their soft blood; and birds,
Perched next her elbow and pecking at her hair,

Stretched their necks more to see her than even to sing.
A sharp thing is it I have need to say;
For Hades holding both white wrists of hers
Unloosed the girdle and with knot by knot
Bound her between his wheels upon the seat,
Bound her pure body, holiest yet and dear
90 To me and God as always, clothed about
With blossoms loosened as her knees went down,
Let fall as she let go of this and this
By tens and twenties, tumbled to her feet,
White waifs or purple of the pasturage.
Therefore with only going up and down
My feet were wasted, and the gracious air,
To me discomfortable and dun, became
As weak smoke blowing in the under world.
And finding in the process of ill days
100 What part had Zeus herein, and how as mate
He coped with Hades, yokefellow in sin,
I set my lips against the meat of gods
And drank not neither ate or slept in heaven.
Nor in the golden greeting of their mouths
Did ear take note of me, nor eye at all
Track my feet going in the ways of them.
Like a great fire on some strait slip of land
Between two washing inlets of wet sea
That burns the grass up to each lip of beach
110 And strengthens, waxing in the growth of wind,
So burnt my soul in me at heaven and earth,
Each way a ruin and a hungry plague,
Visible evil; nor could any night
Put cool between mine eyelids, nor the sun
With competence of gold fill out my want.
Yea so my flame burnt up the grass and stones,
Shone to the salt-white edges of thin sea,
Distempered all the gracious work, and made
Sick change, unseasonable increase of days
120 And scant avail of seasons; for by this
The fair gods faint in hollow heaven: there comes
No taste of burnings of the twofold fat

To leave their palates smooth, nor in their lips
Soft rings of smoke and weak scent wandering;
All cattle waste and rot, and their ill smell
Grows alway from the lank unsavoury flesh
That no man slays for offering; the sea
And waters moved beneath the heath and corn
Preserve the people of fin-twinkling fish,
130 And river-flies feed thick upon the smooth;
But all earth over is no man or bird
(Except the sweet race of the kingfisher)
That lacks not and is wearied with much loss.
Meantime the purple inward of the house
Was softened with all grace of scent and sound
In ear and nostril perfecting my praise;
Faint grape-flowers and cloven honey-cake
And the just grain with dues of the shed salt
Made me content: yet my hand loosened not
140 Its gripe upon your harvest all year long.
While I, thus woman-muffled in wan flesh
And waste externals of a perished face,
Preserved the levels of my wrath and love
Patiently ruled; and with soft offices
Cooled the sharp noons and busied the warm nights
In care of this my choice, this child my choice,
Triptolemus, the king's selected son:
That this fair yearlong body, which hath grown
Strong with strange milk upon the mortal lip
150 And nerved with half a god, might so increase
Outside the bulk and the bare scope of man:
And waxen over large to hold within
Base breath of yours and this impoverished air,
I might exalt him past the flame of stars,
The limit and walled reach of the great world.
Therefore my breast made common to his mouth
Immortal savours, and the taste whereat
Twice their hard life strains out the coloured veins
And twice its brain confirms the narrow shell.
160 Also at night, unwinding cloth from cloth
As who unhusks an almond to the white

And pastures curiously the purer taste,
I bared the gracious limbs and the soft feet,
Unswaddled the weak hands, and in mid ash
Laid the sweet flesh of either feeble side,
More tender for impressure of some touch
Than wax to any pen; and lit around
Fire, and made crawl the white worm-shapen flame,
And leap in little angers spark by spark
170 At head at once and feet; and the faint hair
Hissed with rare sprinkles in the closer curl,
And like scaled oarage of a keen thin fish
In sea-water, so in pure fire his feet
Struck out, and the flame bit not in his flesh,
But like a kiss it curled his lip, and heat
Fluttered his eyelids; so each night I blew
The hot ash red to purge him to full god.
Ill is it when fear hungers in the soul
For painful food, and chokes thereon, being fed;
180 And ill slant eyes interpret the straight sun,
But in their scope its white is wried to black:
By the queen Metaneira mean I this;
For with sick wrath upon her lips, and heart
Narrowing with fear the spleenful passages,
She thought to thread this web's fine ravel out,
Nor leave her shuttle split in combing it;
Therefore she stole on us, and with hard sight
Peered, and stooped close; then with pale open mouth
As the fire smote her in the eyes between
190 Cried, and the child's laugh, sharply shortening
As fire doth under rain, fell off; the flame
Writhed once all through and died, and in thick dark
Tears fell from mine on the child's weeping eyes,
Eyes dispossessed of strong inheritance
And mortal fallen anew. Who not the less
From bud of beard to pale-grey flower of hair
Shall wax vinewise to a lordly vine, whose grapes
Bleed the red heavy blood of swoln soft wine,

Subtle with sharp leaves' intricacy, until
200 Full of white years and blossom of hoary days
I take him perfected; for whose one sake
I am thus gracious to the least who stands
Filleted with white wool and girt upon
As he whose prayer endures upon the lip
And falls not waste: wherefore let sacrifice
Burn and run red in all the wider ways;
Seeing I have sworn by the pale temples' band
And poppied hair of gold Persephone
Sad-tressed and pleached low down about her brows,
210 And by the sorrow in her lips, and death
Her dumb and mournful-mouthèd minister,
My word for you is eased of its harsh weight
And doubled with soft promise; and your king
Triptolemus, this Celeus dead and swathed
Purple and pale for golden burial,
Shall be your helper in my services,
Dividing earth and reaping fruits thereof
In fields where wait, well-girt, well-wreathen, all
The heavy-handed seasons all year through;
220 Saving the choice of warm spear-headed grain,
And stooping sharp to the slant-sided share
All beasts that furrow the remeasured land
With their bowed necks of burden equable.

August

There were four apples on the bough,
Half gold half red, that one might know
The blood was ripe inside the core;
The colour of the leaves was more
Like stems of yellow corn that grow
Through all the gold June meadow's floor.

The warm smell of the fruit was good
To feed on, and the split green wood,
With all its bearded lips and stains
Of mosses in the cloven veins,
Most pleasant, if one lay or stood
In sunshine or in happy rains.

There were four apples on the tree,
Red stained through gold, that all might see
The sun went warm from core to rind;
The green leaves made the summer blind
In that soft place they kept for me
With golden apples shut behind.

The leaves caught gold across the sun,
And where the bluest air begun
Thirsted for song to help the heat;
As I to feel my lady's feet
Draw close before the day were done;
Both lips grew dry with dreams of it.

In the mute August afternoon
They trembled to some undertune
Of music in the silver air;
Great pleasure was it to be there
Till green turned duskier and the moon
Coloured the corn-sheaves like gold hair.

That August time it was delight
To watch the red moons wane to white
'Twixt grey seamed stems of apple-trees;
A sense of heavy harmonies
Grew on the growth of patient night,
More sweet than shapen music is.

But some three hours before the moon
The air, still eager from the noon,
Flagged after heat, not wholly dead;

40   Against the stem I leant my head;
The colour soothed me like a tune,
Green leaves all round the gold and red.

I lay there till the warm smell grew
More sharp, when flecks of yellow dew
Between the round ripe leaves had blurred
The rind with stain and wet; I heard
A wind that blew and breathed and blew,
Too weak to alter its one word.

The wet leaves next the gentle fruit
50   Felt smoother, and the brown tree-root
Felt the mould warmer: I too felt
(As water feels the slow gold melt
Right through it when the day burns mute)
The peace of time wherein love dwelt.

There were four apples on the tree,
Gold stained on red that all might see
The sweet blood filled them to the core:
The colour of her hair is more
Like stems of fair faint gold, that be
60   Mown from the harvest's middle floor.

A Christmas Carol[1]

Three damsels in the queen's chamber,
   The queen's mouth was most fair;
She spake a word of God's mother
   As the combs went in her hair.
     Mary that is of might,
     Bring us to thy Son's sight.

[1]Suggested by a drawing of Mr. D. G. Rossetti's.

They held the gold combs out from her,
    A span's length off her head;
She sang this song of God's mother
10   And of her bearing-bed.
       Mary most full of grace,
       Bring us to thy Son's face.

When she sat at Joseph's hand,
    She looked against her side;
And either way from the short silk band
    Her girdle was all wried.
       Mary that all good may,
       Bring us to thy Son's way.

Mary had three women for her bed,
20   The twain were maidens clean;
The first of them had white and red,
    The third had riven green.
       Mary that is so sweet,
       Bring us to thy Son's feet.

She had three women for her hair,
    Two were gloved soft and shod;
The third had feet and fingers bare,
    She was the likest God.
       Mary that wieldeth land,
30   Bring us to thy Son's hand.

She had three women for her ease,
    The twain were good women:
The first two were the two Maries,
    The third was Magdalen.
       Mary that perfect is,
       Bring us to thy Son's kiss.

Joseph had three workmen in his stall,
    To serve him well upon;
The first of them were Peter and Paul,

40   The third of them was John.
            Mary, God's handmaiden,
            Bring us to thy Son's ken.

'If your child be none other man's,
    But if it be very mine,
The bedstead shall be gold two spans,
    The bedfoot silver fine.'
        Mary that made God mirth,
        Bring us to thy Son's birth.

'If the child be some other man's,
50   And if it be none of mine,
The manger shall be straw two spans,
    Betwixen kine and kine.'
        Mary that made sin cease,
        Bring us to thy Son's peace.

Christ was born upon this wise,
    It fell on such a night,
Neither with sounds of psalteries,
    Nor with fire for light.
        Mary that is God's spouse,
60   Bring us to thy Son's house.

The star came out upon the east
    With a great sound and sweet:
Kings gave gold to make him feast
    And myrrh for him to eat.
        Mary, of thy sweet mood,
        Bring us to thy Son's good.

He had two handmaids at his head,
    One handmaid at his feet;
The twain of them were fair and red,
70   The third one was right sweet.
        Mary that is most wise,
        Bring us to thy Son's eyes.   Amen.

The Masque of Queen Bersabe
A MIRACLE-PLAY

KING DAVID

Knights mine, all that be in hall,
I have a counsel to you all,
Because of this thing God lets fall
    Among us for a sign.
For some days hence as I did eat
From kingly dishes my good meat,
There flew a bird between my feet
    As red as any wine.
This bird had a long bill of red
10 And a gold ring above his head;
Long time he sat and nothing said,
Put softly down his neck and fed
    From the gilt patens fine:
And as I marvelled, at the last
He shut his two keen eyën fast
And suddenly woxe big and brast
    Ere one should tell to nine.

PRIMUS MILES

Sir, note this that I will say;
That Lord who maketh corn with hay
20 And morrows each of yesterday,
    He hath you in his hand.

SECUNDUS MILES (*Paganus quidam*)

By Satan I hold no such thing;
For if wine swell within a king
Whose ears for drink are hot and ring,
The same shall dream of wine-bibbing
    Whilst he can lie or stand.

QUEEN BERSABE

Peace now, lords, for Godis head,
Ye chirk as starlings that be fed
And gape as fishes newly dead;
30 The devil put your bones to bed,
    Lo, this is all to say.

SECUNDUS MILES

By Mahound, lords, I have good will
This devil's bird to wring and spill;
For now meseems our game goes ill,
    Ye have scant hearts to play.

TERTIUS MILES

Lo, sirs, this word is there said,
That Urias the knight is dead
Through some ill craft; by Poulis head,
I doubt his blood hath made so red
40 This bird that flew from the queen's bed
    Whereof ye have such fear.

KING DAVID

Yea, my good knave, and is it said
That I can raise men from the dead?
By God I think to have his head
Who saith words of my lady's bed
    For any thief to hear.
    Et percutiat eum in capite.

QUEEN BERSABE

I wis men shall spit at me,
And say, it were but right for thee
That one should hang thee on a tree;
50 Ho! it were a fair thing to see
The big stones bruise her false body;
    Fie! who shall see her dead?

KING DAVID
I rede you have no fear of this,
For, as ye wot, the first good kiss
I had must be the last of his;
Now are ye queen of mine, I wis,
And lady of a house that is
    Full rich of meat and bread.

PRIMUS MILES
I bid you make good cheer to be
60 So fair a queen as all men see.
And hold us for your lieges free;
By Peter's soul that hath the key,
    Ye have good hap of it.

SECUNDUS MILES
I would that he were hanged and dead
Who hath no joy to see your head
With gold about it, barred on red;
I hold him as a sow of lead
    That is so scant of wit.

Tunc dicat NATHAN *propheta*
O king, I have a word to thee;
70 The child that is in Bersabe
Shall wither without light to see;
This word is come of God by me
    For sin that ye have done.
Because herein ye did not right,
To take the fair one lamb to smite
That was of Urias the knight;
    Ye wist he had but one.
Full many sheep I wot ye had,
And many women, when ye bade,
80 To do your will and keep you glad,
And a good crown about your head
    With gold to show thereon.
This Urias had one poor house

With low-barred latoun shot-windows
And scant of corn to fill a mouse;
And rusty basnets for his brows,
     To wear them to the bone.
Yea the roofs also, as men sain,
Were thin to hold against the rain;
90   Therefore what rushes were there lain
Grew wet withouten foot of men;
The stancheons were all gone in twain
     As sick man's flesh is gone.

Nathless he had great joy to see
The long hair of this Bersabe
Fall round her lap and round her knee
Even to her small soft feet, that be
Shod now with crimson royally
     And covered with clean gold.
100 Likewise great joy he had to kiss
Her throat, where now the scarlet is
Against her little chin, I wis,
     That then was but cold.

No scarlet then her kirtle had
And little gold about it sprad;
But her red mouth was always glad
To kiss, albeit the eyes were sad
     With love they had to hold.

SECUNDUS MILES
How! old thief, thy wits are lame;
110 To clip such it is no shame;
I rede you in the devil's name,
Ye come not here to make men game;
By Termagaunt that maketh grame,
     I shall to–bete thine head.
          Hìc Diabolus capiat eum.
This knave hath sharp fingers, perfay;
Mahound you thank and keep alway,
And give you good knees to pray;
What man hath no lust to play,

The devil wring his ears, I say;
120 There is no more but wellaway,
    For now am I dead.

KING DAVID

Certes his mouth is wried and black,
Full little pence be in his sack;
This devil hath him by the back,
    It is no boot to lie.

NATHAN

Sitteth now still and learn of me;
A little while and ye shall see
The face of God's strength presently.
All queens made as this Bersabe,
130 All that were fair and foul ye be,
    Come hither; it am I.
    Et hìc omnes cantabunt.

HERODIAS

I am the queen Herodias.
This headband of my temples was
    King Herod's gold band woven me.
This broken dry staff in my hand
Was the queen's staff of a great land
    Betwixen Perse and Samarie.
For that one dancing of my feet,
The fire is come in my green wheat,
140   From one sea to the other sea.

AHOLIBAH

I am the queen Aholibah.
My lips kissed dumb the word of *Ah*
    Sighed on strange lips grown sick thereby.
God wrought to me my royal bed;
The inner work thereof was red,
    The outer work was ivory.

My mouth's heat was the heat of flame
For lust towards the kings that came
   With horsemen riding royally.

CLEOPATRA

150   I am the queen of Ethiope.
Love bade my kissing eyelids ope
   That men beholding might praise love.
My hair was wonderful and curled;
My lips held fast the mouth o' the world
   To spoil the strength and speech thereof.
The latter triumph in my breath
Bowed down the beaten brows of death,
   Ashamed they had not wrath enough.

ABIHAIL

I am the queen of Tyrians.
160   My hair was glorious for twelve spans,
   That dried to loose dust afterward.
My stature was a strong man's length:
My neck was like a place of strength
   Built with white walls, even and hard.
Like the first noise of rain leaves catch
One from another, snatch by snatch,
   Is my praise, hissed against and marred.

AZUBAH

I am the queen of Amorites.
My face was like a place of lights
170   With multitudes at festival.
The glory of my gracious brows
Was like God's house made glorious
   With colours upon either wall.
Between my brows and hair there was
A white space like a space of glass
   With golden candles over all.

AHOLAH

I am the queen of Amalek.
There was no tender touch or fleck
    To spoil my body or bared feet.
180   My words were soft like dulcimers,
And the first sweet of grape-flowers
    Made each side of my bosom sweet.
My raiment was as tender fruit
Whose rind smells sweet of spice-tree root,
    Bruised balm-blossom and budded wheat.

AHINOAM

I am the queen Ahinoam.
Like the throat of a soft slain lamb
    Was my throat, softer veined than his:
My lips were as two grapes the sun
190   Lays his whole weight of heat upon
    Like a mouth heavy with a kiss:
My hair's pure purple a wrought fleece,
My temples therein as a piece
    Of a pomegranate's cleaving is.

ATARAH

I am the queen Sidonian.
My face made faint the face of man,
    And strength was bound between my brows.
Spikenard was hidden in my ships,
Honey and wheat and myrrh in strips,
200   White wools that shine as colour does,
Soft linen dyed upon the fold,
Split spice and cores of scented gold,
    Cedar and broken calamus.

SEMIRAMIS

I am the queen Semiramis.
The whole world and the sea that is
    In fashion like a chrysopras,
The noise of all men labouring,

The priest's mouth tired through thanksgiving,
    The sound of love in the blood's pause,
210 The strength of love in the blood's beat,
All these were cast beneath my feet
    And all found lesser than I was.

HESIONE
I am the queen Hesione.
The seasons that increased in me
    Made my face fairer than all men's.
I had the summer in my hair;
And all the pale gold autumn air
    Was as the habit of my sense.
My body was as fire that shone;
220 God's beauty that makes all things one
    Was one among my handmaidens.

CHRYSOTHEMIS
I am the queen of Samothrace.
God, making roses, made my face
    As a rose filled up full with red.
My prows made sharp the straitened seas
From Pontus to that Chersonese
    Whereon the ebbed Asian stream is shed.
My hair was as sweet scent that drips;
Love's breath begun about my lips
230 Kindled the lips of people dead.

THOMYRIS
I am the queen of Scythians.
My strength was like no strength of man's,
    My face like day, my breast like spring.
My fame was felt in the extreme land
That hath sunshine on the one hand
    And on the other star-shining.
Yea, and the wind there fails of breath;
Yea, and there life is waste like death;
    Yea, and there death is a glad thing.

HARHAS

240   I am the queen of Anakim.
In the spent years whose speech is dim,
      Whose raiment is the dust and death,
My stately body without stain
Shone as the shining race of rain
      Whose hair a great wind scattereth.
Now hath God turned my lips to sighs,
Plucked off mine eyelids from mine eyes,
      And sealed with seals my way of breath.

MYRRHA

I am the queen Arabian.
250   The tears wherewith mine eyelids ran
      Smelt like my perfumed eyelids' smell.
A harsh thirst made my soft mouth hard,
That ached with kisses afterward;
      My brain rang like a beaten bell.
As tears on eyes, as fire on wood,
Sin fed upon my breath and blood,
      Sin made my breasts subside and swell.

PASIPHAE

I am the queen Pasiphae.
Not all the pure clean-coloured sea
260   Could cleanse or cool my yearning veins;
Nor any root nor herb that grew,
Flag-leaves that let green water through,
      Nor washing of the dews and rains.
From shame's pressed core I wrung the sweet
Fruit's savour that was death to eat,
      Whereof no seed but death remains.

SAPPHO

I am the queen of Lesbians.
My love, that had no part in man's,
      Was sweeter than all shape of sweet.
270   The intolerable infinite desire

Made my face pale like faded fire
    When the ashen pyre falls through with heat.
My blood was hot wan wine of love,
And my song's sound the sound thereof,
    The sound of the delight of it.

MESSALINA
I am the queen of Italy.
These were the signs God set on me;
    A barren beauty subtle and sleek,
Curled carven hair, and cheeks worn wan
280 With fierce false lips of many a man,
    Large temples where the blood ran weak,
A mouth athirst and amorous
And hungering as the grave's mouth does
    That, being an-hungred, cannot speak.

AMESTRIS
I am the queen of Persians.
My breasts were lordlier than bright swans,
    My body as amber fair and thin.
Strange flesh was given my lips for bread,
With poisonous hours my days were fed,
290   And my feet shod with adder-skin.
In Shushan toward Ecbatane
I wrought my joys with tears and pain,
    My loves with blood and bitter sin.

EPHRATH
I am the queen of Rephaim.
God, that some while refraineth him,
    Made in the end a spoil of me.
My rumour was upon the world
As strong sound of swoln water hurled
    Through porches of the straining sea.
300 My hair was like the flag-flower,
And my breasts carven goodlier
    Than beryl with chalcedony.

PASITHEA

I am the queen of Cypriotes.
Mine oarsmen, labouring with brown throats,
    Sang of me many a tender thing.
My maidens, girdled loose and braced
With gold from bosom to white waist,
    Praised me between their wool-combing.
All that praise Venus all night long
310   With lips like speech and lids like song
    Praised me till song lost heart to sing.

ALACIEL

I am the queen Alaciel.
My mouth was like that moist gold cell
    Whereout the thickest honey drips.
Mine eyes were as a grey-green sea;
The amorous blood that smote on me
    Smote to my feet and finger-tips.
My throat was whiter than the dove,
Mine eyelids as the seals of love,
320   And as the doors of love my lips.

ERIGONE

I am the queen Erigone.
The wild wine shed as blood on me
    Made my face brighter than a bride's.
My large lips had the old thirst of earth,
Mine arms the might of the old sea's girth
    Bound round the whole world's iron sides.
Within mine eyes and in mine ears
Were music and the wine of tears,
    And light, and thunder of the tides.
    Et hìc exeant, et dicat Bersabe regina;

330   Alas, God, for thy great pity
    And for the might that is in thee,
    Behold, I woful Bersabe

Cry out with stoopings of my knee
And thy wrath laid and bound on me
   Till I may see thy love.
Behold, Lord, this child is grown
Within me between bone and bone
To make me mother of a son,
Made of my body with strong moan;
There shall not be another one
   That shall be made hereof.

KING DAVID

Lord God, alas, what shall I sain?
Lo, thou art as an hundred men
Both to break and build again:
The wild ways thou makest plain,
Thine hands hold the hail and rain,
And thy fingers both grape and grain;
Of their largess we be all well fain,
   And of their great pity:
The sun thou madest of good gold,
Of clean silver the moon cold,
All the great stars thou hast told
As thy cattle in thy fold
Every one by his name of old;
Wind and water thou hast in hold,
   Both the land and the long sea;
Both the green sea and the land,
Lord God, thou hast in hand,
Both white water and grey sand;
Upon thy right or thy left hand
There is no man that may stand;
   Lord, thou rue on me.
O wise Lord, if thou be keen
To note things amiss that been,
I am not worth a shell of bean
More than an old mare meagre and lean;
For all my wrong-doing with my queen,
It grew not of our heartès clean,
   But it began of her body.

340

350

360

370   For it fell in the hot May
    I stood within a paven way
    Built of fair bright stone, perfay,
    That is as fire of night and day
        And lighteth all my house.
    Therein be neither stones nor sticks,
    Neither red nor white bricks,
    But for cubits five or six
    There is most goodly sardonyx
        And amber laid in rows.

380   It goes round about my roofs,
    (If ye list ye shall have proofs)
    There is good space for horse and hoofs,
        Plain and nothing perilous.
    For the fair green weather's heat,
    And for the smell of leavès sweet,
    It is no marvel, well ye weet,
        A man to waxen amorous.
    This I say now by my case
    That spied forth of that royal place,

390   There I saw in no great space
    Mine own sweet, both body and face,
    Under the fresh boughs.
    In a water that was there
    She wesshe her goodly body bare
    And dried it with her owen hair:
    Both her arms and her knees fair,
        Both bosom and brows;
    Both shoulders and eke thighs
    Tho she wesshe upon this wise;

400   Ever she sighed with little sighs,
        And ever she gave God thank.
    Yea, God wot I can well see yet
    Both her breast and her sides all wet
    And her long hair withouten let
    Spread sideways like a drawing net;
    Full dear bought and full far fet
    Was that sweet thing there y-set;
    It were a hard thing to forget

How both lips and eyen met,
410   Breast and breath sank.
So goodly a sight as there she was,
Lying looking on her glass
By wan water in green grass,
    Yet saw never man.
So soft and great she was and bright
With all her body waxen white,
I woxe nigh blind to see the light
Shed out of it to left and right;
This bitter sin from that sweet sight
420   Between us twain began.

NATHAN
Now, sir, be merry anon,
For ye shall have a full wise son,
Goodly and great of flesh and bone;
There shall no king be such an one,
    I swear by Godis rood.
Therefore, lord, be merry here,
And go to meat withouten fear,
And hear a mass with goodly cheer;
For to all folk ye shall be dear,
    And all folk of your blood.
    Et tunc dicant Laudamus.

St. Dorothy

It hath been seen and yet it shall be seen
That out of tender mouths God's praise hath been
Made perfect, and with wood and simple string
He hath played music sweet as shawm-playing
To please himself with softness of all sound;
And no small thing but hath been sometime found
Full sweet of use, and no such humbleness
But God hath bruised withal the sentences
And evidence of wise men witnessing;

10   No leaf that is so soft a hidden thing
      It never shall get sight of the great sun;
      The strength of ten has been the strength of one,
      And lowliness has waxed imperious.

        There was in Rome a man Theophilus
      Of right great blood and gracious ways, that had
      All noble fashions to make people glad
      And a soft life of pleasurable days;
      He was a goodly man for one to praise,
      Flawless and whole upward from foot to head;

20   His arms were a red hawk that alway fed
      On a small bird with feathers gnawed upon,
      Beaten and plucked about the bosom-bone
      Whereby a small round fleck like fire there was:
      They called it in their tongue lampadias;
      This was the banner of the lordly man.

      In many straits of sea and reaches wan
      Full of quick wind, and many a shaken firth,
      It had seen fighting days of either earth,
      Westward or east of waters Gaditane

30   (This was the place of sea-rocks under Spain
      Called after the great praise of Hercules)
      And north beyond the washing Pontic seas,
      Far windy Russian places fabulous,
      And salt fierce tides of storm-swoln Bosphorus.

        Now as this lord came straying in Rome town
      He saw a little lattice open down
      And after it a press of maidens' heads
      That sat upon their cold small quiet beds
      Talking, and played upon short-stringèd lutes;

40   And other some ground perfume out of roots
      Gathered by marvellous moons in Asia;
      Saffron and aloes and wild cassia,
      Coloured all through and smelling of the sun;
      And over all these was a certain one
      Clothed softly, with sweet herbs about her hair
      And bosom flowerful; her face more fair

Than sudden-singing April in soft lands:
Eyed like a gracious bird, and in both hands
She held a psalter painted green and red.

50   This Theophile laughed at the heart, and said,
Now God so help me hither and St. Paul,
As by the new time of their festival
I have good will to take this maid to wife.
And herewith fell to fancies of her life
And soft half-thoughts that ended suddenly.
This is man's guise to please himself, when he
Shall not see one thing of his pleasant things,
Nor with outwatch of many travailings
Come to be eased of the least pain he hath

60   For all his love and all his foolish wrath
And all the heavy manner of his mind.
Thus is he like a fisher fallen blind
That casts his nets across the boat awry
To strike the sea, but lo, he striketh dry
And plucks them back all broken for his pain
And bites his beard and casts across again
And reaching wrong slips over in the sea.
So hath this man a strangled neck for fee,
For all his cost he chuckles in his throat.

70   This Theophile that little hereof wote
Laid wait to hear of her what she might be:
Men told him she had name of Dorothy,
And was a lady of a worthy house.
Thereat this knight grew inly glorious
That he should have a love so fair of place.
She was a maiden of most quiet face,
Tender of speech, and had no hardihood
But was nigh feeble of her fearful blood;
Her mercy in her was so marvellous

80   From her least years, that seeing her school-fellows
That read beside her stricken with a rod,
She would cry sore and say some word to God
That he would ease her fellow of his pain.
There is no touch of sun or fallen rain

That ever fell on a more gracious thing.
    In middle Rome there was in stone-working
The church of Venus painted royally.
The chapels of it were some two or three,
In each of them her tabernacle was
90 And a wide window of six feet in glass
Coloured with all her works in red and gold.
The altars had bright cloths and cups to hold
The wine of Venus for the services,
Made out of honey and crushed wood-berries
That shed sweet yellow through the thick wet red,
That on high days was borne upon the head
Of Venus' priest for any man to drink;
So that in drinking he should fall to think
On some fair face, and in the thought thereof
100 Worship, and such should triumph in his love.
For this soft wine that did such grace and good
Was new trans-shaped and mixed with Love's own blood,
That in the fighting Trojan time was bled;
For which came such a woe to Diomed
That he was stifled after in hard sea.
And some said that this wine-shedding should be
Made of the falling of Adonis' blood,
That curled upon the thorns and broken wood
And round the gold silk shoes on Venus' feet;
110 The taste thereof was as hot honey sweet
And in the mouth ran soft and riotous.
This was the holiness of Venus' house.
    It was their worship, that in August days
Twelve maidens should go through those Roman ways
Naked, and having gold across their brows
And their hair twisted in short golden rows,
To minister to Venus in this wise:
And twelve men chosen in their companies
To match these maidens by the altar-stair,
120 All in one habit, crowned upon the hair.
Among these men was chosen Theophile.
    This knight went out and prayed a little while,

Holding queen Venus by her hands and knees;
I will give thee twelve royal images
Cut in glad gold, with marvels of wrought stone
For thy sweet priests to lean and pray upon,
Jasper and hyacinth and chrysopras,
And the strange Asian thalamite that was
Hidden twelve ages under heavy sea
130 Among the little sleepy pearls, to be
A shrine lit over with soft candle-flame
Burning all night red as hot brows of shame,
So thou wilt be my lady without sin.
Goddess that art all gold outside and in,
Help me to serve thee in thy holy way.
Thou knowest, Love, that in my bearing day
There shone a laughter in the singing stars
Round the gold-ceilèd bride-bed wherein Mars
Touched thee and had thee in your kissing wise.
140 Now therefore, sweet, kiss thou my maiden's eyes
That they may open graciously towards me;
And this new fashion of thy shrine shall be
As soft with gold as thine own happy head.
    The goddess, that was painted with face red
Between two long green tumbled sides of sea,
Stooped her neck sideways, and spake pleasantly:
Thou shalt have grace as thou art thrall of mine.
And with this came a savour of shed wine
And plucked-out petals from a rose's head:
150 And softly with slow laughs of lip she said,
Thou shalt have favour all thy days of me.
    Then came Theophilus to Dorothy,
Saying: O sweet, if one should strive or speak
Against God's ways, he gets a beaten cheek
For all his wage and shame above all men.
Therefore I have no will to turn again
When God saith 'go,' lest a worse thing fall out.
Then she, misdoubting lest he went about
To catch her wits, made answer somewhat thus:
160 I have no will, my lord Theophilus,

To speak against this worthy word of yours;
Knowing how God's will in all speech endures,
That save by grace there may no thing be said.
Then Theophile waxed light from foot to head,
And softly fell upon this answering.
It is well seen you are a chosen thing
To do God service in his gracious way.
I will that you make haste and holiday
To go next year upon the Venus stair,
170   Covered none else, but crowned upon your hair,
And do the service that a maiden doth.
She said: but I that am Christ's maid were loth
To do this thing that hath such bitter name.
Thereat his brows were beaten with sore shame
And he came off and said no other word.
Then his eyes chanced upon his banner-bird,
And he fell fingering at the staff of it
And laughed for wrath and stared between his feet,
And out of a chafed heart he spake as thus:
180   Lo how she japes at me Theophilus,
Feigning herself a fool and hard to love;
Yet in good time for all she boasteth of
She shall be like a little beaten bird.
And while his mouth was open in that word
He came upon the house Janiculum,
Where some went busily, and other some
Talked in the gate called the gate glorious.
The emperor, which was one Gabalus,
Sat over all and drank chill wine alone.
190   To whom is come Theophilus anon,
And said as thus: *Beau sire, Dieu vous aide.*
And afterward sat under him, and said
All this thing through as ye have wholly heard.
    This Gabalus laughed thickly in his beard.
Yea, this is righteousness and maiden rule.
Truly, he said, a maid is but a fool.
And japed at them as one full villainous,
In a lewd wise, this heathen Gabalus,

And sent his men to bind her as he bade.
200   Thus have they taken Dorothy the maid,
And haled her forth as men hale pick-purses:
A little need God knows they had of this,
To hale her by her maiden gentle hair.
Thus went she lowly, making a soft prayer,
As one who stays the sweet wine in his mouth,
Murmuring with eased lips, and is most loth
To have done wholly with the sweet of it.

    Christ king, fair Christ, that knowest all men's wit
And all the feeble fashion of my ways,
210   O perfect God, that from all yesterdays
Abidest whole with morrows perfected,
I pray thee by thy mother's holy head
Thou help me to do right, that I not slip:
I have no speech nor strength upon my lip,
Except thou help me who art wise and sweet.
Do this too for those nails that clove thy feet,
Let me die maiden after many pains.
Though I be least among thy handmaidens,
Doubtless I shall take death more sweetly thus.

220   Now have they brought her to King Gabalus,
Who laughed in all his throat some breathing-whiles:
By God, he said, if one should leap two miles,
He were not pained about the sides so much.
This were a soft thing for a man to touch.
Shall one so chafe that hath such little bones?
And shook his throat with thick and chuckled moans
For laughter that she had such holiness.
What aileth thee, wilt thou do services?
It were good fare to fare as Venus doth.

230   Then said this lady with her maiden mouth,
Shamefaced, and something paler in the cheek:
Now, sir, albeit my wit and will to speak
Give me no grace in sight of worthy men,
For all my shame yet know I this again,
I may not speak, nor after downlying
Rise up to take delight in lute-playing,

Nor sing nor sleep, nor sit and fold my hands,
But my soul in some measure understands
God's grace laid like a garment over me.
240 For this fair God that out of strong sharp sea
Lifted the shapely and green-coloured land,
And hath the weight of heaven in his hand
As one might hold a bird, and under him
The heavy golden planets beam by beam
Building the feasting-chambers of his house,
And the large world he holdeth with his brows,
And with the light of them astonisheth
All place and time and face of life and death
And motion of the north wind and the south,
250 And is the sound within his angel's mouth
Of singing words and words of thanksgiving,
And is the colour of the latter spring
And heat upon the summer and the sun,
And is beginning of all things begun
And gathers in him all things to their end,
And with the fingers of his hand doth bend
The stretched-out sides of heaven like a sail,
And with his breath he maketh the red pale
And fills with blood faint faces of men dead,
260 And with the sound between his lips are fed
Iron and fire and the white body of snow,
And blossom of all trees in places low,
And small bright herbs about the little hills,
And fruit pricked softly with birds' tender bills,
And flight of foam about green fields of sea,
And fourfold strength of the great winds that be
Moved always outward from beneath his feet,
And growth of grass and growth of sheavèd wheat
And all green flower of goodly-growing lands;
270 And all these things he gathers with his hands
And covers all their beauty with his wings;
The same, even God that governs all these things,
Hath set my feet to be upon his ways.
Now therefore for no painfulness of days

I shall put off this service bound on me.
Also, fair sir, ye know this certainly,
How God was in his flesh full chaste and meek
And gave his face to shame, and either cheek
Gave up to smiting of men tyrannous.
280   And here with a great voice this Gabalus
Cried out and said: By God's blood and his bones,
This were good game betwixen night and nones
For one to sit and hearken to such saws:
I were as lief fall in some big beast's jaws
As hear these women's jaw-teeth clattering;
By God a woman is the harder thing,
One may not put a hook into her mouth.
Now by St. Luke I am so sore adrouth
For all these saws I must needs drink again.
290   But I pray God deliver all us men
From all such noise of women and their heat.
That is a noble scripture, well I weet,
That likens women to an empty can;
When God said that he was a full wise man.
I trow no man may blame him as for that.
    And herewithal he drank a draught, and spat,
And said: Now shall I make an end hereof.
Come near all men and hearken for God's love,
And ye shall hear a jest or twain, God wot.
300   And spake as thus with mouth full thick and hot;
But thou do this thou shalt be shortly slain.
Lo, sir, she said, this death and all his pain
I take in penance of my bitter sins.
Yea now, quoth Gabalus, this game begins.
Lo, without sin one shall not live a span.
Lo, this is she that would not look on man
Between her fingers folded in thwart wise.
See how her shame hath smitten in her eyes
That was so clean she had not heard of shame.
310   Certes, he said, by Gabalus my name,
This two years back I was not so well pleased.
This were good mirth for sick men to be eased

And rise up whole and laugh at hearing of.
I pray thee show us something of thy love,
Since thou wast maid thy gown is waxen wide.
Yea, maid I am, she said, and somewhat sighed,
As one who thought upon the low fair house
Where she sat working, with soft bended brows
Watching her threads, among the school-maidens.
320   And she thought well now God had brought her thence
She should not come to sew her gold again.
     Then cried King Gabalus upon his men
To have her forth and draw her with steel gins.
And as a man hag-ridden beats and grins
And bends his body sidelong in his bed,
So wagged he with his body and knave's head,
Gaping at her, and blowing with his breath.
And in good time he gat an evil death
Out of his lewdness with his cursèd wives:
330   His bones were hewn asunder as with knives
For his misliving, certes it is said.
But all the evil wrought upon this maid,
It were full hard for one to handle it.
For her soft blood was shed upon her feet,
And all her body's colour bruised and faint.
But she, as one abiding God's great saint,
Spake not nor wept for all this travail hard.
Wherefore the king commanded afterward
To slay her presently in all men's sight.
340   And it was now an hour upon the night
And winter-time, and a few stars began.
The weather was yet feeble and all wan
For beating of a weighty wind and snow.
And she came walking in soft wise and slow,
And many men with faces piteous.
Then came this heavy cursing Gabalus,
That swore full hard into his drunken beard;
And faintly after without any word
Came Theophile some paces off the king.
350   And in the middle of this wayfaring

Full tenderly beholding her he said:
    There is no word of comfort with men dead
Nor any face and colour of things sweet;
But always with lean cheeks and lifted feet
These dead men lie all aching to the blood
With bitter cold, their brows withouten hood
Beating for chill, their bodies swathed full thin:
Alas, what hire shall any have herein
To give his life and get such bitterness?
360 Also the soul going forth bodiless
Is hurt with naked cold, and no man saith
If there be house or covering for death
To hide the soul that is discomforted.
    Then she beholding him a little said:
Alas, fair lord, ye have no wit of this;
For on one side death is full poor of bliss
And as ye say full sharp of bone and lean:
But on the other side is good and green
And hath soft flower of tender-coloured hair
370 Grown on his head, and a red mouth as fair
As may be kissed with lips; thereto his face
Is as God's face, and in a perfect place
Full of all sun and colour of straight boughs
And waterheads about a painted house
That hath a mile of flowers either way
Outward from it, and blossom-grass of May
Thickening on many a side for length of heat,
Hath God set death upon a noble seat
Covered with green and flowered in the fold,
380 In likeness of a great king grown full old
And gentle with new temperance of blood;
And on his brows a purfled purple hood,
They may not carry any golden thing;
And plays some tune with subtle fingering
On a small cithern, full of tears and sleep
And heavy pleasure that is quick to weep
And sorrow with the honey in her mouth;
And for this might of music that he doth

Are all souls drawn toward him with great love
390   And weep for sweetness of the noise thereof
And bow to him with worship of their knees;
And all the field is thick with companies
Of fair-clothed men that play on shawms and lutes
And gather honey of the yellow fruits
Between the branches waxen soft and wide:
And all this peace endures in either side
Of the green land, and God beholdeth all.
And this is girdled with a round fair wall
Made of red stone and cool with heavy leaves
400   Grown out against it, and green blossom cleaves
To the green chinks, and lesser wall-weed sweet,
Kissing the crannies that are split with heat,
And branches where the summer draws to head.

   And Theophile burnt in the cheek, and said:
Yea, could one see it, this were marvellous.
I pray you, at your coming to this house,
Give me some leaf of all those tree-branches;
Seeing how so sharp and white our weather is,
There is no green nor gracious red to see.
410   Yea, sir, she said, that shall I certainly.
And from her long sweet throat without a fleck
Undid the gold, and through her stretched-out neck
The cold axe clove, and smote away her head:
Out of her throat the tender blood full red
Fell suddenly through all her long soft hair.
And with good speed for hardness of the air
Each man departed to his house again.

   Lo, as fair colour in the face of men
At seed-time of their blood, or in such wise
420   As a thing seen increaseth in men's eyes,
Caught first far off by sickly fits of sight,
So a word said, if one shall hear aright,
Abides against the season of its growth.
This Theophile went slowly, as one doth
That is not sure for sickness of his feet;
And counting the white stonework of the street,

Tears fell out of his eyes for wrath and love,
Making him weep more for the shame thereof
Than for true pain: so went he half a mile.
430　And women mocked him, saying: Theophile,
Lo, she is dead; what shall a woman have
That loveth such an one? so Christ me save,
I were as lief to love a man new-hung.
Surely this man has bitten on his tongue,
This makes him sad and writhled in his face.
　　And when they came upon the paven place
That was called sometime the place amorous
There came a child before Theophilus
Bearing a basket, and said suddenly:
440　Fair sir, this is my mistress Dorothy
That sends you gifts; and with this he was gone.
In all this earth there is not such an one
For colour and straight stature made so fair.
The tender growing gold of his pure hair
Was as wheat growing, and his mouth as flame.
God called him Holy after his own name;
With gold cloth like fire burning he was clad.
But for the fair green basket that he had,
It was filled up with heavy white and red;
450　Great roses stained still where the first rose bled,
Burning at heart for shame their heart withholds:
And the sad colour of strong marigolds
That have the sun to kiss their lips of love;
The flower that Venus' hair is woven of,
The colour of fair apples in the sun,
Late peaches gathered when the heat was done
And the slain air got breath; and after these
The fair faint-headed poppies drunk with ease,
And heaviness of hollow lilies red.
460　　Then cried they all that saw these things, and said
It was God's doing, and was marvellous.
And in brief while this knight Theophilus
Is waxen full of faith, and witnesseth
Before the king of God and love and death,

For which the king bade hang him presently.
A gallows of a goodly piece of tree
This Gabalus hath made to hang him on.
Forth of this world lo Theophile is gone
With a wried neck, God give us better fare
470 Than his that hath a twisted throat to wear;
But truly for his love God hath him brought
There where his heavy body grieves him nought
Nor all the people plucking at his feet;
But in his face his lady's face is sweet,
And through his lips her kissing lips are gone:
God send him peace, and joy of such an one.
    This is the story of St. Dorothy.
I will you of your mercy pray for me
Because I wrote these sayings for your grace,
480 That I may one day see her in the face.

The Two Dreams
(FROM BOCCACCIO)

I will that if I say a heavy thing
Your tongues forgive me; seeing ye know that spring
Has flecks and fits of pain to keep her sweet,
And walks somewhile with winter-bitten feet.
Moreover it sounds often well to let
One string, when ye play music, keep at fret
The whole song through; one petal that is dead
Confirms the roses, be they white or red;
Dead sorrow is not sorrowful to hear
10 As the thick noise that breaks mid weeping were;
The sick sound aching in a lifted throat
Turns to sharp silver of a perfect note;
And though the rain falls often, and with rain
Late autumn falls on the old red leaves like pain,
I deem that God is not disquieted.
Also while men are fed with wine and bread,

They shall be fed with sorrow at his hand.
   There grew a rose-garden in Florence land
More fair than many; all red summers through
20 The leaves smelt sweet and sharp of rain, and blew
Sideways with tender wind; and therein fell
Sweet sound wherewith the green waxed audible,
As a bird's will to sing disturbed his throat
And set the sharp wings forward like a boat
Pushed through soft water, moving his brown side
Smooth-shapen as a maid's, and shook with pride
His deep warm bosom, till the heavy sun's
Set face of heat stopped all the songs at once.
The ways were clean to walk and delicate;
30 And when the windy white of March grew late,
Before the trees took heart to face the sun
With ravelled raiment of lean winter on,
The roots were thick and hot with hollow grass.

   Some roods away a lordly house there was,
Cool with broad courts and latticed passage wet
From rush-flowers and lilies ripe to set,
Sown close among the strewings of the floor;
And either wall of the slow corridor
Was dim with deep device of gracious things;
40 Some angel's steady mouth and weight of wings
Shut to the side; or Peter with straight stole
And beard cut black against the aureole
That spanned his head from nape to crown; thereby
Mary's gold hair, thick to the girdle-tie
Wherein was bound a child with tender feet;
Or the broad cross with blood nigh brown on it.

   Within this house a righteous lord abode,
Ser Averardo; patient of his mood,
And just of judgment; and to child he had
50 A maid so sweet that her mere sight made glad
Men sorrowing, and unbound the brows of hate;
And where she came, the lips that pain made strait
Waxed warm and wide, and from untender grew
Tender as those that sleep brings patience to.

Such long locks had she, that with knee to chin
She might have wrapped and warmed her feet therein.
Right seldom fell her face on weeping wise;
Gold hair she had, and golden-coloured eyes,
Filled with clear light and fire and large repose

60 Like a fair hound's; no man there is but knows
Her face was white, and thereto she was tall;
In no wise lacked there any praise at all
To her most perfect and pure maidenhood;
No sin I think there was in all her blood.

    She, where a gold grate shut the roses in,
Dwelt daily through deep summer weeks, through green
Hushed hours of rain upon the leaves; and there
Love made him room and space to worship her
With tender worship of bowed knees, and wrought

70 Such pleasure as the pained sense palates not
For weariness, but at one taste undoes
The heart of its strong sweet, is ravenous
Of all the hidden honey; words and sense
Fail through the tune's imperious prevalence.

    In a poor house this lover kept apart,
Long communing with patience next his heart
If love of his might move that face at all,
Tuned evenwise with colours musical;
Then after length of days he said thus: 'Love,

80 For love's own sake and for the love thereof
Let no harsh words untune your gracious mood;
For good it were, if anything be good,
To comfort me in this pain's plague of mine;
Seeing thus, how neither sleep nor bread nor wine
Seems pleasant to me, yea no thing that is
Seems pleasant to me; only I know this,
Love's ways are sharp for palms of piteous feet
To travel, but the end of such is sweet:
Now do with me as seemeth you the best.'

90 She mused a little, as one holds his guest
By the hand musing, with her face borne down:
Then said: 'Yea, though such bitter seed be sown,

Have no more care of all that you have said;
Since if there is no sleep will bind your head,
Lo, I am fain to help you certainly;
Christ knoweth, sir, if I would have you die;
There is no pleasure when a man is dead.'
Thereat he kissed her hands and yellow head
And clipped her fair long body many times;
100 I have no wit to shape in written rhymes
A scanted tithe of this great joy they had.

    They were too near love's secret to be glad;
As whoso deems the core will surely melt
From the warm fruit his lips caress, hath felt
Some bitter kernel where the teeth shut hard:
Or as sweet music sharpens afterward,
Being half disrelished both for sharp and sweet;
As sea-water, having killed over-heat
In a man's body, chills it with faint ache;
110 So their sense, burdened only for love's sake,
Failed for pure love; yet so time served their wit,
They saved each day some gold reserves of it,
Being wiser in love's riddle than such be
Whom fragments feed with his chance charity.
All things felt sweet were felt sweet overmuch;
The rose-thorn's prickle dangerous to touch,
And flecks of fire in the thin leaf-shadows;
Too keen the breathèd honey of the rose,
Its red too harsh a weight on feasted eyes;
120 They were so far gone in love's histories,
Beyond all shape and colour and mere breath,
Where pleasure has for kinsfolk sleep and death,
And strength of soul and body waxen blind
For weariness, and flesh entoiled with mind,
When the keen edge of sense foretasteth sin.

    Even this green place the summer caught them in
Seemed half deflowered and sick with beaten leaves
In their strayed eyes; these gold flower-fumèd eves
Burnt out to make the sun's love-offering,
130 The midnoon's prayer, the rose's thanksgiving,

The trees' weight burdening the strengthless air,
The shape of her stilled eyes, her coloured hair,
Her body's balance from the moving feet –
All this, found fair, lacked yet one grain of sweet
It had some warm weeks back: so perisheth
On May's new lip the tender April breath:
So those same walks the wind sowed lilies in
All April through, and all their latter kin
Of languid leaves whereon the Autumn blows –
140 The dead red raiment of the last year's rose –
The last year's laurel, and the last year's love,
Fade, and grow things that death grows weary of.

What man will gather in red summer-time
The fruit of some obscure and hoary rhyme
Heard last midwinter, taste the heart in it,
Mould the smooth semitones afresh, refit
The fair limbs ruined, flush the dead blood through
With colour, make all broken beauties new
For love's new lesson – shall not such find pain
150 When the marred music labouring in his brain
Frets him with sweet sharp fragments, and lets slip
One word that might leave satisfied his lip –
One touch that might put fire in all the chords?
This was her pain: to miss from all sweet words
Some taste of sound, diverse and delicate –
Some speech the old love found out to compensate
For seasons of shut lips and drowsiness –
Some grace, some word the old love found out to bless
Passionless months and undelighted weeks.
160 The flowers had lost their summer-scented cheeks,
Their lips were no more sweet than daily breath:
The year was plagued with instances of death.

So fell it, these were sitting in cool grass
With leaves about, and many a bird there was
Where the green shadow thickliest impleached
Soft fruit and writhen spray and blossom bleached
Dry in the sun or washed with rains to white:
Her girdle was pure silk, the bosom bright

With purple as purple water and gold wrought in.
170 One branch had touched with dusk her lips and chin,
Made violet of the throat, abashed with shade
The breast's bright plaited work: but nothing frayed
The sun's large kiss on the luxurious hair.
Her beauty was new colour to the air
And music to the silent many birds.
Love was an-hungred for some perfect words
To praise her with; but only her low name
'Andrevuola' came thrice, and thrice put shame
In her clear cheek, so fruitful with new red
180 That for pure love straightway shame's self was dead.
    Then with lids gathered as who late had wept
She began saying: 'I have so little slept
My lids drowse now against the very sun;
Yea, the brain aching with a dream begun
Beats like a fitful blood; kiss but both brows,
And you shall pluck my thoughts grown dangerous
Almost away.' He said thus, kissing them:
'O sole sweet thing that God is glad to name,
My one gold gift, if dreams be sharp and sore
190 Shall not the waking time increase much more
With taste and sound, sweet eyesight or sweet scent?
Has any heat too hard and insolent
Burnt bare the tender married leaves, undone
The maiden grass shut under from the sun?
Where in this world is room enough for pain?'
    The feverish finger of love had touched again
Her lips with happier blood; the pain lay meek
In her fair face, nor altered lip nor cheek
With pallor or with pulse; but in her mouth
200 Love thirsted as a man wayfaring doth,
Making it humble as weak hunger is.
She lay close to him, bade do this and this,
Say that, sing thus: then almost weeping-ripe
Crouched, then laughed low. As one that fain would wipe
The old record out of old things done and dead,
She rose, she heaved her hands up, and waxed red

For wilful heart and blameless fear of blame;
Saying 'Though my wits be weak, this is no shame
For a poor maid whom love so punisheth
210   With heats of hesitation and stopped breath
That with my dreams I live yet heavily
For pure sad heart and faith's humility.
Now be not wroth and I will show you this.

    'Methought our lips upon their second kiss
Met in this place, and a fair day we had
And fair soft leaves that waxed and were not sad
With shaken rain or bitten through with drouth;
When I, beholding ever how your mouth
Waited for mine, the throat being fallen back,
220   Saw crawl thereout a live thing flaked with black
Specks of brute slime and leper-coloured scale,
A devil's hide with foul flame-writhen grail
Fashioned where hell's heat festers loathsomest;
And that brief speech may ease me of the rest,
Thus were you slain and eaten of the thing.
My waked eyes felt the new day shuddering
On their low lids, felt the whole east so beat,
Pant with close pulse of such a plague-struck heat,
As if the palpitating dawn drew breath
230   For horror, breathing between life and death,
Till the sun sprang blood-bright and violent.'

    So finishing, her soft strength wholly spent,
She gazed each way, lest some brute-hoovèd thing,
The timeless travail of hell's childbearing,
Should threat upon the sudden: whereat he,
For relish of her tasted misery
And tender little thornprick of her pain,
Laughed with mere love. What lover among men
But hath his sense fed sovereignly 'twixt whiles
240   With tears and covered eyelids and sick smiles
And soft disaster of a painèd face?
What pain, established in so sweet a place,
But the plucked leaf of it smells fragrantly?
What colour burning man's wide-open eye

But may be pleasurably seen? what sense
Keeps in its hot sharp extreme violence
No savour of sweet things? The bereaved blood
And emptied flesh in their most broken mood
Fail not so wholly, famish not when thus
250   Past honey keeps the starved lip covetous.
　　Therefore this speech from a glad mouth began,
Breathed in her tender hair and temples wan
Like one prolonged kiss while the lips had breath.
'Sleep, that abides in vassalage of death
And in death's service wears out half his age,
Hath his dreams full of deadly vassalage,
Shadow and sound of things ungracious;
Fair shallow faces, hooded bloodless brows,
And mouths past kissing; yea, myself have had
260   As harsh a dream as holds your eyelids sad.
　　'This dream I tell you came three nights ago;
In full mid sleep I took a whim to know
How sweet things might be; so I turned and thought;
But save my dream all sweet availed me not.
First came a smell of pounded spice and scent
Such as God ripens in some continent
Of utmost amber in the Syrian sea;
And breaths as though some costly rose could be
Spoiled slowly, wasted by some bitter fire
270   To burn the sweet out leaf by leaf, and tire
The flower's poor heart with heat and waste, to make
Strong magic for some perfumed woman's sake.
Then a cool naked sense beneath my feet
Of bud and blossom; and sound of veins that beat
As if a lute should play of its own heart
And fearfully, not smitten of either part;
And all my blood it filled with sharp and sweet
As gold swoln grain fills out the huskèd wheat;
So I rose naked from the bed, and stood
280   Counting the mobile measure in my blood
Some pleasant while, and through each limb there came
Swift little pleasures pungent as a flame,

Felt in the thrilling flesh and veins as much
As the outer curls that feel the comb's first touch
Thrill to the roots and shiver as from fire;
And blind between my dream and my desire
I seemed to stand and held my spirit still
Lest this should cease. A child whose fingers spill
Honey from cells forgotten of the bee
290   Is less afraid to stir the hive and see
Some wasp's bright back inside, than I to feel
Some finger-touch disturb the flesh like steel.
I prayed thus; Let me catch a secret here
So sweet, it sharpens the sweet taste of fear
And takes the mouth with edge of wine; I would
Have here some colour and smooth shape as good
As those in heaven whom the chief garden hides
With low grape-blossom veiling their white sides
And lesser tendrils that so bind and blind
300   Their eyes and feet, that if one come behind
To touch their hair they see not, neither fly;
This would I see in heaven and not die.
So praying, I had nigh cried out and knelt,
So wholly my prayer filled me: till I felt
In the dumb night's warm weight of glowing gloom
Somewhat that altered all my sleeping-room,
And made it like a green low place wherein
Maids mix to bathe: one sets her small warm chin
Against a ripple, that the angry pearl
310   May flow like flame about her: the next curl
Dips in some eddy coloured of the sun
To wash the dust well out; another one
Holds a straight ankle in her hand and swings
With lavish body sidelong, so that rings
Of sweet fierce water, swollen and splendid, fail
All round her fine and floated body pale,
Swayed flower-fashion, and her balanced side
Swerved edgeways lets the weight of water slide,
As taken in some underflow of sea
320   Swerves the banked gold of sea-flowers; but she

Pulls down some branch to keep her perfect head
Clear of the river: even from wall to bed,
I tell you, was my room transfigured so.
Sweet, green and warm it was, nor could one know
If there were walls or leaves, or if there was
No bed's green curtain, but mere gentle grass.
There were set also hard against the feet
Gold plates with honey and green grapes to eat,
With the cool water's noise to hear in rhymes:
330   And a wind warmed me full of furze and limes
And all hot sweets the heavy summer fills
To the round brim of smooth cup-shapen hills.
Next the grave walking of a woman's feet
Made my veins hesitate, and gracious heat
Made thick the lids and leaden on mine eyes:
And I thought ever, surely it were wise
Not yet to see her: this may last (who knows?)
Five minutes; the poor rose is twice a rose
Because it turns a face to her, the wind
340   Sings that way; hath this woman ever sinned,
I wonder? as a boy with apple-rind,
I played with pleasures, made them to my mind,
Changed each ere tasting. When she came indeed,
First her hair touched me, then I grew to feed
On the sense of her hand; her mouth at last
Touched me between the cheek and lip and past
Over my face with kisses here and there
Sown in and out across the eyes and hair.
Still I said nothing; till she set her face
350   More close and harder on the kissing-place,
And her mouth caught like a snake's mouth, and stung
So faint and tenderly, the fang scarce clung
More than a bird's foot: yet a wound it grew,
A great one, let this red mark witness you
Under the left breast; and the stroke thereof
So clove my sense that I woke out of love
And knew not what this dream was nor had wit;
But now God knows if I have skill of it.'

Hereat she laid one palm against her lips
360   To stop their trembling; as when water slips
Out of a beak-mouthed vessel with faint noise
And chuckles in the narrowed throat and cloys
The carven rims with murmuring, so came
Words in her lips with no word right of them,
A beaten speech thick and disconsolate,
Till his smile ceasing waxed compassionate
Of her sore fear that grew from anything –
The sound of the strong summer thickening
In heated leaves of the smooth apple-trees:
370   The day's breath felt about the ash-branches,
And noises of the noon whose weight still grew
On the hot heavy-headed flowers, and drew
Their red mouths open till the rose-heart ached;
For eastward all the crowding rose was slaked
And soothed with shade: but westward all its growth
Seemed to breathe hard with heat as a man doth
Who feels his temples newly feverous.
And even with such motion in her brows
As that man hath in whom sick days begin,
380   She turned her throat and spake, her voice being thin
As a sick man's, sudden and tremulous;
'Sweet, if this end be come indeed on us,
Let us love more;' and held his mouth with hers.
As the first sound of flooded hill-waters
Is heard by people of the meadow-grass,
Or ever a wandering waif of ruin pass
With whirling stones and foam of the brown stream
Flaked with fierce yellow: so beholding him
She felt before tears came her eyelids wet,
390   Saw the face deadly thin where life was yet,
Heard his throat's harsh last moan before it clomb:
And he, with close mouth passionate and dumb,
Burned at her lips: so lay they without speech,
Each grasping other, and the eyes of each
Fed in the other's face: till suddenly
He cried out with a little broken cry

This word, 'O help me, sweet, I am but dead.'
And even so saying, the colour of fair red
Was gone out of his face, and his blood's beat
400 Fell, and stark death made sharp his upward feet
And pointed hands; and without moan he died.
Pain smote her sudden in the brows and side,
Strained her lips open and made burn her eyes:
For the pure sharpness of her miseries
She had no heart's pain, but mere body's wrack;
But at the last her beaten blood drew back
Slowly upon her face, and her stunned brows
Suddenly grown aware and piteous
Gathered themselves, her eyes shone, her hard breath
410 Came as though one nigh dead came back from death;
Her lips throbbed, and life trembled through her hair.
    And in brief while she thought to bury there
The dead man that her love might lie with him
In a sweet bed under the rose-roots dim
And soft earth round the branchèd apple-trees,
Full of hushed heat and heavy with great ease,
And no man entering divide him thence.
Wherefore she bade one of her handmaidens
To be her help to do upon this wise.
420 And saying so the tears out of her eyes
Fell without noise and comforted her heart:
Yea, her great pain eased of the sorest part
Began to soften in her sense of it.
There under all the little branches sweet
The place was shapen of his burial;
They shed thereon no thing funereal,
But coloured leaves of latter rose-blossom,
Stems of soft-grass, some withered red and some
Fair and fresh-blooded; and spoil splendider
430 Of marigold and great spent sunflower.
    And afterward she came back without word
To her own house; two days went, and the third
Went, and she showed her father of this thing.
And for great grief of her soul's travailing

He gave consent she should endure in peace
Till her life's end; yea, till her time should cease,
She should abide in fellowship of pain.
And having lived a holy year or twain
She died of pure waste heart and weariness.
440   And for love's honour in her love's distress
This word was written over her tomb's head;
'Here dead she lieth, for whose sake Love is dead.'

Aholibah

In the beginning God made thee
   A woman well to look upon,
Thy tender body as a tree
   Whereon cool wind hath always blown
   Till the clean branches be well grown.

There was none like thee in the land;
   The girls that were thy bondwomen
Did bind thee with a purple band
   Upon thy forehead, that all men
10   Should know thee for God's handmaiden.

Strange raiment clad thee like a bride,
   With silk to wear on hands and feet
And plates of gold on either side:
   Wine made thee glad, and thou didst eat
   Honey, and choice of pleasant meat.

And fishers in the middle sea
   Did get thee sea-fish and sea-weeds
In colour like the robes on thee;
   And curious work of plaited reeds,
20   And wools wherein live purple bleeds.

And round the edges of thy cup
   Men wrought thee marvels out of gold,
Strong snakes with lean throats lifted up,
   Large eyes whereon the brows had hold,
   And scaly things their slime kept cold.

For thee they blew soft wind in flutes
   And ground sweet roots for cunning scent;
Made slow because of many lutes,
   The wind among thy chambers went
30   Wherein no light was violent.

God called thy name Aholibah,
   His tabernacle being in thee,
A witness through waste Asia;
   Thou wert a tent sewn cunningly
   With gold and colours of the sea.

God gave thee gracious ministers
   And all their work who plait and weave:
The cunning of embroiderers
   That sew the pillow to the sleeve,
40   And likeness of all things that live.

Thy garments upon thee were fair
   With scarlet and with yellow thread;
Also the weaving of thine hair
   Was as fine gold upon thy head,
   And thy silk shoes were sewn with red.

All sweet things he bade sift, and ground
   As a man grindeth wheat in mills
With strong wheels alway going round;
   He gave thee corn, and grass that fills
50   The cattle on a thousand hills.

The wine of many seasons fed
   Thy mouth, and made it fair and clean;
Sweet oil was poured out on thy head
   And ran down like cool rain between
   The strait close locks it melted in.

The strong men and the captains knew
   Thy chambers wrought and fashioned
With gold and covering of blue,
   And the blue raiment of thine head
60   Who satest on a stately bed.

All these had on their garments wrought
   The shape of beasts and creeping things,
The body that availeth not,
   Flat backs of worms and veinèd wings,
   And the lewd bulk that sleeps and stings.

Also the chosen of the years,
   The multitude being at ease,
With sackbuts and with dulcimers
   And noise of shawms and psalteries
70   Made mirth within the ears of these.

But as a common woman doth,
   Thou didst think evil and devise;
The sweet smell of thy breast and mouth
   Thou madest as the harlot's wise,
   And there was painting on thine eyes.

Yea, in the woven guest-chamber
   And by the painted passages
Where the strange gracious paintings were,
   State upon state of companies,
80   There came on thee the lust of these.

Because of shapes on either wall
   Sea-coloured from some rare blue shell
At many a Tyrian interval,
   Horsemen on horses, girdled well,
   Delicate and desirable,

Thou saidest: I am sick of love:
   Stay me with flagons, comfort me
With apples for my pain thereof
   Till my hands gather in his tree
90   That fruit wherein my lips would be.

Yea, saidest thou, I will go up
   When there is no more shade than one
May cover with a hollow cup,
   And make my bed against the sun
   Till my blood's violence be done.

Thy mouth was leant upon the wall
   Against the painted mouth, thy chin
Touched the hair's painted curve and fall;
   Thy deep throat, fallen lax and thin,
100   Worked as the blood's beat worked therein.

Therefore, O thou Aholibah,
   God is not glad because of thee;
And thy fine gold shall pass away
   Like those fair coins of ore that be
   Washed over by the middle sea.

Then will one make thy body bare
   To strip it of all gracious things,
And pluck the cover from thine hair,
   And break the gift of many kings,
110   Thy wrist-rings and thine ankle-rings.

Likewise the man whose body joins
   To thy smooth body, as was said,
Who hath a girdle on his loins
   And dyed attire upon his head –
   The same who, seeing, worshipped,

Because thy face was like the face
   Of a clean maiden that smells sweet,
Because thy gait was as the pace
   Of one that opens not her feet
120   And is not heard within the street –

Even he, O thou Aholibah,
   Made separate from thy desire,
Shall cut thy nose and ears away
   And bruise thee for thy body's hire
   And burn the residue with fire.

Then shall the heathen people say,
   The multitude being at ease;
Lo, this is that Aholibah
   Whose name was blown among strange seas,
130   Grown old with soft adulteries.

Also her bed was made of green,
   Her windows beautiful for glass
That she had made her bed between:
   Yea, for pure lust her body was
   Made like white summer-coloured grass.

Her raiment was a strong man's spoil;
   Upon a table by a bed
She set mine incense and mine oil
   To be the beauty of her head
140   In chambers walled about with red.

Also between the walls she had
    Fair faces of strong men portrayed;
All girded round the loins, and clad
    With several cloths of woven braid
    And garments marvellously made.

Therefore the wrath of God shall be
    Set as a watch upon her way;
And whoso findeth by the sea
    Blown dust of bones will hardly say
150   If this were that Aholibah.

Love and Sleep

Lying asleep between the strokes of night
    I saw my love lean over my sad bed,
    Pale as the duskiest lily's leaf or head,
Smooth-skinned and dark, with bare throat made to bite,
Too wan for blushing and too warm for white,
    But perfect-coloured without white or red.
    And her lips opened amorously, and said –
I wist not what, saving one word – Delight.
And all her face was honey to my mouth,
10   And all her body pasture to mine eyes;
        The long lithe arms and hotter hands than fire,
The quivering flanks, hair smelling of the south,
    The bright light feet, the splendid supple thighs
        And glittering eyelids of my soul's desire.

Madonna Mia

Under green apple-boughs
That never a storm will rouse,
My lady hath her house
    Between two bowers;

In either of the twain
Red roses full of rain;
She hath for bondwomen
    All kind of flowers.

She hath no handmaid fair
To draw her curled gold hair
Through rings of gold that bear
    Her whole hair's weight;
She hath no maids to stand
Gold-clothed on either hand;
In all the great green land
    None is so great.

She hath no more to wear
But one white hood of vair
Drawn over eyes and hair,
    Wrought with strange gold,
Made for some great queen's head,
Some fair great queen since dead;
And one strait gown of red
    Against the cold.

Beneath her eyelids deep
Love lying seems asleep,
Love, swift to wake, to weep,
    To laugh, to gaze;
Her breasts are like white birds,
And all her gracious words
As water-grass to herds
    In the June-days.

To her all dews that fall
And rains are musical;
Her flowers are fed from all,
    Her joy from these;

In the deep-feathered firs
Their gift of joy is hers,
In the least breath that stirs
40   Across the trees.

She grows with greenest leaves,
Ripens with reddest sheaves,
Forgets, remembers, grieves,
      And is not sad;
The quiet lands and skies
Leave light upon her eyes;
None knows her, weak or wise,
      Or tired or glad.

None knows, none understands,
50   What flowers are like her hands;
Though you should search all lands
      Wherein time grows,
What snows are like her feet,
Though his eyes burn with heat
Through gazing on my sweet,
      Yet no man knows.

Only this thing is said;
That white and gold and red,
God's three chief words, man's bread
60   And oil and wine,
Were given her for dowers,
And kingdom of all hours,
And grace of goodly flowers
      And various vine.

This is my lady's praise:
God after many days
Wrought her in unknown ways,
      In sunset lands;

This was my lady's birth;
70　God gave her might and mirth
And laid his whole sweet earth
　　Between her hands.

Under deep apple-boughs
My lady hath her house;
She wears upon her brows
　　The flower thereof;
All saying but what God saith
To her is as vain breath;
She is more strong than death,
80　　Being strong as love.

The King's Daughter

We were ten maidens in the green corn,
　　Small red leaves in the mill-water:
Fairer maidens never were born,
　　Apples of gold for the king's daughter.

We were ten maidens by a well-head,
　　Small white birds in the mill-water:
Sweeter maidens never were wed,
　　Rings of red for the king's daughter.

The first to spin, the second to sing,
10　　Seeds of wheat in the mill-water;
The third may was a goodly thing,
　　White bread and brown for the king's daughter.

The fourth to sew and the fifth to play,
　　Fair green weed in the mill-water;
The sixth may was a goodly may,
　　White wine and red for the king's daughter.

The seventh to woo, the eighth to wed,
    Fair thin reeds in the mill-water;
The ninth had gold work on her head,
20   Honey in the comb for the king's daughter.

The ninth had gold work round her hair,
    Fallen flowers in the mill-water;
The tenth may was goodly and fair,
    Golden gloves for the king's daughter.

We were ten maidens in a field green,
    Fallen fruit in the mill-water;
Fairer maidens never have been,
    Golden sleeves for the king's daughter.

By there comes the king's young son,
30   A little wind in the mill-water;
'Out of ten maidens ye'll grant me one,'
    A crown of red for the king's daughter.

'Out of ten mays ye'll give me the best,'
    A little rain in the mill-water;
A bed of yellow straw for all the rest,
    A bed of gold for the king's daughter.

He's ta'en out the goodliest,
    Rain that rains in the mill-water;
A comb of yellow shell for all the rest,
40   A comb of gold for the king's daughter.

He's made her bed to the goodliest,
    Wind and hail in the mill-water;
A grass girdle for all the rest,
    A girdle of arms for the king's daughter.

He's set his heart to the goodliest,
    Snow that snows in the mill-water;
Nine little kisses for all the rest,
    An hundredfold for the king's daughter.

He's ta'en his leave at the goodliest,
50   Broken boats in the mill-water;
Golden gifts for all the rest,
    Sorrow of heart for the king's daughter.

'Ye'll make a grave for my fair body,'
    Running rain in the mill-water;
'And ye'll streek my brother at the side of me,'
    The pains of hell for the king's daughter.

After Death

The four boards of the coffin lid
Heard all the dead man did.

The first curse was in his mouth,
Made of grave's mould and deadly drouth.

The next curse was in his head,
Made of God's work discomfited.

The next curse was in his hand,
Made out of two grave-bands.

The next curse was in his feet,
10   Made out of a grave-sheet.

'I had fair coins red and white,
And my name was as great light;

I had fair clothes green and red,
And strong gold bound round my head.

But no meat comes in my mouth,
Now I fare as the worm doth;

And no gold binds in my hair,
Now I fare as the blind fare.

My live thews were of great strength,
20   Now am I waxen a span's length;

My live sides were full of lust,
Now are they dried with dust.'

The first board spake and said:
'Is it best eating flesh or bread?'

The second answered it:
'Is wine or honey the more sweet?'

The third board spake and said:
'Is red gold worth a girl's gold head?'

The fourth made answer thus:
30   'All these things are as one with us.'

The dead man asked of them:
'Is the green land stained brown with flame?

Have they hewn my son for beasts to eat,
And my wife's body for beasts' meat?

Have they boiled my maid in a brass pan,
And built a gallows to hang my man?'

The boards said to him:
'This is a lewd thing that ye deem.

Your wife has gotten a golden bed,
40   All the sheets are sewn with red.

Your son has gotten a coat of silk,
The sleeves are soft as curded milk.

Your maid has gotten a kirtle new,
All the skirt has braids of blue.

Your man has gotten both ring and glove,
Wrought well for eyes to love.'

The dead man answered thus:
'What good gift shall God give us?'

The boards answered him anon:
50   'Flesh to feed hell's worm upon.'

May Janet
(BRETON)

'Stand up, stand up, thou May Janet,
    And go to the wars with me.'
He's drawn her by both hands
    With her face against the sea.

'He that strews red shall gather white,
    He that sows white reap red,
Before your face and my daughter's
    Meet in a marriage-bed.

'Gold coin shall grow in the yellow field,
10   Green coin in the green sea-water,
And red fruit grow of the rose's red,
    Ere your fruit grow in her.'

'But I shall have her by land,' he said,
    'Or I shall have her by sea,
Or I shall have her by strong treason
    And no grace go with me.'

Her father's drawn her by both hands,
    He's rent her gown from her,
He's ta'en the smock round her body,
20   Cast in the sea-water.

The captain's drawn her by both sides
    Out of the fair green sea;
'Stand up, stand up, thou May Janet,
    And come to the war with me.'

The first town they came to
    There was a blue bride-chamber;
He clothed her on with silk
    And belted her with amber.

The second town they came to
30   The bridesmen feasted knee to knee;
He clothed her on with silver,
    A stately thing to see.

The third town they came to
    The bridesmaids all had gowns of gold;
He clothed her on with purple,
    A rich thing to behold.

The last town they came to
    He clothed her white and red,
With a green flag either side of her
40   And a gold flag overhead.

The Bloody Son
(FINNISH)

'O where have ye been the morn sae late,
    My merry son, come tell me hither?
O where have ye been the morn sae late?

And I wot I hae not anither.'
'By the water-gate, by the water-gate,
    O dear mither.'

'And whatten kin' o' wark had ye there to make,
    My merry son, come tell me hither?
And whatten kin' o' wark had ye there to make?
10   And I wot I hae not anither.'
'I watered my steeds with water frae the lake,
    O dear mither.'

'Why is your coat sae fouled the day,
    My merry son, come tell me hither?
Why is your coat sae fouled the day?
    And I wot I hae not anither.'
'The steeds were stamping sair by the weary banks of clay,
    O dear mither.'

'And where gat ye thae sleeves of red,
20   My merry son, come tell me hither?
And where gat ye thae sleeves of red?
    And I wot I hae not anither.'
'I have slain my ae brither by the weary water-head,
    O dear mither.'

'And where will ye gang to mak your mend,
    My merry son, come tell me hither?
And where will ye gang to mak your mend?
    And I wot I hae not anither.'
'The warldis way, to the warldis end,
30   O dear mither.'

'And what will ye leave your father dear,
    My merry son, come tell me hither?
And what will ye leave your father dear?
    And I wot I hae not anither.'
'The wood to fell and the logs to bear,
For he'll never see my body mair,
    O dear mither.'

'And what will ye leave your mither dear,
   My merry son, come tell me hither?
40   And what will ye leave your mither dear?
    And I wot I hae not anither.'
'The wool to card and the wool to wear,
For ye'll never see my body mair,
   O dear mither.'

'And what will ye leave for your wife to take,
   My merry son, come tell me hither?
And what will ye leave for your wife to take?
    And I wot I hae not anither.'
'A goodly gown and a fair new make,
50 For she'll do nae mair for my body's sake,
   O dear mither.'

'And what will ye leave your young son fair,
   My merry son, come tell me hither?
And what will ye leave your young son fair?
    And I wot ye hae not anither.'
'A twiggen school-rod for his body to bear,
Though it garred him greet he'll get nae mair,
   O dear mither.'

'And what will ye leave your little daughter sweet,
60   My merry son, come tell me hither?
And what will ye leave your little daughter sweet?
    And I wot ye hae not anither.'
'Wild mulberries for her mouth to eat,
She'll get nae mair though it garred her greet,
   O dear mither.'

'And when will ye come back frae roamin',
   My merry son, come tell me hither?
And when will ye come back frae roamin'?
    And I wot I hae not anither.'
70 'When the sunrise out of the north is comen,
   O dear mither.'

'When shall the sunrise on the north side be,
   My merry son, come tell me hither?
When shall the sunrise on the north side be?
   And I wot I hae not anither.'
'When chuckie-stanes shall swim in the sea,
   O dear mither.'

'When shall stanes in the sea swim,
   My merry son, come tell me hither?
80 When shall stanes in the sea swim?
   And I wot I hae not anither.'
'When birdies' feathers are as lead therein,
   O dear mither.'

'When shall feathers be as lead,
   My merry son, come tell me hither?
When shall feathers be as lead?
   And I wot I hae not anither.'
'When God shall judge between the quick and dead,
   O dear mither.'

The Sea-Swallows

This fell when Christmas lights were done,
   (Red rose leaves will never make wine)
But before the Easter lights begun;
   The ways are sair fra' the Till to the Tyne.

Two lovers sat where the rowan blows
   And all the grass is heavy and fine,
By the gathering-place of the sea-swallows
   When the wind brings them over Tyne.

Blossom of broom will never make bread,
10   Red rose leaves will never make wine;
Between her brows she is grown red,
   That was full white in the fields by Tyne.

'O what is this thing ye have on,
   Show me now, sweet daughter of mine?'
'O father, this is my little son
   That I found hid in the sides of Tyne.

'O what will ye give my son to eat,
   Red rose leaves will never make wine?'
'Fen-water and adder's meat.'
20   The ways are sair fra' the Till to the Tyne.

'Or what will ye get my son to wear?'
   (Red rose leaves will never make wine.)
'A weed and a web of nettle's hair.'
   The ways are sair fra' the Till to the Tyne.

'Or what will ye take to line his bed?'
   (Red rose leaves will never make wine.)
'Two black stones at the kirkwall's head.'
   The ways are sair fra' the Till to the Tyne.

'Or what will ye give my son for land?'
30   (Red rose leaves will never make wine.)
'Three girl's paces of red sand.'
   The ways are sair fra' the Till to the Tyne.

'Or what will ye give me for my son?'
   (Red rose leaves will never make wine.)
'Six times to kiss his young mouth on.'
   The ways are sair fra' the Till to the Tyne.

'But what have ye done with the bearing-bread,
   And what have ye made of the washing-wine?
Or where have ye made your bearing-bed,
40   To bear a son in the sides of Tyne?'

'The bearing-bread is soft and new,
   There is no soil in the straining wine;
The bed was made between green and blue,
   It stands full soft by the sides of Tyne.

'The fair grass was my bearing-bread,
    The well-water my washing-wine;
The low leaves were my bearing-bed,
    And that was best in the sides of Tyne.'

'O daughter, if ye have done this thing,
50   I wot the greater grief is mine;
This was a bitter child-bearing,
    When ye were got by the sides of Tyne.

'About the time of sea-swallows
    That fly full thick by six and nine,
Ye'll have my body out of the house,
    To bury me by the sides of Tyne.

'Set nine stones by the wall for twain,'
    (Red rose leaves will never make wine)
'For the bed I take will measure ten.'
60   The ways are sair fra' the Till to the Tyne.

'Tread twelve girl's paces out for three,'
    (Red rose leaves will never make wine)
'For the pit I made has taken me.'
    The ways are sair fra' the Till to the Tyne.

The Year of Love

There were four loves that one by one,
Following the seasons and the sun,
Passed over without tears, and fell
Away without farewell.

The first was made of gold and tears,
The next of aspen-leaves and fears,
The third of rose-boughs and rose-roots,
The last love of strange fruits.

These were the four loves faded. Hold
10   Some minutes fast the time of gold
When our lips each way clung and clove
To a face full of love.

The tears inside our eyelids met,
Wrung forth with kissing, and wept wet
The faces cleaving each to each
Where the blood served for speech.

The second, with low patient brows
Bound under aspen-coloured boughs
And eyes made strong and grave with sleep
20   And yet too weak to weep –

The third, with eager mouth at ease
Fed from late autumn honey, lees
Of scarce gold left in latter cells
With scattered flower-smells –

Hair sprinkled over with spoilt sweet
Of ruined roses, wrists and feet
Slight-swathed, as grassy-girdled sheaves
Hold in stray poppy-leaves –

The fourth, with lips whereon has bled
30   Some great pale fruit's slow colour, shed
From the rank bitten husk whence drips
Faint blood between her lips –

Made of the heat of whole great Junes
Burning the blue dark round their moons
(Each like a mown red marigold)
So hard the flame keeps hold –

These are burnt thoroughly away.
Only the first holds out a day
Beyond these latter loves that were
40   Made of mere heat and air.

And now the time is winterly
The first love fades too: none will see,
When April warms the world anew,
The place wherein love grew.

Dedication
1865

The sea gives her shells to the shingle,
    The earth gives her streams to the sea;
They are many, but my gift is single,
    My verses, the firstfruits of me.
Let the wind take the green and the grey leaf,
    Cast forth without fruit upon air;
Take rose-leaf and vine-leaf and bay-leaf
    Blown loose from the hair.

The night shakes them round me in legions,
    Dawn drives them before her like dreams;
Time sheds them like snows on strange regions,
    Swept shoreward on infinite streams;
Leaves pallid and sombre and ruddy,
    Dead fruits of the fugitive years;
Some stained as with wine and made bloody,
    And some as with tears.

Some scattered in seven years' traces,
    As they fell from the boy that was then;
Long left among the idle green places,
    Or gathered but now among men;
On seas full of wonder and peril,
    Blown white round the capes of the north;
Or in islands where myrtles are sterile
    And loves bring not forth.

O daughters of dreams and of stories
    That life is not wearied of yet,
Faustine, Fragoletta, Dolores,
    Félise and Yolande and Juliette,
Shall I find you not still, shall I miss you,
30   When sleep, that is true or that seems,
Comes back to me hopeless to kiss you,
    O daughters of dreams?

They are past as a slumber that passes,
    As the dew of a dawn of old time;
More frail than the shadows on glasses,
    More fleet than a wave or a rhyme.
As the waves after ebb drawing seaward,
    When their hollows are full of the night,
So the birds that flew singing to me-ward
40   Recede out of sight.

The songs of dead seasons, that wander
    On wings of articulate words;
Lost leaves that the shore-wind may squander,
    Light flocks of untameable birds;
Some sang to me dreaming in class-time
    And truant in hand as in tongue;
For the youngest were born of boy's pastime,
    The eldest are young.

Is there shelter while life in them lingers,
50   Is there hearing for songs that recede,
Tunes touched from a harp with man's fingers
    Or blown with boy's mouth in a reed?
Is there place in the land of your labour,
    Is there room in your world of delight,
Where change has not sorrow for neighbour
    And day has not night?

In their wings though the sea-wind yet quivers,
    Will you spare not a space for them there
Made green with the running of rivers
60   And gracious with temperate air;
In the fields and the turreted cities,
    That cover from sunshine and rain
Fair passions and bountiful pities
    And loves without stain?

In a land of clear colours and stories,
    In a region of shadowless hours,
Where earth has a garment of glories
    And a murmur of musical flowers;
In woods where the spring half uncovers
70   The flush of her amorous face,
By the waters that listen for lovers,
    For these is there place?

For the song-birds of sorrow, that muffle
    Their music as clouds do their fire:
For the storm-birds of passion, that ruffle
    Wild wings in a wind of desire;
In the stream of the storm as it settles
    Blown seaward, borne far from the sun,
Shaken loose on the darkness like petals
80   Dropt one after one?

Though the world of your hands be more gracious
    And lovelier in lordship of things
Clothed round by sweet art with the spacious
    Warm heaven of her imminent wings,
Let them enter, unfledged and nigh fainting,
    For the love of old loves and lost times;
And receive in your palace of painting
    This revel of rhymes.

Though the seasons of man full of losses
90   Make empty the years full of youth,
If but one thing be constant in crosses,
      Change lays not her hand upon truth;
Hopes die, and their tombs are for token
      That the grief as the joy of them ends
Ere time that breaks all men has broken
      The faith between friends.

Though the many lights dwindle to one light,
      There is help if the heaven has one;
Though the skies be discrowned of the sunlight
100   And the earth dispossessed of the sun,
They have moonlight and sleep for repayment,
      When, refreshed as a bride and set free,
With stars and sea-winds in her raiment,
      Night sinks on the sea.

ATALANTA IN CALYDON

A TRAGEDY

Τοὺς ζῶντας εὖ δρᾶν· κατθανὼν δὲ πᾶς ἀνὴρ
Γῆ καὶ σκιά· τὸ μηδὲν εἰς οὐδὲν ῥέπει

EUR. *Fr. Mel.* 20 (537)

TO THE MEMORY

OF

WALTER SAVAGE LANDOR

I NOW DEDICATE, WITH EQUAL AFFECTION, REVERENCE, AND
REGRET, A FORM INSCRIBED TO HIM WHILE YET ALIVE IN WORDS
WHICH ARE NOW RETAINED BECAUSE THEY WERE LAID BEFORE
HIM; AND TO WHICH, RATHER THAN CANCEL THEM, I HAVE ADDED
SUCH OTHERS AS WERE EVOKED BY THE NEWS OF HIS DEATH:
THAT THOUGH LOSING THE PLEASURE I MAY NOT LOSE THE
HONOUR OF INSCRIBING IN FRONT OF MY WORK THE HIGHEST OF
CONTEMPORARY NAMES.

ᾤχεο δὴ Βορέηθεν ἀπότροπος· ἀλλά σε Νύμφαι
    ἤγαγον ἀσπασίαν ἡδύπνοοι καθ' ἅλα,
πληροῦσαι μέλιτος θεόθεν στόμα, μή τι Ποσειδῶν
    βλάψῃ, ἐν ὠσὶν ἔχων σὴν μελίγηρυν ὄπα.
τοῖος ἀοιδὸς ἔφυς· ἡμεῖς δ' ἔτι κλαίομεν, οἵ σου
    δευόμεθ' οἰχομένου, καί σε ποθοῦμεν ἀεί.
εἶπε δὲ Πιερίδων τις ἀναστρεφθεῖσα πρὸς ἄλλην·
    ἦλθεν, ἰδού, πάντων φίλτατος ἦλθε βροτῶν,
στέμματα δρεψάμενος νεοθηλέα χερσὶ γεραιαῖς,
    καὶ πολιὸν δάφναις ἀμφεκάλυψε κάρα,
ἡδύ τι Σικελικαῖς ἐπὶ πηκτίσιν, ἡδύ τι χόρδαις,
    ἀσόμενος· πολλὴν γὰρ μετέβαλλε λύραν,
πολλάκι δ' ἐν βήσσαισι καθήμενον εὗρεν Ἀπόλλων,
    ἄνθεσι δ' ἔστεψεν, τερπνὰ δ' ἔδωκε λέγειν,
Πᾶνα τ' ἀείμνηστόν τε Πίτυν Κόρυθόν τε δύσεδρον,
    ἥν τ' ἐφίλησε θεὰν θνητὸς Ἀμαδρύαδα·
πόντου δ' ἐν μεγάροισιν ἐκοίμισε Κυμοδάμειαν,
    τήν τ' Ἀγαμεμνονίαν παῖδ' ἀπέδωκε πατρί,
πρὸς δ' ἱεροὺς Δελφοὺς θεόπληκτον ἔπεμψεν Ὀρέστην,
    τειρόμενον στυγεραῖς ἔνθα καὶ ἔνθα θεαῖς.

ᾤχεο δὴ καὶ ἄνευθε φίλων καὶ ἄνευθεν ἀοιδῆς,
  δρεψόμενος μαλακῆς ἄνθεα Περσεφόνης.
ᾤχεο· κοὐκ ἔτ' ἔσει, κοὐκ αὖ ποτέ σοι παρεδοῦμαι
  ἁζόμενος, χειρῶν χερσὶ θιγὼν ὁσίαις·
νῦν δ' αὖ μνησάμενον γλυκύπικρος ὑπήλυθεν αἰδώς,
  οἷα τυχὼν οἵου πρὸς σέθεν οἷος ἔχω·
οὔποτε σοῖς, γέρον, ὄμμα φίλοις φίλον ὄμμασι τέρψω,
  σῆς, γέρον, ἁψάμενος, φίλτατε, δεξιτερᾶς.
ἢ ψαφαρὰ κόνις, ἢ ψαφαρὸς βίος ἐστι· τί τούτων
  μεῖον ἐφημερίων; οὐ κόνις ἀλλὰ βίος.
ἀλλά μοι ἡδύτερός γε πέλεις πολὺ τῶν ἔτ' ἐόντων,
  ἔπλεο γάρ· σοὶ μὴν ταῦτα θανόντι φέρω,
παῦρα μὲν, ἀλλ' ἀπὸ κῆρος ἐτήτυμα· μηδ' ἀποτρεφθῇς,
  πρὸς δὲ βαλὼν ἔτι νῦν ἥσυχον ὄμμα δέχου.
οὐ γὰρ ἔχω, μέγα δή τι θέλων, σέθεν ἄξια δοῦναι,
  θαπτομένου περ ἀπών· οὐ γὰρ ἔνεστιν ἐμοί·
οὐδὲ μελικρήτου παρέχειν γάνος· εἰ γὰρ ἐνείη
  καί σε χεροῖν ψαῦσαι καί σέ ποτ' αὖθις ἰδεῖν,
δάκρυσί τε σπονδαῖς τε κάρα φίλον ἀμφιπολεύειν
  ὀφθαλμούς θ' ἱεροὺς σοὺς ἱερόν τε δέμας.
εἴθ' ὄφελον· μάλα γὰρ τάδ' ἂν ἀμπαύσειε μερίμνης·
  νῦν δὲ πρόσωθεν ἄνευ σήματος οἶκτον ἄγω·
οὐδ' ἐπιτυμβίδιον θρηνῶ μέλος, ἀλλ' ἀπαμυνθεὶς,
  ἀλλ' ἀπάνευθεν ἔχων ἀμφιδάκρυτα πάθη.
ἀλλὰ σὺ χαῖρε θανὼν, καὶ ἔχων γέρας ἴσθι πρὸς ἀνδρῶν
  πρός τε θεῶν, ἐνέροις εἴ τις ἔπεστι θεός.
χαῖρε, γέρον, φίλε χαῖρε πάτερ, πολὺ φέρτατ' ἀοιδῶν
  ὧν ἴδομεν, πολὺ δὴ φέρτατ' ἀεισομένων·
χαῖρε, καὶ ὄλβον ἔχοις, οἷόν γε θανόντες ἔχουσιν,
  ἡσυχίαν ἔχθρας καὶ φιλότητος ἄτερ.

σήματος οἰχομένου σοι μνήματ' ἐς ὕστερον ἔσται,
  σοί τε φίλη μνήμη μνήματος οἰχομένου·
ὃν Χάριτες κλαίουσι θεαί, κλαίει δ' Ἀφροδίτη
  καλλιχόροις Μουσῶν τερψαμένη στεφάνοις·
οὐ γὰρ ἅπαξ ἱερούς ποτε γῆρας ἔτριψεν ἀοιδούς·
  τήνδε τὸ σὸν φαίνει μνῆμα τόδ' ἀγλαΐαν.
ἢ φίλος ἦς μακάρεσσι βροτός, σοὶ δ' εἴ τινι Νύμφαι
  δῶρα ποθεινὰ νέμειν, ὕστατα δῶρ', ἔδοσαν.
τὰς νῦν χάλκεος ὕπνος ἔβη καὶ ἀνήνεμος αἰὼν,
  καὶ συνθαπτομέναι μοῖραν ἔχουσι μίαν.
εὕδεις καὶ σύ, καλὸν καὶ ἀγάκλυτον ἐν χθονὶ κοίλῃ
  ὕπνον ἐφικόμενος, σῆς ἀπόνοσφι πάτρας,
τῆλε παρὰ ξανθοῦ Τυρσηνικὸν οἶδμα καθεύδεις
  νάματος, ἡ δ' ἔτι σὴ μαῖά σε γαῖα ποθεῖ,
ἀλλ' ἀπέχεις, καὶ πρόσθε φιλόπτολις ὤν περ ἀπεῖπας·
  εὗδε· μάκαρ δ' ἡμῖν οὐδ' ἀμέγατος ἔσει.
βαιὸς ἐπιχθονίων γε χρόνος καὶ μοῖρα κρατήσει,
  τοὺς δέ ποτ' εὐφροσύνη τοὺς δέ ποτ' ἄλγος ἔχει·
πολλάκι δ' ἢ βλάπτει φάος ἢ σκότος ἀμφικαλύπτει
  μυρομένους, δάκνει δ' ὕπνος ἐγρηγορότας·
οὐδ' ἔθ' ὅτ' ἐν τύμβοισι κατέδραθεν ὄμμα θανόντων
  ἢ σκότος ἤ τι φάος δήξεται ἠελίου·
οὐδ' ὄναρ ἐννύχιον καὶ ἐνύπνιον οὐδ' ὕπαρ ἔσται
  ἢ ποτε τερπομένοις ἤ ποτ' ὀδυρομένοις·
ἀλλ' ἕνα πάντες ἀεὶ θᾶκον συνέχουσι καὶ ἕδραν
  ἀντὶ βροτῆς ἄβροτον, κάλλιμον ἄντι κακῆς.

THE ARGUMENT

Althæa, daughter of Thestius and Eurythemis, queen of Calydon, being with child of Meleager her first-born son, dreamed that she brought forth a brand of burning; and upon his birth came the three Fates and prophesied of him three things, namely these; that he should have great strength of his hands, and good fortune in this life, and that he should live no longer when the brand then in the fire were consumed: wherefore his mother plucked it forth and kept it by her. And the child being a man grown sailed with Jason after the fleece of gold, and won himself great praise of all men living; and when the tribes of the north and west made war upon Ætolia, he fought against their army and scattered it. But Artemis, having at the first stirred up these tribes to war against Œneus king of Calydon, because he had offered sacrifice to all the gods saving her alone, but her he had forgotten to honour, was yet more wroth because of the destruction of this army, and sent upon the land of Calydon a wild boar which slew many and wasted all their increase, but him could none slay, and many went against him and perished. Then were all the chief men of Greece gathered together, and among them Atalanta daughter of Iasius the Arcadian, a virgin; for whose sake Artemis let slay the boar, seeing she favoured the maiden greatly; and Meleager having despatched it gave the spoil thereof to Atalanta, as one beyond measure enamoured of her; but the brethren of Althæa his mother, Toxeus and Plexippus, with such others as misliked that she only should bear off the praise whereas many had borne the labour, laid wait for her to take away her spoil; but Meleager fought against them and slew them: whom when Althæa their sister beheld and knew to be slain of her son, she waxed for wrath and sorrow like as one mad, and taking the brand whereby the measure of her son's life was meted to him, she cast it upon a fire; and with the wasting thereof his life likewise wasted away, that being brought back to his father's house he died in a brief space; and his mother also endured not long after for very sorrow; and this was his end, and the end of that hunting.

THE PERSONS

CHIEF HUNTSMAN
CHORUS
ALTHÆA
MELEAGER
ŒNEUS
ATALANTA
TOXEUS
PLEXIPPUS
HERALD
MESSENGER
SECOND MESSENGER

ἴστω δ’ ὅστις οὐχ ὑπόπτερος
φροντίσιν δαεὶς,
τὰν ἁ παιδολύμας τάλαινα Θεστιὰς μήσατο
πυρδαῆ τινα πρόνοιαν,
καταίθουσα παιδὸς δαφοινὸν
δαλὸν ἥλικ’, ἐπεὶ μολὼν
ματρόθεν κελάδησε
σύμμετρόν τε διαὶ βίου
μοιρόκραντον ἐς ἆμαρ.

ÆSCH. *Cho.* 602–612.

ATALANTA IN CALYDON

CHIEF HUNTSMAN

Maiden, and mistress of the months and stars
Now folded in the flowerless fields of heaven,
Goddess whom all gods love with threefold heart,
Being treble in thy divided deity,
A light for dead men and dark hours, a foot
Swift on the hills as morning, and a hand
To all things fierce and fleet that roar and range
Mortal, with gentler shafts than snow or sleep;
Hear now and help and lift no violent hand,
But favourable and fair as thine eye's beam
Hidden and shown in heaven; for I all night
Amid the king's hounds and the hunting men
Have wrought and worshipped toward thee; nor shall man
See goodlier hounds or deadlier edge of spears;
But for the end, that lies unreached at yet
Between the hands and on the knees of gods.
O fair-faced sun, killing the stars and dews
And dreams and desolation of the night!
Rise up, shine, stretch thine hand out, with thy bow
Touch the most dimmest height of trembling heaven,
And burn and break the dark about thy ways,
Shot through and through with arrows; let thine hair
Lighten as flame above that flameless shell
Which was the moon, and thine eyes fill the world
And thy lips kindle with swift beams; let earth
Laugh, and the long sea fiery from thy feet
Through all the roar and ripple of streaming springs
And foam in reddening flakes and flying flowers
Shaken from hands and blown from lips of nymphs
Whose hair or breast divides the wandering wave
With salt close tresses cleaving lock to lock,
All gold, or shuddering and unfurrowed snow;
And all the winds about thee with their wings,
And fountain-heads of all the watered world;
Each horn of Acheloüs, and the green

Euenus, wedded with the straitening sea.
For in fair time thou comest; come also thou,
Twin-born with him, and virgin, Artemis,
And give our spears their spoil, the wild boar's hide,
40   Sent in thine anger against us for sin done
And bloodless altars without wine or fire.
Him now consume thou; for thy sacrifice
With sanguine-shining steam divides the dawn,
And one, the maiden rose of all thy maids,
Arcadian Atalanta, snowy-souled,
Fair as the snow and footed as the wind,
From Ladon and well-wooded Mænalus
Over the firm hills and the fleeting sea
Hast thou drawn hither, and many an armèd king,
50   Heroes, the crown of men, like gods in fight.
Moreover out of all the Ætolian land,
From the full-flowered Lelantian pasturage
To what of fruitful field the son of Zeus
Won from the roaring river and labouring sea
When the wild god shrank in his horn and fled
And foamed and lessened through his wrathful fords
Leaving clear lands that steamed with sudden sun,
These virgins with the lightening of the day
Bring thee fresh wreaths and their own sweeter hair,
60   Luxurious locks and flower-like mixed with flowers,
Clean offering, and chaste hymns; but me the time
Divides from these things; whom do thou not less
Help and give honour, and to mine hounds good speed,
And edge to spears, and luck to each man's hand.

CHORUS

When the hounds of spring are on winter's traces,
    The mother of months in meadow or plain
Fills the shadows and windy places
    With lisp of leaves and ripple of rain;
And the brown bright nightingale amorous
70   Is half assuaged for Itylus,
For the Thracian ships and the foreign faces,
    The tongueless vigil, and all the pain.

Come with bows bent and with emptying of quivers,
  Maiden most perfect, lady of light,
With a noise of winds and many rivers,
  With a clamour of waters, and with might;
Bind on thy sandals, O thou most fleet,
Over the splendour and speed of thy feet;
For the faint east quickens, the wan west shivers,
80   Round the feet of the day and the feet of the night.

Where shall we find her, how shall we sing to her,
  Fold our hands round her knees, and cling?
O that man's heart were as fire and could spring to her,
  Fire, or the strength of the streams that spring!
For the stars and the winds are unto her
As raiment, as songs of the harp-player;
For the risen stars and the fallen cling to her,
  And the southwest-wind and the west-wind sing.

For winter's rains and ruins are over,
90   And all the season of snows and sins;
The days dividing lover and lover,
  The light that loses, the night that wins;
And time remembered is grief forgotten,
And frosts are slain and flowers begotten,
And in green underwood and cover
  Blossom by blossom the spring begins.

The full streams feed on flower of rushes,
  Ripe grasses trammel a travelling foot,
The faint fresh flame of the young year flushes
100   From leaf to flower and flower to fruit;
And fruit and leaf as are gold and fire,
And the oat is heard above the lyre,
And the hoofèd heel of a satyr crushes
  The chestnut-husk at the chestnut-root.

And Pan by noon and Bacchus by night,
  Fleeter of foot than the fleet-foot kid,
Follows with dancing and fills with delight

      The Mænad and the Bassarid;
      And soft as lips that laugh and hide
110   The laughing leaves of the trees divide,
      And screen from seeing and leave in sight
         The god pursuing, the maiden hid.

      The ivy falls with the Bacchanal's hair
         Over her eyebrows hiding her eyes;
      The wild vine slipping down leaves bare
         Her bright breast shortening into sighs;
      The wild vine slips with the weight of its leaves,
      But the berried ivy catches and cleaves
      To the limbs that glitter, the feet that scare
120   The wolf that follows, the fawn that flies.

ALTHÆA
What do ye singing? what is this ye sing?

CHORUS
Flowers bring we, and pure lips that please the gods,
And raiment meet for service: lest the day
Turn sharp with all its honey in our lips.

ALTHÆA
Night, a black hound, follows the white fawn day,
Swifter than dreams the white flown feet of sleep;
Will ye pray back the night with any prayers?
And though the spring put back a little while
Winter, and snows that plague all men for sin,
130   And the iron time of cursing, yet I know
Spring shall be ruined with the rain, and storm
Eat up like fire the ashen autumn days.
I marvel what men do with prayers awake
Who dream and die with dreaming; any god,
Yea the least god of all things called divine,
Is more than sleep and waking; yet we say,
Perchance by praying a man shall match his god.
For if sleep have no mercy, and man's dreams
Bite to the blood and burn into the bone,

140   What shall this man do waking? By the gods,
      He shall not pray to dream sweet things to-night,
      Having dreamt once more bitter things than death.

      CHORUS
      Queen, but what is it that hath burnt thine heart?
      For thy speech flickers like a blown-out flame.

      ALTHÆA
      Look, ye say well, and know not what ye say;
      For all my sleep is turned into a fire,
      And all my dreams to stuff that kindles it.

      CHORUS
      Yet one doth well being patient of the gods.

      ALTHÆA
      Yea, lest they smite us with some four-foot plague.

      CHORUS
150   But when time spreads find out some herb for it.

      ALTHÆA
      And with their healing herbs infect our blood.

      CHORUS
      What ails thee to be jealous of their ways?

      ALTHÆA
      What if they give us poisonous drinks for wine?

      CHORUS
      They have their will; much talking mends it not.

      ALTHÆA
      And gall for milk, and cursing for a prayer?

      CHORUS
      Have they not given life, and the end of life?

ALTHÆA

Lo, where they heal, they help not; thus they do,
They mock us with a little piteousness,
And we say prayers, and weep; but at the last,
160 Sparing awhile, they smite and spare no whit.

CHORUS

Small praise man gets dispraising the high gods:
What have they done that thou dishonourest them?

ALTHÆA

First Artemis for all this harried land
I praise not, and for wasting of the boar
That mars with tooth and tusk and fiery feet
Green pasturage and the grace of standing corn
And meadow and marsh with springs and unblown leaves,
Flocks and swift herds and all that bite sweet grass,
I praise her not; what things are these to praise?

CHORUS

170 But when the king did sacrifice, and gave
Each god fair dues of wheat and blood and wine,
Her not with bloodshed nor burnt-offering
Revered he, nor with salt or cloven cake;
Wherefore being wroth she plagued the land; but now
Takes off from us fate and her heavy things.
Which deed of these twain were not good to praise?
For a just deed looks always either way
With blameless eyes, and mercy is no fault.

ALTHÆA

Yea, but a curse she hath sent above all these
180 To hurt us where she healed us; and hath lit
Fire where the old fire went out, and where the wind
Slackened, hath blown on us with deadlier air.

CHORUS

What storm is this that tightens all our sail?

ALTHÆA
Love, a thwart sea-wind full of rain and foam.

CHORUS
Whence blown, and born under what stormier star?

ALTHÆA
Southward across Euenus from the sea.

CHORUS
Thy speech turns toward Arcadia like blown wind.

ALTHÆA
Sharp as the north sets when the snows are out.

CHORUS
Nay, for this maiden hath no touch of love.

ALTHÆA
190   I would she had sought in some cold gulf of sea
Love, or in dens where strange beasts lurk, or fire,
Or snows on the extreme hills, or iron land
Where no spring is; I would she had sought therein
And found, or ever love had found her here.

CHORUS
She is holier than all holy days or things,
The sprinkled water or fume of perfect fire;
Chaste, dedicated to pure prayers, and filled
With higher thoughts than heaven; a maiden clean,
Pure iron, fashioned for a sword; and man
200   She loves not; what should one such do with love?

ALTHÆA
Look you, I speak not as one light of wit,
But as a queen speaks, being heart-vexed; for oft
I hear my brothers wrangling in mid hall,
And am not moved; and my son chiding them,
And these things nowise move me, but I know

Foolish and wise men must be to the end,
And feed myself with patience; but this most,
This moves me, that for wise men as for fools
Love is one thing, an evil thing, and turns
210   Choice words and wisdom into fire and air.
And in the end shall no joy come, but grief,
Sharp words and soul's division and fresh tears
Flower-wise upon the old root of tears brought forth,
Fruit-wise upon the old flower of tears sprung up,
Pitiful sighs, and much regrafted pain.
These things are in my presage, and myself
Am part of them and know not; but in dreams
The gods are heavy on me, and all the fates
Shed fire across my eyelids mixed with night,
220   And burn me blind, and disilluminate
My sense of seeing, and my perspicuous soul
Darken with vision; seeing I see not, hear
And hearing am not holpen, but mine eyes
Stain many tender broideries in the bed
Drawn up about my face that I may weep
And the king wake not; and my brows and lips
Tremble and sob in sleeping, like swift flames
That tremble, or water when it sobs with heat
Kindled from under; and my tears fill my breast
230   And speck the fair dyed pillows round the king
With barren showers and salter than the sea,
Such dreams divide me dreaming; for long since
I dreamed that out of this my womb had sprung
Fire and a firebrand; this was ere my son,
Meleager, a goodly flower in fields of fight,
Felt the light touch him coming forth, and wailed
Childlike; but yet he was not; and in time
I bare him, and my heart was great; for yet
So royally was never strong man born,
240   Nor queen so nobly bore as noble a thing
As this my son was: such a birth God sent
And such a grace to bear it. Then came in
Three weaving women, and span each a thread,
Saying This for strength and That for luck, and one

Saying Till the brand upon the hearth burn down,
So long shall this man see good days and live.
And I with gathered raiment from the bed
Sprang, and drew forth the brand, and cast on it
Water, and trod the flame bare-foot, and crushed
250 With naked hand spark beaten out of spark
And blew against and quenched it; for I said,
These are the most high Fates that dwell with us,
And we find favour a little in their sight,
A little, and more we miss of, and much time
Foils us; howbeit they have pitied me, O son,
And thee most piteous, thee a tenderer thing
Than any flower of fleshly seed alive.
Wherefore I kissed and hid him with my hands,
And covered under arms and hair, and wept,
260 And feared to touch him with my tears, and laughed;
So light a thing was this man, grown so great
Men cast their heads back, seeing against the sun
Blaze the armed man carven on his shield, and hear
The laughter of little bells along the brace
Ring, as birds singing or flutes blown, and watch,
High up, the cloven shadow of either plume
Divide the bright light of the brass, and make
His helmet as a windy and wintering moon
Seen through blown cloud and plume-like drift, when ships
270 Drive, and men strive with all the sea, and oars
Break, and the beaks dip under, drinking death;
Yet was he then but a span long, and moaned
With inarticulate mouth inseparate words,
And with blind lips and fingers wrung my breast
Hard, and thrust out with foolish hands and feet,
Murmuring; but those grey women with bound hair
Who fright the gods frighted not him; he laughed
Seeing them, and pushed out hands to feel and haul
Distaff and thread, intangible; but they
280 Passed, and I hid the brand, and in my heart
Laughed likewise, having all my will of heaven.
But now I know not if to left or right
The gods have drawn us hither; for again

I dreamt, and saw the black brand burst on fire
As a branch bursts in flower, and saw the flame
Fade flower-wise, and Death came and with dry lips
Blew the charred ash into my breast; and Love
Trampled the ember and crushed it with swift feet.
This I have also at heart; that not for me,
290   Not for me only or son of mine, O girls,
The gods have wrought life, and desire of life,
Heart's love and heart's division; but for all
There shines one sun and one wind blows till night.
And when night comes the wind sinks and the sun,
And there is no light after, and no storm,
But sleep and much forgetfulness of things.
In such wise I gat knowledge of the gods
Years hence, and heard high sayings of one most wise,
Eurythemis my mother, who beheld
300   With eyes alive and spake with lips of these
As one on earth disfleshed and disallied
From breath or blood corruptible; such gifts
Time gave her, and an equal soul to these
And equal face to all things; thus she said.
But whatsoever intolerable or glad
The swift hours weave and unweave, I go hence
Full of mine own soul, perfect of myself,
Toward mine and me sufficient; and what chance
The gods cast lots for and shake out on us,
310   That shall we take, and that much bear withal.
And now, before these gather to the hunt,
I will go arm my son and bring him forth,
Lest love or some man's anger work him harm.

CHORUS
Before the beginning of years
   There came to the making of man
Time, with a gift of tears;
   Grief, with a glass that ran;

Pleasure, with pain for leaven;
   Summer, with flowers that fell;
320 Remembrance fallen from heaven,
   And madness risen from hell;
Strength without hands to smite;
   Love that endures for a breath:
Night, the shadow of light,
   And life, the shadow of death.

And the high gods took in hand
   Fire, and the falling of tears,
And a measure of sliding sand
   From under the feet of the years;
330 And froth and drift of the sea;
   And dust of the labouring earth;
And bodies of things to be
   In the houses of death and of birth;
And wrought with weeping and laughter,
   And fashioned with loathing and love,
With life before and after
   And death beneath and above,
For a day and a night and a morrow,
   That his strength might endure for a span
340 With travail and heavy sorrow,
   The holy spirit of man.

From the winds of the north and the south
   They gathered as unto strife;
They breathed upon his mouth,
   They filled his body with life;
Eyesight and speech they wrought
   For the veils of the soul therein,
A time for labour and thought,
   A time to serve and to sin;
350 They gave him light in his ways,
   And love, and a space for delight,
And beauty and length of days,
   And night, and sleep in the night.

His speech is a burning fire;
   With his lips he travaileth;
In his heart is a blind desire,
   In his eyes foreknowledge of death;
He weaves, and is clothed with derision;
   Sows, and he shall not reap;
360 His life is a watch or a vision
   Between a sleep and a sleep.

MELEAGER

O sweet new heaven and air without a star,
Fair day, be fair and welcome, as to men
With deeds to do and praise to pluck from thee.
Come forth a child, born with clear sound and light,
With laughter and swift limbs and prosperous looks;
That this great hunt with heroes for the hounds
May leave thee memorable and us well sped.

ALTHÆA

Son, first I praise thy prayer, then bid thee speed;
370 But the gods hear men's hands before their lips,
And heed beyond all crying and sacrifice
Light of things done and noise of labouring men.
But thou, being armed and perfect for the deed,
Abide; for like rain-flakes in a wind they grow,
The men thy fellows, and the choice of the world,
Bound to root out the tuskèd plague, and leave
Thanks and safe days and peace in Calydon.

MELEAGER

For the whole city and all the low-lying land
Flames, and the soft air sounds with them that come;
380 The gods give all these fruit of all their works.

ALTHÆA

Set thine eye thither and fix thy spirit and say
Whom there thou knowest; for sharp mixed shadow and
                    wind
Blown up between the morning and the mist,

With steam of steeds and flash of bridle or wheel,
And fire, and parcels of the broken dawn,
And dust divided by hard light, and spears
That shine and shift as the edge of wild beasts' eyes,
Smite upon mine; so fiery their blind edge
Burns, and bright points break up and baffle day.

MELEAGER

390 The first, for many I know not, being far off,
Peleus the Larissæan, couched with whom
Sleeps the white sea-bred wife and silver-shod,
Fair as fled foam, a goddess; and their son
Most swift and splendid of men's children born,
Most like a god, full of the future fame.

ALTHÆA

Who are these shining like one sundered star?

MELEAGER

Thy sister's sons, a double flower of men.

ALTHÆA

O sweetest kin to me in all the world,
O twin-born blood of Leda, gracious heads
400 Like kindled lights in untempestuous heaven,
Fair flower-like stars on the iron foam of fight,
With what glad heart and kindliness of soul,
Even to the staining of both eyes with tears
And kindling of warm eyelids with desire,
A great way off I greet you, and rejoice
Seeing you so fair, and moulded like as gods.
Far off ye come, and least in years of these,
But lordliest, but worth love to look upon.

MELEAGER

Even such (for sailing hither I saw far hence,
410 And where Eurotas hollows his moist rock
Nigh Sparta with a strenuous-hearted stream)
Even such I saw their sisters; one swan-white,

The little Helen, and less fair than she
Fair Clytæmnestra, grave as pasturing fawns
Who feed and fear some arrow; but at whiles,
As one smitten with love or wrung with joy,
She laughs and lightens with her eyes, and then
Weeps; whereat Helen, having laughed, weeps too,
And the other chides her, and she being chid speaks nought,
420   But cheeks and lips and eyelids kisses her,
Laughing; so fare they, as in their bloomless bud
And full of unblown life, the blood of gods.

ALTHÆA
Sweet days befall them and good loves and lords,
And tender and temperate honours of the hearth,
Peace, and a perfect life and blameless bed.
But who shows next an eagle wrought in gold,
That flames and beats broad wings against the sun
And with void mouth gapes after emptier prey?

MELEAGER
Know by that sign the reign of Telamon
430   Between the fierce mouths of the encountering brine
On the strait reefs of twice-washed Salamis.

ALTHÆA
For like one great of hand he bears himself,
Vine-chapleted, with savours of the sea,
Glittering as wine and moving as a wave.
But who girt round there roughly follows him?

MELEAGER
Ancæus, great of hand, an iron bulk,
Two-edged for fight as the axe against his arm,
Who drives against the surge of stormy spears
Full-sailed; him Cepheus follows, his twin-born,
440   Chief name next his of all Arcadian men.

ALTHÆA

Praise be with men abroad; chaste lives with us,
Home-keeping days and household reverences.

MELEAGER

Next by the left unsandalled foot know thou
The sail and oar of this Ætolian land,
Thy brethren, Toxeus and the violent-souled
Plexippus, over-swift with hand and tongue;
For hands are fruitful, but the ignorant mouth
Blows and corrupts their work with barren breath.

ALTHÆA

Speech too bears fruit, being worthy; and air blows down
450 Things poisonous, and high-seated violences,
And with charmed words and songs have men put out
Wild evil, and the fire of tyrannies.

MELEAGER

Yea, all things have they, save the gods and love.

ALTHÆA

Love thou the law and cleave to things ordained.

MELEAGER

Law lives upon their lips whom these applaud.

ALTHÆA

How sayest thou these? what god applauds new things?

MELEAGER

Zeus, who hath fear and custom under foot.

ALTHÆA

But loves not laws thrown down and lives awry.

MELEAGER

Yet is not less himself than his own law.

ALTHÆA

460   Nor shifts and shuffles old things up and down.

MELEAGER

But what he will remoulds and discreates.

ALTHÆA

Much, but not this, that each thing live its life.

MELEAGER

Nor only live, but lighten and lift up higher.

ALTHÆA

Pride breaks itself, and too much gained is gone.

MELEAGER

Things gained are gone, but great things done endure.

ALTHÆA

Child, if a man serve law through all his life
And with his whole heart worship, him all gods
Praise; but who loves it only with his lips,
And not in heart and deed desiring it
470   Hides a perverse will with obsequious words,
Him heaven infatuates and his twin-born fate
Tracks, and gains on him, scenting sins far off,
And the swift hounds of violent death devour.
Be man at one with equal-minded gods,
So shall he prosper; not through laws torn up,
Violated rule and a new face of things.
A woman armed makes war upon herself,
Unwomanlike, and treads down use and wont
And the sweet common honour that she hath,
480   Love, and the cry of children, and the hand
Trothplight and mutual mouth of marriages.
This doth she, being unloved; whom if one love,
Not fire nor iron and the wide-mouthed wars
Are deadlier than her lips or braided hair.
For of the one comes poison, and a curse

Falls from the other and burns the lives of men.
But thou, son, be not filled with evil dreams,
Nor with desire of these things; for with time
Blind love burns out; but if one feed it full
490   Till some discolouring stain dyes all his life,
He shall keep nothing praiseworthy, nor die
The sweet wise death of old men honourable,
Who have lived out all the length of all their years
Blameless, and seen well-pleased the face of gods,
And without shame and without fear have wrought
Things memorable, and while their days held out
In sight of all men and the sun's great light
Have gat them glory and given of their own praise
To the earth that bare them and the day that bred,
500   Home friends and far-off hospitalities,
And filled with gracious and memorial fame
Lands loved of summer or washed by violent seas,
Towns populous and many unfooted ways,
And alien lips and native with their own.
But when white age and venerable death
Mow down the strength and life within their limbs,
Drain out the blood and darken their clear eyes,
Immortal honour is on them, having past
Through splendid life and death desirable
510   To the clear seat and remote throne of souls,
Lands indiscoverable in the unheard-of west,
Round which the strong stream of a sacred sea
Rolls without wind for ever, and the snow
There shows not her white wings and windy feet,
Nor thunder nor swift rain saith anything,
Nor the sun burns, but all things rest and thrive;
And these, filled full of days, divine and dead,
Sages and singers fiery from the god,
And such as loved their land and all things good
520   And, best beloved of best men, liberty,
Free lives and lips, free hands of men free-born,
And whatsoever on earth was honourable
And whosoever of all the ephemeral seed,
Live there a life no liker to the gods

But nearer than their life of terrene days.
Love thou such life and look for such a death.
But from the light and fiery dreams of love
Spring heavy sorrows and a sleepless life,
Visions not dreams, whose lids no charm shall close
530   Nor song assuage them waking; and swift death
Crushes with sterile feet the unripening ear,
Treads out the timeless vintage; whom do thou
Eschewing embrace the luck of this thy life,
Not without honour; and it shall bear to thee
Such fruit as men reap from spent hours and wear,
Few men, but happy; of whom be thou, O son,
Happiest, if thou submit thy soul to fate,
And set thine eyes and heart on hopes high-born
And divine deeds and abstinence divine.
540   So shalt thou be toward all men all thy days
As light and might communicable, and burn
From heaven among the stars above the hours,
And break not as a man breaks nor burn down:
For to whom other of all heroic names
Have the gods given his life in hand as thine?
And gloriously hast thou lived, and made thy life
To me that bare thee and to all men born
Thankworthy, a praise for ever; and hast won fame
When wild wars broke all round thy father's house,
550   And the mad people of windy mountain ways
Laid spears against us like a sea, and all
Ætolia thundered with Thessalian hoofs;
Yet these, as wind baffles the foam, and beats
Straight back the relaxed ripple, didst thou break
And loosen all their lances, till undone
And man from man they fell; for ye twain stood
God against god, Ares and Artemis,
And thou the mightier; wherefore she unleashed
A sharp-toothed curse thou too shalt overcome;
560   For in the greener blossom of thy life
Ere the full blade caught flower, and when time gave
Respite, thou didst not slacken soul nor sleep,
But with great hand and heart seek praise of men

Out of sharp straits and many a grievous thing,
Seeing the strange foam of undivided seas
On channels never sailed in, and by shores
Where the old winds cease not blowing, and all the night
Thunders, and day is no delight to men.

CHORUS
Meleager, a noble wisdom and fair words
570   The gods have given this woman; hear thou these.

MELEAGER
O mother, I am not fain to strive in speech
Nor set my mouth against thee, who art wise
Even as they say and full of sacred words.
But one thing I know surely, and cleave to this;
That though I be not subtle of wit as thou
Nor womanlike to weave sweet words, and melt
Mutable minds of wise men as with fire,
I too, doing justly and reverencing the gods,
Shall not want wit to see what things be right.
580   For whom they love and whom reject, being gods,
There is no man but seeth, and in good time
Submits himself, refraining all his heart.
And I too as thou sayest have seen great things;
Seen otherwhere, but chiefly when the sail
First caught between stretched ropes the roaring west,
And all our oars smote eastward, and the wind
First flung round faces of seafaring men
White splendid snow-flakes of the sundering foam,
And the first furrow in virginal green sea
590   Followed the plunging ploughshare of hewn pine,
And closed, as when deep sleep subdues man's breath
Lips close and heart subsides; and closing, shone
Sunlike with many a Nereid's hair, and moved
Round many a trembling mouth of doubtful gods,
Risen out of sunless and sonorous gulfs
Through waning water and into shallow light,
That watched us; and when flying the dove was snared
As with men's hands, but we shot after and sped

Clear through the irremeable Symplegades;
600 And chiefliest when hoar beach and herbless cliff
Stood out ahead from Colchis, and we heard
Clefts hoarse with wind, and saw through narrowing reefs
The lightning of the intolerable wave
Flash, and the white wet flame of breakers burn
Far under a kindling south-wind, as a lamp
Burns and bends all its blowing flame one way;
Wild heights untravelled of the wind, and vales
Cloven seaward by their violent streams, and white
With bitter flowers and bright salt scurf of brine;
610 Heard sweep their sharp swift gales, and bowing birdwise
Shriek with birds' voices, and with furious feet
Tread loose the long skirts of a storm; and saw
The whole white Euxine clash together and fall
Full-mouthed, and thunderous from a thousand throats:
Yet we drew thither and won the fleece and won
Medea, deadlier than the sea; but there
Seeing many a wonder and fearful things to men
I saw not one thing like this one seen here,
Most fair and fearful, feminine, a god,
620 Faultless; whom I that love not, being unlike,
Fear, and give honour, and choose from all the gods.

ŒNEUS

Lady, the daughter of Thestius, and thou, son,
Not ignorant of your strife nor light of wit,
Scared with vain dreams and fluttering like spent fire,
I come to judge between you, but a king
Full of past days and wise from years endured.
Nor thee I praise, who art fain to undo things done:
Nor thee, who art swift to esteem them overmuch.
For what the hours have given is given, and this
630 Changeless; howbeit these change, and in good time
Devise new things and good, not one thing still.
Us have they sent now at our need for help
Among men armed a woman, foreign born,
Virgin, not like the natural flower of things
That grows and bears and brings forth fruit and dies;

Unlovable, no light for a husband's house,
Espoused; a glory among unwedded girls,
And chosen of gods who reverence maidenhood.
These too we honour in honouring her; but thou,
640   Abstain thy feet from following, and thine eyes
From amorous touch; nor set toward hers thine heart,
Son, lest hate bear no deadlier fruit than love.

ALTHÆA

O king, thou art wise, but wisdom halts; and just,
But the gods love not justice more than fate,
And smite the righteous and the violent mouth,
And mix with insolent blood the reverent man's,
And bruise the holier as the lying lips.
Enough; for wise words fail me, and my heart
Takes fire and trembles flamewise, O my son,
650   O child, for thine head's sake; mine eyes wax thick,
Turning toward thee, so goodly a weaponed man,
So glorious; and for love of thine own eyes
They are darkened, and tears burn them, fierce as fire,
And my lips pause and my soul sinks with love.
But by thine hand, by thy sweet life and eyes,
By thy great heart and these clasped knees, O son,
I pray thee that thou slay me not with thee.
For there was never a mother woman-born
Loved her sons better; and never a queen of men
660   More perfect in her heart toward whom she loved.
For what lies light on many and they forget,
Small things and transitory as a wind o' the sea,
I forget never; I have seen thee all thine years
A man in arms, strong and a joy to men
Seeing thine head glitter and thine hand burn its way
Through a heavy and iron furrow of sundering spears;
But always also a flower of three suns old,
The small one thing that lying drew down my life
To lie with thee and feed thee; a child and weak,
670   Mine, a delight to no man, sweet to me.
Who then sought to thee? who gat help? who knew
If thou wert goodly? nay, no man at all.

Or what sea saw thee, or sounded with thine oar,
Child? or what strange land shone with war through thee?
But fair for me thou wert, O little life,
Fruitless, the fruit of mine own flesh, and blind,
More than much gold, ungrown, a foolish flower.
For silver nor bright snow nor feather of foam
Was whiter, and no gold yellower than thine hair,
680 O child, my child; and now thou art lordlier grown,
Not lovelier, nor a new thing in mine eyes,
I charge thee by thy soul and this my breast,
Fear thou the gods and me and thine own heart,
Lest all these turn against thee; for who knows
What wind upon what wave of altering time
Shall speak a storm and blow calamity?
And there is nothing stabile in the world
But the gods break it; yet not less, fair son,
If but one thing be stronger, if one endure,
690 Surely the bitter and the rooted love
That burns between us, going from me to thee,
Shall more endure than all things. What dost thou,
Following strange loves? why wilt thou kill mine heart?
Lo, I talk wild and windy words, and fall
From my clear wits, and seem of mine own self
Dethroned, dispraised, disseated; and my mind,
That was my crown, breaks, and mine heart is gone,
And I am naked of my soul, and stand
Ashamed, as a mean woman; take thou thought:
700 Live if thou wilt, and if thou wilt not, look,
The gods have given thee life to lose or keep,
Thou shalt not die as men die, but thine end
Fallen upon thee shall break me unaware.

MELEAGER

Queen, my whole heart is molten with thy tears,
And my limbs yearn with pity of thee, and love
Compels with grief mine eyes and labouring breath;
For what thou art I know thee, and this thy breast
And thy fair eyes I worship, and am bound
Toward thee in spirit and love thee in all my soul.

710 For there is nothing terribler to men
Than the sweet face of mothers, and the might.
But what shall be let be; for us the day
Once only lives a little, and is not found.
Time and the fruitful hour are more than we,
And these lay hold upon us; but thou, God,
Zeus, the sole steersman of the helm of things,
Father, be swift to see us, and as thou wilt
Help: or if adverse, as thou wilt, refrain.

CHORUS

We have seen thee, O Love, thou art fair; thou art goodly,
        O Love;
720 Thy wings make light in the air as the wings of a dove.
Thy feet are as winds that divide the stream of the sea;
Earth is thy covering to hide thee, the garment of thee.
Thou art swift and subtle and blind as a flame of fire;
Before thee the laughter, behind thee the tears of desire;
And twain go forth beside thee, a man with a maid;
Her eyes are the eyes of a bride whom delight makes afraid;
As the breath in the buds that stir is her bridal breath:
But Fate is the name of her; and his name is Death.

    For an evil blossom was born
730   Of sea-foam and the frothing of blood,
        Blood-red and bitter of fruit,
            And the seed of it laughter and tears,
And the leaves of it madness and scorn;
        A bitter flower from the bud,
            Sprung of the sea without root,
                Sprung without graft from the years.

    The weft of the world was untorn
        That is woven of the day on the night,
        The hair of the hours was not white
740   Nor the raiment of time overworn,

When a wonder, a world's delight,
A perilous goddess was born;
    And the waves of the sea as she came
Clove, and the foam at her feet,
    Fawning, rejoiced to bring forth
    A fleshly blossom, a flame
Filling the heavens with heat
    To the cold white ends of the north.

And in air the clamorous birds,
750   And men upon earth that hear
Sweet articulate words
    Sweetly divided apart,
And in shallow and channel and mere
The rapid and footless herds,
    Rejoiced, being foolish of heart.

For all they said upon earth,
    She is fair, she is white like a dove,
    And the life of the world in her breath
Breathes, and is born at her birth;
760   For they knew thee for mother of love,
    And knew thee not mother of death.

What hadst thou to do being born,
    Mother, when winds were at ease,
As a flower of the springtime of corn,
    A flower of the foam of the seas?
For bitter thou wast from thy birth,
    Aphrodite, a mother of strife;
For before thee some rest was on earth,
    A little respite from tears,
770   A little pleasure of life;
For life was not then as thou art,
    But as one that waxeth in years
Sweet-spoken, a fruitful wife;
    Earth had no thorn, and desire

No sting, neither death any dart;
   What hadst thou to do amongst these,
     Thou, clothed with a burning fire,
Thou, girt with sorrow of heart,
   Thou, sprung of the seed of the seas
780 As an ear from a seed of corn,
     As a brand plucked forth of a pyre,
As a ray shed forth of the morn,
   For division of soul and disease,
For a dart and a sting and a thorn?
What ailed thee then to be born?

Was there not evil enough,
   Mother, and anguish on earth
   Born with a man at his birth,
Wastes underfoot, and above
790   Storm out of heaven, and dearth
Shaken down from the shining thereof,
     Wrecks from afar overseas
   And peril of shallow and firth,
    And tears that spring and increase
   In the barren places of mirth,
That thou, having wings as a dove,
   Being girt with desire for a girth
    That thou must come after these,
That thou must lay on him love?

800 Thou shouldst not so have been born:
   But death should have risen with thee,
    Mother, and visible fear,
     Grief, and the wringing of hands,
And noise of many that mourn;
   The smitten bosom, the knee
    Bowed, and in each man's ear
     A cry as of perishing lands,

A moan as of people in prison,
  A tumult of infinite griefs;
810   And thunder of storm on the sands,
    And wailing of wives on the shore;
And under thee newly arisen
  Loud shoals and shipwrecking reefs,
      Fierce air and violent light;
  – Sail rent and sundering oar,
      Darkness, and noises of night;
Clashing of streams in the sea,
  Wave against wave as a sword,
    Clamour of currents, and foam;
820   Rains making ruin on earth,
    Winds that wax ravenous and roam
As wolves in a wolfish horde;
Fruits growing faint in the tree,
      And blind things dead in their birth;
    Famine, and blighting of corn,
    When thy time was come to be born.

All these we know of; but thee
  Who shall discern or declare?
In the uttermost ends of the sea
830   The light of thine eyelids and hair,
    The light of thy bosom as fire
      Between the wheel of the sun
And the flying flames of the air?
    Wilt thou turn thee not yet nor have pity,
But abide with despair and desire
  And the crying of armies undone,
      Lamentation of one with another
      And breaking of city by city;
    The dividing of friend against friend,
840   The severing of brother and brother;
    Wilt thou utterly bring to an end?
      Have mercy, mother!

> For against all men from of old
>> Thou hast set thine hand as a curse,
>>> And cast out gods from their places.
>>>> These things are spoken of thee.
> Strong kings and goodly with gold
>> Thou hast found out arrows to pierce,
>>> And made their kingdoms and races
850 >>>> As dust and surf of the sea.
> All these, overburdened with woes
>> And with length of their days waxen weak,
>>> Thou slewest; and sentest moreover
>>>> Upon Tyro an evil thing,
> Rent hair and a fetter and blows
>> Making bloody the flower of the cheek,
>>> Though she lay by a god as a lover,
>>>> Though fair, and the seed of a king.
> For of old, being full of thy fire,
860 >> She endured not longer to wear
>>> On her bosom a saffron vest,
>>>> On her shoulder an ashwood quiver;
> Being mixed and made one through desire
>> With Enipeus, and all her hair
>>> Made moist with his mouth, and her breast
>>>> Filled full of the foam of the river.

ATALANTA

Sun, and clear light among green hills, and day
Late risen and long sought after, and you just gods
Whose hands divide anguish and recompense,
870 But first the sun's white sister, a maid in heaven,
On earth of all maids worshipped – hail, and hear,
And witness with me if not without sign sent,
Not without rule and reverence, I a maid
Hallowed, and huntress holy as whom I serve,
Here in your sight and eyeshot of these men
Stand, girt as they toward hunting, and my shafts
Drawn; wherefore all ye stand up on my side,
If I be pure and all ye righteous gods,
Lest one revile me, a woman, yet no wife,

880 That bear a spear for spindle, and this bow strung
     For a web woven; and with pure lips salute
     Heaven, and the face of all the gods, and dawn
     Filling with maiden flames and maiden flowers
     The starless fold o' the stars, and making sweet
     The warm wan heights of the air, moon-trodden ways
     And breathless gates and extreme hills of heaven.
     Whom, having offered water and bloodless gifts,
     Flowers, and a golden circlet of pure hair,
     Next Artemis I bid be favourable
890 And make this day all golden, hers and ours,
     Gracious and good and white to the unblamed end.
     But thou, O well-beloved, of all my days
     Bid it be fruitful, and a crown for all,
     To bring forth leaves and bind round all my hair
     With perfect chaplets woven for thine of thee.
     For not without the word of thy chaste mouth,
     For not without law given and clean command,
     Across the white straits of the running sea
     From Elis even to the Acheloïan horn,
900 I with clear winds came hither and gentle gods,
     Far off my father's house, and left uncheered
     Iasius, and uncheered the Arcadian hills
     And all their green-haired waters, and all woods
     Disconsolate, to hear no horn of mine
     Blown, and behold no flash of swift white feet.

MELEAGER

     For thy name's sake and awe toward thy chaste head,
     O holiest Atalanta, no man dares
     Praise thee, though fairer than whom all men praise,
     And godlike for thy grace of hallowed hair
910 And holy habit of thine eyes, and feet
     That make the blown foam neither swift nor white
     Though the wind winnow and whirl it; yet we praise
     Gods, found because of thee adorable
     And for thy sake praiseworthiest from all men:
     Thee therefore we praise also, thee as these,
     Pure, as a light lit at the hands of gods.

TOXEUS

How long will ye whet spears with eloquence,
Fight, and kill beasts dry-handed with sweet words?
Cease, or talk still and slay thy boars at home.

PLEXIPPUS

920 Why, if she ride among us for a man,
Sit thou for her and spin; a man grown girl
Is worth a woman weaponed; sit thou here.

MELEAGER

Peace, and be wise; no gods love idle speech.

PLEXIPPUS

Nor any man a man's mouth woman-tongued.

MELEAGER

For my lips bite not sharper than mine hands.

PLEXIPPUS

Nay, both bite soft, but no whit softly mine.

MELEAGER

Keep thine hands clean; they have time enough to stain.

PLEXIPPUS

For thine shall rest and wax not red to-day.

MELEAGER

Have all thy will of words; talk out thine heart.

ALTHÆA

930 Refrain your lips, O brethren, and my son,
Lest words turn snakes and bite you uttering them.

TOXEUS

Except she give her blood before the gods,
What profit shall a maid be among men?

PLEXIPPUS

Let her come crowned and stretch her throat for a knife,
Bleat out her spirit and die, and so shall men
Through her too prosper and through prosperous gods,
But nowise through her living; shall she live
A flower-bud of the flower-bed, or sweet fruit
For kisses and the honey-making mouth,
940   And play the shield for strong men and the spear?
Then shall the heifer and her mate lock horns,
And the bride overbear the groom, and men
Gods; for no less division sunders these;
Since all things made are seasonable in time,
But if one alter unseasonable are all.
But thou, O Zeus, hear me that I may slay
This beast before thee and no man halve with me
Nor woman, lest these mock thee, though a god,
Who hast made men strong, and thou being wise be held
950   Foolish; for wise is that thing which endures.

ATALANTA

Men, and the chosen of all this people, and thou,
King, I beseech you a little bear with me.
For if my life be shameful that I live,
Let the gods witness and their wrath; but these
Cast no such word against me. Thou, O mine,
O holy, O happy goddess, if I sin
Changing the words of women and the works
For spears and strange men's faces, hast not thou
One shaft of all thy sudden seven that pierced
960   Seven through the bosom or shining throat or side,
All couched about one mother's loosening knees,
All holy born, engraffed of Tantalus?
But if toward any of you I am overbold
That take thus much upon me, let him think
How I, for all my forest holiness,
Fame, and this armed and iron maidenhood,
Pay thus much also; I shall have no man's love
For ever, and no face of children born
Or feeding lips upon me or fastening eyes

970   For ever, nor being dead shall kings my sons
      Mourn me and bury, and tears on daughters' cheeks
      Burn; but a cold and sacred life, but strange,
      But far from dances and the back-blowing torch,
      Far off from flowers or any bed of man,
      Shall my life be for ever: me the snows
      That face the first o' the morning, and cold hills
      Full of the land-wind and sea-travelling storms
      And many a wandering wing of noisy nights
      That know the thunder and hear the thickening wolves –
980   Me the utmost pine and footless frost of woods
      That talk with many winds and gods, the hours
      Re-risen, and white divisions of the dawn,
      Springs thousand-tongued with the intermitting reed
      And streams that murmur of the mother snow –
      Me these allure, and know me; but no man
      Knows, and my goddess only. Lo now, see
      If one of all you these things vex at all.
      Would God that any of you had all the praise
      And I no manner of memory when I die,
990   So might I show before her perfect eyes
      Pure, whom I follow, a maiden to my death.
      But for the rest let all have all they will;
      For is it a grief to you that I have part,
      Being woman merely, in your male might and deeds
      Done by main strength? yet in my body is throned
      As great a heart, and in my spirit, O men,
      I have not less of godlike. Evil it were
      That one a coward should mix with you, one hand
      Fearful, one eye abase itself; and these
1000 Well might ye hate and well revile, not me.
      For not the difference of the several flesh
      Being vile or noble or beautiful or base
      Makes praiseworthy, but purer spirit and heart
      Higher than these meaner mouths and limbs, that feed,
      Rise, rest, and are and are not; and for me,
      What should I say? but by the gods of the world
      And this my maiden body, by all oaths
      That bind the tongue of men and the evil will,

I am not mighty-minded, nor desire
1010 Crowns, nor the spoil of slain things nor the fame;
Feed ye on these, eat and wax fat; cry out,
Laugh, having eaten, and leap without a lyre,
Sing, mix the wind with clamour, smite and shake
Sonorous timbrels and tumultuous hair,
And fill the dance up with tempestuous feet,
For I will none; but having prayed my prayers
And made thank-offering for prosperities,
I shall go hence and no man see me more.
What thing is this for you to shout me down,
1020 What, for a man to grudge me this my life
As it were envious of all yours, and I
A thief of reputations? nay, for now,
If there be any highest in heaven, a god
Above all thrones and thunders of the gods
Throned, and the wheel of the world roll under him,
Judge he between me and all of you, and see
If I transgress at all: but ye, refrain
Transgressing hands and reinless mouths, and keep
Silence, lest by much foam of violent words
1030 And proper poison of your lips ye die.

OENEUS

O flower of Tegea, maiden, fleetest foot
And holiest head of women, have good cheer
Of thy good words: but ye, depart with her
In peace and reverence, each with blameless eye
Following his fate; exalt your hands and hearts,
Strike, cease not, arrow on arrow and wound on wound,
And go with gods and with the gods return.

CHORUS

Who hath given man speech? or who hath set therein
A thorn for peril and a snare for sin?
1040 For in the word his life is and his breath,
    And in the word his death,
That madness and the infatuate heart may breed
    From the word's womb the deed

And life bring one thing forth ere all pass by,
Even one thing which is ours yet cannot die —
Death. Hast thou seen him ever anywhere,
Time's twin-born brother, imperishable as he
Is perishable and plaintive, clothed with care
    And mutable as sand,
1050 But death is strong and full of blood and fair
And perdurable and like a lord of land?
Nay, time thou seest not, death thou wilt not see
Till life's right hand be loosened from thine hand
    And thy life-days from thee.
For the gods very subtly fashion
    Madness with sadness upon earth:
Not knowing in any wise compassion,
    Nor holding pity of any worth;
And many things they have given and taken,
1060   And wrought and ruined many things;
The firm land have they loosed and shaken,
    And sealed the sea with all her springs;
They have wearied time with heavy burdens
    And vexed the lips of life with breath:
Set men to labour and given them guerdons,
    Death, and great darkness after death:
Put moans into the bridal measure
    And on the bridal wools a stain;
And circled pain about with pleasure,
1070   And girdled pleasure about with pain;
And strewed one marriage-bed with tears and fire
For extreme loathing and supreme desire.

What shall be done with all these tears of ours?
    Shall they make watersprings in the fair heaven
To bathe the brows of morning? or like flowers
Be shed and shine before the starriest hours,
    Or made the raiment of the weeping Seven?
Or rather, O our masters, shall they be
Food for the famine of the grievous sea,
1080   A great well-head of lamentation
Satiating the sad gods? or fall and flow

Among the years and seasons to and fro,
    And wash their feet with tribulation
And fill them full with grieving ere they go?
    Alas, our lords, and yet alas again,
Seeing all your iron heaven is gilt as gold
    But all we smite thereat in vain;
Smite the gates barred with groanings manifold,
    But all the floors are paven with our pain.
1090 Yea, and with weariness of lips and eyes,
With breaking of the bosom, and with sighs,
    We labour, and are clad and fed with grief
And filled with days we would not fain behold
And nights we would not hear of; we wax old,
    All we wax old and wither like a leaf.
We are outcast, strayed between bright sun and moon;
    Our light and darkness are as leaves of flowers,
Black flowers and white, that perish; and the noon
    As midnight, and the night as daylight hours.
1100 A little fruit a little while is ours,
    And the worm finds it soon.

But up in heaven the high gods one by one
    Lay hands upon the draught that quickeneth,
Fulfilled with all tears shed and all things done,
    And stir with soft imperishable breath
    The bubbling bitterness of life and death,
And hold it to our lips and laugh; but they
Preserve their lips from tasting night or day,
    Lest they too change and sleep, the fates that spun,
1110 The lips that made us and the hands that slay;
    Lest all these change, and heaven bow down to none,
Change and be subject to the secular sway
    And terrene revolution of the sun.
Therefore they thrust it from them, putting time away.

I would the wind of time, made sharp and sweet
    With multitudinous days and nights and tears
    And many mixing savours of strange years,
Were no more trodden of them under feet,

Cast out and spilt about their holy places:
1120   That life were given them as a fruit to eat
And death to drink as water; that the light
Might ebb, drawn backward from their eyes, and night
    Hide for one hour the imperishable faces.
That they might rise up sad in heaven, and know
Sorrow and sleep, one paler than young snow,
    One cold as blight of dew and ruinous rain;
Rise up and rest and suffer a little, and be
Awhile as all things born with us and we,
    And grieve as men, and like slain men be slain.

1130   For now we know not of them; but one saith
    The gods are gracious, praising God; and one,
When hast thou seen? or hast thou felt his breath
    Touch, nor consume thine eyelids as the sun,
Nor fill thee to the lips with fiery death?
    None hath beheld him, none
Seen above other gods and shapes of things,
Swift without feet and flying without wings,
Intolerable, not clad with death or life,
    Insatiable, not known of night or day,
1140   The lord of love and loathing and of strife
    Who gives a star and takes a sun away;
Who shapes the soul, and makes her a barren wife
    To the earthly body and grievous growth of clay;
Who turns the large limbs to a little flame
    And binds the great sea with a little sand;
Who makes desire, and slays desire with shame;
    Who shakes the heaven as ashes in his hand;
Who, seeing the light and shadow for the same,
    Bids day waste night as fire devours a brand,
1150   Smites without sword, and scourges without rod;
    The supreme evil, God.

Yea, with thine hate, O God, thou hast covered us,
    One saith, and hidden our eyes away from sight,
And made us transitory and hazardous,
    Light things and slight;

Yet have men praised thee, saying, He hath made man thus,
    And he doeth right.
Thou hast kissed us, and hast smitten; thou hast laid
Upon us with thy left hand life, and said,
1160 Live: and again thou hast said, Yield up your breath,
And with thy right hand laid upon us death.
Thou hast sent us sleep, and stricken sleep with dreams,
    Saying, Joy is not, but love of joy shall be;
Thou hast made sweet springs for all the pleasant streams,
    In the end thou hast made them bitter with the sea.
Thou hast fed one rose with dust of many men;
    Thou hast marred one face with fire of many tears;
Thou hast taken love, and given us sorrow again;
    With pain thou hast filled us full to the eyes and ears.
1170 Therefore because thou art strong, our father, and we
    Feeble; and thou art against us, and thine hand
Constrains us in the shallows of the sea
    And breaks us at the limits of the land;
Because thou hast bent thy lightnings as a bow,
    And loosed the hours like arrows; and let fall
Sins and wild words and many a wingèd woe
    And wars among us, and one end of all;
Because thou hast made the thunder, and thy feet
    Are as a rushing water when the skies
1180 Break, but thy face as an exceeding heat
    And flames of fire the eyelids of thine eyes;
Because thou art over all who are over us;
    Because thy name is life and our name death;
Because thou art cruel and men are piteous,
    And our hands labour and thine hand scattereth;
Lo, with hearts rent and knees made tremulous,
    Lo, with ephemeral lips and casual breath,
      At least we witness of thee ere we die
That these things are not otherwise, but thus;
1190   That each man in his heart sigheth, and saith,
      That all men even as I,
All we are against thee, against thee, O God most high.

But ye, keep ye on earth
    Your lips from over-speech,
Loud words and longing are so little worth;
    And the end is hard to reach.
For silence after grievous things is good,
    And reverence, and the fear that makes men whole,
And shame, and righteous governance of blood,
1200   And lordship of the soul.
But from sharp words and wits men pluck no fruit,
And gathering thorns they shake the tree at root;
    For words divide and rend;
But silence is most noble till the end.

ALTHÆA
I heard within the house a cry of news
And came forth eastward hither, where the dawn
Cheers first these warder gods that face the sun
And next our eyes unrisen; for unaware
Came clashes of swift hoofs and trampling feet
1210 And through the windy pillared corridor
Light sharper than the frequent flames of day
That daily fill it from the fiery dawn;
Gleams, and a thunder of people that cried out,
And dust and hurrying horsemen; lo their chief,
That rode with Œneus rein by rein, returned.
What cheer, O herald of my lord the king?

HERALD
Lady, good cheer and great; the boar is slain.

CHORUS
Praised be all gods that look toward Calydon.

ALTHÆA
Good news and brief; but by whose happier hand?

HERALD
1220 A maiden's and a prophet's and thy son's.

ALTHÆA
Well fare the spear that severed him and life.

HERALD
Thine own, and not an alien, hast thou blest.

ALTHÆA
Twice be thou too for my sake blest and his.

HERALD
At the king's word I rode afoam for thine.

ALTHÆA
Thou sayest he tarrieth till they bring the spoil?

HERALD
Hard by the quarry, where they breathe, O queen.

ALTHÆA
Speak thou their chance; but some bring flowers and crown
These gods and all the lintel, and shed wine,
Fetch sacrifice and slay; for heaven is good.

HERALD
1230   Some furlongs northward where the brakes begin
West of that narrowing range of warrior hills
Whose brooks have bled with battle when thy son
Smote Acarnania, there all they made halt,
And with keen eye took note of spear and hound,
Royally ranked; Laertes island-born,
The young Gerenian Nestor, Panopeus,
And Cepheus and Ancæus, mightiest thewed,
Arcadians; next, and evil-eyed of these,
Arcadian Atalanta, with twain hounds
1240   Lengthening the leash, and under nose and brow
Glittering with lipless tooth and fire-swift eye;
But from her white braced shoulder the plumed shafts
Rang, and the bow shone from her side; next her
Meleager, like a sun in spring that strikes

Branch into leaf and bloom into the world,
A glory among men meaner; Iphicles,
And following him that slew the biform bull
Pirithous, and divine Eurytion,
And, bride-bound to the gods, Æacides.
1250 Then Telamon his brother, and Argive-born
The seer and sayer of visions and of truth,
Amphiaraus; and a four-fold strength,
Thine, even thy mother's and thy sister's sons.
And recent from the roar of foreign foam
Jason, and Dryas twin-begot with war,
A blossom of bright battle, sword and man
Shining; and Idas, and the keenest eye
Of Lynceus, and Admetus twice-espoused,
And Hippasus and Hyleus, great in heart.
1260 These having halted bade blow horns, and rode
Through woods and waste lands cleft by stormy streams,
Past yew-trees and the heavy hair of pines,
And where the dew is thickest under oaks,
This way and that; but questing up and down
They saw no trail nor scented; and one said,
Plexippus, Help, or help not, Artemis,
And we will flay thy boarskin with male hands;
But saying, he ceased and said not that he would,
Seeing where the green ooze of a sun-struck marsh
1270 Shook with a thousand reeds untunable,
And in their moist and multitudinous flower
Slept no soft sleep, with violent visions fed,
The blind bulk of the immeasurable beast.
And seeing, he shuddered with sharp lust of praise
Through all his limbs, and launched a double dart.
And missed; for much desire divided him,
Too hot of spirit and feebler than his will,
That his hand failed, though fervent; and the shaft,
Sundering the rushes, in a tamarisk stem
1280 Shook, and stuck fast; then all abode save one,
The Arcadian Atalanta; from her side
Sprang her hounds, labouring at the leash, and slipped,
And plashed ear-deep with plunging feet; but she

Saying, Speed it as I send it for thy sake,
Goddess, drew bow and loosed; the sudden string
Rang, and sprang inward, and the waterish air
Hissed, and the moist plumes of the songless reeds
Moved as a wave which the wind moves no more.
But the boar heaved half out of ooze and slime
1290   His tense flank trembling round the barbèd wound,
Hateful; and fiery with invasive eyes
And bristling with intolerable hair
Plunged, and the hounds clung, and green flowers and white
Reddened and broke all round them where they came.
And charging with sheer tusk he drove, and smote
Hyleus; and sharp death caught his sudden soul,
And violent sleep shed night upon his eyes.
Then Peleus, with strong strain of hand and heart,
Shot; but the sidelong arrow slid, and slew
1300   His comrade born and loving countryman,
Under the left arm smitten, as he no less
Poised a like arrow; and bright blood brake afoam,
And falling, and weighed back by clamorous arms,
Sharp rang the dead limbs of Eurytion.
Then one shot happier, the Cadmean seer,
Amphiaraus; for his sacred shaft
Pierced the red circlet of one ravening eye
Beneath the brute brows of the sanguine boar,
Now bloodier from one slain; but he so galled
1310   Sprang straight, and rearing cried no lesser cry
Than thunder and the roar of wintering streams
That mix their own foam with the yellower sea;
And as a tower that falls by fire in fight
With ruin of walls and all its archery,
And breaks the iron flower of war beneath,
Crushing charred limbs and molten arms of men;
So through crushed branches and the reddening brake
Clamoured and crashed the fervour of his feet,
And trampled, springing sideways from the tusk,
1320   Too tardy a moving mould of heavy strength,
Ancæus; and as flakes of weak-winged snow
Break, all the hard thews of his heaving limbs

Broke, and rent flesh fell every way, and blood
Flew, and fierce fragments of no more a man.
Then all the heroes drew sharp breath, and gazed,
And smote not; but Meleager, but thy son,
Right in the wild way of the coming curse
Rock-rooted, fair with fierce and fastened lips,
Clear eyes, and springing muscle and shortening limb –
1330 With chin aslant indrawn to a tightening throat,
Grave, and with gathered sinews, like a god, –
Aimed on the left side his well-handled spear
Grasped where the ash was knottiest hewn, and smote,
And with no missile wound, the monstrous boar
Right in the hairiest hollow of his hide
Under the last rib, sheer through bulk and bone,
Deep in; and deeply smitten, and to death,
The heavy horror with his hanging shafts
Leapt, and fell furiously, and from raging lips
1340 Foamed out the latest wrath of all his life.
And all they praised the gods with mightier heart,
Zeus and all gods, but chiefliest Artemis,
Seeing; but Meleager bade whet knives and flay,
Strip and stretch out the splendour of the spoil;
And hot and horrid from the work all these
Sat, and drew breath and drank and made great cheer
And washed the hard sweat off their calmer brows.
For much sweet grass grew higher than grew the reed,
And good for slumber, and every holier herb,
1350 Narcissus, and the low-lying melilote,
And all of goodliest blade and bloom that springs
Where, hid by heavier hyacinth, violet buds
Blossom and burn; and fire of yellower flowers
And light of crescent lilies, and such leaves
As fear the Faun's and know the Dryad's foot;
Olive and ivy and poplar dedicate,
And many a well-spring overwatched of these.
There now they rest; but me the king bade bear
Good tidings to rejoice this town and thee.
1360 Wherefore be glad, and all ye give much thanks,
For fallen is all the trouble of Calydon.

ALTHÆA

Laud ye the gods; for this they have given is good,
And what shall be they hide until their time.
Much good and somewhat grievous hast thou said,
And either well; but let all sad things be,
Till all have made before the prosperous gods
Burnt-offering, and poured out the floral wine.
Look fair, O gods, and favourable; for we
Praise you with no false heart or flattering mouth,
1370 Being merciful, but with pure souls and prayer.

HERALD

Thou hast prayed well; for whoso fears not these,
But once being prosperous waxes huge of heart,
Him shall some new thing unaware destroy.

CHORUS

O that I now, I too were
By deep wells and water-floods,
Streams of ancient hills, and where
All the wan green places bear
Blossoms cleaving to the sod,
Fruitless fruit, and grasses fair,
1380 Or such darkest ivy-buds
As divide thy yellow hair,
Bacchus, and their leaves that nod
Round thy fawnskin brush the bare
Snow-soft shoulders of a god;
There the year is sweet, and there
Earth is full of secret springs,
And the fervent rose-cheeked hours,
Those that marry dawn and noon,
There are sunless, there look pale
1390 In dim leaves and hidden air,
Pale as grass or latter flowers
Or the wild vine's wan wet rings
Full of dew beneath the moon,

And all day the nightingale
Sleeps, and all night sings;
There in cold remote recesses
That nor alien eyes assail,
Feet, nor imminence of wings,
Nor a wind nor any tune,
1400   Thou, O queen and holiest,
Flower the whitest of all things,
With reluctant lengthening tresses
And with sudden splendid breast
Save of maidens unbeholden,
There art wont to enter, there
Thy divine swift limbs and golden
Maiden growth of unbound hair,
Bathed in waters white,
Shine, and many a maid's by thee
1410   In moist woodland or the hilly
Flowerless brakes where wells abound
Out of all men's sight;
Or in lower pools that see
All their marges clothed all round
With the innumerable lily,
Whence the golden-girdled bee
Flits through flowering rush to fret
White or duskier violet,
Fair as those that in far years
1420   With their buds left luminous
And their little leaves made wet,
From the warmer dew of tears,
Mother's tears in extreme need,
Hid the limbs of Iamus,
Of thy brother's seed;
For his heart was piteous
Toward him, even as thine heart now
Pitiful toward us;
Thine, O goddess, turning hither
1430   A benignant blameless brow;
Seeing enough of evil done
And lives withered as leaves wither

In the blasting of the sun;
Seeing enough of hunters dead,
Ruin enough of all our year,
Herds and harvests slain and shed,
Herdsmen stricken many an one,
Fruits and flocks consumed together,
And great length of deadly days.
1440 Yet with reverent lips and fear
Turn we toward thee, turn and praise
For this lightening of clear weather
And prosperities begun.
For not seldom, when all air
As bright water without breath
Shines, and when men fear not, fate
Without thunder unaware
Breaks, and brings down death.
Joy with grief ye great gods give,
1450 Good with bad, and overbear
All the pride of us that live,
All the high estate,
As ye long since overbore,
As in old time long before,
Many a strong man and a great,
All that were.
But do thou, sweet, otherwise,
Having heed of all our prayer,
Taking note of all our sighs;
1460 We beseech thee by thy light,
By thy bow, and thy sweet eyes,
And the kingdom of the night,
Be thou favourable and fair;
By thine arrows and thy might
And Orion overthrown;
By the maiden thy delight,
By the indissoluble zone
And the sacred hair.

MESSENGER

Maidens, if ye will sing now, shift your song,
1470   Bow down, cry, wail for pity; is this a time
For singing? nay, for strewing of dust and ash,
Rent raiment, and for bruising of the breast.

CHORUS

What new thing wolf-like lurks behind thy words?
What snake's tongue in thy lips? what fire in the eyes?

MESSENGER

Bring me before the queen and I will speak.

CHORUS

Lo, she comes forth as from thank-offering made.

MESSENGER

A barren offering for a bitter gift.

ALTHÆA

What are these borne on branches, and the face
Covered? no mean men living, but now slain
1480   Such honour have they, if any dwell with death.

MESSENGER

Queen, thy twain brethren and thy mother's sons.

ALTHÆA

Lay down your dead till I behold their blood
If it be mine indeed, and I will weep.

MESSENGER

Weep if thou wilt, for these men shall no more.

ALTHÆA

O brethren, O my father's sons, of me
Well loved and well reputed, I should weep
Tears dearer than the dear blood drawn from you

But that I know you not uncomforted,
Sleeping no shameful sleep, however slain,
1490 For my son surely hath avenged you dead.

MESSENGER
Nay, should thine own seed slay himself, O queen?

ALTHÆA
Thy double word brings forth a double death.

MESSENGER
Know this then singly, by one hand they fell.

ALTHÆA
What mutterest thou with thine ambiguous mouth?

MESSENGER
Slain by thy son's hand; is that saying so hard?

ALTHÆA
Our time is come upon us: it is here.

CHORUS
O miserable, and spoiled at thine own hand.

ALTHÆA
Wert thou not called Meleager from this womb?

CHORUS
A grievous huntsman hath it bred to thee.

ALTHÆA
1500 Wert thou born fire, and shalt thou not devour?

CHORUS
The fire thou madest, will it consume even thee?

ALTHÆA
My dreams are fallen upon me; burn thou too.

CHORUS
Not without God are visions born and die.

ALTHÆA
The gods are many about me; I am one.

CHORUS
She groans as men wrestling with heavier gods.

ALTHÆA
They rend me, they divide me, they destroy.

CHORUS
Or one labouring in travail of strange births.

ALTHÆA
They are strong, they are strong; I am broken, and these
        prevail.

CHORUS
The god is great against her; she will die.

ALTHÆA
1510   Yea, but not now; for my heart too is great.
I would I were not here in sight of the sun.
But thou, speak all thou sawest, and I will die.

MESSENGER
O queen, for queenlike hast thou borne thyself,
A little word may hold so great mischance.
For in division of the sanguine spoil
These men thy brethren wrangling bade yield up
The boar's head and the horror of the hide
That this might stand a wonder in Calydon,
Hallowed; and some drew toward them; but thy son
1520   With great hands grasping all that weight of hair
Cast down the dead heap clanging and collapsed
At female feet, saying This thy spoil not mine,
Maiden, thine own hand for thyself hath reaped,

And all this praise God gives thee: she thereat
Laughed, as when dawn touches the sacred night
The sky sees laugh and redden and divide
Dim lips and eyelids virgin of the sun,
Hers, and the warm slow breasts of morning heave,
Fruitful, and flushed with flame from lamp-lit hours,
1530 And maiden undulation of clear hair
Colour the clouds; so laughed she from pure heart,
Lit with a low blush to the braided hair,
And rose-coloured and cold like very dawn,
Golden and godlike, chastely with chaste lips,
A faint grave laugh; and all they held their peace,
And she passed by them. Then one cried Lo now,
Shall not the Arcadian shoot out lips at us,
Saying all we were despoiled by this one girl?
And all they rode against her violently
1540 And cast the fresh crown from her hair, and now
They had rent her spoil away, dishonouring her,
Save that Meleager, as a tame lion chafed,
Bore on them, broke them, and as fire cleaves wood
So clove and drove them, smitten in twain; but she
Smote not nor heaved up hand; and this man first,
Plexippus, crying out This for love's sake, sweet,
Drove at Meleager, who with spear straightening
Pierced his cheek through; then Toxeus made for him,
Dumb, but his spear spake; vain and violent words.
1550 Fruitless; for him too stricken through both sides
The earth felt falling, and his horse's foam
Blanched thy son's face, his slayer; and these being slain,
None moved nor spake; but Œneus bade bear hence
These made of heaven infatuate in their deaths,
Foolish; for these would baffle fate, and fell.
And they passed on, and all men honoured her,
Being honourable, as one revered of heaven.

ALTHÆA

What say you, women? is all this not well done?

CHORUS
No man doth well but God hath part in him.

ALTHÆA
1560 But no part here; for these my brethren born
Ye have no part in, these ye know not of
As I that was their sister, a sacrifice
Slain in their slaying. I would I had died for these;
For this man dead walked with me, child by child,
And made a weak staff for my feebler feet
With his own tender wrist and hand, and held
And led me softly and shewed me gold and steel
And shining shapes of mirror and bright crown
And all things fair; and threw light spears, and brought
1570 Young hounds to huddle at my feet and thrust
Tame heads against my little maiden breasts
And please me with great eyes; and those days went
And these are bitter and I a barren queen
And sister miserable, a grievous thing
And mother of many curses; and she too,
My sister Leda, sitting overseas
With fair fruits round her, and her faultless lord,
Shall curse me, saying A sorrow and not a son,
Sister, thou barest, even a burning fire,
1580 A brand consuming thine own soul and me.
But ye now, sons of Thestius, make good cheer,
For ye shall have such wood to funeral fire
As no king hath; and flame that once burnt down
Oil shall not quicken or breath relume or wine
Refresh again; much costlier than fine gold,
And more than many lives of wandering men.

CHORUS
O queen, thou hast yet with thee love-worthy things,
Thine husband, and the great strength of thy son.

ALTHÆA

Who shall get brothers for me while I live?
1590   Who bear them? who bring forth in lieu of these?
Are not our fathers and our brethren one,
And no man like them? are not mine here slain?
Have we not hung together, he and I,
Flowerwise feeding as the feeding bees,
With mother-milk for honey? and this man too,
Dead, with my son's spear thrust between his sides,
Hath he not seen us, later born than he,
Laugh with lips filled, and laughed again for love?
There were no sons then in the world, nor spears,
1600   Nor deadly births of women; but the gods
Allowed us, and our days were clear of these.
I would I had died unwedded, and brought forth
No swords to vex the world; for these that spake
Sweet words long since and loved me will not speak
Nor love nor look upon me; and all my life
I shall not hear nor see them living men.
But I too living, how shall I now live?
What life shall this be with my son, to know
What hath been and desire what will not be,
1610   Look for dead eyes and listen for dead lips,
And kill mine own heart with remembering them,
And with those eyes that see their slayer alive
Weep, and wring hands that clasp him by the hand?
How shall I bear my dreams of them, to hear
False voices, feel the kisses of false mouths
And footless sound of perished feet, and then
Wake and hear only it may be their own hounds
Whine masterless in miserable sleep,
And see their boar-spears and their beds and seats
1620   And all the gear and housings of their lives
And not the men? shall hounds and horses mourn,
Pine with strange eyes, and prick up hungry ears,
Famish and fail at heart for their dear lords,
And I not heed at all? and those blind things
Fall off from life for love's sake, and I live?
Surely some death is better than some life,

Better one death for him and these and me
For if the gods had slain them it may be
I had endured it; if they had fallen by war
1630 Or by the nets and knives of privy death
And by hired hands while sleeping, this thing too
I had set my soul to suffer; or this hunt,
Had this despatched them under tusk or tooth
Torn, sanguine, trodden, broken; for all deaths
Or honourable or with facile feet avenged
And hands of swift gods following, all save this,
Are bearable; but not for their sweet land
Fighting, but not a sacrifice, lo these
Dead; for I had not then shed all mine heart
1640 Out at mine eyes: then either with good speed,
Being just, I had slain their slayer atoningly,
Or strewn with flowers their fire and on their tombs
Hung crowns, and over them a song, and seen
Their praise outflame their ashes: for all men,
All maidens, had come thither, and from pure lips
Shed songs upon them, from heroic eyes
Tears; and their death had been a deathless life;
But now, by no man hired nor alien sword,
By their own kindred are they fallen, in peace,
1650 After much peril, friendless among friends,
By hateful hands they loved; and how shall mine
Touch these returning red and not from war,
These fatal from the vintage of men's veins,
Dead men my brethren? how shall these wash off
No festal stains of undelightful wine,
How mix the blood, my blood on them, with me,
Holding mine hand? or how shall I say, son,
That am no sister? but by night and day
Shall we not sit and hate each other, and think
1660 Things hate-worthy? not live with shamefast eyes,
Brow-beaten, treading soft with fearful feet,
Each unupbraided, each without rebuke
Convicted, and without a word reviled
Each of another? and I shall let thee live
And see thee strong and hear men for thy sake

Praise me, but these thou wouldest not let live
No man shall praise for ever? these shall lie
Dead, unbeloved, unholpen, all through thee?
Sweet were they toward me living, and mine heart
1670 Desired them, but was then well satisfied,
That now is as men hungered; and these dead
I shall want always to the day I die.
For all things else and all men may renew;
Yea, son for son the gods may give and take,
But never a brother or sister any more.

CHORUS
Nay, for the son lies close about thine heart,
Full of thy milk, warm from thy womb, and drains
Life and the blood of life and all thy fruit,
Eats thee and drinks thee as who breaks bread and eats,
1680 Treads wine and drinks, thyself, a sect of thee;
And if he feed not, shall not thy flesh faint?
Or drink not, are not thy lips dead for thirst?
This thing moves more than all things, even thy son,
That thou cleave to him; and he shall honour thee,
Thy womb that bare him and the breasts he knew,
Reverencing most for thy sake all his gods.

ALTHÆA
But these the gods too gave me, and these my son,
Not reverencing his gods nor mine own heart
Nor the old sweet years nor all venerable things,
1690 But cruel, and in his ravin like a beast,
Hath taken away to slay them: yea, and she
She the strange woman, she the flower, the sword,
Red from spilt blood, a mortal flower to men,
Adorable, detestable – even she
Saw with strange eyes and with strange lips rejoiced,
Seeing these mine own slain of mine own, and me
Made miserable above all miseries made,
A grief among all women in the world,
A name to be washed out with all men's tears.

CHORUS

1700 Strengthen thy spirit; is this not also a god,
Chance, and the wheel of all necessities?
Hard things have fallen upon us from harsh gods,
Whom lest worse hap rebuke we not for these.

ALTHÆA

My spirit is strong against itself, and I
For these things' sake cry out on mine own soul
That it endures outrage, and dolorous days,
And life, and this inexpiable impotence.
Weak am I, weak and shameful; my breath drawn
Shames me, and monstrous things and violent gods.

1710 What shall atone? what heal me? what bring back
Strength to the foot, light to the face? what herb
Assuage me? what restore me? what release?
What strange thing eaten or drunken, O great gods,
Make me as you or as the beasts that feed,
Slay and divide and cherish their own hearts?
For these ye show us; and we less than these
Have not wherewith to live as all these things
Which all their lives fare after their own kind
As who doth well rejoicing; but we ill,

1720 Weeping or laughing, we whom eyesight fails,
Knowledge and light of face and perfect heart,
And hands we lack, and wit; and all our days
Sin, and have hunger, and die infatuated.
For madness have ye given us and not health,
And sins whereof we know not; and for these
Death, and sudden destruction unaware.
What shall we say now? what thing comes of us?

CHORUS

Alas, for all this all men undergo.

ALTHÆA

Wherefore I will not that these twain, O gods,
1730 Die as a dog dies, eaten of creeping things,
Abominable, a loathing; but though dead

Shall they have honour and such funereal flame
As strews men's ashes in their enemies' face
And blinds their eyes who hate them: lest men say,
'Low how they lie, and living had great kin,
And none of these hath pity of them, and none
Regards them lying, and none is wrung at heart,
None moved in spirit for them, naked and slain,
Abhorred, abased, and no tears comfort them:'
1740   And in the dark this grieve Eurythemis,
Hearing how these her sons come down to her
Unburied, unavenged, as kinless men,
And had a queen their sister. That were shame
Worse than this grief. Yet how to atone at all
I know not; seeing the love of my born son,
A new-made mother's new-born love, that grows
From the soft child to the strong man, now soft
Now strong as either, and still one sole same love,
Strives with me, no light thing to strive withal;
1750   This love is deep, and natural to man's blood,
And ineffaceable with many tears.
Yet shall not these rebuke me though I die,
Nor she in that waste world with all her dead,
My mother, among the pale flocks fallen as leaves,
Folds of dead people, and alien from the sun;
Nor lack some bitter comfort, some poor praise,
Being queen, to have borne her daughter like a queen,
Righteous; and though mine own fire burn me too,
She shall have honour and these her sons, though dead.
1760   But all the gods will, all they do, and we
Not all we would, yet somewhat; and one choice
We have, to live and do just deeds and die.

CHORUS
Terrible words she communes with, and turns
Swift fiery eyes in doubt against herself,
And murmurs as who talks in dreams with death.

ALTHÆA

For the unjust also dieth, and him all men
Hate, and himself abhors the unrighteousness,
And seeth his own dishonour intolerable.
But I being just, doing right upon myself,
1770 Slay mine own soul, and no man born shames me.
For none constrains nor shall rebuke, being done,
What none compelled me doing; thus these things fare.
Ah, ah, that such things should so fare; ah me,
That I am found to do them and endure,
Chosen and constrained to choose, and bear myself
Mine own wound through mine own flesh to the heart
Violently stricken, a spoiler and a spoil,
A ruin ruinous, fallen on mine own son.
Ah, ah, for me too as for these; alas,
1780 For that is done that shall be, and mine hand
Full of the deed, and full of blood mine eyes,
That shall see never nor touch anything
Save blood unstanched and fire unquenchable.

CHORUS

What wilt thou do? what ails thee? for the house
Shakes ruinously; wilt thou bring fire for it?

ALTHÆA

Fire in the roofs, and on the lintels fire.
Lo ye, who stand and weave, between the doors,
There; and blood drips from hand and thread, and stains
Threshold and raiment and me passing in
1790 Flecked with the sudden sanguine drops of death.

CHORUS

Alas that time is stronger than strong men,
Fate than all gods: and these are fallen on us.

ALTHÆA

A little since and I was glad; and now
I never shall be glad or sad again.

CHORUS
Between two joys a grief grows unaware.

ALTHÆA
A little while and I shall laugh; and then
I shall weep never and laugh not any more.

CHORUS
What shall be said? for words are thorns to grief.
Withhold thyself a little and fear the gods.

ALTHÆA
1800   Fear died when these were slain; and I am as dead,
And fear is of the living; these fear none.

CHORUS
Have pity upon all people for their sake.

ALTHÆA
It is done now; shall I put back my day?

CHORUS
An end is come, an end; this is of God.

ALTHÆA
I am fire, and burn myself; keep clear of fire.

CHORUS
The house is broken, is broken; it shall not stand.

ALTHÆA
Woe, woe for him that breaketh; and a rod
Smote it of old, and now the axe is here.

CHORUS
     Not as with sundering of the earth
1810   Nor as with cleaving of the sea
     Nor fierce foreshadowings of a birth
        Nor flying dreams of death to be

Nor loosening of the large world's girth
And quickening of the body of night,
  And sound of thunder in men's ears
And fire of lightning in men's sight,
  Fate, mother of desires and fears,
  Bore unto men the law of tears;
But sudden, an unfathered flame,
1820   And broken out of night, she shone,
She, without body, without name,
  In days forgotten and foregone;
And heaven rang round her as she came
Like smitten cymbals, and lay bare;
  Clouds and great stars, thunders and snows,
The blue sad fields and folds of air,
  The life that breathes, the life that grows,
  All wind, all fire, that burns or blows,
Even all these knew her: for she is great;
1830   The daughter of doom, the mother of death,
The sister of sorrow; a lifelong weight
  That no man's finger lighteneth,
Nor any god can lighten fate;
A landmark seen across the way
  Where one race treads as the other trod;
An evil sceptre, an evil stay,
  Wrought for a staff, wrought for a rod,
  The bitter jealousy of God.

For death is deep as the sea,
1840   And fate as the waves thereof.
Shall the waves take pity on thee
  Or the southwind offer thee love?
Wilt thou take the night for thy day
Or the darkness for light on thy way,
  Till thou say in thine heart Enough?
Behold, thou art over fair, thou art over wise;
The sweetness of spring in thine hair, and the light in thine
        eyes.
The light of the spring in thine eyes, and the sound in thine
        ears;

Yet thine heart shall wax heavy with sighs and thine eyelids
    with tears.

1850 Wilt thou cover thine hair with gold, and with silver thy
    feet?

Hast thou taken the purple to fold thee, and made thy
    mouth sweet?

Behold, when thy face is made bare, he that loved thee shall
    hate;

Thy face shall be no more fair at the fall of thy fate.

For thy life shall fall as a leaf and be shed as the rain;

And the veil of thine head shall be grief; and the crown shall
    be pain.

ALTHÆA

Ho, ye that wail, and ye that sing, make way
Till I be come among you. Hide your tears,
Ye little weepers, and your laughing lips,
Ye laughers for a little; lo mine eyes
1860 That outweep heaven at rainiest, and my mouth
That laughs as gods laugh at us. Fate's are we,
Yet fate is ours a breathing-space; yea, mine,
Fate is made mine for ever; he is my son,
My bedfellow, my brother. You strong gods,
Give place unto me; I am as any of you,
To give life and to take life. Thou, old earth,
That hast made man and unmade; thou whose mouth
Looks red from the eaten fruits of thine own womb;
Behold me with what lips upon what food
1870 I feed and fill my body; even with flesh
Made of my body. Lo, the fire I lit
I burn with fire to quench it; yea, with flame
I burn up even the dust and ash thereof.

CHORUS

Woman, what fire is this thou burnest with?

ALTHÆA

Yea to the bone, yea to the blood and all.

CHORUS
For this thy face and hair are as one fire.

ALTHÆA
A tongue that licks and beats upon the dust.

CHORUS
And in thine eyes are hollow light and heat.

ALTHÆA
Of flame not fed with hand or frankincense.

CHORUS
1880   I fear thee for the trembling of thine eyes.

ALTHÆA
Neither with love they tremble nor for fear.

CHORUS
And thy mouth shuddering like a shot bird.

ALTHÆA
Not as the bride's mouth when man kisses it.

CHORUS
Nay, but what thing is this thing thou hast done?

ALTHÆA
Look, I am silent, speak your eyes for me.

CHORUS
I see a faint fire lightening from the hall.

ALTHÆA
Gaze, stretch your eyes, strain till the lids drop off.

CHORUS
Flushed pillars down the flickering vestibule.

ALTHÆA

Stretch with your necks like birds: cry, chirp as they.

CHORUS

1890   And a long brand that blackens: and white dust.

ALTHÆA

O children, what is this ye see? your eyes
Are blinder than night's face at fall of moon.
That is my son, my flesh, my fruit of life,
My travail, and the year's weight of my womb,
Meleager, a fire enkindled of mine hands
And of mine hands extinguished; this is he.

CHORUS

O gods, what word has flown out at thy mouth?

ALTHÆA

I did this and I say this and I die.

CHORUS

Death stands upon the doorway of thy lips
1900   And in thy mouth has death set up his house.

ALTHÆA

O death, a little, a little while, sweet death,
Until I see the brand burnt down and die.

CHORUS

She reels as any reed under the wind,
And cleaves unto the ground with staggering feet.

ALTHÆA

Girls, one thing will I say and hold my peace.
I that did this will weep not nor cry out,
Cry ye and weep: I will not call on gods,
Call ye on them; I will not pity man,
Shew ye your pity. I know not if I live;
1910   Save that I feel the fire upon my face

And on my cheek the burning of a brand.
Yea the smoke bites me, yea I drink the steam
With nostril and with eyelid and with lip
Insatiate and intolerant; and mine hands
Burn, and fire feeds upon mine eyes; I reel
As one made drunk with living, whence he draws
Drunken delight; yet I, though mad for joy,
Loathe my long living and am waxen red
As with the shadow of shed blood; behold,
1920 I am kindled with the flames that fade in him,
I am swollen with subsiding of his veins,
I am flooded with his ebbing; my lit eyes
Flame with the falling fire that leaves his lids
Bloodless; my cheek is luminous with blood
Because his face is ashen. Yet, O child,
Son, first-born, fairest – O sweet mouth, sweet eyes,
That drew my life out through my suckling breast,
That shone and clove mine heart through – O soft knees
Clinging, O tender treadings of soft feet,
1930 Cheeks warm with little kissings – O child, child,
What have we made each other? Lo, I felt
Thy weight cleave to me, a burden of beauty, O son,
Thy cradled brows and loveliest loving lips,
The floral hair, the little lightening eyes,
And all thy goodly glory; with mine hands
Delicately I fed thee, with my tongue
Tenderly spake, saying, Verily in God's time,
For all the little likeness of thy limbs,
Son, I shall make thee a kingly man to fight,
1940 A lordly leader; and hear before I die,
'She bore the goodliest sword of all the world.'
Oh! oh! For all my life turns round on me;
I am severed from myself, my name is gone,
My name that was a healing, it is changed,
My name is a consuming. From this time,
Though mine eyes reach to the end of all these things,
My lips shall not unfasten till I die.

SEMICHORUS

She has filled with sighing the city,
    And the ways thereof with tears;
1950   She arose, she girdled her sides,
    She set her face as a bride's;
    She wept, and she had no pity;
        Trembled, and felt no fears.

SEMICHORUS

Her eyes were clear as the sun,
    Her brows were fresh as the day;
She girdled herself with gold,
Her robes were manifold;
But the days of her worship are done,
    Her praise is taken away.

SEMICHORUS

1960   For she set her hand to the fire,
    With her mouth she kindled the same;
As the mouth of a flute-player,
So was the mouth of her;
With the might of her strong desire
    She blew the breath of the flame.

SEMICHORUS

She set her hand to the wood,
    She took the fire in her hand;
As one who is nigh to death,
She panted with strange breath;
1970   She opened her lips unto blood,
    She breathed and kindled the brand.

SEMICHORUS

As a wood-dove newly shot,
    She sobbed and lifted her breast;
She sighed and covered her eyes,
Filling her lips with sighs;
She sighed, she withdrew herself not,
    She refrained not, taking not rest;

SEMICHORUS

But as the wind which is drouth,
    And as the air which is death,
As storm that severeth ships,
Her breath severing her lips,
The breath came forth of her mouth
    And the fire came forth of her breath.

SECOND MESSENGER

Queen, and you maidens, there is come on us
A thing more deadly than the face of death;
Meleager the good lord is as one slain.

SEMICHORUS

Without sword, without sword is he stricken;
    Slain, and slain without hand.

SECOND MESSENGER

For as keen ice divided of the sun
His limbs divide, and as thawed snow the flesh
Thaws from off all his body to the hair.

SEMICHORUS

He wastes as the embers quicken;
    With the brand he fades as a brand.

SECOND MESSENGER

Even while they sang and all drew hither and he
Lifted both hands to crown the Arcadian's hair
And fix the looser leaves, both hands fell down.

SEMICHORUS

With rending of cheek and of hair
    Lament ye, mourn for him, weep.

SECOND MESSENGER

Straightway the crown slid off and smote on earth,
First fallen; and he, grasping his own hair, groaned
And cast his raiment round his face and fell.

SEMICHORUS
> Alas for visions that were,
> > And soothsayings spoken in sleep.

SECOND MESSENGER
But the king twitched his reins in and leapt down
And caught him, crying out twice 'O child' and thrice,
So that men's eyelids thickened with their tears.

SEMICHORUS
> Lament with a long lamentation,
> > Cry, for an end is at hand.

SECOND MESSENGER
O son, he said, son, lift thine eyes, draw breath,
2010 Pity me; but Meleager with sharp lips
Gasped, and his face waxed like as sunburnt grass.

SEMICHORUS
> Cry aloud, O thou kingdom, O nation,
> > O stricken, a ruinous land.

SECOND MESSENGER
Whereat king Œneus, straightening feeble knees,
With feeble hands heaved up a lessening weight,
And laid him sadly in strange hands, and wept.

SEMICHORUS
> Thou art smitten, her lord, her desire,
> > Thy dear blood wasted as rain.

SECOND MESSENGER
And they with tears and rendings of the beard
2020 Bear hither a breathing body, wept upon
And lightening at each footfall, sick to death.

SEMICHORUS
> Thou madest thy sword as a fire,
> > With fire for a sword thou art slain.

SECOND MESSENGER

And lo, the feast turned funeral, and the crowns
Fallen; and the huntress and the hunter trapped;
And weeping and changed faces and veiled hair.

MELEAGER

    Let your hands meet
      Round the weight of my head;
    Lift ye my feet
2030   As the feet of the dead;
For the flesh of my body is molten, the limbs of it molten as
        lead.

CHORUS

    O thy luminous face,
      Thine imperious eyes!
    O the grief, O the grace,
      As of day when it dies!
Who is this bending over thee, lord, with tears and
        suppression of sighs?

MELEAGER

    Is a bride so fair?
      Is a maid so meek?
    With unchapleted hair,
2040   With unfilleted cheek,
Atalanta, the pure among women, whose name is as blessing
        to speak.

ATALANTA

    I would that with feet
      Unsandalled, unshod,
    Overbold, overfleet,
      I had swum not nor trod
From Arcadia to Calydon northward, a blast of the envy of
        God.

MELEAGER

Unto each man his fate;
Unto each as he saith
In whose fingers the weight
2050   Of the world is as breath;
Yet I would that in clamour of battle mine hands had laid
hold upon death.

CHORUS

Not with cleaving of shields
And their clash in thine ear,
When the lord of fought fields
Breaketh spearshaft from spear,
Thou art broken, our lord, thou art broken, with travail and
labour and fear.

MELEAGER

Would God he had found me
Beneath fresh boughs!
Would God he had bound me
2060   Unawares in mine house,
With light in mine eyes, and songs in my lips, and a crown
on my brows!

CHORUS

Whence art thou sent from us?
Whither thy goal?
How art thou rent from us,
Thou that wert whole,
As with severing of eyelids and eyes, as with sundering of
body and soul!

MELEAGER

My heart is within me
As an ash in the fire;
Whosoever hath seen me,
2070   Without lute, without lyre,
Shall sing of me grievous things, even things that were ill to
desire.

CHORUS

> Who shall raise thee
>> From the house of the dead?
> Or what man praise thee
>> That thy praise may be said?
> Alas thy beauty! alas thy body! alas thine head!

MELEAGER

> But thou, O mother,
>> The dreamer of dreams,
> Wilt thou bring forth another
2080 >> To feel the sun's beams
> When I move among shadows a shadow, and wail by
>> impassable streams?

ŒNEUS

> What thing wilt thou leave me
>> Now this thing is done?
> A man wilt thou give me,
>> A son for my son,
> For the light of mine eyes, the desire of my life, the
>> desirable one?

CHORUS

> Thou wert glad above others,
>> Yea, fair beyond word;
> Thou wert glad among mothers;
2090 >> For each man that heard
> Of thee, praise there was added unto thee, as wings to the
>> feet of a bird.

ŒNEUS

> Who shall give back
>> Thy face of old years
> With travail made black,
>> Grown grey among fears
> Mother of sorrow, mother of cursing, mother of tears?

MELEAGER

   Though thou art as fire
    Fed with fuel in vain,
   My delight, my desire,
    Is more chaste than the rain,
More pure than the dewfall, more holy than stars are that
    live without stain.

ATALANTA

   I would that as water
    My life's blood had thawn,
   Or as winter's wan daughter
    Leaves lowland and lawn
Spring-stricken, or ever mine eyes had beheld thee made
    dark in thy dawn.

CHORUS

   When thou dravest the men
    Of the chosen of Thrace,
   None turned him again
    Nor endured he thy face
Clothed round with the blush of the battle, with light from a
    terrible place.

ŒNEUS

   Thou shouldst die as he dies
    For whom none sheddeth tears;
   Filling thine eyes
    And fulfilling thine ears
With the brilliance of battle, the bloom and the beauty, the
    splendour of spears.

CHORUS

   In the ears of the world
    It is sung, it is told,
   And the light thereof hurled
    And the noise thereof rolled
From the Acroceraunian snow to the ford of the fleece of
    gold.

MELEAGER

    Would God ye could carry me
        Forth of all these;
    Heap sand and bury me
        By the Chersonese
Where the thundering Bosphorus answers the thunder of
            Pontic seas.

ŒNEUS

    Dost thou mock at our praise
        And the singing begun
    And the men of strange days
2130   Praising my son
In the folds of the hills of home, high places of Calydon?

MELEAGER

    For the dead man no home is;
        Ah, better to be
    What the flower of the foam is
        In fields of the sea,
That the sea-waves might be as my raiment, the gulf-stream
            a garment for me.

CHORUS

    Who shall seek thee and bring
        And restore thee thy day,
    When the dove dipt her wing
2140   And the oars won their way
Where the narrowing Symplegades whitened the straits of
            Propontis with spray?

MELEAGER

    Will ye crown me my tomb
        Or exalt me my name,
    Now my spirits consume,
        Now my flesh is a flame?
Let the sea slake it once, and men speak of me sleeping to
            praise me or shame.

CHORUS

> Turn back now, turn thee,
>> As who turns him to wake;
> Though the life in thee burn thee,
2150 >> Couldst thou bathe it and slake
> Where the sea-ridge of Helle hangs heavier, and east upon
>> west waters break?

MELEAGER

> Would the winds blow me back
>> Or the waves hurl me home?
> Ah, to touch in the track
>> Where the pine learnt to roam
> Cold girdles and crowns of the sea-gods, cool blossoms of
>> water and foam!

CHORUS

> The gods may release
>> That they made fast;
> Thy soul shall have ease
2160 >> In thy limbs at the last;
> But what shall they give thee for life, sweet life that is
>> overpast?

MELEAGER

> Not the life of men's veins,
>> Not of flesh that conceives;
> But the grace that remains,
>> The fair beauty that cleaves
> To the life of the rains in the grasses, the life of the dews on
>> the leaves.

CHORUS

> Thou wert helmsman and chief;
>> Wilt thou turn in an hour,
> Thy limbs to the leaf,
2170 >> Thy face to the flower,
> Thy blood to the water, thy soul to the gods who divide and
>> devour?

MELEAGER

    The years are hungry,
      They wail all their days;
    The gods wax angry,
      And weary of praise;
And who shall bridle their lips? and who shall straiten their
        ways?

CHORUS

    The gods guard over us
      With sword and with rod;
    Weaving shadow to cover us,
2180   Heaping the sod,
That law may fulfil herself wholly, to darken man's face
      before God.

MELEAGER

O holy head of Œneus, lo thy son
Guiltless, yet red from alien guilt, yet foul
With kinship of contaminated lives,
Lo, for their blood I die; and mine own blood
For bloodshedding of mine is mixed therewith,
That death may not discern me from my kin.
Yet with clean heart I die and faultless hand,
Not shamefully; thou therefore of thy love
2190 Salute me, and bid fare among the dead
Well, as the dead fare; for the best man dead
Fares sadly; nathless I now faring well
Pass without fear where nothing is to fear
Having thy love about me and thy goodwill,
O father, among dark places and men dead.

ŒNEUS

Child, I salute thee with sad heart and tears,
And bid thee comfort, being a perfect man
In fight, and honourable in the house of peace.
The gods give thee fair wage and dues of death,
2200 And me brief days and ways to come at thee.

MELEAGER

Pray thou thy days be long before thy death,
And full of ease and kingdom; seeing in death
There is no comfort and none aftergrowth,
Nor shall one thence look up and see day's dawn
Nor light upon the land whither I go.
Live thou and take thy fill of days and die
When thy day comes; and make not much of death
Lest ere thy day thou reap an evil thing.
Thou too, the bitter mother and mother-plague
2210 Of this my weary body – thou too, queen,
The source and end, the sower and the scythe,
The rain that ripens and the drought that slays,
The sand that swallows and the spring that feeds,
To make me and unmake me – thou, I say,
Althæa, since my father's ploughshare, drawn
Through fatal seedland of a female field,
Furrowed thy body, whence a wheaten ear
Strong from the sun and fragrant from the rains
I sprang and cleft the closure of thy womb,
2220 Mother, I dying with unforgetful tongue
Hail thee as holy and worship thee as just
Who art unjust and unholy; and with my knees
Would worship, but thy fire and subtlety,
Dissundering them, devour me; for these limbs
Are as light dust and crumblings from mine urn
Before the fire has touched them; and my face
As a dead leaf or dead foot's mark on snow,
And all this body a broken barren tree
That was so strong, and all this flower of life
2230 Disbranched and desecrated miserably,
And minished all that god-like muscle and might
And lesser than a man's: for all my veins
Fail me, and all mine ashen life burns down.
I would thou hadst let me live; but gods averse,
But fortune, and the fiery feet of change,
And time, these would not, these tread out my life,
These and not thou; me too thou hast loved, and I
Thee; but this death was mixed with all my life,

Mine end with my beginning: and this law,
2240 This only, slays me, and not my mother at all.
And let no brother or sister grieve too sore,
Nor melt their hearts out on me with their tears,
Since extreme love and sorrowing overmuch
Vex the great gods, and overloving men
Slay and are slain for love's sake; and this house
Shall bear much better children; why should these
Weep? but in patience let them live their lives
And mine pass by forgotten: thou alone,
Mother, thou sole and only, thou not these,
2250 Keep me in mind a little when I die
Because I was thy first-born; let thy soul
Pity me, pity even me gone hence and dead,
Though thou wert wroth, and though thou bear again
Much happier sons, and all men later born
Exceedingly excel me; yet do thou
Forget not, nor think shame; I was thy son.
Time was I did not shame thee; and time was
I thought to live and make thee honourable
With deeds as great as these men's; but they live,
2260 These, and I die; and what thing should have been
Surely I know not; yet I charge thee, seeing
I am dead already, love me not the less,
Me, O my mother; I charge thee by these gods,
My father's, and that holier breast of thine,
By these that see me dying, and that which nursed,
Love me not less, thy first-born: though grief come,
Grief only, of me, and of all these great joy,
And shall come always to thee; for thou knowest,
O mother, O breasts that bare me, for ye know,
2270 O sweet head of my mother, sacred eyes,
Ye know my soul albeit I sinned, ye know
Albeit I kneel not neither touch thy knees,
But with my lips I kneel, and with my heart
I fall about thy feet and worship thee.
And ye farewell now, all my friends; and ye,
Kinsmen, much younger and glorious more than I,
Sons of my mother's sister; and all farewell

That were in Colchis with me, and bare down
The waves and wars that met us: and though times
2280 Change, and though now I be not anything,
Forget not me among you, what I did
In my good time; for even by all those days,
Those days and this, and your own living souls,
And by the light and luck of you that live,
And by this miserable spoil, and me
Dying, I beseech you, let my name not die.
But thou, dear, touch me with thy rose-like hands,
And fasten up mine eyelids with thy mouth,
A bitter kiss; and grasp me with thine arms,
2290 Printing with heavy lips my light waste flesh,
Made light and thin by heavy-handed fate,
And with thine holy maiden eyes drop dew,
Drop tears for dew upon me who am dead,
Me who have loved thee; seeing without sin done
I am gone down to the empty weary house
Where no flesh is nor beauty nor swift eyes
Nor sound of mouth nor might of hands and feet.
But thou, dear, hide my body with thy veil,
And with thy raiment cover foot and head,
2300 And stretch thyself upon me and touch hands
With hands and lips with lips: be pitiful
As thou art maiden perfect; let no man
Defile me to despise me, saying, This man
Died woman-wise, a woman's offering, slain
Through female fingers in his woof of life,
Dishonourable; for thou hast honoured me.
And now for God's sake kiss me once and twice
And let me go; for the night gathers me,
And in the night shall no man gather fruit.

ATALANTA

2310 Hail thou: but I with heavy face and feet
Turn homeward and am gone out of thine eyes.

CHORUS

Who shall contend with his lords
  Or cross them or do them wrong?
Who shall bind them as with cords?
  Who shall tame them as with song?
Who shall smite them as with swords?
  For the hands of their kingdom are strong.

NOTES

POEMS AND BALLADS

A Ballad of Life and A Ballad of Death

Swinburne relished the most lurid accounts of Lucrezia Borgia's cruelty and sexual adventurousness, as in Victor Hugo's *Lucrèce Borgia* (1833), which he read at Eton, and Alexandre Dumas's *Crimes Célèbres* (1839–1842). He would also have known of Byron's theft of a strand of her hair and the poem by Landor which it inspired, 'On Seeing a Hair of Lucretia Borgia' (1825, 1846). In the early 1860s he had written part of a projected long story about Borgia; Randolph Hughes, who edited the fragment in 1942, sifts through the evidence for Swinburne's sources for that work. The two poems open *Poems and Ballads* with Swinburne's favourite *femme fatale* and, in addition, introduce the volume as a whole; the roses in the envoy to the first poem refer to the poems in the collection.

A central figure in the brilliant court at Ferrara, Borgia had received sophisticated verse in her praise (from Bembo and Ariosto among others). Swinburne's two poems are 'Italian *canzoni* of the exactest type', in the words of William Rossetti, who adds that they have taken 'the tinge which works of this class have assumed in Mr. Dante G. Rossetti's volume of translations *The Early Italian Poets* [1861]'. That is, they consist of several stanzas in a rhyme scheme which is unique to each poem, include both pentameter and trimeter lines, and conclude with an envoy. Rossetti's drawing of a woman playing a lute surrounded by three lecherous men, a work that evolved into his watercolour of Borgia, has also been adduced as an influence (cf. Virginia Surtees' *catalogue raisonné* of Dante Gabriel Rossetti's paintings and drawings, catalogue numbers 47 and 48).

The rhyme 'moon' and 'swoon' (lines 5–6, 'A Ballad of Life') occurs in Tennyson's 'Fatima' (1832), an adaptation of Sappho. For the blue eye-lids (line 8, 'A Ballad of Life') as a sign of either fatigue or pregnancy, see Leah Marcus, *Unediting the Renaissance*, 1996, pp. 5–17. The phrase 'whole soul' (line 65, 'A Ballad of Life') is common in Tennyson and Browning as well as in Swinburne; it occurs twice in 'Fatima'. 'Sendaline' (line 41, 'A Ballad of Death') is sendal, a thin rich silken material (the *OED* cites Swinburne alone for the form 'sendaline'). The phrase 'who knows not this' (cf. line 86, 'A Ballad of Death') appears in Edward Young's *Night Thoughts* (Night II, line 386) and Dante Gabriel Rossetti's translation of a sonnet by Bonaggiunta Urbiciani, da Lucca, 'Of Wisdom and Foresight' (1861).

The diction is frequently biblical: for example, 'righteous' (line 70, 'A Ballad of Life'), 'lift up thine eyes' (line 54, 'A Ballad of Death'), 'vesture' (line 79, 'A Ballad of Death'). 'Honeycomb', 'spikenard', and 'frankincense' (lines 64–7, 'A Ballad of Death') appear in the Song of Solomon. Swinburne's diction throughout the collection is influenced by the Authorized Version; I have usually given references only in cases of allusion. In 1876, Swinburne planned to 'subjoin in the *very smallest* capitals' the words 'In honorem D. Lucretiae Estensis Borgiae' and 'In obitum D. Lucretiae Estensis Borgiae' under the titles of the respective poems (Lang, 3, 200).

Some copies of the 1904 *Poems* print 'curled air' rather than 'curled hair' ('A Ballad of Death', line 36).

Laus Veneris

The 'Praise of Venus' is Swinburne's adaptation of the Tannhäuser legend, which emerged shortly after the time of the minnesinger's death (*c.* 1270) in an anonymous ballad that tells the story of the knight who had been living in Venus Mountain but who, sated with pleasure, feels remorse and travels to Rome in order to obtain absolution. The pope, leaning on a dry dead staff, tells him that it will sprout leaves before the poet receive God's grace. Swinburne's fictitious French epigraph takes up the story at this point:

Then he said weeping, Alas, too unhappy a man and a cursed sinner, I shall never see the mercy and pity of God. Now I shall go from here and hide myself within Mount Horsel [Venus Mountain], entreating my sweet lady Venus of her favour and loving mercy, since for her love I shall be damned to Hell for all eternity. This is the end of all my feats of arms and all my pretty songs. Alas, too beautiful was the face and the eyes of my lady, it was on an evil day that I saw them. Then he went away groaning and returned to her, and lived sadly there in great love with his lady. Afterward it happened that the pope one day saw fine red and white flowers and many leafy buds break forth from his staff, and in this way he saw all the bark become green again. Of which he was much afraid and moved, and he took great pity on this knight who had departed without hope like a man who is miserable and damned. Therefore he sent many messengers after him to bring him back, saying that he would have God's grace and good absolution for his great sin of love. But they never

saw him; for this poor knight remained forever beside Venus, the high strong
goddess, in the amorous mountainside.

> Book of the great wonders of love, written in Latin and
> French by Master Antoine Gaget. 1530.

The story was popular among German Romantic writers. Ludwig Tieck
introduced it in his story 'Der getreue Eckart und der Tannhäuser' (1799);
Swinburne may have read the translation Thomas Carlyle made in 1827.
The ballad itself became well known early in the century when it was
printed in a collection of folksongs in 1806 and retold later by Grimm;
Clemens Brentano, E. T. A. Hoffmann, Joseph von Eichendorff, Franz
Grillparzer, and others also made use of it. Heinrich Heine's poem 'Der
Tannhäuser. Eine Legende' (1847) was a source for Wagner's opera, which
Baudelaire defended in La Revue européenne after its first performance in
Paris in 1861. However, neither Wagner nor Baudelaire's comment were
direct sources for Swinburne; at most he could have read about the opera,
and he received Baudelaire's pamphlet only after he had written the poem.
(See, however, Anne Walder, Swinburne's Flowers of Evil, 1976, p. 88.)
Swinburne may have known William Morris's 'The Hill of Venus' (pub-
lished in 1870 in The Earthly Paradise but according to his daughter written
in the early sixties).

Clyde Hyder in 'Swinburne's Laus Veneris and the Tannhäuser Legend'
(PMLA, 45:4, December 1930, 1202–13) sorts out the different cases for
influences and sources, one of which he identifies as a translation of the
Tannhäuser ballad that appeared in the newspaper Once a Week on 17
August 1861. For Burne-Jones's paintings of the subject (the earliest
begun in 1861, the most famous painted in 1873–8) and their relation to
Swinburne, see Kirsten Powell, 'Burne-Jones, Swinburne, and Laus Ven-
eris' (in Pre-Raphaelitism and Medievalism in the Arts, ed. Liana Cheney,
1992). While visiting Fantin-Latour's studio in Paris in 1863, Swinburne
saw a sketch of the Tannhäuser in the Venusberg. J. W. Thomas in
Tannhäuser: Man and Legend (1974) provides information about
Tannhäuser, the legend, and its later uses.

The poem is a dramatic monologue written in the stanza Edward Fitz-
Gerald used to translate the Rubáiyát of Omar Khayyám (1859); Swinburne,
however, links pairs of stanzas by rhyming their third lines. In the poem,
Venus has survived into the Middle Ages, but her stature has been dimin-
ished; nonetheless, we have glimpses of her former power both in its
destructive aspect (lines 117–37, for example, include Adonis, the favourite
of Aphrodite, killed by a boar) and in her incarnation as Venus Anadyomene,
rising from the sea (lines 389–92).

Swinburne's vision of hell is indebted to Dante's second circle of hell,
reserved for lustful sinners. Helen, Cleopatra, and Semiramis in lines 193–

204 recall the sequence Semiramis, Cleopatra, and Helen in *Inferno* 5: 52–63. Swinburne's description of Semiramis draws loosely on Assyrian art, knowledge of which, thanks to Henry Layard and the British Museum, had entered both popular culture and works by Tennyson and Rossetti. The line immediately following the description of the lustful sinners in Swinburne, 'Yea, with red sin the faces of them shine' (line 205), is modelled on the line 'culpa rubet vultus meus' from 'Dies Irae', as Lafourcade points out.

'Great-chested' in line 204 does not appear in the *OED*, but 'deep-chested' occurs in Landor, Tennyson and Longfellow. For the 'long lights' of line 216, cf. the 'long light' of Tennyson's *The Princess* (1847; the song between Parts 3 and 4). 'Doubt' in line 252 means 'suspect', and 'teen' in that line means 'grief'. 'Slotwise' in line 267, for which the *OED* gives Swinburne as the first citation, is derived from 'slot', the track of an animal. 'Springe' and 'gin' in lines 271–2 are both snares, the latter in this case for men. 'Vair' in line 278 is fur from squirrel. The elder-tree of line 305 is the European *Sambucus nigra* and not the American *Sambucus canadensis*, which does not grow large. 'To save my soul alive' (line 331) resembles Dante Gabriel Rossetti's line 'To save his dear son's soul alive' in 'Sister Helen', line 192 (1853, 1857, 1870; see also his translation of Cavalcanti's sonnet to Pope Boniface VIII, 1861, line 13). It derives from Ezekiel 18:27. 'Wizard' in line 338 is an adjective meaning 'bewitched' or 'enchanted'. Lines 369–70 recall James Shirley's couplet 'Only the actions of the just / Smell sweet, and blossom in their dust', from one of his most famous lyrics, 'The glories of our blood and state', at the end of *The Contention of Ajax and Ulysses*.

'Explicit' in the closing formula is a medieval Latin word which came to be regarded as a verb in the third person singular, meaning 'here ends' (a book, piece, etc.). It was current until the sixteenth century.

See 'Notes on Poems and Reviews' (Appendix 1) for Swinburne's own discussion of the poem. William Empson discusses lines 49–56 in *Seven Types of Ambiguity*, 3rd ed. 1953, pp. 163–5.

There is a reproduction of the first four stanzas of a manuscript of 'Laus Veneris' in Wise's 1919 *Bibliography*.

Phædra

Euripides, Seneca and Racine wrote the major extant dramas about Hippolytus and Phaedra, but the combination of masochism and sexual aggressiveness in Swinburne's Phaedra is not derived from his models. Despite his contempt for Euripides and very limited esteem of Racine, he includes a discriminating comparison of *Hippolytus* and *Phèdre* in his essay on Philip Massinger (1889; reprinted in *Contemporaries of Shakespeare*, pp. 201–2).

Hippolytus, the son of Theseus and the Amazon Hippolyta (line 56), has been raised by Theseus's grandfather Pittheus (line 176) in Troezen, a town in the Peloponnese. Phaedra is the daughter of King Minos of Crete and Pasiphae (line 35; Pasiphae is the daughter of the sun, line 53). She is the wife of Theseus, who marries her after his most famous exploit: killing the minotaur, the offspring of Pasiphae by a handsome bull, and thus the half-brother of Phaedra (line 181). King Minos had regularly fed it a tribute of Athenian youth (cf. lines 179–81), but Theseus defeats it and escapes from the labyrinth that contained it with the help of Ariadne, Phaedra's sister; he leaves Crete with Ariadne but later abandons her and marries Phaedra. He rules in Athens but is obliged to move temporarily to Troezen, where Aphrodite, revenging herself on Hippolytus for his excessive devotion to Artemis, inspires Phaedra to love her stepson passionately. In most versions of the story, Theseus has been away from Troezen for a time (consulting an oracle or waiting for Heracles to release him from hell).

'Have' in line 5 is in the subjunctive mood. The comparison of grass and the colour of flesh (line 27) recalls Sappho (φαίνεταί μοι), and the periphrastic address to divinity in lines 29–30 is like Aeschylus, *Agamemnon*, lines 160–2. Line 47 echoes Christ's words 'Woman, what have I to do with thee?' (John 2:4). The evil born with all its teeth (line 73) recalls Richard III (see Shakespeare, *Henry VI, Part 3*, Act 5, Scene 6). 'Ate' (line 139) is the passionate derangement of the mind and senses that leads to ruin. Amathus (line 139), on Cyprus, is the site of a famous shrine to Aphrodite. 'Lies' (line 155) are strata or layers, masses that lie, according to the *OED*, which cites Swinburne's usage. The sea is hollow (line 165) when the troughs between waves are very deep.

Swinburne's note to line 97 signals that the next six lines are a translation of a fragment of *Niobe*, a lost play by Aeschylus:

> μόνος θεῶν γὰρ Θάνατος οὐ δώρων ἐρᾷ,
> οὔτ' ἄν τι θύων οὔτ' ἐπισπένδων ἄνοις,
> οὐ βωμός ἐστιν οὐδὲ παιωνίζεται·
> μόνου δὲ Πειθὼ δαιμόνων ἀποστατεῖ.

('Death alone of all gods does not love gifts, neither by sacrifice nor by libation would you accomplish anything, he has no altar nor is he praised; from him alone among gods, does Persuasion stand apart.' The text is taken from Dindorf's 1851 *Poetae Scenici Graeci*.)

For possible echoes from Beaumont and Fletcher's *Maid's Tragedy*, see Mario Praz, 'Le Tragedie "Greche" di A. C. Swinburne', *Atene e Roma*, No. 7–8–9 (July–August–September 1922), p. 185n2.

The poem, in blank verse, is an imitation of an episode of Greek tragedy;

the use of stikhomythia (one- or two-line exchanges between characters) and the oblique naming of a divinity (lines 29–30) are characteristic of Greek tragedy.

The Triumph of Time

Recent biographers have interpreted 'The Triumph of Time' as a *cri de coeur* provoked by the engagement of Swinburne's greatest romantic interest, his cousin Mary Gordon, to Colonel Robert Disney Leith, who was twenty-one years older than she was.

The 'sea-daisies' (line 56) are also known as sea-pinks. The 'third wave' (line 83) derives from the Greek τριχυμία, originally meaning a group of three waves; later it comes to mean a large or irresistible wave (cf. *Prometheus Bound*, line 1015, Euripides' *Hippolytus*, line 1213, Plato's *Republic*, 472a). The *OED* credits Swinburne with the first citation for this meaning of 'third'. 'Flesh of his flesh' (line 102) is an adaptation of Genesis 2:23. The narrow gate of line 168 recalls Matthew 7:13–14 and Luke 13:24, where it leads to life. The pleonastic phrase 'royal king's' (line 220) may be an echo of 'royal kings' in Shakespeare, *Antony and Cleopatra* (Act V, Scene 2, line 326). Line 223 may recall 'What hath night to do with sleep' of Milton's 'Comus' (line 122). The quotation in line 237 is from Hamlet's lines to Ophelia beginning 'Get thee to a nunnery' (Act 3, Scene 1). Line 253 is indebted to Dante Gabriel Rossetti's 'The Blessed Damozel' (1850, 1856, 1870), 'And the stars in her hair were seven' (line 6). Line 273 is similar to Tennyson's *Maud* (1855), 'But only moves with the moving eye' (Part II, line 85). The 'midland sea' (line 322) is the Mediterranean. 'Or ever' (line 332) is emphatic for 'before'. 'Overwatching' (line 374) can mean both 'keeping watch over' and 'fatiguing by excessive watching'.

The 'singer in France of old' (line 321) is the troubadour Jaufre Rudel, who lived in the south of France in the twelfth century. His thirteenth-century *vida* explains:

Jaufre Rudel, Prince of Blaye, was a very noble man. And he fell in love with the Countess of Tripoli, without having seen her, because of the great goodness and courtliness which he heard tell of her from the pilgrims who came from Antioch. And he wrote many good songs about her, with good melodies and poor words. And because of his desire, he took the cross and set sail to go to see her. But in the ship he fell very ill, to the point where those who were with him thought he was dead. However, they got him – a dead man, as they thought – to Tripoli, to an inn. And it was made known to the Countess, and she came to his bedside, and took him in her arms. And he knew she was the Countess, and recovered sight [*or*, hearing] and smell, and praised God because He had kept him alive until he had seen her. And so he died in the arms of the lady. And she had him buried with honour in the Temple at Tripoli. Then, the same day, she became a nun because of the grief which she felt for him and for his death.

(George Wolf and Roy Rosenstein, *The Poetry of Cercamon and Jaufre Rudel*, 1983. See also *The Vidas of the Troubadours*, Margarita Egan, 1984.)

The story of this troubadour is present elsewhere in nineteenth-century literature; we find it in Stendhal (in *De l'amour*, 1822), Heine (in *Romanzero*, 1851), and Browning ('Rudel and the Lady of Tripoli', 1842). The story remains current after Swinburne: Carducci, Rostand, Pound and Döblin were drawn to it. Swinburne's 'The Death of Rudel', apparently written during his college years, is printed in the first volume of the Bonchurch edition of his works.

The stanza consists of tetrameter lines of both iambs and anapests and rhymes *ababccab*; it is the same stanza used for the first choral ode of *Atalanta in Calydon*. George Saintsbury, in *A History of English Prosody* (1906, Vol. 3, p. 233), sees 'The Triumph of Time' as an improvement, prosodically and otherwise, on Browning's 'The Worst of It' (1864). The title derives ultimately from Petrarch's allegorical *Trionfi* (his 'Triumph of Love' mentions Rudel). There are triumphs of time by Robert Greene (Swinburne praised his prose romance *Pandosto, The Triumph of Time* in 1908), Beaumont and Fletcher, and Handel.

Cecil Lang, in 'A Manuscript, a Mare's-Nest, and a Mystery' (*Yale University Library Gazette*, Vol. 31, 1957, pp. 163–71), prints an early fragment of the poem. The first page of the poem in manuscript is reproduced in Rooksby, p. 104.

Les Noyades

For a time, the noyade was as famous as the guillotine, both being methods of mass execution introduced during the French Revolution. Jean-Baptiste Carrier arrived in Nantes in October 1793 as the representative of the Committee of Public Safety to control the insurrection in the Vendée. He soon introduced the mass drownings of prisoners, who were confined to boats that were then sunk in the Loire. He was recalled to Paris in February 1795 and eventually tried and executed. Among the charges he faced were 'republican marriages', the binding of a naked man and woman together before they were drowned. Some historians have subsequently disputed that any republican marriages actually occurred, but at the time it was sensational news. James Schmidt, in a discussion of the noyade in the development of Hegel's thought ('Cabbage Heads and Gulps of Water', *Political Theory*, 26:1, February 1998, pp. 4–32), sets out the historical background of Carrier's activities and also reproduces a contemporary illustration of the republican marriages.

Swinburne probably knew Carlyle's *French Revolution* (1837), Part 3, Book 5, Chapter 3:

Nantes town is sunk in sleep; but *Représentant* Carrier is not sleeping, the wool-capped Company of Marat is not sleeping. Why unmoors that flatbottomed craft, that *gabarre*; about eleven at night; with Ninety Priests under hatches? They are going to Belle Isle? In the middle of the Loire stream, on signal given, the gabarre is scuttled; she sinks with all her cargo. 'Sentence of deportation', writes Carrier, 'was executed *vertically*'. The Ninety Priests, with their gabarre-coffin lie deep! It is the first of the *Noyades*, what we may call *Drownages*, of Carrier; which have become famous forever . . .

Or why waste a gabarre, sinking it with them? Fling them out; fling them out, with their hands tied; pour a continual hail of lead over all the space, till the last struggler of them be sunk! Unsound sleepers of Nantes, and the Sea-Villages thereabouts, hear the musketry amid the night-winds; wonder what the meaning of it is. And women were in that gabarre; whom the Red Nightcaps were stripping naked; who begged, in their agony, that their smocks not be stript from them . . .

By degrees, daylight itself witnesses Noyades: woman and men are tied together, feet and feet, hands and hands; and flung in: this they call *Mariage Républicain*, Republican Marriage.

'Mean' (line 53) refers to the speaker's inferior social rank. The poem is in rhyming quatrains (*abab*) of tetrameter lines of both iambs and anapests.

A Leave-Taking

'All we' (lines 5 and 20): formerly used for 'we all' or 'all of us' (*OED*, 'all', 2c). 'Thrust in thy sickle and reap' (line 18) echoes Revelation 14:15.

Cecil Lang ('A Manuscript, A Mare's-Nest, and A Mystery', *Yale University Library Gazette*, Vol. 31, 1957, pp. 163–71) publishes early drafts of the poem.

Each stanza rhymes *aababaa*; the *a* rhyme of one stanza becomes the *b* rhyme of the next. Swinburne modifies such forms as the rondeau and its relatives or the villanelle, which have the same two rhymes throughout an entire poem. In other ways, too, the poem recalls early French stanza forms: it has a refrain, like the ballade or chant royal (though the last word of the refrain changes), and the shortness of the refrain is like the *rentrement* of a rondeau, though here it responds to the second half of the first line of the stanza rather than the first half. It is suggestive of the French *formes fixes* without being directly imitative of them.

Itylus

The poem is a monologue by Philomela, the sister of Procne, who is the wife of Tereus, the king of Thrace (line 48). He lusts after Philomela, rapes her, and then cuts off her tongue and hides her. Philomela tells her story by weaving the events in the design of a tapestry (line 52), which she sends to Procne. The sisters revenge themselves by killing Itylus, the son of Tereus and Procne, and cooking him. Procne feeds him to Tereus and afterwards reveals what they have done; Tereus pursues them in a rage, but they are saved by the gods, who turn Philomela into a nightingale (line 19) and Procne into a swallow.

In Daulis (line 48), in central Greece, the women murdered Itylus, according to Thucydides (ii. 29). Swinburne appears to locate it on the Thracian coast, perhaps mistaking a detail from Matthew Arnold's 'Philomela' (1853). The wet roofs and lintels (line 51) may suggest the blood of Itylus; cf. Ovid's *Metamorphoses*, Book 6, line 646 ('manant penetralia tabo', 'the room drips with gore'). 'Itylus' is the name in Homer; 'Itys' is more common. In Greek poetry, it is Procne who becomes the nightingale.

Ovid's *Metamorphoses*, Book 6, is the major source of the story. There are references to it in Homer (*Odyssey*, Book 19, lines 518–523), Aeschylus (*Agamemnon*, lines 1140–9 and *Suppliants*, lines 58–67), and Apollodorus. In addition to Matthew Arnold, Catulle Mendès was inspired by the legend; see 'Le Rossignol' in *Philoméla* (1863), which appeared shortly before Swinburne wrote his poem.

Swinburne combines iambs and anapests in stanzas of six tetrameters rhyming *abcabc*. 'Swallow' is a constant feminine rhyme in each stanza.

Anactoria

Swinburne's admiration for Sappho was unbounded. In a posthumously published appreciation ('Sappho', *The Saturday Review*, 21 February 1914, p. 228) he wrote:

Judging even from the mutilated fragments fallen within our reach from the broken altar of her sacrifice of song, I for one have always agreed with all Grecian tradition in thinking Sappho to be beyond all question and comparison the very greatest poet that ever lived. Æschylus is the greatest poet who ever was also a prophet; Shakespeare is the greatest dramatist who ever was also a poet; but Sappho is simply nothing less – as she is certainly nothing more – than the greatest poet who ever was at all. Such at least is the simple and sincere profession of my lifelong faith.

(See also Lang, 4, 124 and Swinburne's defence of the poem in 'Notes on Poems and Reviews', Appendix 1.)

Her ode beginning 'φαίνεταί μοι', known to Swinburne as the 'Ode to Anactoria', provides the context of this poem: Sappho suffers intense erotic jealousy because of Anactoria's infidelity to her. In Swinburne's dramatic monologue, Sappho addresses Anactoria in an attempt to win her back. He works some of Sappho's own words into the address. (The standard text of Sappho at the time was Theodor Bergk's *Poetae Lyrici Graeci*, revised in 1853; citations to Bergk's edition are accompanied by those to the Loeb text, edited and translated by David A. Campbell, *Greek Lyric*, volume 1.)

line 63: 'For I beheld in sleep'; cf. 'In a dream I spoke with the Cyprus-born' (Bergk 86; Campbell 134).

line 70: 'a mind of many colours'; translates ποικίλοφρον, found in the first line of some texts of the Aphrodite ode.

lines 73–4: 'Who doth thee wrong, Sappho?' translates lines 19–20 of the Aphrodite ode.

lines 81–4 are a translation of the sixth stanza of the Aphrodite ode.

lines 189–200 are an expansion of Bergk 68, Campbell 55.

line 221: 'sleepless moon' conflates the moon and the sleepless speaker of one of the most famous fragments, though now denied by many to Sappho; Bergk 52, Campbell 168B.

In addition, Sappho's boasts that she will be remembered after death have been amplified in lines 203–14. The names Erinna (line 22) and Atthis (line 286) occur in some fragments. The name 'Erotion' (line 22) presumably refers to a male lover; see the note to Swinburne's poem 'Erotion'. Lines 260–5 allude to the legend of Sappho's suicide by drowning as the result of an unhappy love affair with Phaon.

The epigraph is an emendation, perhaps Swinburne's own, of a corrupt line in the Aphrodite ode; Swinburne's version means 'Whose love have you caught in vain by persuasion?' (Sappho calls Persuasion the daughter of Aphrodite; see Bergk 133, Campbell 200.)

'Reluctation' (line 33) means 'struggle, resistance, opposition' (*OED*: 'somewhat rare'; 'obsolete' with reference to bodily organs). Aphrodite's 'amorous girdle' (line 45) makes her irresistible; in lines 49–50, we are given the account of her birth from the ocean (Aphrodite Anadyomene); Paphos, line 64, is the site of her famous sanctuary on Cyprus. 'Storied' (line 68) means either 'ornamented with scenes from history or legend' or 'celebrated in history or story'. 'Flies' (line 81) means 'flees'. Swinburne activates the etymology of 'disastrous' in 'disastrous stars' (line 164); 'comet' and 'hair' (lines 161–2) are also connected etymologically. Pieria is a district in Thessaly associated with the Muses, and so the 'high Pierian flower' (line 195) is a poem as well as the garland for the victorious poet. 'Reflex' (line 198) is a reflection of light. In line 302, the lotus produces dreamy forgetfulness, and Lethe is the river of oblivion.

Timothy A. J. Burnett, in 'Swinburne at Work: The First Page of "Anactoria"' (in *The Whole Music of Passion*, eds Rikky Rooksby and Nicholas Shrimpton, 1993), discusses and reproduces a draft of the first page of the poem. It is also reproduced in Yopie Prins, *Victorian Sappho* (1999), p. 118. Edmund Gosse discusses a first version of the poem in 'The First Draft of Swinburne's "Anactoria"' (*Modern Language Review*, 14, 1919, pp. 271-7).

The poem is in heroic couplets; all sentences come to a stop at the end of a line.

Hymn to Proserpine

Constantine I, the first Christian Roman emperor, issued the Edict of Milan in 313 with the Eastern Roman emperor Licinus; it established religious toleration of Christians and protected their legal rights. Constantine's policy went further than official toleration, and he began to establish Rome as a Christian state. His nephew Julian (emperor from 361 to 363) announced his conversion to paganism in 361 and hence is known as Julian the Apostate (see L. M. Findlay, 'The Art of Apostasy', *Victorian Poetry* 28:1, Spring 1990, pp. 69-78, for the Victorian controversies over 'national apostasy' and the image of Julian). He became a fierce opponent of Christians, but his opposition had no lasting effect; his legendary dying words ('Vicisti, Galilaee', 'Thou hast conquered, Galilean') were reported in Greek by Theodoret, the Bishop of Cyrrhus, in the fifth century.

Proserpine, or Persephone, is the wife of Hades and the queen (lines 2, 92) of the underworld; the river Lethe (line 36) and poppies (line 97) are associated with the oblivion of death. She is also Kore, a maiden (lines 2, 92) and the daughter of Demeter, the earth (line 93). She and Demeter are the subject of the mysteries at Eleusis. Swinburne contrasts the new queen of heaven (line 76), the Jewish (line 85, 'slave among slaves') virgin (lines 75, 81) mother of Christ, with Venus, the former queen. Venus is described as she rose from the sea (lines 78, 86-9); she is the 'mother of Rome' (line 80) both as Aeneas's mother and as Venus Genetrix; and she is called Cytherean (line 73) after her birthplace in Cythera.

'I have lived long enough' (line 1) quotes Macbeth's line from Act V, Scene 3, line 22. 'Galilean' (lines 23, 35, 74) is 'used by pagans as a contemptuous designation for Christ' (*OED*). In Greek 'unspeakable things' (line 52, ἄρρητα) can refer to the Eleusinian mysteries. L. M. Findlay (Swinburne, *Selected Poems*, 1982, pp. 257-8) suggests that the description of the wave of the world (line 54) is indebted to Turner's painting *The Slave Ship* (1834) and Ruskin's defence of the painting in *Modern Painters* (1843). 'Viewless ways' (line 87) may have been influenced by Shakespeare's 'viewless winds' (*Measure for Measure*, Act III, Scene 1, line 124) or Keats's 'viewless wings' ('Ode to a Nightingale', line 33, 1820). The footnote in Greek by Epictetus is the source of Swinburne's line 108; the remark survives in Marcus Aurelius's *Meditations*, 4.41.

Robert Peters ('A. C. Swinburne's "Hymn to Proserpine": The Work Sheets', *PMLA* 83, October 1968, pp. 1400–6) discusses the work sheets to the poem and reproduces some of the manuscripts. Bernard Richards (*English Verse: 1830–1890*, 1980, p. 465) warns that there are errors in Peters's transcription.

The metre is hexameter with both iambs and anapests. The rhyme is in couplets, and there is an internal rhyme at the end of the third foot. All sentences come to a full stop at the end of a metrical line except for line 105.

Ilicet

'Ilicet' is a Latin exclamation of dismay, 'It's all over.'

The stooped urn (line 49) is tilted, inclined (the only *OED* citation for this meaning); to 'flash' is to rise and dash, as with the tide. 'Date' (line 105) is the 'limit, term or end of a period of time' (obsolete or archaic, *OED*).

For 'No memory, no memorial' (line 39), cf. Milton, *Paradise Lost* Book 1, line 362 and Nehemiah 2:20. 'Blood-red' (line 74) is a common colour in Shelley, Tennyson, and Morris. For watching and not sleeping (line 123), cf. 1 Thessalonians 5:6 and recall Gethsemane.

The metre is iambic tetrameter; the six-line stanza rhymes *aabccb*, where 'a' and 'c' are feminine rhymes.

Hermaphroditus

Swinburne's appended note 'At Museum of the Louvre, March 1863' indicates that the poem is a response to the Hellenistic sculpture of the sleeping Hermaphrodite, in the Louvre. On the topic of the androgyne and hermaphrodite in this period, see A. J. L. Busst, 'The Image of the Androgyne in the Nineteenth Century' in Ian Fletcher's *Romantic Myth-ologies* (1967), and Franca Franchi's *Le Metamorfosi di Zambinella* (1991). Busst contrasts the theme of hermaphrodite as the perfection of human existence (the androgynous universal man of the Saint-Simonians and others), current in the first half of the nineteenth century, with the decadent hermaphrodite of the later nineteenth century. The latter was popularized by Henri de Latouche's once famous *Fragoletta* (1829); Gautier (*Mademoiselle de Maupin*, 1836, and 'Contralto', 1852), Balzac (*Séraphîta*, 1835, and *La Fille aux yeux d'or*, 1835), and Baudelaire ('Les Bijoux', 1857) were also influenced by it.

In defence of his choice of subject, Swinburne quotes from Shelley's description in 'The Witch of Atlas' (1820) of the Louvre sculpture; see 'Notes on Poems and Reviews' (Appendix 1). For hermaphroditism in Swinburne's early unpublished *Laugh and Lie Down*, see Edward Philip Schuldt, *Four Early Unpublished Plays of Algernon Charles Swinburne* (doctoral dissertation from the University of Reading, 1976), pp. 206–10; he corrects all previous discussions. In *Lesbia Brandon*, begun in 1864, Swinburne emphasizes the feminine aspects of Herbert Seyton's appearance and his likeness to his sister (see, for example, pp. 3, 16, 30, 34 and 164 in Hughes's edition, 1952).

Ovid (*Metamorphoses*, Book 4) is the main source for the story of Hermaphroditus. Salamacis (line 53), the nymph of a spring, falls in love with him, but he rejects her. She prays that the gods will unite them; the gods do so, forming one being.

For the figurative use of 'pleasure-house' (line 24), contrast Tennyson, 'The Palace of Art' (1832, 1842): 'I built my soul a lordly pleasure-house, / Wherein at ease for aye to dwell' (lines 1–2).

The four sonnets are of the Italian kind, with two quatrains and two tercets. Note that Swinburne only uses four rhymes per sonnet, as Rossetti does occasionally in *A House of Love* (including several early sonnets). The first three sonnets rhyme *abba abba cdc dcd*; the last rhymes *abba abba cdd ccd*.

Fragoletta

William Rossetti writes that the poem 'has to be guessed at, and *is* guessed at with varying degrees of horror and repugnance: it is only readers of De Latouche's novel of the same name who can be certain that they see how much it does, and how much else it does in no wise, mean.' Latouche's novel (1829) narrates the story of the hermaphrodite Fragoletta (the name is a diminutive of the Italian word for strawberry and occurs in Casanova and elsewhere); much of the plot is concerned with the complications of bisexual love. Swinburne was dismissive of Latouche's art, and in *A Note on Charlotte Brontë*, 1877, he referred to the 'Rhadamanthine author of "Fragoletta"; who certainly, to judge by his own examples of construction, had some right to pronounce with authority how a novel ought *not* to be written'; nonetheless, he was more excited in private, as when he wrote that he dare not trust another work of Latouche's out of his sight (Lang, 1, 46). Swinburne read Gautier's 1839 review of a drama of the same name as Latouche's novel, in which he wrote that the '*Fragoletta* est un titre pimpant, égrillard, croustilleux, qui promet beaucoup de choses très-difficile à dire, et surtout à représenter' ('*Fragoletta* is a chic, ribald, spicy title which promises many things very difficult to say and above all to represent').

The five-line iambic stanza consists of two tetrameters, two trimeters, and a dimeter, rhyming *abaab*.

Rondel

The rondel is Swinburne's naturalization of the French rondeau, a fixed form that nonetheless has had many variations. Clément Marot and others established the most common formula: a poem in octosyllabic or decasyllabic lines, consisting of three stanzas made of five, three and five lines respectively. There are only two rhymes, and a refrain (called the *rentrement*) made from the first half of the first line is added, unrhymed, to the end of the second and third stanzas. Much of the skill of the rondeau is in placing the *rentrement* in new contexts. The form was popular in the first half of the sixteenth century in France, but was disdained by the Pléiade and long thereafter. Alfred de Musset used it for some of his light verse in the nineteenth century. Théodore de Banville included four rondeaux in his first book, *Les Cariatides* (1842); Swinburne referred to Banville's 'most flexible and brilliant style' (though one which 'hardly carries weight enough to tell across the Channel') in his 1862 essay on Baudelaire.

'These many years' is a biblical phrase; see Ezra 5:11, Luke 15:29 (the parable of the prodigal son) and Romans 15:23.

Swinburne adapts the form by using one constant rhyme throughout the poem (in iambic pentameter) and one new rhyme per stanza. The *rentrement* becomes a rhymed iambic dimeter at the end of each stanza. Two manuscripts of the poem are reproduced in John S. Mayfield's *These Many Years* (1947).

Satia Te Sanguine

The title, 'glut thyself with blood', derives from the phrase 'satia te sanguine quem sitisti' ('glut thyself with the blood for which thou hast thirsted'), uttered by Queen Tomyris of the Massagetai as she dropped the severed head of Cyrus, the great Persian king who had treacherously killed her son, into a bowl of human blood. The story is recounted by Herodotus (at the end of the first book of his *History*) and other ancient sources (see *Paulys*

Real-Encyclopädie der Classischen Altertumswissenschaft, second series); the Latin words are derived from medieval authors like Marcus Junianus Justinus or Paulus Orosius. Tomyris eventually evolves into a virtuous heroine, as in Dante's *Purgatorio*, the *Speculum humanae salvationis*, or Rubens's painting *Queen Tomyris with the Head of Cyrus* (see Paget Toynbee, *A Dictionary of Proper Names and Notable Matters in the Works of Dante*, revised by Charles S. Singleton, 1968, p. 596, and Robert W. Berger, 'Rubens's "Queen Tomyris with the Head of Cyrus"', *Bulletin of the Museum of Fine Arts, Boston*, Vol. 77, 1979, pp. 4–35). Swinburne uses the Latin words without alluding to the story and inverts any virtuous connotation they might have. The title and theme are also reminiscent of Baudelaire's 'Sed non Satiata' (1857). Tomyris appears in the procession of women in 'The Masque of Queen Bersabe' (p. 176).

For Sappho's suicide (third stanza), see note to 'Anactoria'. For line 16, cf. Ezekiel 2:10, 'and there was written therein lamentations, and mourning, and woe'.

The poem is in quatrains, rhyming *abab*; the lines are trimeter and combine iambs and anapests.

A Litany

A litany is 'an appointed form of public prayer, usually of a penitential character, consisting of a series of supplications, deprecations, or intercessions in which the clergy lead and the people respond, the same formula of response being repeated for several successive clauses' (*OED*). The poem consists of antiphones (perhaps Swinburne wrote the older form 'antiphone' rather than 'antiphon' in a mistaken attempt to reproduce the Greek form of the term; the medieval Latin singular 'antiphona' comes in fact from the Greek plural τὰ ἀντίφωνα). That is, it is to be sung by two voices or choirs. William Rossetti calls the poem 'a cross between the antiphonal hymnal form and the ideas and phraseology of the Old Testament'. To the influence of the Old Testament, we should add the ideas and phraseology of Revelation. The wine-press of lines 62 and 78 (and likewise 'that hour' of line 81) refers to the wrath of God at the Last Judgement; cf. Revelation 14:19–20: 'And the angel thrust in his sickle into the earth, and gathered the vine of the earth, and cast it into the great winepress of the wrath of God. And the winepress was trodden without the city, and blood came out of the winepress, even unto the horse bridles, by the space of a thousand and six hundred furlongs.'

The *Anthologia Sacra* appears to be Swinburne's invention; his Greek means 'the shining lights in heaven I shall hide from you, for one night you will have seven, etc.' Metrically, the first line consists of an iamb and a bacchiac; the second line appears to be a variant of the first. The third line is iambic trimeter.

'Skirts' (line 4) are 'the beginning or end of a period of time' (*OED* 9b). 'Thick darkness' (line 36) is a recurrent phrase in the Old Testament. For 'before' and 'behind' (lines 37 and 38), cf. Psalms 139:5, 'Thou hast beset me behind and before.' 'Remnant' (line 39), according to the *OED*, can mean by allusion to Isaiah 10:22, 'a small number of Jews that survives persecution, in whom future hope is vested'. 'Put away' (line 87) commonly means 'divorce' in the Bible. Line 127 derives from Ezekiel 34:16, 'I . . . will bind up that which was broken.'

The poem consists of alternating trimeter and dimeter lines of both iambs and anapests. The stanza rhymes *ababcdcd*; note the double and triple rhymes 'over thee', 'cover thee' / 'over us', 'cover us'; 'love thee', 'above thee' / 'love us', 'above us'; 'sunder thee', 'under thee' / 'sunder us', 'under us'; 'reach me', 'beseech me' / 'reach thee', 'beseech thee'; 'gold on you', 'hold on you' / 'gold on us', 'hold on us'. The antiphony is both semantic (as even-numbered antiphones recall the wording of the previous odd-numbered antiphones) and rhythmic (many of the rhyme-words are repeated in the pairs of antiphones, with one or two new rhymes introduced in the successor).

A Lamentation

The poem invokes the lamentation of Thetis (line 114) over her dead son Achilles, which Homer recounts in the *Odyssey* (at the beginning of Book 24), and also the dead Heracles (line 122), killed unintentionally by his wife Deianira; the chorus in Sophocles's *Women of Trachis* laments both Heracles and Deianira. (Matthew Arnold's 'Fragment of a Chorus of a "Dejaneira"', though probably written much earlier, was published only in 1867.) Lamentations, one of the books of the Old Testament, is Jeremiah's lament over the destruction of Jerusalem; the Lamentation, one of the lessons read during Holy Week, is taken from it.

The phrase 'the desire of mine eyes' (line 56) is related to the phrases 'the desire of thine eyes', 'the desire of your eyes', and 'the desire of their eyes', which all occur in Ezekiel 24 (and nowhere else in the Bible).

The metre and the rhyme scheme vary among the sections. The three stanzas of the first section are all trimeter lines of both iambs and anapests. Note the *abcabc* rhymes in the first stanza and the *abcdabcd* rhymes in the second. The second section consists of several stanzas. The first rhymes *abaab* and consists of tetrameters (iambo-anapestic); 'travail' (line 48) is stressed on the first syllable. The second stanza consists of alternating trimeter and dimeter lines, each consisting of both iambs and anapests. It is composed of nine quatrains with cross rhymes. The remaining stanzas of the section are made of tetrameter lines of both iambs and anapests rhyming *abcabc*. The third section consists of iambic trimeter lines in stanzas rhyming *abcabcabc*.

Anima Anceps

The title means literally 'two-fold soul'. The source is a formula which Victor Hugo is likely to have invented, in Book 8, Chapter 6 of *Notre-Dame de Paris* (1831):

Alors levant la main sur l'égyptienne il s'écria d'une voix funèbre: «*I nunc, anima anceps, et sit tibi Deus misericors!*»
 C'était la redoutable formule dont on avait coutume de clore ces sombres céré-monies. C'était le signal convenu du prêtre au bourreau.

[Then he raised his hand over the gypsy girl and pronounced sombrely: 'Go there-fore, divided soul, and may God be merciful to you.' It was the awful formula by which it was customary to conclude these grim ceremonies. It was the appointed signal of the priest to the hangman.]

Parts of Arthur Clough's *Dipsychus* (1865; the title means 'double-minded' or 'double-souled') were published in 1862 and 1863; Swinburne frequently quotes from the poem in his later letters, while maintaining reservations about Clough's merits.
 For the address to the soul, cf. Hadrian's lines 'Animula, vagula, bland-ula', translated by Matthew Prior, Byron and others. For the rhyme 'rafter' and 'laughter' (lines 34 and 35), cf. Shelley's 'Lines ("When the lamp is shattered")' (1824), lines 29 and 31.
 It is written in iambic dimeter; the rhyme scheme is *aaabcccbdddbeeeb*. All rhymes except for *b* are feminine.

In the Orchard

The poem is inspired by an anonymous Provençal alba, or dawn-song (a genre without a fixed metre or form in which a lover laments the imminent separation from the other lover at the break of day). It begins 'En un vergier' ('In an orchard') and consists of six stanzas of four lines each; the last line of each stanza is the refrain 'Oy Dieus, oy Dieus, de l'abla!, tan tost ve' ('Ah God, ah God, the dawn! it comes so fast'). The text was available in editions like F. J. M. Raynouard's *Choix des poésies originales des troubadours*

(1821) and C. A. F. Mahn's *Gedichte der Troubadours* (1856). A convenient modern edition is R. T. Hill and T. C. Bergin, *Anthology of the Provençal Troubadours* (2nd ed., 1973). For more information about the genre, see *Eos: An Enquiry into the Theme of Lovers' Meetings and Partings at Dawn in Poetry*, ed. Arthur T. Hatto, 1965. Pound translated the alba as 'Alba Innominata' in 1910. By 'Provençal burden' Swinburne indicates that he is adopting the music or undersong of Provençal lyric, rather than offering a translation. 'Burden', in addition, refers to the refrain at the end of each stanza.

The *OED* gives no instance of 'plenilune' (line 23) between *c.* 1600 and Swinburne in 1878.

The poem is in iambic pentameter and rhymes *aabab*; the *b* rhyme ('soon' in the refrain) is constant throughout.

A Match

'Closes' (line 5) are enclosures. The reference in lines 35–6 is to dice and cards, respectively.

The metre is iambic trimeter, the rhyme scheme is *abccabab*. The *a* and *c* rhymes are feminine.

Swinburne writes several lyrics in iambic trimeter octaves: 'A Match', 'Rococo', 'Before Dawn', 'The Garden of Proserpine'; cf. 'Madonna Mia'. Katherine Williams (in her 1986 doctoral dissertation from CUNY, *'Song New-Born': Renaissance Forms in Swinburne's Lyrics*) adduces Keats's poem beginning 'In a drear nighted December' (1829) and Shelley's poem 'The Indian Serenade' (1824) as other examples of iambic trimeter octaves.

Faustine

Published in the *Spectator*, 31 May 1862.

In *Notes on Poems and Reviews* (Appendix 1) Swinburne explains that 'the idea that gives [these verses] such life as they have is simple enough: the transmigration of a single soul, doomed as though by accident from the first to all evil and no good, through many ages and forms, but clad always in the same type of fleshly beauty. The chance which suggested to me this poem was one which may happen any day to any man – the sudden sight of a living face which recalled the well-known likeness of another dead for centuries: in this instance, the noble and faultless type of the elder Faustina, as seen in coin and bust.' (According to the *Encyclopaedia Britannica*, the elder Faustina's coiffure is depicted with a coronal of plaits on top; the younger Faustina's with rippling side waves and a small bun at the nape of the neck.)

The elder Faustina is Annia Galeria Faustina, who married the future emperor Antoninus Pius. She was the aunt of Marcus Aurelius, whom her daughter, also named Annia Galeria Faustina, married. Ancient historians like Cassius Dio and the authors of the *Historia Augusta* established the reputation of both women for treachery and licentiousness. The latter work reports many amours of the younger Faustina (including an affair with her son-in-law, whom it says she may have poisoned). The discrepancy between the characters of Marcus Aurelius and his son was explained by postulating a liaison between Faustina and a gladiator; she is said to have preferred sailors and gladiators. Gibbon summarizes: 'the grave simplicity of the philosopher was ill calculated to engage her wanton levity, or to fix that unbounded passion for variety, which often discovered personal merit in the meanest of mankind. The Cupid of the ancients was, in general, a very sensual deity; and the amours of an empress, as they exact on her side the plainest advances, are seldom susceptible of much sentimental delicacy' (*The History of the Decline and Fall of the Roman Empire*, Chapter 4). Neither Gibbon nor Swinburne was aware of the fictitious nature of much of the *Historia Augusta*, which was revealed by Hermann Dessau in 1889. According to Dio, she died either of the gout or by suicide.

Satan won the contest with God over Faustina's soul 'this time' (line 25); the contest over Job was the previous time. The combats of gladiators are described in lines 65–80; the words '*morituri te salutant*' of the epigraph (in full, 'Hail, empress Faustina, they who are about to die salute you') are the traditional greeting of gladiators (see H. J. Leon, 'Morituri Te Salutamus', *Transactions of the American Philological Association* 70, 1939, pp. 46–50; cf. Jean Gérôme's painting *Ave Cæsar, Morituri Te Salutant* exhibited in 1859). She is a Bacchanal (line 99), a votary of Bacchus and so a drunken reveller, but she is also a votary of Priapus, the ithyphallic god whose cult diffused from the region of Lampsacus (line 146), as well as a lesbian like Sappho of Mitylene (lines 117–24). Priapus 'metes the gardens with his rod' (line 147) because, as a garden god, his image was usually situated in the garden; cf. Catullus's 'Priapean' poems (18, 19, and 20), usually regarded as spurious; Swinburne read Catullus with 'delight and wonder' at Eton (unpublished letter quoted in Rooksby, p. 30).

'Dust and din' (line 82) is a Victorian collocation: cf. Tennyson, *In Memoriam* (1850) LXXXIX.8, and Arnold, *Empedocles on Etna* (1852) Act 1, Scene 2, line 206. 'Dashed with dew' (line 103) recalls Tennyson's 'Dashed together in blinding dew', from 'A Vision of Sin' (1842), line 42. 'Serene' (line 114), in reference to heavenly bodies, means 'shining with a clear and tranquil light' (*OED*, 1b). 'Pulseless' (line 115) can mean 'unfeeling, pitiless' as well as 'devoid of life'.

The metre is iambic; 'devil' in line 19 ought to be scanned as a monosyllable. The four-line quatrains rhyme *abab* and alternate between tetrameter and dimeter lines. The last word of each quatrain is 'Faustine', for which Swinburne finds forty-one rhymes.

A Cameo

A description of a cameo, with the allegorical figures of Desire, Pain, Pleasure, Satiety, Hate and Death, as well as a crowd of senses, sorrows, sins and strange loves. Strictly speaking, cameos are not painted (line 2). For the title, compare Gautier's *Émaux et Camées* (1852) and his intention that 'chaque pièce [of that collection] devait être un médaillon'. For contemporary sonnets on works of art, recall Rossetti's 'Sonnets for Pictures', published in 1850. For the topic of ekphrasis in general, see John Hollander's *The Gazer's Spirit* (1995).

'Pash' (line 8), to smash violently, may be influenced by the intransitive use of the word 'said of the dashing action of sudden heavy rain . . . and of the action of beating or striking water as by the feet of the horse' (*OED*).

The sonnet is of the Italian sort; it rhymes *abba abba cde cde*.

Song Before Death

The poem is a translation from a song in Letter 68 of Sade's *Aline et Valcour*, his philosophical epistolary novel published in 1795:

Air: *Romance de Nina*.

Mère adorée, en un moment
La mort t'enlève à ma tendresse!
Toi qui survis, ô mon amant!
Reviens consoler ta maîtresse.
Ah! qu'il revienne (*bis*), hélas! hélas!
Mais le bien-aimé ne vient pas.

Comme la rose au doux printemps
S'entrouvre au souffle du zéphyre,
Mon âme à ces tendres accents
S'ouvrirait de même au délire.
En vain, j'écoute: hélas! hélas!
Le bien-aimé ne parle pas.

> Vous qui viendrez verser des pleurs
> Sur ce cercueil où je repose,
> En gémissant sur mes douleurs,
> Dites a l'amant qui les cause
> Qu'il fut sans cesse, hélas! hélas!
> Le bien-aimé jusqu'au trépas.

In a letter of 1862 (Lang, 1, 58), Swinburne describes the song as 'about the most exquisite piece of simple finished language and musical effect in all 18th century French literature'. On Swinburne's initial reading of Sade, see Rooksby, pp. 75–7. For his abiding interest, consult the index to the letters.

The title and the date '1795' indicate that the speaker is anticipating execution during the French Revolution.

Swinburne translates into iambic tetrameter lines in stanzas that rhyme *ababcc*.

Wise reproduces the manuscript of the poem in the 1919 *Bibliography* (p. 110).

Rococo

In the nineteenth century the term could mean merely 'old-fashioned', and even when applied to French decoration, it did not specifically refer to the florid, light style conceived in reaction to the official baroque of Louis XIV. The *OED*'s first citation for 'rococo' is dated 1836. Swinburne invokes Juliette (line 62), whose name recalls the depraved heroine of Sade's novel, published in 1797.

On the newly recovered fashion for the rococo in French culture in the nineteenth century, see the chapter 'Age of Rococo' in Maxine G. Cutler's *Evocations of the Eighteenth Century in French Poetry, 1800–1869* (1970). Gautier was central in the new appreciation for it; see his poems 'Rocaille', 'Pastel' (originally called 'Roccoco'), 'Watteau', etc. Banville and Hugo ('La Fête chez Thérèse') were also important in its recovery, as were Baudelaire and the Goncourt brothers.

'Sanguine' (line 8) means 'of blood-red colour', but the sense 'blood-thirsty, delighting in bloodshed' is not absent. Both meanings were literary uses of the word when Swinburne wrote the poem.

The poem is written in iambic trimeter; the stanzas rhyme *ababcdcd*, where *a* and *c* have feminine endings. The last two rhymes of each stanza alternate between 'pleasure/pain' and 'remember/forget'. On iambic trimeter octaves, see the note to 'A Match'.

Wise reproduces a manuscript of the poem in the 1919 *Bibliography* (p. 113).

Stage Love

Bacon, in his essay on love, offers one of the classical contrasts between stage love and love in life: 'The stage is more beholding to love, than the life of man. For as to the stage, love is ever matter of comedies, and now and then of tragedies; but in life it doth much mischief: sometimes like a siren; sometimes like a fury.'

The poem is written in trochaics with six stresses (the last unstressed syllable is sometimes omitted, as often in trochaic verse); the stanzas rhyme *aabb*, where *b* is feminine. Trochaics are among the most enduring metres of classical poetry: Archilochus wrote in trochaics, the metre occurred regularly in Greek and Latin tragedy and comedy and also in late works like the *Pervigilium Veneris*, and it was used in goliardic verse. In English, by the eighteenth century, the trochaic had typically been used for lighter purposes. William Blake's songs in trochees, like 'The Tyger', introduced a new weight and flexibility to the metre. Tennyson's 'Locksley Hall' (1842), Longfellow's 'The Song of Hiawatha' (1855), and Browning's 'A Toccata of Galuppi's' (1855) were recent poems in trochaics.

Wise prints a manuscript of the poem in his 1919 *Bibliography* (p. 113) and in *A Swinburne Library*, facing page 25.

The Leper

Swinburne invents a French source for the story, which he offers in a note at the end: 'At that time there was in this land a great number of lepers, which greatly displeased the king, seeing that because of them the Lord must have been grievously wroth. Now it happened that a noble lady named Yolande de Sallières was afflicted and utterly ravaged by this base sickness; all her friends and relatives, with the fear of the Lord before their eyes, made her quit their houses and would never receive or help a thing cursed of God, stinking and abominable to all men. This lady had been very beautiful and graceful of figure; she was generous of body and lascivious in her life. However, none of the lovers who had often embraced and kissed her very tenderly would shelter any longer such an ugly woman and such a detestable sinner. One clerk alone who had been at first her servant and her intermediary in the matter of love took her in, hiding her in a small hut. There the villainous woman died of great misery and an evil death:

and after her, the aforesaid clerk died, who had of his great love for six months tended, washed, dressed and undressed her with his own hands every day. They even say that this wicked man and cursed clerk, calling to mind the great beauty of this woman, now gone by and ravaged, delighted many times to kiss her on her foul, leprous mouth and to embrace her gently with loving hands. Thus, he died of the same abominable malady. This happened near Fontainebellant in Gastinois. And when King Philip heard this story, he was greatly astonished.'

Clyde K. Hyder ('The Medieval Background of Swinburne's *The Leper*', *PMLA* 46, December 1931, pp. 1280–8) identifies a source behind various details of Swinburne's archaic French; he also notes correspondences between the poem and the medieval poem *Amis and Amiloun*, which Swinburne read in Henry Weber's *Metrical Romances* (1810).

William Empson discusses the word 'delicate' (line 3) in *The Structure of Complex Words* (1951, p. 78), where he writes that in this poem 'the sadism is adequately absorbed or dramatised into a story where both characters are humane, and indeed behave better than they think; Swinburne nowhere else (that I have read him) succeeds in imagining two people.'

The metre is iambic tetrameter; the stanza is a quatrain rhyming *abab*.

An early version of the poem, entitled 'A Vigil', was transcribed by T. J. Wise in *A Swinburne Library* (p. 2) and by Lafourcade (Vol. 2, pp. 63–4 and 573). Cecil Lang warns that the transcriptions are inaccurate (*The Pre-Raphaelites and their Circle*, 1975, p. 521). There is a reproduction of the first four stanzas of 'A Vigil' in T. Earle Welby's *A Study of Swinburne* (1976), p. 60.

A Ballad of Burdens

'Ballad' indicates that the poem is a ballade, the form of which was standardized by Guillaume de Machaut and Eustache Deschamps in the fourteenth century: three stanzas of either eight octosyllabic lines or ten decasyllabic lines; usually with an envoy at the end; having a refrain or *rebriche* as the last line of each stanza and of the envoy; and maintaining the same rhymes for each stanza. The greatest ballades were written by Villon in the fifteenth century and by Charles d'Orléans in the sixteenth. Despite efforts by Chaucer and Gower, the form was never naturalized in English; in France it fell into disuse in the later sixteenth and seventeenth centuries. Gautier's essay on Villon in *Les Grotesques* (1844) was influential in establishing Villon's reputation in the nineteenth century. (Although Banville was composing ballades 'after the manner of Villon' at the same time as Swinburne, they were not published until 1873; his polemical *Petit traité de poésie française*, insisting on the necessity of returning to forms like the rondeau, triolet, and ballade, appeared in 1872.) Swinburne's enthusiasm for the fifteenth-century French poet was longstanding; in the early 1860s, he and Rossetti planned to translate all of Villon's work. His translation from this period entitled 'The Ballad of Villon and Fat Madge', like 'A Ballad of Burdens', does not preserve the same rhymes in each stanza; in contrast, his translations of Villon's ballades published in *Poems and Ballads, Second Series* (1878) adhere to the stricter rhyme scheme. 'A Ballad of Burdens' is a triple ballade; the stanza rhymes *ababbcbc*, and *c* is constant in each stanza.

'Burden', besides meaning 'refrain' and 'accompanying song', is used in the English Bible (like *onus* in the Vulgate) to render Hebrew *massa*, which was generally taken in English to mean a 'burdensome or heavy lot or fate'. See Isaiah 13:1 and *OED*, 'burden' 8. Dante Gabriel Rossetti's 'The Burden of Nineveh', as printed in 1856, added below the title ' "*Burden*. Heavy calamity; the chorus of a song." – *Dictionary*.'

For 'the burden of fair women' (line 1), cf. Tennyson's title, 'A Dream of Fair Women' (1832). Compare the repeated line 'I would that I were dead' of Tennyson's 'Mariana' (1830) with line 28.

Rondel

See note to the first rondel (p. 337), and recall that the form of the rondeau was very fluid before the time of Marot. The poem is in two stanzas, like Villon's rondeau on death, which Rossetti translated in 1869. The metre is iambic pentameter, the rhyme scheme is *aabbcc* (*c* is the same rhyme in both stanzas), the *rentrement* is iambic dimeter.

'White death' (line 11) occurs twice in Shelley, in *Prometheus Unbound* (1820) Act 4, line 424 and *Adonais* (1821), line 66. It is most likely an equivalent to the more common poetic phrase 'pale death'.

Wise prints a manuscript of the poem in his 1919 *Bibliography* (p. 109) and in *A Swinburne Library*, facing page 24.

Before the Mirror

The poem was written for Whistler's *The Little White Girl: Symphony in White no. 2* (1864), now in the Tate Gallery, the second of the series Whistler only later called 'symphonies in white'. (Whistler may have taken his synaesthetic title from Gautier's 'Symphonie en blanc majeur', or perhaps from a critic's description of *The White Girl: Symphony in White, no. 1*, 1862.) A girl in white leans on a white mantelpiece, extending one arm along it, holds a fan in the hand of her other arm, and looks at a Japanese vase at the end of the mantelpiece. Her head is inclined to the mirror above the mantel; her reflection is sadder than her face. Swinburne wrote to Whistler in 1865 (Lang, 1, 118–20): 'I know [the idea of the poem] was entirely and only suggested to me by the picture, where I found at once the metaphor of the rose and the notion of sad and glad mystery in the face languidly contemplative of its own phantom and all other things seen by their phantoms.' Whistler liked the verses; the fourth and sixth stanzas were printed in the Royal Academy catalogue of 1865; and he had the poem printed on gold paper and fastened to the frame (Frederick A. Sweet, *James McNeill Whistler*, 1968, p. 57). John Hollander (*The Gazer's Spirit*, 1995) suggests that this last fact may account for the poem's subtitle. See also Linda Merrill, *The Peacock Room: A Cultural Biography* (1998), pp. 62–6, 357.

'Behind the veil' (line 8) recalls Tennyson's *In Memoriam* (1850) LVI, 28 ('Behind the veil, behind the veil'), as well as the metaphysical veils of Coleridge and Shelley, and also Hebrews 6:19.

The poem is iambic; the length of the lines varies. The rhyme scheme is $a_3b_2a_3b_2c_3c_3b_5$. Note that there is an internal c rhyme after the third foot in the last line of each stanza. Hollander remarks on the third section of the poem: 'The poem now moves inside the girl's reveries to the traces of the past that must inevitably emerge from its depths, even as – in Swinburne's verse throughout this poem – the internal rhymes emerge in the ultimate line of each stanza.'

Erotion

Swinburne explained that he wrote this poem as a comment on Simeon Solomon's painting *Damon and Aglae*:

a picture of two young lovers in fresh fullness of first love crossed and troubled visibly by the mere shadow and the mere breath of doubt, the dream of inevitable change to come which dims the longing eyes of the girl with a ghostly foreknowledge that this too shall pass away, as with arms half clinging and half repellent she seems at once to hold off and to hold fast the lover whose bright youth for the moment is smiling back in the face of hers – a face full of the soft fear and secret certitude of future things which I have tried elsewhere to render in the verse called 'Erotion' written as a comment on this picture, with design to express the subtle passionate sense of mortality in love itself which wells up from 'the middle spring of pleasure', yet cannot quite kill the day's delight or eat away with the bitter poison of doubt the burning faith and self-abandoned fondness of the hour; since, at least, though the future be for others, and the love now here turn elsewhere to seek pasture in fresh fields from other flowers, the vows and kisses of these present lips are not theirs but hers, as the memory of his love and the shadow of his youth shall be hers for ever. (Swinburne, 'Simeon Solomon: Notes on His "Vision of Love" and Other Studies', *The Dark Blue*, July 1871, p. 574)

The first eight lines of Swinburne's poem were printed in the 1866 exhibition catalogue of the Royal Academy of Arts under the entry for *Damon and Aglae*. The painting was sold at Sotheby's in 1978.

'Erotion' is a Greek name, a diminutive of 'Eros'. Although here and in 'Anactoria' the name is presumably applied to a man, in Martial, for example, it is applied to a young slave girl (5.34, 5.37, 10.61).

Swinburne ended his close association and friendship with Solomon after Solomon was arrested in 1873 for soliciting outside a public lavatory.

The poem is in heroic couplets. Complete sentences fit into either couplets or quatrains. There is little enjambment.

A facsimile of a manuscript of the poem is provided in Harry B. Smith's *A Sentimental Library* (1914), facing p. 202.

In Memory of Walter Savage Landor

Swinburne's veneration of Landor began in his Eton days (Rooksby, p. 30). He admired Landor's classicism and republicanism. They met in Florence ('flower-town', line 1) in March 1864. Landor accepted the dedication of *Atalanta in Calydon* but died before it could reach him in print. In the article he contributed to the ninth edition of the *Encyclopaedia Britannica* (1882), Swinburne praised Landor's ideal of civic and heroic life, his 'passionate compassion, his bitter and burning pity for all wrongs endured in all the world', and his loyalty and liberality; and he particularly admired his *Hellenics* (1847) and *Imaginary Conversations of Greeks and Romans* (1853).

Landor was eighty-nine years old when they met, and Swinburne was about to turn twenty-seven (line 23). The address 'Look earthward now' (line 34) recalls Milton's 'Lycidas', line 163, 'Look homeward Angel now', and it may also be influenced by Christina Rossetti, 'Your eyes look earthward', in 'The Convent Threshold' (1862), line 17. 'Dedicated' (line 47) means 'consecrated'.

The poem is written in quatrains consisting of alternate iambic tetrameter and iambic dimeter lines; they rhyme *abab*.

A Song in Time of Order. *1852* and *A Song in Time of Revolution. 1860*

'A Song in Time of Order. 1852' was published in the *Spectator*, 26 April 1862, and 'A Song in Time of Revolution. 1860' in the *Spectator*, 28 June 1862.

Both poems are expressions of Swinburne's republican convictions. The date appended to the title of the first poem indicates that his target is Louis Napoleon, who became emperor of France in 1852. He had been elected president of France in 1848, backed by the newly founded 'Party of Order'; 'order' was one of his political slogans. In 1851, when his term as president expired, he staged a successful *coup d'état*; the next year he began to deport his enemies to Algeria and French Guiana; later that year, he was proclaimed emperor. He also sent convicts with long sentences to French Guiana; Cayenne (line 50) became known as the 'city of the condemned'. See Hugo's 'Hymne des Transportés' (1853). Austria (line 50) dominated the disunited Italian states (until 1859). Louis Napoleon's parentage had been a topic of contemporary gossip (line 39, 'Buonaparte the bastard'). The revolution that Swinburne praises in the second poem is Garibaldi's successful offensive into Italy: capturing first Sicily and then Naples in 1860, he handed both over to Victor Emmanuel and greeted him as the king of a united Italy.

Contrast the title with the occasional prayers of the *Book of Common Prayer*, for example, 'In the Time of War and Tumults'. Lines 29–30 of the first poem and lines 19–20 of the second are reminiscent of God's power in Job; see, for example, Job 38:8 and 41:1. See, too, Hugo's 'Lux' (1853) line 202–6. 'Reins' (line 27, 'A Song in Time of Revolution') means 'loins'.

For Swinburne, Victor Hugo's collection of poems denouncing Louis Napoleon, *Les Châtiments* (1853), was a crucial example of republicanism in poetry. (Much of Swinburne's critical work on Hugo, including comments on *Les Châtiments*, is reprinted in the Bonchurch edition of his works, volume 13. However, that volume includes works now known not to have been written by Swinburne, and it is misleading in other respects, too; see Clyde Hyder, *Swinburne as Critic*, 1972.) Lafourcade points to the influence of Hugo's 'Ultima Verba' in particular. Consider Hugo's last stanza in relation to the lines 'While three men hold together, The kingdoms are less by three' ('A Song in Time of Order'):

> Si l'on n'est plus que mille, eh bien, j'en suis! Si même
> Ils ne sont plus que cent, je brave encor Sylla;
> S'il en demeure dix, je serai le dixième;
> Et s'il n'en reste qu'un, je serai celui-là!

(Sylla, or Sulla, the Roman tyrant, is one of Hugo's names for Louis Napoleon.)

'A Song in Time of Order' is in quatrains of trimeter lines that combine iambs and anapests; 'gunwale' (line 12) is pronounced as a strong trochee, not as a spondee. The quatrains rhyme *abab*. 'A Song in Time of Revolution' is in hexameter rhyming couplets, combining anapests and iambs; there is a rhyme after the third foot as well as at the end of the line.

To Victor Hugo

Throughout his life Swinburne was passionately enthusiastic about Victor Hugo. In this poem, he recalls Hugo's childhood during the Napoleonic period and pays tribute to Hugo's self-enforced, principled exile (forced into exile after he resisted Louis Napoleon's *coup d'état*, he refused to enter France after the general amnesty of 1859). In his prose works of 1852, *Napoléon le Petit* and *Histoire d'un crime*, he indicted Napoleon III, and in 1853 he wrote a book of satirical poems condemning him, *Les Châtiments*. Swinburne praises the principles of the French Revolution (line 99) and the democratic uprisings of 1848, while lamenting their apparent political failure. He contrasts the political pessimism of his generation (lines 124–6) with Hugo's optimism (line 153). The tenth stanza recalls the exile of Swinburne's ancestors during the English Civil War. The eighteenth stanza invokes Prometheus.

Contrast the opening two lines with Tennyson, 'Ode on the Death of the Duke of Wellington' (1852), line 266: 'On God and Godlike men we build our trust.' 'Uplift' in lines 50 and 128 is an older form of 'uplifted'; it survived in nineteenth-century poetry. Compare line 99 with Genesis 1:3, 'And God said, Let there be light; and there was light.' Swinburne refers to 'the vast and various universe created by the *fiat lux* of Victor Hugo' (*Studies in Prose and Poetry*, [1889] 1894, p. 277). Line 166 recalls Shakespeare's Macbeth, 'I gin to be a-weary of the sun' (Act V, Scene 5, line 49).

Swinburne sent a copy of *Poems and Ballads* to Hugo, who could not read English but who asked a friend to translate this poem. He wrote graciously to Swinburne about 'les nobles et magnifiques strophes que vous m'adressez' (Lang, 1, 248n2).

The poem is written in iambics; the eight-line stanza consists of two trimeter lines, a pentameter, two trimeters, a pentameter, a tetrameter, and a pentameter; rhyming *aabccbdd*. The stanza is very like that of Milton's hymn in 'On the Morning of Christ's Nativity', except that Milton's last line is a hexameter.

Before Dawn

The metre is iambic trimeter. The stanza rhymes *aaabcccb*, where *a* and *c* have feminine endings. On rhyming triplets, see Swinburne's discussion of Robert Herrick (1891; reprinted in *Studies in Prose and Poetry*, 1894). With 'no abiding' (line 71), compare 1 Chronicles 29:15, 'our days on the earth are as a shadow, and there is none abiding'.

Dolores

Dolores is Swinburne's anti-madonna; her name derives from the phrase 'Our Lady of the Seven Sorrows' (which, in French, is Swinburne's sub-title). 'Our Lady of Pain', Swinburne's pagan darker Venus, is his answer to the Christian 'Our Lady of Sorrows', although his paganism is tinged with his own interest in sadomasochism (see Lang, 1, 123). Words and phrases from the Bible (lines 10 and 439: Matthew 18:21–2; line 137: Matthew 9:17 and elsewhere; lines 371–2: Exodus 7:9–12; line 328: Matthew 13:24–40), the Loreto Litany of the Blessed Virgin (line 19 and 'tower of ivory'; line 21 and 'mystical rose'; line 22 and 'house of gold'), the prayers of the Mass (e.g. lines 133–4 and the taking of communion), the 'Ave Maria' (line 39 and 'blessed among women'), and the Lord's Prayer (lines 279 and 391) are blasphemously deployed. Baudelaire's poems 'À une Madonne' and 'Les Litanies de Satan' (1857) are models for Swinburne; he writes admiringly about these two poems in particular in his 1862 *Spectator* review of *Les Fleurs du Mal*.

Libitina (lines 51, 423) is the Roman goddess of burials, misidentified since antiquity with Venus; Priapus (lines 51, 423) is the ithyphallic god of gardens (lines 303, 313), whose cult was centred in Lampsacus (line 405). The prayer to Dolores to intercede with her father Priapus on our behalf (line 311) is a parody of Catholic prayer. Priapus is the subject of three poems once attributed to Catullus (line 340); Swinburne quotes two lines of one of these in a note to line 307: 'for in its cities the coast of the Hellespont, more oysterous than most, honours you particularly'. One of his lyrics (*Carmina* 32) is addressed to the girl Ipsitilla (cf. Swinburne's line 326).

Swinburne reverses the usual associations of cypress and myrtle in lines 175–6. The Thalassian in line 223 is Aphrodite Anadyomene, risen again in Roman cruelty. The gladiatorial combats follow in the next stanzas, for which Lafourcade adduces the preface to Gautier's *Mademoiselle de Maupin* (1835) as an influence. Nero is introduced in lines 249–56 (see Linda Dowling, 'Nero and the Aesthetics of Torture', *The Victorian Newsletter*,

Fall 1984, pp. 2–5, on the aestheticized Nero in the nineteenth century). Alciphron and Arisbe (line 299) are names that occur in Greek history and mythology, but Swinburne is most likely using them simply as the names of a male and a female lover.

The stanzas beginning at line 329 describe Cybele, the 'Great Mother of the Gods', whose worship, characterized by ecstatic states and insensibility to pain, arose in Phrygia (line 330), where her main cult was located on Mount Dindymus (line 345). It later spread to Greece and Rome, where one of her Latin names was the 'Idaean Mother' (line 333). Her priests castrated themselves as Cybele's lover, Attis, did; Catullus, *Carmina* 63, relates that legend (line 340). In 'Notes on Poems and Reviews' (Appendix 1), Swinburne contrasts Dolores, 'the darker Venus', with both the Virgin Mary and Cybele.

Cotys or Cotyto (line 409, Cotytto) was a Thracian goddess later worshipped orgiastically in Corinth and Sicily as well as in Thrace. Astarte (in Greek) or Ashtaroth (in the Bible) are names for Ishtar, the Mesopotamian goddess of love and war. Privately, Swinburne associates the 'Europian Cotytto' and the 'Asiatic Aphrodite of Aphaca' (Lang, 1, 406) with Sade and with sadomasochistic indulgence (see Lang, 1, 312).

'Seventy times seven' (lines 10 and 439) recalls Matthew 18:22. J. C. Maxwell (*Notes and Queries*, Vol. 21, January 1974, p. 15) offers a parallel to and possible source of line 159 in Thackeray's *The Newcomes* (1855), Chapter 65, 'before marriages and cares and divisions had separated us'. Perhaps 'live torches' (line 245) refer to humans burnt alive; however, the *OED* offers no example of such a usage. A 'visible God' (line 320) echoes *Timon of Athens*, Act 4, Scene 3. The rod in lines 371–2 recalls Aaron's rod in Exodus 7. Line 379 may invoke Sade, and line 380 alludes to the allegory of sin and death in *Paradise Lost*, Book 2; the *OED* records an obsolete usage of 'incestuous' meaning 'begotten of incest'. The tares and grain of line 438 recall Christ's parable in Matthew 13.

The metre combines iambs and anapests in seven trimeter lines concluded by the dimeter eighth line, which always consists of an iamb followed by an anapest; in every other stanza, the refrain is 'Our Lady of Pain'. The rhyme scheme is *ababcdcd*, where *a* and *c* are regularly feminine; 'Dolores' appears nine times in this position. The metre and stanza is very close to those of some poems by William Praed, such as 'Song for the Fourteenth of February' (1827), except that Swinburne's last line is shorter by a foot than Praed's and so clinches each stanza. Swinburne read Praed at school and respected his work (Lang, 3, 314), though coolly (*Studies in Prose and Poetry* [1891] 1894, p. 100). Byron used the same versification (that is, with the trimeter final line) in 'Stanzas to [Augusta]' (1816); however, Swinburne was critical of Byron for 'having . . . so bad an ear for metre' (*Essays and*

Studies, [1866] 1875, p. 251). Saintsbury, in *A History of English Prosody* (1906, Vol. 3, p. 344), reviews Swinburne's antecedents:

The initial 'rumtity-tumtity-tum' of Shenstone and Cowper; the comic improve-ments of Gay and others; the apparently casual inspiration which made Byron get rid of the jolt and jingle, by the simple expedient of alternative double rhyme, in Haidée's 'Garden of Roses'; the perfecting of this form by Praed – these surely form a genealogical tree of sufficient interest as they stand.

A. E. Housman refers to this stanza 'which Swinburne dignified and strengthened till it yielded a combination of speed and magnificence which nothing in English had possessed before' (lecture on Swinburne delivered in 1910).

There is a reproduction of two stanzas of 'Dolores' in Wise's 1919 *Bibliography,* p. 160.

The Garden of Proserpine

See 'Hymn to Proserpine' (page 334) for the figure of Proserpine, who in this poem stands at the garden-entrance to the world of the dead, wear-ing a crown of poppies and having prepared a wine of oblivion from the poppies.

At a dinner party in the 1870s, while speaking about *Poems and Ballads* in relation to his experiences, Swinburne said that there were three poems

which beyond all the rest were autobiographical – 'The Triumph of Time', 'Dolores', and 'The Garden of Proserpine'. 'The Triumph of Time' was a monument to the sole real love of his life – a love which had been the tragic destruction of all his faith in women. 'Dolores' expressed the passion with which he had sought relief, in the madnesses of the fleshly Venus, from his ruined dreams of the heavenly. 'The Garden of Proserpine' expressed his revolt against the flesh and its fevers, and his longing to find a refuge from them in a haven of undisturbed rest . . .

(W. H. Mallock, *Memoirs of Life and Literature,* 1920; quoted in Rooksby, p. 102.)

Wordsworth's 'A slumber did my spirit seal' (1800) and Keats's 'Ode to a Nightingale' (1819) famously invoke the easeful or restful condition of death. Tennyson's 'The Lotos-Eaters' (1832), Matthew Arnold's 'Requies-cat' (1853), and Christina Rossetti's sonnet 'Rest' (1862) continue this Romantic theme.

The imagery of line 76 derives from falconry. 'Diurnal' (line 94) may recall Wordsworth ('A slumber did my spirit seal').

The metre is iambic trimeter, and the rhyme scheme is *ababcccb*, where *b* is the only masculine rhyme. Christina Rossetti frequently used three consecutive rhymes in poems, though not with feminine endings; cf. a poem in a similar mood, 'Dream-Land' (1862). Swinburne discusses the triplet rhyme in a short piece on Robert Herrick (*Studies in Prose and Poetry*, [1891] 1894, p. 46), where he praises an instance of it in Herrick as 'worthy of Miss Rossetti herself; and praise of such work can go no higher'. See the note to 'A Match' for examples of iambic trimeter octaves. The octave of 'The Garden of Proserpine' is identical to the stanza of Dryden's song 'Farewell ungrateful traitor' from Act 5 of *The Spanish Fryar*. Saintsbury, in *A History of English Prosody* (1906, Vol. 2, p. 379), writes that Dryden's song 'joins the music of the seventeenth century to that of the nineteenth, and Dryden to Swinburne'.

Hesperia

Hesperia, the west, is the location of the Fortunatae Insulae (line 35), the 'Islands of the Blest', home of the happy dead; see *Atalanta in Calydon*, lines 510–25. Both Dolores, 'Our Lady of Pain' (line 60), and Proserpine, 'Our Lady of Sleep' (line 72), are invoked here.

In 1887, Swinburne opposed the inclusion of 'Hesperia' in a selection of his poems on the ground that it was 'too long, too vague, and too dependent on the two preceding poems' (Lang, 5, 208); William Rossetti, in his criticism of 1866, made similar comments.

The metre may be described as a modification of accentual dactylic hexameter / xx / xx / xx / xx / xx //. However, Swinburne had a strong antipathy to the dactyl. In an essay on Coleridge, he disparaged the 'feeble and tuneless form of metre called hexameters in English; if form of metre that may be called which has neither metre nor form' (*Essays and Studies*, [1869] 1875, p. 272). In his preface to his translation in anapests of the 'Grand Chorus of Birds' from Aristophanes (1880), he famously declared that in English 'all variations and combinations of anapæstic, iambic, or trochaic metre are as natural and pliable as all dactylic and spondaic forms of verse are unnatural and abhorrent'.

In this poem he modified the classical metre in two ways: first, his verses rhyme *ababcdcd* . . . , where feminine and masculine endings, respectively, alternate. Thus, in every other line, the last foot consists of a single stressed syllable, rather than of two syllables (i.e., it is catalectic). Second, Swinburne introduced 'anacrustic' syllables, as the term then was; that is, he added to the beginning of a line one or two unstressed syllables which precede the six metrical feet and which are not part of the scansion. Otherwise, Swinburne stayed close to the classical metre: he substituted spondees for dactyls, and his caesuras, sometimes more than one in a line, never coincide with the end of a metrical foot. Here are the first eight lines scanned; anacrustic words are italicized:

```
  /   x  x | /   x   x x| /   /   | /  /    x    x | /   x   x |
```
Out of the golden remote wild west where the sea without
```
        /        /
```
shore is,
```
   /   x   x | /   x   x   | /   x  x| /   x    x | / x   x | /
```
Full of the sunset, and sad, if at all, with the fulness of joy,
```
    /    /  | /  x   x | / x     x | /    x  x |
```
As a wind sets in with the autumn that blows from the
```
   /   x   x | /
```
region of stories,
```
  /     x   x | / x   x | /   x   x | /   x  x| / /
```
Blows with a perfume of songs and of memories beloved
```
    x   x | /
```
from a boy,
```
  /    x    x   x| /  /   x  x| /  x  x |/  x  x  x | / x   x
```
Blows from the capes of the past oversea to the bays of the
```
  | / /
```
present,
```
  /    x   x  | / x   x | / | /  x   x x| / / x   x| / x x
```
Filled as with shadow of sound with the pulse of invisible
```
         /
```
feet,
```
   /   x  x x| / / x   x  x | / / x  x x | / x   x x | /
```
Far out to the shallows and straits of the future, by rough
```
  x   x | / / /
```
ways or pleasant,
```
     /  x   x | / /   / | /  / x x | / x  x | / x   x|
```
Is it thither the wind's wings beat? is it hither to me, O my
```
          /
```
sweet?

('Passionate', line 30, presents a problem; perhaps it is to be scanned with three stresses. 'Sonorous', line 80, is stressed on the second syllable, like Latin sonōrus, and as it is pronounced in Milton and Pope. Note that consecutive vowels are sometimes elided and that the last syllable counts as stressed by convention, regardless of its intrinsic accent.)

The poem can be understood as dactylic hexameter with these two modifications. However, these innovations make the lines scan much more anapestically. Every other line has a masculine ending, and so in half the

lines the last three syllables can be heard as an anapest. When two unstressed
anacrustic syllables are added to the beginning of a line with a masculine
ending, that line can be scanned as an exact anapestic hexameter (with
spondaic substitution); there are thirteen such lines in 'Hesperia'.

However, the confusion of dactylic and anapestic metres is exactly what
Swinburne complained of in Arnold's hexameters (*Essays and Studies*,
[1867] 1875, pp. 163–4), which, he writes, he has 'tried in vain to reduce
by scansion into any metrical feet at all':

They look like nothing on earth, and sound like anapæsts broken up and driven
wrong; neither by ear nor by finger can I bring them to any reckoning. I am sure of
one thing, that some of them begin with a pure and absolute anapæst; and how a
hexameter can do this it passes my power to conceive. And at best what ugly bastards
of verse are these self-styled hexameters! how human tongues or hands could utter
or write them except by way of burlesque improvisation I could never imagine, and
never shall. Once only, to be candid – and I will for once show all possible loyalty
and reverence to past authority – once only, as far as I know, in Dr. Hawtrey's
delicate and fluent verse, has the riddle been resolved; the verses are faultless, are
English; are hexametric; but this is simply a graceful interlude of pastime, a well-
played stroke in a game of skill played with language. Such as pass elsewhere for
English hexameters I do hope and suppose impossible at Eton. Mr. Clough's I will
not presume to be serious attempts or studies in any manner of metre; they are
admirable studies in graduated prose, full of fine sound and effect. Even Mr.
Kingsley's 'Andromeda', the one good poem extant in that pernicious metre, for all
its spirit and splendour, for all the grace and glory and exultation of its rushing and
ringing words, has not made possible the impossible thing. Nothing but loose
rhymeless anapæsts can be made of the language in that way; and we hardly want
these, having infinite command and resource of metre without them, and rhyme
thrown in to turn the overweighted scale.

The scansion has been controversial. I believe that it is best to identify the
metre as modified dactylic hexameter because the opening lines of the poem
are straightforwardly scanned as such (the anacrustic syllables become
much more frequent later in the poem) and because the caesuras occur in
the middle of the metrical feet when so scanned; the metrical taxonomy,
however, is less important than the movement of the verse, which is both
dactylic and anapestic.

Love at Sea

The poem is a free imitation of Gautier's 'Barcarolle' (originally a song sung by Venetian *barcaruoli*, gondoliers, the barcarole was featured in a number of operas and other musical compositions in the eighteenth and nineteenth centuries):

> Dites, la jeune belle,
> Où voulez-vous aller?
> La voile ouvre son aile,
> La brise va souffler!
>
> L'aviron est d'ivoire,
> Le pavillon de moire,
> Le gouvernail d'or fin;
> J'ai pour lest une orange,
> Pour voile une aile d'ange,
10 Pour mousse un séraphin.
>
> Dites, la jeune belle,
> Où voulez-vous aller?
> La voile ouvre son aile,
> La brise va souffler!
>
> Est-ce dans la Baltique,
> Sur la mer Pacifique,
> Dans l'île de Java?
> Ou bien dans la Norwège,
> Cueillir la fleur de neige,
20 Ou la fleur d'Angsoka?
>
> Dites, la jeune belle,
> Où voulez-vous aller?
> La voile ouvre son aile,
> La brise va souffler!
>
> Menez-moi, dit la belle,
> A la rive fidèle
> Où l'on aime toujours.
> – Cette rive, ma chère,
> On ne la connaît guère
30 Au pays des amours.

Gautier published the lyric in 1835. (It was one of the six lyrics by Gautier that Berlioz set to music in his song cycle 'Les Nuits d'Été', 1841; according to Philip Henderson, *Swinburne: Portrait of a Poet*, 1974, p. 140, Swinburne felt a special affinity to Berlioz.) 'Angsoka' (line 20) is the Malay word for the flower *Pavetta indica*, of the Rubiaceae family; it makes another appearance in Banville's poem 'À Auguste Supersac' in *Les Cariatides*, 1842. For Swinburne's 'fire-flowers' (line 26, evidently his translation of 'la fleur d'Angsoka') cf. Hugo's 'fleur de feu' in 'Mille Chemins, Un Sel But' (1840).

Swinburne's third stanza may recall the cancelled opening stanza of Keats's 'Ode on Melancholy' (published in 1848).

The stanza and metre of 'Love at Sea' are more intricate than those of Gautier's 'Barcarolle'. Swinburne's basic form, used for all the stanzas but the first, consists of six lines: $a_3a_3b_2c_3c_3b_2$. The three middle stanzas add a refrain which either repeats or offers slight variations of the first line of the poem. The metre is iambic.

The first stanza rhymes $ABabaaAB$, where the capital letters indicate that the whole line is repeated (sometimes with slight variation in subsequent stanzas). Line A later serves as the refrain. The repetition of the first two lines at the end of a stanza recalls the rondel and the triolet; the use of the first line as a refrain recalls the villanelle. Swinburne, however, is not employing a *forme fixe* but suggesting the musical repetitions that lie behind such forms.

April

A vidame was a feudal officer, originally appointed by a bishop but later hereditary, who held lands from a bishop and was his representative in secular matters. This thirteenth-century vidame of Chartres (died *c.* 1219) was Guillaume de Ferrières, whose works were edited and published by Louis Lacour in 1856. Swinburne translates the seventh poem in that collection, from the section *Saluts d'Amour* (amatory epistles):

> Quant florissent li boscage,
> Que pré sont vert et flori
> Et cil oisellon sauvage
> Chantent au dous tems seri,
> Et je plus plaing mon damage.
> Quant plus je et chant et ri,
> Moins ai joie en mon corage

Et si me muir por celi
Qui n'en daigne avoir merci:
10   Si ne me tieng pas à sage.

Seur tous connois mon folage
Moi que chant, je sai de si
Qu'amer à tel seignorage,
Qu'il le m'estuet fere ainsi.
Si servirai mon eage
Tant qu'elle ait de moi merci
La belle, la preus, la sage,
Pour qui j'ai soulas guerpi;
Dont fine amour m'a traï
20   Qui m'occhist en son hommage.

Amours en vostre servise
Me suis mis en non chaloir:
Si sai bien qu'en nule guise
Ne me porroie mouvoir;
Ains me convient à devise
Quanque vous voulés voloir.
Mis sui en vostre franchise
Loiaument, sans decevoir,
Mais ne me puis apercevoir
30   Que pitiés vous en soit prise.

Moult ai en vous pitié quise
C'onques ne li poi véoir.
S'en cele ne l'avés mise
Qui tout le mont set voloir:
Bien avès ma mort emprise
Ne le ne puet remanoir;
Car trop ai m'entente mise
En ce qui me fet doloir,
Et quant plus me desespoir
40   Plus me truis en sa justice.

Dame de valour est la moie,
Car tant en ai le mal chier,
Que tout le mont n'en prendroie
S'il me convenoit changier.
Las! qu'ai dit? Je ne porroie,
Ne jà volenté n'en quier,

Et ne porquant toute voie
Me fait penser et veillier;
Mais ne me puis esloignier
50   De li, se morir devoie.

Dame, voir, tous i morroie,
Quant je ne vous os prier,
S'en chantant ne vos disoie
Ce dont j'ai greignor mestier.
Belle à qui mes cuers s'outroie
Tuit mi celei de si errier
Sont de vous, où que je soie,
Seulement tant vous requier
Que me feissiez cuidier,
60   La votre amour avanroie.

Maint felon et losengier
Auront fait maint destorbier
A ces qui amours maiscroie.

Swinburne translates into ten-line stanzas plus an envoy, but the metre and
rhyme scheme of his stanzas vary. The metre consists of iambs and anapests
in lines either dimeter or trimeter, or occasionally tetrameter. The basic
rhyme scheme is *ababbcdcdc*, with variations in stanza one and three. The
envoy rhymes *ddc* (its rhyme are those of the previous stanza) and consists
of a trimeter, dimeter and trimeter line, each combining one anapest with
one or two iambs.

Before Parting

Published in the *Spectator*, 17 May 1862.

On purple-coloured hair (line 32), see Ahinoam in 'The Masque of
Queen Bersabe' and Alexander Theroux, *The Secondary Colors* (1996),
pp. 138–9, who mentions purple hair in works by Marvell and Ovid and in
the wigs of fashionable ladies under Napoleon. We should add Baudelaire
and Swinburne to Theroux's list of 'very purple poets', including Keats,
Edgar Allan Poe and Tennyson. See also Vladimir Nabokov, *Eugene Onegin*
(rev. ed., 1975) volume 2, pp. 520–21, on the confusion among kinds of
purple.

In 1878, Swinburne published the poem 'At Parting' and boasted to
Joseph Knight about it: 'I pique myself on its moral tone; in an age when
all other lyrists, from Tennyson to Rossetti, go in (metrically) for constancy

and eternity of attachment and reunion in future lives, etc., etc., I limit love, honestly and candidly, to 24 hours' (Lang, 3, 44).

There existed a Provençal tradition of 'reverse albas'; see, for example, Guiraut Riquier's poem with the refrain 'e dezir vezer l'alba'.

The six-line stanza rhymes *abbacc*. The lines are iambic pentameter except for the fifth or sixth line of each stanza, one of which is iambic trimeter.

The Sundew

Published in the *Spectator*, 20 June 1862.

'Sundew' commonly refers to the members of the *Drosera* genus; Vernon Rendall, in *Wild Flowers in Literature* (1934), identifies it as *Drosera rotundifolia*. It is an insectivore; its leaves, covered with red glandular hairs, exude a sticky substance that attracts and traps insects. It is small and glistens in the sun; it has a small, five-petalled white flower. The sundew is a perennial that grows in boggy regions. In 'Winter in Northumberland' (1878) Swinburne recalls the sundew hiding under the heather in winter; he also associates the flower with the borders in Lang, 4, 121.

Rendall notes the appearance of the sundew in George Crabbe, *The Borough* (Letter 1); Swinburne respected Crabbe (Lang, 5, 135). Rendall also reminds us that the traditional contrast between flowers that revive every year and man for whom death is final (stanza 3) is found in Moschus's 'Lament for Bion':

Alas the mallows, when they wither in the garden, and the green parsley and the flourishing curled dill, they live anew and grow another year; but we men, great and mighty in our wisdom, when once we die, unhearing in the hollow earth we sleep the long long sleep that knows no waking.

In his review 'The Poems of Dante Gabriel Rossetti', Swinburne admired the 'keen truthfulness and subtle sincerity' of Rossetti's 'A Young Fir-Wood', 'The Honeysuckle', and 'The Woodspurge', poems written by 1856 (*Essays and Studies*, [1870] 1875, pp. 70–1). In 1880, he protested against Henry Arthur Bright's too exclusive commendation of Tennyson's floriculture and cited the flower called by its Spanish name in Browning's 'Garden Fancies' (1845) and the 'plant . . . yielding a three-leaved bell' in *Sordello* (1840, Book 2, line 290), Dante Gabriel Rossetti's 'The Woodspurge' and 'The Honeysuckle', Morris's good words for the sunflower (perhaps in 'A Good Knight in Prison', 1858, but cf. 'The Gilliflower of Gold', 1858), as well as his own 'Sundew' (see Lang, 4, 121). For the French background, see Philip Knight's *Flower Poetics in Nineteenth-Century France* (1986). Swinburne disparaged his poem later in life (Lang, 5, 40, 70; 6, 153).

The metre is iambic tetrameter; the stanza rhymes *abbab*.

Félise

The epigraph is the refrain (*rebriche*) of Villon's 'Ballade des dames du temps jadis' from *Le Testament*: Rossetti translates it in 1869 as 'But where are the snows of yester-year.' ('Antan' derives from *ante annum*.)

Line 61, 'You loved me and you loved me not', might recall the formula used in children's divining-games, but the *OED* gives as the earliest written reference to it the 1909 *Old Hampshire Singing Games*. The *OED* gives no instance of 'fledge' used intransitively after 1637 except for line 69. Line 76 recalls Shakespeare, *The Tempest*, 'deeper than e'er plummet sounded' (Act III, Scene 3, line 101) and 'deeper than did ever plummet sound' (Act V, Scene 1, line 56). Line 134 may have been influenced by Keats's remark in a letter to Benjamin Bailey dated 22 November 1817: 'The Imagination may be compared to Adam's dream – he awoke and found it truth.' Lines 136–7 recall Isaiah 6:6–7. Lines 234–5 are reminiscent of Shakespeare, *King Lear*, Act I, Scene 4, 'beat at this gate that let thy folly in'. Lines 229 and 236 recall Matthew 23:17 and 19. Line 244 echoes Shakespeare, *Macbeth*, Act II, Scene 2, line 60 ('making the green one red') and line 245 recalls one of the temptations of Christ in the desert, Matthew 4:3.

Swinburne defends 'Félise' in a letter to John Ruskin in 1866 (Lang, 1, 160):

I recalcitrate vigorously against your opinion of 'Félise', which is rather a favourite child of mine. As to the subject, I thought it clear enough, and likely to recall to most people a similar passage of experience. A young fellow is left alone with a woman rather older, whom a year since he violently loved. Meantime he has been in town, she in the country; and in the year's lapse they have had time, he to become tired of her memory, she to fall in love with his. Surely I have explained this plainly and 'cynically' enough! Last year I loved you, and you were puzzled, and didn't love me – quite. This year (I perceive) you love me, and I feel puzzled, and don't love you – quite. 'Sech is life,' as Mrs. Gamp says [in Dickens's *Martin Chuzzlewit*, Chapter 29]; '*Deus vult* ['it is God's will', not in Dickens]; it can't be helped.' As to the flowers and hours [lines 91, 93], they rhyme naturally, being the sweetest and most transient things that exist – when they *are* sweet. And the poem, it seems to me, is not long enough to explain what it has to say.

See also his letter to William Rossetti, Lang, 1, 193.

The stanza consists of four iambic tetrameter lines followed by an iambic dimeter, rhyming *ababb*. However, the two stanzas starting at line 116 rhyme *abaab*, where the lines in *b* are iambic trimeter. Swinburne occasionally substitutes an anapest for an iamb or elides consecutive vowels. 'Félise' is used six times as a rhyme (three times with 'seas').

An Interlude

The 'flag-flowers' of line 11 belong to the yellow flag (*Iris pseudacorus*), common in wet meadows. Vernon Rendall in *Wild Flowers in Literature* (1934) records the appearance of flag-flowers in John Clare's 'Recollections after a Ramble' (1821) and Tennyson's 'The Miller's Daughter' (1832), to which we might add Southey's *Thalaba* (1801, Book 11, line 431), John Clare's 'Summer Evening' (1821) and 'The Wild Flower Nosegay' (1821), and Shelley's 'The Question' (1824). The meadow-sweet (line 12) is *Spiraea ulmaria*, of the same order as roses; it grows to about two feet and has creamy-white, strongly scented flowers; it is common in damp ground such as in moist meadows or along river-banks. It is not the species *Spiraea salicifolia*, which the name denotes in the United States. Rendall notes the meadow-sweets in Clare, Tennyson, Meredith and Arnold.

The lines are trimeter, and the metre consists of both iambs and anapests. The rhyme is *abab*, where *a* has a feminine ending.

Hendecasyllabics

The name ('eleven syllables') refers to the metre of the line:

– – – ⏑ ⏑ – ⏑ – ⏑ – –

with two possible variations, each occurring within the first two syllables:

– ⏑ – ⏑ ⏑ – ⏑ – ⏑ – –
⏑ – – ⏑ ⏑ – ⏑ – ⏑ – .

The metre was favoured by Catullus, who used it in about two-thirds of his lyric poems. In English, the stress replaces the quantity of classical verse, though quantity must still be reckoned with. Coleridge's 'Catullian Hendecasyllabics' (a reworking of the hendecasyllabic line into twelve syllables and running / x x / x x / x / x / /) was first published in 1834; Tennyson's 'Hendecasyllabics' ('all in quantity') in 1863.

George M. Ridenour ('Swinburne's Imitations of Catullus', *Victorian Newsletter* 74, Fall 1998, pp. 51–7) sees the poem's welcome to autumn in relation to Catullus's poem 46, which welcomes spring and is written in hendecasyllabics; he also takes lines 19–25 to be a reversal of the welcome to the beloved in the spring ('For, lo, the winter is past . . .'), in the Song of Solomon 2:11–13. The metaphorical use of eyelids (line 6) perhaps recalls Milton, 'Lycidas' (line 26), 'under the opening eyelids of the morn'.

In 1875, Swinburne objected to Gosse's reference to the 'laborious versification' of Catullus, 'whom I should have called the least laborious, and the most spontaneous in his godlike and birdlike melody, of all lyrists known to me except Sappho and Shelley: I should as soon call a lark's note laboured as his' (Lang, 3, 1).

Sapphics

Sappho's stanza was modified by Horace, and the modified form became the basis for most English sapphics before Swinburne. Among the Elizabethan experiments with the sapphic, Philip Sidney's and Thomas Campion's are the most famous. Sidney's most successful effort, 'If mine eyes can speak,' like Campion's paraphrase of Psalm 19 ('Come, let us sound'), adopts the scansion of the Horatian sapphic:

$$- \cup - - \cup \cup - \cup - -$$
$$- \cup - - \cup \cup - \cup - -$$
$$- \cup - - \cup \cup - \cup - -$$
$$- \cup \cup - -.$$

A caesura is mandatory after the fifth or sixth syllable. In English, stress replaces quantity; nonetheless, Swinburne, like Tennyson, was attentive to quantity and would not have demurred at Cowper's admonition: 'without close attention to syllabic quantity in the construction of our verse, we can give it neither melody nor dignity.'

In his *Observations in the Art of English Poesie*, Campion offers freer versions of the stanza, so that it consists of trochaics with an initial spondee, 'to make the number more grave'. Although these freer versions had little subsequent influence, the insistence on gravity was important. Later sapphic stanzas were frequently weighty, as for example poems by Isaac Watts ('The Day of Judgment') and William Cowper ('Lines Written During a Period of Insanity'). Robert Southey employed it to describe the death of an abandoned, homeless woman in 'The Widow' (1795). In Shelley's 'The Crisis' (in the *Esdaile Notebook*, not published until the twentieth century) the theme is political injustice.

Swinburne bypasses this way of treating the metre, and returns to its form in Sappho rather than Horace. The scansion (marked in terms of accent rather than quantity, where x́ indicates a variable syllable) is

$$/ x / \acute{x} / x x / x / /$$
$$/ x / \acute{x} / x x / x / /$$
$$/ x / \acute{x} / x x / x / /$$
$$/ x x / /.$$

The Greek form differs from the Latin in having a variable fourth foot (in Horace it is always long) and in not requiring a caesura after the fifth or sixth syllable, so that the line flows more freely.

Théodore de Banville did not break with the traditional French form in his two sapphic poems 'Idolâtrie' and 'À Victor Hugo' in *Les Cariatides* (1842), but the first is an attempt to return to Sappho via sapphics:

> Mètre divin, mètre de bonne race,
> Que nous rapporte un poëte nouveau,
> Toi qui jadis combattais pour Horace,
>   Rhythme de Sappho!

Sappho, of Mitylene (line 16) in Lesbos (lines 15, 30, 49), was called the 'Tenth Muse' (lines 26–30) in antiquity (*Greek Anthology*, 9.506; the expression is used by Shakespeare in Sonnet 38).

One of the interlocutors in Jerome J. McGann's *Swinburne: An Experiment in Criticism* (1972) sees the poem as a conscious imitation with a reversal and further development of the 'Ode to Aphrodite', in which Aphrodite implores Sappho's attention, not vice versa, etc. (p. 112).

At Eleusis

With some changes of detail, the poem keeps close to the story of Demeter as it is told in the *Homeric Hymn to Demeter* (which had been translated by Shelley around 1818 and published in 1839): after Hades abducts Persephone, her mother Demeter, hearing the echo of her voice, goes to seek her. No one will tell Demeter what happened until she meets Hecate, who takes her to the sun, who explains that Zeus gave her daughter to Hades. She is angry and distraught; disguised as an old woman, she wanders the earth until she meets the daughters of Celeus, a ruler of Eleusis. They are respectful and kind to her, and she becomes a nurse to Demophon, the infant son of Celeus and Metaneira. She tries to make him immortal by burning away his mortality; however, she is interrupted by Metaneira. (In later versions, Demophon is replaced by Triptolemus, as in Swinburne.) In the hymn, Demeter then reveals herself and begins to instruct the Eleusinians in her worship. She leaves then and instigates a year-long universal famine to force Zeus and Hades to release her daughter. A compromise is reached: Persephone is to spend part of each year with her mother. Demeter then renews the earth and teaches the Eleusinians to perform her mysteries.

Swinburne adopted some of the Greek phrases of the original: 'τῆς δ' αὐτίκα γούνατ' ἔλυντο' (line 281), 'and right away her knees were loosened'; compare this with Swinburne's lines 23 and 91. 'Cope' (line 101) is obsolete for 'to meet' or 'to have a relation with'; it is used with this meaning in Shakespeare. 'Competence' (line 115) means sufficiency. The kingfisher (line 132) is the Greek mythical bird, the Halcyon. 'Pleached' (line 209) means interlaced. Lines 214–15 are an absolute construction, 'when Celeus is dead and swathed . . .'

William Rossetti wrote that ' "At Eleusis" is an exceptionally long speech spoken by Demeter, as from a Greek tragedy – recalling also such modern work as some of Landor's *Hellenics* [1847], or Browning's so-called "Artemis Prologizes" [1842].' It is written in blank verse. 'Perfecting' (line 136) and 'perfected' (line 201) are stressed on the first syllable.

Two pages from a manuscript are reproduced and discussed in John Hollander, 'Algernon Charles Swinburne's "At Eleusis" ', in the *Paris Review* 154 (Spring 2000) 246–51.

August

Published in the *Spectator*, 6 September 1862.

For a discussion of the motif of the orchard, 'the favourite Pre-Raphaelite refuge after 1850', see Lothar Hönnighausen's *The Symbolist Tradition in English Literature* (1988), pp. 141–2.

Keats in 'To Autumn' (1820) is Swinburne's great predecessor in descriptions of ripeness.

The metre is iambic tetrameter; the stanza rhymes *aabbab*. Lines 1–2, 13–14, and 55–6 are repetitions with variations.

A manuscript is reproduced in P. J. Croft's *Autograph Poetry in the English Language* (1973), pp. 139–40 (and facing pages).

A Christmas Carol

There was a revival of interest in Christmas carols in the mid-nineteenth century. Davies Gilbert published the first modern collection of carols in 1822; the next collector, William Sandys, published his in 1833; both men anticipated that carol singing would become extinct (see the preface to *The*

Oxford Book of Carols, 1928). But scholarly interest in them, which would prompt Thomas Wright to publish several collections of early carols; romantic medievalism, which would inspire William Morris's carols published in 1860; and the rise of Anglo-Catholicism following the decline of the Evangelical movement, all helped to revive the form as part of the 'Victorian "reinvention" of Christmas' (see the introduction to *The New Oxford Book of Carols*, 1992).

In 1884, in response to a request to reprint the poem, Swinburne indicated that his three favourite carols were William Morris's 'Masters in this hall' (published around 1860 in Edmund Sedding's *Nine Antient and Goodly Carols for the Merry Tide of Christmass*; Swinburne said it was worth '1,000,000,000 of mine'); 'As Joseph was a-walking' ('which everybody knows'); and 'I sing a mayden' (published in 1856 by Thomas Wright; 'I picked up the pamphlet by accident years ago'); see Lang, 5, 74–5).

The drawing by Rossetti which suggested the poem is presumably related to the watercolour *A Christmas Carol*, dated on the upper left side 'Xmas 1857–58', which shows a young woman playing a clavicord decorated with Christmas scenes and having her hair combed by two women.

The metre is predominantly iambic. The rhyme scheme is $a_4b_3a_4b_3c_3c_3$. The last two lines of each stanza form a variable refrain.

The Masque of Queen Bersabe

Although the story of David's adultery with Bathsheba, his sending her husband Uriah to death in war, and the public exposure of his sins by Nathan (2 Samuel 11–12), does not seem to be among the extant miracle plays in English, the subject nonetheless is part of the sacred history upon which the cycle of miracle plays is based. However, since David was seen typologically as a figure of Christ in the Middle Ages, the story tended to be evaded or allegorized. Even in later English literature, George Peele's *The Love of King David and Fair Bethsabe* has few parallels. (The drama was the subject of qualified praise by Swinburne in his essay 'Christopher Marlowe in Relation to Greene, Peele, and Lodge', *Contemporaries of Shakespeare*, [1916] 1919.) Nothing like the procession of the twenty-two women occurs in the extant miracle plays (not even the names of the women, including Bersabe, appear in the York, Chester or Towneley plays, at least). Still the cycles usually included a procession of prophets, sometimes including David. Bathsheba had a greater vogue in medieval and later art and in continental drama. For further information, see Elmer Blistein, 'David in the Drama before 1600', *The Dramatic Works of George Peele*, 1970, pp. 165–76.

The renewed appreciation and publication of medieval dramas was a recent phenomenon. The Shakespeare Society published some of the first modern editions of miracle plays ('mysteries') in 1841 (Coventry plays) and 1843–7 (Chester plays). John Hall in his *Chronicles* dated the introduction of the masque in England to 1513, and the word itself, according to the *OED*, first appears in print in 1514.

The Latin names of characters and stage directions are typical of such plays:

'PRIMUS [etc.] MILES' = 'first [etc.] soldier'; '*Paganus quidam*' = 'a pagan.'
Et percutiat eum in capite = And let him strike him in the head.
Tunc dicat NATHAN *propheta* = Then let the prophet Nathan speak.
Hìc Diabolus capiat eum = Here let the Devil take him.
Et hìc omnes cantabunt = And here everyone will sing.
Et hìc exeant, et dicat Bersabe regina = And here let them leave, and let Queen Bersabe say.
Et tunc dicant Laudamus = And then let them say the 'Laudamus'.

The vocabulary is often archaic: 'patens' (line 13) = shallow dishes; 'brast' (line 16) = burst; 'chirk' (line 28) = chirp; 'By Mahound' (line 32; cf. line 116) = By Mahomet, an oath common in miracle plays, where Mahomet is taken to be a pagan god; 'spill' (line 33) = kill; 'Poulis' (line 38) = Paul's; 'I wis' (lines 47, 56, 102) = certainly; 'rede' (lines 53, 111) = suppose; 'sow of lead' (line 67) = 'large oblong mass of metal, as obtained from the smelting-surface' (*OED* 'sow' 6a; cf. 'pig' sb. 1.7); 'latoun' (line 84) = made of latten, a metal like brass; 'shot-windows' (line 84) = windows opened on a hinge; 'scant' (line 85) = scanty supply; 'basnets' (line 86) = small, light headpiece; 'stancheons' (line 92) = upright supports; 'kirtle' (line 104) = skirt or outer petticoat; 'Termagaunt' (line 113) = 'name of an imaginary deity held in medieval Christendom to be worshipped by Muslims' (*OED*); 'to-bete' (line 114) = beat violently; 'perfay' (line 115) = by my faith (the *OED* gives this example as the first since the sixteenth century); 'it is no boot' (line 125) = it is no use.

'As red as any' (line 8) is an old comparison; it occurs, for example, in Langland, *Piers Plowman* B, Passus II, line 12. Lines 127–8 echo John 16:19.

The procession of women includes both classical and biblical names, sometimes with no particular reference or allusion implied:

HERODIAS. The wife of Herod Antipas (the son of Herod I), she seems in Swinburne's poem to have performed herself the dance that the gospels attribute to her daughter Salome, for which Herod agreed to give her the severed head of John the Baptist. The subject was very popular in the second half of the nineteenth century; Heinrich Heine's *Atta Troll* (1843) helped to introduce it.

AHOLIBAH. Along with her sister Aholah, a whore in the allegory of Ezekiel 23, to be brought to judgement. 'She doted upon the Assyrians her neighbours, captains and rulers clothed most gorgeously, horsemen riding upon horses, all of them desirable young men' (Ezekiel 23:12). See Swinburne's poem 'Aholibah', p. 214.

CLEOPATRA. Also the subject of Swinburne's poem 'Cleopatra' (1866); she committed suicide rather than be taken captive. Cf. Gautier's *Une Nuit de Cléopâtre* (1845).

ABIHAIL. The name occurs in the Old Testament (e.g. the mother of Esther, among others). Isaiah 23 contains 'the burden of Tyre'.

AZUBAH. An Old Testament name; Amorites were enemies of the Jews.

AHOLAH. See Aholibah. The city of Amalek was hostile to the Jews; see 1 Samuel 15.

AHINOAM. Two women in the Bible shared the name, a wife of Saul and a wife of David.

ATARAH. One mention in the Old Testament (1 Chronicles 2:26). Sidon is a Phoenician city.

SEMIRAMIS. Assyrian queen and heroine. See note to 'Laus Veneris'. 'Chrysophras' (line 6): 'the ancient name of a golden-green precious stone . . . It was one of the stones to which in the Middle Ages was attributed the faculty of shining in the dark' (*OED*).

HESIONE. Daughter of Laomedon, king of Troy; saved by Heracles from a sea monster. Among various medieval accounts, there is Gower's in *Confessio Amantis*.

CHRYSOTHEMIS. Daughter of Agamemnon. Samothrace is an island in the Aegean.

THOMYRIS OF SCYTHIANS. Queen who defeated Cyrus of Persia; see note to 'Satia Te Sanguine'.

HARHAS. Mentioned once at 2 Kings 22:14. The Anakim are traditionally the surviving descendants of the giants of Genesis 6. (Tennyson: 'I felt the thews of Anakim', *In Memoriam*, 1850, CIII, 31.)

MYRRHA. Daughter and lover of Cinyras, of Panchaia, fabulous island between Arabia and India. The story is told in Ovid's *Metamorphoses*, Book 10.

PASIPHAE. Cretan queen. See note to 'Phædra'.

SAPPHO. Poet from Lesbos. See notes to 'Anactoria' and 'Sapphics'.

MESSALINA. Wife of the Roman emperor Claudius; licentious and ambitious; one of the targets of Juvenal's *Satires* 6 and 10.

AMESTRIS. Wife of Xerxes I, the Persian king. In 'Notes on Designs of the Old Masters at Florence' (*Essays and Studies*, [1868] 1875, p. 320), Swinburne describes a drawing of a woman's head by Michelangelo as 'the deadlier Venus incarnate', namely such women as Lamia or Cleopatra or 'the Persian Amestris, watching the only breasts on earth more beautiful than her own cut off from her rival's living bosom'. The story is in Herodotus 9.112. Susa (Biblical Shushan) and Ecbatana are Persian cities in the time of Xerxes I.

EPHRATH. In 1 Chronicles 2:19, Ephrath replaces Azubah after her death. The valley of Rephaim makes several appearances in the Old Testament.

PASITHEA. The name of one of the Graces.

ALACIEL. The daughter of the Sultan of Babylon and eventual wife of the King of Algarve, who slept with nine men but was still taken for a virgin. The story is in Boccaccio's *Decameron*, the seventh story of the second day. She also figures in Banville's 'Nadar' of 1859.

ERIGONE. Daughter of Icarius, who was taught by Dionysus how to make wine. She killed herself when she found the body of her father, whom shepherds murdered in their drunken confusion. The story is told by Landor in the *Hellenics* (1847); it also influenced a composition by Berlioz (1841) and is represented in a painting by Gustave Moreau (1855).

Although the verse of the miracle plays is not iambic – instead interspersing an irregular number of unstressed syllables among the stressed syllables – Swinburne's verse is mainly iambic. The stanza forms of the miracle plays are numerous and include the *rime coué* of this poem (and of Tennyson's 'The Lady of Shalott', 1832).

St. Dorothy

Swinburne knew the treatment of the martyrdom of St Dorothy in Thomas Dekker and Philip Massinger's *The Virgin Martyr*, a source for his early unpublished play 'The Unhappy Revenge' (see Edward Philip Schuldt's dissertation *Four Early Unpublished Plays of Algernon Charles Swinburne*, 1976, pp. 118–24). Charles Lamb had praised *The Virgin Martyr* in his *Specimens of English Dramatic Poets* (1808), and several editions of Massinger's complete plays were published in the first half of the nineteenth century. The martyrdom is recorded in many editions of the *Golden Legend*. In 1861 Swinburne wrote to Lady Trevelyan about 'St. Dorothy': 'I wanted to try my heathen hands at a Christian subject, you comprehend, and give a pat to the Papist interest' (Lang, 1, 38).

Norman H. MacKenzie (in an essay in *Vital Candle*, edited by John S. North and Michael D. Moore, 1981) explores the context of the mid-century interest in St Dorothy and adduces, in addition to Swinburne, Christina Rossetti's 'A Shadow of Dorothea' (dated November 1858),

Burne-Jones's watercolour eventually called *Theophilus and the Angel* (1863–7), William Morris's intention to include her among the stories in his *Earthly Paradise*, and early work by Gerard Hopkins.

A 'shawm' (lines 4, 393) is a medieval oboe. 'Lampadias' (line 24) is in Pliny a kind of comet or meteor (*Natural History* 2.90). 'Lattice' (line 36) is a window of lattice-work, and 'after' (line 37) means 'behind'. 'Other some' (line 40) means 'some others'. 'Outwatch' (line 58) is the only *OED* citation for the act of outwatching, that is, watching until the object watched disappears (cf. Milton's 'Il Penseroso', line 87). 'Middle Rome' (line 86) = 'the middle of Rome', an archaic partitive usage revived, on the evidence of the *OED*, by Byron. Diomedes (line 104) wounded Aphrodite in battle during the Trojan war. A 'thalamite' (line 128) is a rower of a trireme; either Swinburne or Theophilus seems not to be using the word precisely. To 'turn again' (line 156) is to turn back. The 'Janiculum' (line 185) is the hill on which tradition locates the crucifixion of St Peter. The French in line 191 means 'Good sir, God keep you.' 'Nones' (line 282), the daily ecclesiastical office said at the ninth hour (about 3 p.m.), can in later use sometimes be said earlier, according to the *OED*, which quotes this line from Swinburne. 'Saws' (lines 283, 289) are stories or sayings; the word was obsolete though current in Shakespeare. The *OED* does not record the form 'adrouth' (line 288) from 'drouth', archaic for thirst. Although 'hag' meaning 'nightmare' was obsolete in Swinburne's time, 'hag-ridden' (line 324), 'afflicted by nightmare', was still current usage. 'Wit' in line 365 is knowledge (*OED* 11b, the last citation is from 1648). Of 'waterheads' (line 374), Norman H. MacKenzie notes in his *Poetical Works of Gerard Manley Hopkins* (1990, p. 240): 'Swinburne . . . uses it vaguely, probably for water-falls or springs.' 'Purfled' (line 382), 'having a decorative or ornamental border', was revived as an archaism in the nineteenth century. 'Wall-weed' (line 401) appears to be Swinburne's new term for the wallflower.

To my knowledge, there is no scripture that likens woman to an empty can (lines 292–3) and no 'place amorous' (line 437) in ancient or modern Rome. 'Scripture', however, once had the more general meaning of any written composition.

Line 12 may recall Tennyson, 'Sir Galahad' (1842, line 3), 'My strength is as the strength of ten.' 'Eyed like a gracious bird' (line 48) recalls Keats, 'Lamia' (1820, line 50), 'Eyed like a peacock.' 'When God saith, "Go"' (line 157) may recall Matthew 8:13, 'And Jesus said unto the centurion, Go thy way.' Line 287 recalls the leviathan of Job 41:1–2.

William Rossetti observed that ' "St. Dorothy" is Chaucerian work, even to the extent of intentional anachronisms in the designations of the personages and otherwise.' Gabalus, in particular, presumably the Roman emperor Heliogabalus (204–22), known for his cruelty, homosexual orgies, and worship of Baal, stands in anachronistically for the proconsul Sapricius under the Emperor Diocletian (245–316), who is Dorothy's traditional tormentor. (Heliogabalus appears in Gautier's *Mademoiselle de Maupin*, 1835 and *Une Nuit de Cléopâtre*, 1845; Edgar Allan Poe's 'William Wilson', 1839; and Flaubert's *L'Éducation Sentimentale*, 1845. Simeon Solomon painted a *Heliogabalus* in 1866. See also Lang, 1, 57.) Theophilus's prayer to Venus (lines 123–51) is reminiscent of Arcite's prayer to Mars in *The Knight's Tale*. Rossetti referred to the 'intimate and indwelling Chaucerism' of 'St. Dorothy'. Still, much of the archaic vocabulary is early modern English rather than Chaucerian: 'Gaditane' (line 29, of Cadiz), 'trans-shape' (line 102, transform), 'gold-ceiled' (line 138), 'downlying' (line 235), 'sheaved' (line 268, gathered into a sheaf), 'weet' (line 292, know), and 'writhled' (line 435, wrinkled) date from the sixteenth or very early seventeenth centuries, according to the evidence of the *OED*.

The poem is in rhyming couplets of iambic pentameter; the metre is more regularly iambic than Chaucer's. Sequences of sentences beginning with 'And' occur in both 'St. Dorothy' and Chaucer, but Swinburne's series tend to be longer.

The Two Dreams

The poem is an adaptation of the sixth story of the fourth day of Boccaccio's *Decameron*:

Andriula loves Gabriotto: she tells him a dream she has had and he tells her another he has had; he dies suddenly in her arms; while she is carrying him to his house with one of her servants, they are arrested by the authorities and she explains how things stand; the mayor tries to violate her, but she will not have it; her father hears this and frees her when she is found innocent; altogether refusing to live in the world any longer, she becomes a nun.

Swinburne's changes include changing Andriula and Gabriotto into lovers rather than a secretly married couple and, in general, heightening the sensuality of the landscape and of the dreams.

William Rossetti wrote that ' "The Two Dreams", from Boccaccio, is almost in equal measure Keatsian.' Keats's 'Isabella' (1820) derives from the fifth story of the fourth day of the *Decameron*.

Dante Gabriel Rossetti's painting *Bocca Baciata* (1859) takes its title from Boccaccio; his *Fiammetta* dates from 1866. He published his translation of six sonnets by Boccaccio in 1861. See Herbert G. Wright's *Boccaccio in England* (1957) for more information about the reception and influence of Boccaccio in this period. Tennyson's 'The Golden Supper' was first published in 1869.

Landor's *Pentameron* (1837) consists of imaginary conversations between Petrarch and Boccaccio over five days; on the first day, Petrarch praises Boccaccio's depiction of Andriula's dream.

In his preface to Charles Well's *Joseph and His Brethren* (1876), Swinburne referred to the 'direct aim and clear comprehension of story which are never wanting in Boccaccio' and to the 'perfect narrative power which sustains the most poetical stories even of the fifth day of the Decameron, keeping always in full view the simple prose of the event'.

'Somewhile' (line 4) is sometimes. A 'rood' (line 34) is a measure of six to eight yards. 'Prevalence' (line 74) is mastery. 'Evenwise' (line 78) means 'in like manner'. 'Scanted' in line 101 (stinted) is the first use since the seventeenth century, according to the *OED*, which describes 'impleached' (line 165) as 'poet. rare' and cites only Shakespeare, Tennyson and Swinburne. 'Mere' (line 238) is pure. 'Chuckles' (line 362) is the only *OED* citation for this usage.

The description of Ser Averardo's house may owe something to the description of Madeline's casement in Keats's 'The Eve of St. Agnes' (1820).

The metre is iambic pentameter, in rhyming couplets.

Aholibah

Aholibah, in the allegory of Ezekiel 23, is unfaithful to God and consorts first with Assyrians and then with Babylonians:

12 She doted upon the Assyrians her neighbours, captains and rulers clothed most gorgeously, horsemen riding upon horses, all of them desirable young men.

13 Then I saw that she was defiled, that they [she and her sister Aholah] took both one way,

14 And that she increased her whoredoms: for when she saw men portrayed upon the wall, the images of the Chaldeans portrayed with vermilion,

15 Girdled with girdles upon their loins, exceeding in dyed attire upon their heads, all of them princes to look to, after the manner of the Babylonians of Chaldea, the land of their nativity:

16 And as soon as she saw them with her eyes, she doted upon them, and sent messengers unto them into Chaldea.

17 And the Babylonians came to her into the bed of love, and they defiled her with their whoredom, and she was polluted with them, and her mind was alienated from them.

[. . .]

22 Therefore, O Aholibah, thus saith the Lord God; Behold, I will raise up thy

lovers against thee, from whom thy mind is alienated, and I will bring them against thee on every side;

23 The Babylonians, and all the Chaldeans, Pekod, and Shoa, and Koa, and all the Assyrians with them: all of them desirable young men, captains and rulers, great lords and renowned, all of them riding upon horses.

24 And they shall come against thee with chariots, wagons, and wheels, and with an assembly of people, which shall set against thee buckler and shield and helmet round about: and I will set judgement before them, and they shall judge thee according to their judgements.

25 And I will set my jealousy against thee, and they shall deal furiously with thee: they shall take away thy nose and thine ears; and thy remnant shall fall by the sword: they shall take thy sons and thy daughters; and thy residue shall be devoured by the fire.

26 They shall also strip thee out of thy clothes, and take away thy fair jewels.

[. . .]

40 And furthermore, that ye have sent for men to come from far, unto whom a messenger was sent; and lo, they came: for whom thou didst wash thyself, paintedst thy eyes, and deckedst thyself with ornaments,

41 And satest upon a stately bed, and a table prepared before it, whereupon thou hast set mine incense and mine oil.

42 And a voice of a multitude being at ease was with her: and with the men of the common sort were brought Sabeans from the wilderness, which put bracelets upon their hands, and beautiful crowns upon their heads.

43 Then I said unto her that was old in adulteries, Will they now commit whoredoms with her, and she with them?

Many details of phrasing are taken from Ezekiel 23: line 60 from verse 41; lines 67 and 127 from verse 42; line 84 from verse 12; line 113 from verse 15; lines 123–5 from verse 25; line 130 from verse 43; and line 138 from verse 41. Lines 86–8 are taken from Song of Solomon 2:5. Some phrases like 'creeping things' (line 62) and 'I will go up' (line 91) occur in several places in the Bible. The 'middle sea' (line 16) is the Mediterranean; the 'sackbut' (line 67) is a Renaissance trumpet.

Line 34 is reminiscent of the first line of Donne's sonnet, 'I am a little world made cunningly', as line 65 is of Pope's line 'This painted child of dirt that stinks and stings', from the 'Epistle to Dr. Arbuthnot' (line 310). 'Strange seas' (line 129) recalls Wordsworth, *The Prelude*, Book III, line 63 (1850).

The citizens in Swinburne's *Chastelard* (1865) Act 5, Scene 1, discuss a sermon about Aholah and Aholibah.

The poem is in iambic tetrameter, and the stanzas rhyme *ababb*.

Love and Sleep

The conjunction of love and sleep is traditional; cf. Pope's *Iliad*, Book 14, line 405, 'with Love and Sleep's soft Pow'r opprest'; Burns's 'On a Bank of Flowers' (1790), line 4, 'With love and sleep opprest'; Shelley's 'The Sunset' (1824) lines 24–5, 'the youth and lady mingled lay in love and sleep' and *Homeric Hymn to the Moon* (1839), line 21, 'The Son of Saturn with this glorious Power Mingled in love and sleep.'

The sonnet is Petrarchan, rhyming *abba abba cde cde*.

Madonna Mia

The phrase 'madonna mia', an address to the beloved, is not uncommon in Italian duecento poetry. Dante Gabriel Rossetti translates it as 'my lady mine' in his version of Jacobo da Lentino [Giacomo da Lentini], 'Of his lady', in 1861; he gives the Italian in a footnote.

Douglas C. Fricke compares the poem to Wordsworth's Lucy poems, especially 'Three years she grew in sun and shower', in his 1971 doctoral dissertation from Pennsylvania State University, *A Critical Study of Swinburne's Poems and Ballads* (1866).

The metre is iambic; the stanza rhymes *aaabcccb*, where *a* and *c* are trimeters and *b* is dimeter.

The King's Daughter

Swinburne's interest in ballads began in his childhood and endured throughout his life. In 1861 he began to prepare his own collection of mostly northern ballads, relying heavily on Francis Child's 1861 edition of *English and Scottish Ballads*, and also on Walter Scott's *Minstrelsy of the Scottish Border* (1802) and Peter Buchan's *Ancient Ballads and Songs of the North of Scotland* (1828); he abandoned the project shortly after. (See Anne Henry Ehrenpreis's 'Swinburne's Edition of Popular Ballads', *Publications of the Modern Language Association* 78:5, December 1963, 559–71.)

'The King's Daughter' is the first of five consecutive ballads in *Poems and Ballads*. The tradition of the literary ballad includes works by many of the major Romantic writers (Coleridge, Wordsworth, Scott, Keats) as well as Tennyson and, nearer to Swinburne's time, William Morris and Dante Gabriel Rossetti. (Swinburne praised Rossetti's 'Sister Helen' intensely, in *Essays in Studies*, [1870] 1875, p. 86.) See Anne Henry Ehrenpreis's anthology *The Literary Ballad*, 1966.

In her anthology, Ehrenpreis writes of 'The King's Daughter':

The most interesting contribution of literary balladists is what might be called the modulated refrain. As the plot unfolds, the wording of the accompanying refrain changes from stanza to stanza. The tedium of straight repetition is replaced by a shifting commentary on the action. This effect, which is not found in the traditional ballads, is generally associated with the Pre-Raphaelites, but there are earlier instances of it given in these pages, the first that I have found being in Tennyson's ballad 'The Sisters' . . .

More complicated is Swinburne's internal refrain in 'The King's Daughter', where the objects 'in the mill-water' and 'for the king's daughter' change significantly with each stanza. The coming disaster is heralded by 'A little wind in the mill-water' on the arrival of the king's son; when incest is disclosed there is 'Running rain in the mill-water'. The catalogue of bright objects associated with the king's daughter – rings of red, golden gloves, a crown of red, etc. – is abruptly interrupted in the final refrain by 'The pains of hell for the king's daughter'. The refrain does far more than help to create atmosphere; it is as essential to the story as to the sound.

For the theme of incest, compare this poem with 'The Bonny Hind', which Scott introduced apologetically in his collection as 'a fair sample of a certain class of songs and tales, turning upon incidents the most horrible and unnatural'. 'Castle Ha's Daughter' in Peter Buchan's anthology is another example.

Compare the poem's first line with the opening of Tennyson's 'The Sisters' (1832), 'We were two daughters of one race'. 'May' (lines 11, 15, 23, 33) is maiden; 'streek' (line 55) is to lay out (as a corpse).

The lines have four stresses, and the quatrains rhyme *abab*. The *b* rhymes are constant: 'mill-water' and 'king's daughter'.

After Death

Published in the *Spectator*, 24 May 1862.

Clyde K. Hyder, in 'Swinburne and the Popular Ballad', *PMLA*, 49 (March 1934), pp. 302-3, compares the language of the poem to riddling ballads; he also compares the spirit of the poem to 'The Twa Corbies'. Compare it also with that of 'The Lyke-Wake Dirge'; both ballads are in Scott's *Minstrelsy of the Scottish Border*.

Lafourcade compares the poem to Hugo, *Les Contemplations* (1856), Book 6, lines 382-90, in which the four boards of the coffin address the dead man. Recall, too, 'les quatres planches du cercueil' in which Jean Valjean is confined in *Les Misérables* (1862), Part 2, Book 8, Chapters 6 ('Entre quatre planches') and 7.

Quatrains are by far the most common ballad stanza, but couplets with refrains are not uncommon, and Francis Child has a few examples of ballads in couplets without refrains. The lines have three or four stresses.

May Janet

Brittany took on the role of a French Scotland for French Romantics, its antiquities and oral tradition providing the subject of imagination and research. Théodore-Claude-Henri Hersart de la Villemarqué's bilingual edition of Breton ballads, *Barzaz-Breiz* (1840, 1845, 1867), translated into German in 1859 and English in 1865, was enthusiastically received. See Mary-Ann Constantine's *Breton Ballads* (1996). When 'After Death' was first published in the *Spectator* (24 May 1862), its title was 'After Death (Breton)' and a footnote indicated a bogus source: 'From the *Recueil de Chants Bretons*, edited by Félicien Cossu, première série (no more published), p. 89. Paris, 1858.' In 1865, Swinburne dropped the indication of a Breton source for 'After Death'; 'May Janet' now has it instead.

Clyde K. Hyder, in 'Swinburne and the Popular Ballad', *PMLA*, 49 (March 1934), p. 305, offers the following comments on the poem:

The poem tells of two lovers who have been forbidden to marry. The girl's impetuous father, hearing of the young man's determination to have her, tears off his daughter's gown and casts her in the water. Her lover rescues her. Their subsequent journey together becomes a triumphal procession. They travel to four different towns, and at each the lover purchases something for the bride's wardrobe. The series of statements, 'The first town they came to', 'The second town they came to', is similar to a commonplace which occurs, for example, in *Johnie Scot* and *The Fause Lover*.

The quatrains consist of lines rhyming *abcb*, of either three or four stresses.

The Bloody Son

Published as 'The Fratricide' in *Once a Week*, 15 February 1862.

Clyde K. Hyder, in 'Swinburne and the Popular Ballad', *PMLA*, 49 (March 1934), p. 303, identified the original of the poem: a Finnish ballad had been translated into German in H. R. van Schröter's *Finnische Runen* (1834), and the German was then translated in all editions of Francis Child's *English and Scottish Ballads*. He also points to the influence of the versification of the ballad 'Edward, Edward' (2, 25 in the 1861 edition of Child). Compare the opening of 'The Bloody Son' with the first line of

'Lord Randal', ' "O where hae ye been, Lord Randal, my son?" ' (in Scott's *Minstrelsy of the Scottish Border*).

'Make' (line 49) is mate or companion; 'garred' (lines 57, 64), the *OED* states, is 'wrongly used for: to be amiss with, to ail'. 'Chuckie-stanes' (line 76) are rounded pebbles used in a game.

The stanzas are six and sometimes seven lines long. The second, fourth and last lines are constant. The number of stresses per line varies from two to six, and the first line of each stanza is repeated as the third. The stanzas rhyme *ababab* or *ababaab*.

The Sea-Swallows

The Till and the Tyne are rivers in Northumberland. 'Bearing-bread' and 'washing-wine' (lines 37-8, 45-6), according to Anne Henry Ehrenpreis (*The Literary Ballad*, 1966, p. 174) are 'bread and wine ritually connected with childbearing'. Weed (line 23) is a triple pun: the plant, an article of clothing and a mourning garment.

It is not always obvious who is speaking. Lines 13-14, 19, 23, 27, 31, 35, 37-40, 49-57 and 59 belong to the father, who predicts his own death when the sea-swallows return and plans to be buried with his dead grandson. Lines 15-18, 21, 25, 29, 33, 41-8, 61 and 63 belong to the daughter, who predicts her own death at the same time and plans to join her father and her son.

Ehrenpreis compares the 'revelation of a macabre situation through question and answer between parent and child' to the popular ballads 'Edward, Edward' and 'Lord Randal'.

The lines have four stresses; the quatrain rhymes *abab*.

The Year of Love

In 1860, William Caldwell Roscoe published a poem entitled 'The Year of Love' in his *Poems and Essays*.

The stanza consists of three iambic tetrameters and one iambic trimeter, rhyming *aabb*.

Dedication, 1865

Swinburne dedicated *Poems and Ballads* to his friend Edward Burne Jones (later Burne-Jones), whom he had met at Oxford where Burne-Jones, Morris, Rossetti, and others were painting Arthurian murals. When he was living in London in 1861, he saw Burne-Jones and his wife frequently ('sometimes twice or three times a day he would come in', Georgiana Burne-Jones recalled in 1905). They remained friends until Burne-Jones's death in 1898.

Yolande (line 28) appears in the French text appended to 'The Leper'. Banville in 'Loys' (1842) refers to a Yolande 'dans un ancien poëme', and there is a Yolande in Gautier's *Le Capitaine Fracasse* (1863), set in the time of Louis XIII. Juliette (line 28) appears in 'Rococo'.

The stanza and metre here are the same as those of 'Dolores'.

ATALANTA IN CALYDON

Published in March 1865 by Edward Moxon & Co., probably in an edition of 500 copies (see Lang, 2, 213). 'It was a small quarto of 125 pages (xiv + 111), bound in cream-coloured buckram boards, bevelled edges, with three gold roundels on the front cover designed by Dante Gabriel Rossetti' (John S. Mayfield, *Swinburneiana*, 1974, p. 157). The cost of the first edition was defrayed by Swinburne's father (Lang, 2, 213). A commercial second edition was published in the same year.

Composition. Swinburne seems to have begun the play in the autumn of 1863, around the time of the death of his sister Edith. He paused in his work on it when he went abroad in February 1864 (he visited Landor in Florence in late March), returning in August. Towards the end of August he went to North Cornwall for a three-month stay and finished the play there. He was reading proofs in February 1865. See Lang, 1, 114–15, Philip Henderson, *Swinburne: Portrait of a Poet* (1974), pp. 106–7, and Rooksby, pp. 88–91, 94–7.

Sources of the story. Ovid, *Metamorphoses*, Book 8, lines 273–544 and Apollodorus 1.7.7–1.8.3. Swinburne also drew on fragments of the lost tragedy *Meleager* by Euripides (included in Dindorf's 1851 *Poetae Scenici Graeci*) and fables of Hyginus, 171–4. In an appendix to *Swinburne: A Nineteenth-Century Hellene* (1931), William R. Rutland collected the principal ancient sources of the Meleager story.

The story of Atalanta's race is well known and has been the subject of paintings and works of literature, including Walter Savage Landor's 'Hippomenes and Atalanta' (1863) and William Morris's 'Atalanta's Race' (1868, though written earlier), for which Edward Burne-Jones drew eight illustrations; however, the story of the Calydonian hunt has much less frequently inspired artists or writers.

Manuscripts. Studies of the manuscripts include: Georges Lafourcade, 'Atalanta in Calydon: Le Manuscrit. – Les Sources', *Revue anglo-américaine* 3 (October 1925), pp. 34–47 and 3 (December 1925), pp. 128–33; Mario Praz, 'Il manoscritto dell' "Atalanta in Calydon"', *La Cultura* 8 (July 1929), pp. 405–15; Cecil Y. Lang, 'The First Chorus of Swinburne's *Atalanta*', *Yale University Library Gazette* 27 (January 1953), pp. 119–22; Cecil Y. Lang, 'Some Swinburne Manuscripts', *Journal of the Rutgers University Library* 18 (December 1954), pp. 1–11; Paull F. Baum, 'The Fitzwilliam Manuscript of Swinburne's "Atalanta", Verses 1038–1204', *Modern Language Review* 54 (1959); Cecil Y. Lang, '*Atalanta* in Manuscript', *Yale University Library Gazette* 37 (July 1962), pp. 19–24.

Commentary. Bruno Herlet, *Versuch eines Kommentars zu Swinburnes Atalanta* (1909) and Mario Praz, 'Le tragedie "Greche" di A. C. Swinburne e le fonti dell' "Atalanta in Calydon"', *Atene e Roma* n.s. 3 (July–August–September 1922), pp. 157–89 are the most complete.

Influences. Handel: Lang, 1, 93: 'My greatest pleasure just now is when [Mary Gordon] practises Handel on the organ . . . It crams and crowds me with old and new verses, half-remembered and half-made, which new ones will hardly come straight afterwards: but under their influence I have done some more of my Atalanta . . .'

The sea: *Atalanta* was begun and later finished by the sea. Rooksby quotes Lafourcade, 'a keen sea breeze blows through the lines of *Atalanta*', and discusses the marine influences on pages 110–11 of his biography.

Sade: Lang, 1, 125: '[Sade was] the poet, thinker, and man of the world from whom the theology of my poem is derived.' (Swinburne's theology also derives from Blake; his critical study of Blake was begun in the early 1860s, though not published until 1867.)

Shelley: *Atalanta* is, in part, Swinburne's response to *Prometheus Unbound*. The Greek structure of his drama contrasts with acts and scenes of Shelley's drama in English form, and his dark antitheism contrasts with Shelley's 'philanthropic doctrinaire views' (Lang, 1, 115). See also Terry L. Meyers, 'Shelley's Influence on *Atalanta in Calydon*', *Victorian Poetry* 14 (1976), pp. 150–4.

Elizabethan tragedy and the Bible: Much of Swinburne's diction, in *Atalanta in Calydon* as elsewhere, is archaic. One indication of this is how often the *OED* offers no citation between a seventeenth-century (or earlier) use of word in a particular sense and Swinburne's similar use. For instance, 'fleet-foot', line 106; 'perspicuous', line 221; 'disfleshed', line 301; 'disallied', line 301 (cf. Milton, *Samson Agonistes*, line 1022); 'native', line 504 (cf. *Hamlet*, Act I, Scene 2, line 47); 'loosed', line 1061; 'water-floods', line 1375; 'privy', line 1630 (cf. Milton, 'Lycidas', line 128); 'unholpen', line 1668; 'sect', line 1680 (cf. *Othello*, Act I, Scene 3); 'consuming', line 1945; 'unfasten', line 1947; 'crumblings', line 2225. Generally, allusions from Shakespeare and the Bible have been glossed, but not Shakespearean or biblical language.

Greek tragedy: The most important influences are the language, conventions and structure of Greek tragedy. As an anonymous reviewer wrote in the *Saturday Review*, 'A careful study of the Attic dramatists has enabled him to catch their manner, and to reproduce felicitously many of their terms of expression. The scholar is struck, every few lines, by some phrase which he can fancy a direct translation from the Greek . . .' (*Critical Heritage*, ed. Clyde Hyder, 1970, p. 10). Swinburne's frequent compound epithets and adjectives in 'un-' and 'dis-', use of litotes, inversions of word order, complex syntax, long periods, and omissions of subject or verb are consistent with the elevated language of Greek tragedy. Moreover, his use of the participle (e.g., 'sin done', 'things done', 'men born', 'children born', 'men dead', etc.), his naturalization of the distinctive Greek usage in which two nouns appear connected by 'of' rather than more idiomatically as an adjective with a noun (as in 'bind on thy sandals . . . over the . . . speed of thy feet' rather than 'over thy speedy feet', lines 77–8), and other features, continually suggest the influence of Greek.

Swinburne also adopts the conventions of Greek tragedy. For the kommos, see the note to the fifth episode. He employs stikhomythia, that is, dialogue delivered in alternate lines, which is frequently compressed and oblique. Elaborate invocation to deities and a messenger's speech recounting violent actions that took place offstage are also features of both *Atalanta* and Greek tragedy. However, Swinburne modifies Greek conventions when it suits him. The choral odes do not follow the Greek structure of strophe, antistrophe, and epode; he introduces more characters on stage than Greek drama allows; and his tragedy is significantly longer than the longest extant Greek tragedy.

The structure of Greek tragedy is unlike English drama, which is divided into acts and scenes. To use the traditional terms for the parts of Greek drama, *Atalanta* consists of the following sections:

Prologue (1–64)
Parodos (65–120)
First episode (121–313)
First stasimon (314–61)
Second episode (362–718)
Second stasimon (719–866)

Third episode (867-1037)
Third stasimon (1038-1204)
Fourth episode (1205-1373)
Fourth stasimon (1374-1468)
Fifth episode (1469-1808)
Fifth stasimon (1809-55)
Exodus (1856-2317).

TITLE PAGE

The Greek is taken from Euripides' *Meleager*, which survives only in fragments. The text is identical to that in Dindorf's *Poetae Scenici Graeci* (1851), where it is number 537 of Euripides' fragments and number 20 of the fragments of *Meleager*. (Rooksby notes that Dindorf's collection was given to Swinburne by schoolfriends when he left Eton. The full title is *Poetarum Scenicorum Græcorum, Aeschyli, Sophoclis, Euripidis et Aristophanis, Fabulæ Superstites et Perditarum Fragmenta*.)

The fragment does not provide enough context to be certain of the translation. Perhaps: 'The living fare well, but every man when he is dead is earth and shade: nothingness turns to nothing.' The first clause might also be translated as 'do good to them that live'.

DEDICATORY GREEK VERSES

As Swinburne writes in the dedication, he had written the first of his Greek elegies while Landor was still alive and had shown it to him; he wrote the second after his death. In the 1904 *Poems* the Greek verses are arranged on the page so that they appear to be three elegies, rather than two. This arrangement on the page is reproduced here. The few minor errors introduced into the Greek of the 1904 edition have been corrected by restoring the 1865 text.

Arthur Beatty (*Swinburne's Dramas*, 1909), William R. Rutland (*Swinburne: A Nineteenth-Century Hellene*, 1931) and Apostolos and Lilika Marmaras (in *Aeolian Harps*, ed. Fricke, 1976) have translated the Greek poems, Beatty the most accurately.

Although Swinburne's Greek has often been praised, John Churton Collins, who knew both Swinburne and Greek, describes his knowledge of Greek as very imperfect (*Life and Memoirs*, p. 49). H. Bryan Donkin recalls the story that before publication Swinburne sent the Greek elegiacs to Richard Shilleto at Cambridge, who admired them but thought them filled with errors (letter to the *Spectator*, 14 October 1911). Other classicists have found the grammar unobjectionable but the verses repetitious and empty of content, as Greek verse is not.

First page of Greek (page 242):

You have gone, turned away from the north, but the Nymphs with their sweet breath led you over the welcoming sea, filling your mouth with divine honey, lest Poseidon, hearing your melodious voice, harm you. So great a singer were you. We still mourn for you now that you are gone and long for you always. One of the Muses turning to another said, 'Look, he has gone, the best loved of all men has gone. He gathered fresh-budding garlands with his old hands and he covered his grey head with laurel, to sing some sweet song upon Sicilian harps and strings. For he varied the tunes he played on his great lyre, and often Apollo found him seated in a glen and crowned him with flowers, and gave him delightful things to say: Pan never to be forgotten and Pitys, and unhappy Corythos, and the goddess Hamadryad whom a mortal loved. He lulled Cymodameia to sleep in the chambers of the sea; he restored Agamemnon's daughter to her father; and to sacred Delphi he sent Orestes, stricken by god, distressed here and there by the hateful goddesses.'

Commentary: 'Turned away from the North' refers to Landor's residence in Italy; 'fresh-budding garlands' refer to *Heroic Idylls*, which appeared in 1863, when Landor was eighty-eight. Landor tells the story of Pan and Pitys, Corythos, the Hamadryad, and Cymodameia respectively in 'Pan and Pitys' (Latin, 1815, English, 1847), 'Corythos' (Latin, 1815, English, 1847), 'The Hamadryad' (1842), and 'Enallos and Cymodameia' (1846). Iphigenia is restored to her father Agamemnon in the afterlife in 'Shades of Agamemnon and Iphigeneia' (1836). The Furies' assault upon Orestes and his recovery are described in 'The Madness of Orestes' (1837) and 'The Prayer of Orestes' (1846). See also the commentary to 'In Memory of Walter Savage Landor'.

Second page of Greek (page 243):

You have gone away from friends and from song, to gather the flowers of gentle Persephone. You have gone, you will live no more, and never again will I sit next to you in awe, touching your hands with my devout hands. Bitter-sweet reverent awe has now again stolen over me, as I remember what I, such as I am, received from the man that you were. Never, old man, will my loving eyes take delight in your loved eyes, as I grasp, beloved old man, your right hand. Ah, dust crumbles, life crumbles: which of these passing things is less? Not dust but life. Yet you are far dearer to me than those who still live, for once you lived. I bring to you in death these things, few but from the heart; do not turn away. Take them, casting even now a gentle look. I cannot, greatly though I wish it, give you what you deserve, since I am far from where you are buried, for it is not in my power. Nor can I provide a gleaning libation of milk and honey. O that it were possible to touch you with my hands and see you once again, to tend upon your dear head with tears and libations and your holy eyes and holy body. O that I could, for this would greatly relieve my sorrow. Now far away from your grave I make my lament, and do not keen the dirge over your tomb, but I am kept apart, with tears of sorrow. Farewell to you in death; know that you are honoured by men and gods, if any god is set over those below. Farewell, old man, farewell dear father, greatest of singers we have seen, greatest of singers to come. Farewell, may you have such happiness as dead men have, peace without hatred and without love.

Third page of Greek (page 244):

When your tomb has vanished, there will be monuments to you; there will be loving memory of you when your monument has vanished. You the divine Graces mourn and Aphrodite mourns, she who took delight in the Muses' garlands and lovely dances. Never once has old age worn away holy singers. Your monument reveals this splendour. You were a mortal dear indeed to the blessed ones, and to you if to any the Nymphs gave their lovely, their final gifts, to possess. On them has brazen sleep come, and windless eternity; buried with you they share one fate. You too sleep, having come upon lovely and glorious sleep in the hollow earth, far away from your country, by the Etruscan wave of a golden stream, but still your mother land longs for you; but you keep apart, you renounced her of old, though you loved her. Sleep; blessed not wretched will you be to us. Brief is the time of mortals, and fate will master them. Gladness sometimes possesses them, grief sometimes. Many times the light harms them or the dark shrouds them when they weep, and sleep stings those who are awake. But when the eyes of the dead have fallen asleep in their graves, neither the dark nor the light of the sun will sting. No dream vision at night nor waking vision will ever be theirs when they rejoice or mourn. But all keep together one seat and abode forever, immortal instead of mortal, beautiful instead of evil.

ARGUMENT

Greek plays were supplied with the ὑπόθεσις, a summary of the action, in Alexandrian times. The argument to Milton's *Samson Agonistes* serves the same purpose.

GREEK EPIGRAPH

The text is that of Dindorf's *Poetae Scenici Graeci* (1851) and varies somewhat from modern editions. Thestia is Althaea, the daughter of Thestius. 'This,' in the first sentence, refers to the violent passion of women, the subject of the choral ode from which the passage is taken.

Let him who is not light-witted know this, by learning of the plot of burning in the fire which the reckless killer of her son, Thestia, devised, burning the tawny brand coeval with the life of her son, from the time when with a cry he came from his mother's womb until the day appointed by fate.

Prologue (lines 1–64)

Chief Huntsman.

At dawn, the chief huntsman prays to Artemis, who has sent the wild boar to ravage Aetolia. She is treble (line 4) because she is Artemis on earth, Selene in heaven, and Hecate in the underworld (cf. Horace, *Odes* III 22, line 4 and Ovid, *Metamorphoses* Book 7, lines 94, 177 and 194). 'A light for dead men and dark hours' (line 5) characterizes her under the Hecate and Selene aspects respectively, while 'a foot swift' (lines 5–6) and 'a hand . . . mortal' (lines 6–8) present her as Artemis, goddess of the hunt. At line 17, Apollo is invoked, and at line 37, the hunter returns to Artemis, for whom a sacrifice is now prepared; the Aetolian virgins (who constitute the chorus) will offer her hymns, flowers and locks of their hair.

For place-names, see the map in the appendix. Achelous and Euenus are rivers in Aetolia; Ladon is a river, and Maenalus is a mountain, in Arcadia. The struggle between Heracles and Achelous for Deianira, alluded to in lines 53–57, is recounted in Sophocles, *Trachiniae*, lines 497–530. Deianira is Meleager's sister. Euenus is wedded with the straitening sea (line 36) because it flows into a narrow part of the Corinthian gulf. The plain near the river Lelantus (line 52) is actually in Euboea; Herlet finds that the Greek geographer Strabo (10.3.6) may have led Swinburne into error.

Sometimes Swinburne's diction draws directly on Greek literature. Artemis's shafts are said to be gentler than snow or sleep (line 8) because in Homer her shafts, like those of Apollo, are described as gentle, bringing an easy death. The expression 'on the knees of gods' (line 16) is also Homeric, and lines 25–6 may recall the *Iliad*, Book 19, line 362, where the earth laughs. The laughter of the sea is mentioned in *Prometheus Bound*, line 90. In Greek and Latin, the horns of a river (line 35) refer to its branches (see *OED* 20c). Swinburne also used 'full-flowered' (line 52) in his translation of Euripides' ποιηροὺς . . . νομούς (*Cyclops*, line 61): 'full-flowered pasture-grasses' ('Notes on the Text of Shelley', *Essays and Studies*, [1869] 1875, p. 207). More generally, the opening scene resembles that of Aeschylus' *Agamemnon*, in which the watchman likewise prays to the gods.

Among English writers, Shelley most influenced Swinburne's language and imagery. Stars led at dawn into the folds of the fields of heaven (line 2, and see also line 884) recall *Prometheus Unbound* (1820) Act 4, lines 1–3 and also Shelley's 'Lines Written on Hearing the News of the Death of Napoleon' (1824), line 5; the image also derives from the 'unfolded star' of Shakespeare, *Measure for Measure* Act IV, Scene 2. The 'mistress of the months' (line 1) is similar to the 'mother of months' (line 66), an expression for the moon that Shelley uses repeatedly (see commentary on the parodos). Compare the redundant 'most dimmest' (line 20) with Shakespeare, *King Lear*, Act II, Scene 3, line 7, 'most poorest'. The appositional phrase 'All gold' (line 32) may recall the phrase in the fifth line of Milton's translation of Horace, *Odes* I 5.

The grammar is sometimes compressed and elliptical. In lines 25–36, 'let laugh' has for its subject earth, the long sea, all the winds and fountainheads, each horn of Achelous, and the green Euenus. Lines 30–2 might be rephrased as 'whose hair with salt close tresses cleaving lock to lock, all like gold, or whose breast, shuddering and like unfurrowed snow, divides the wandering wave'.

Parodos (lines 65–120)

The first stanza tells the story of Procne and Philomela; see the notes on 'Itylus'. The nightingale is 'brown bright' (line 69), Swinburne's translation of the adjective (ξουθά) that Aeschylus uses for it in *Agamemnon*, line 1142. The Maenad (line 108), Bassarid (line 108), and Bacchanal (line 113) are all votaries of Bacchus. According to the *OED*, 'Bassarid' was first used by Swinburne.

The advent of spring is being celebrated. The meadow or plain (line 66) is where the signs of spring are first evident. Lines 79–80 imply that the day is gathering in strength and the night is declining, the reverse of line 92. It is time for rural celebration, and here the oat pipes of rustic festivals are more prominent than the sophisticated lyre (line 102; cf. Milton, *Lycidas*, lines 32–4 and 88). It is also time for amorous pursuits; lines 111–12 can be glossed as 'the leaves of the tree screen the maiden from being seen by the god and leave in her sight the god pursuing'.

Artemis is the 'mother of months' (line 66), a Shelleyan expression for the moon; see *The Revolt of Islam* (1818) Canto IV, stanza 1, line 7, *Prometheus Unbound* (1820) Act 4, line 207, and 'The Witch of Atlas' (1824), line 73. 'All the pain' recalls 'all that pain' of Ceres in Milton, *Paradise Lost* Book 4, line 271. 'Fleet-foot' (line 106) echoes the ὠκύπους of Homer (an epithet of horses) and Sophocles (applied to deer in *Oedipus at Colonus*, line 1093), as well as the 'fleet-foot roe' of Shakespeare, *Venus and Adonis*, line 561.

The stanzas consist of eight lines rhyming *ababccab*, where *a* may be a single, double or a triple rhyme. Each line is tetrameter, and the feet are either iambs or anapests. This combination allows a variety of rhythmical effects, though here the anapest dominates. This variety is a feature of Greek choral lyric, which combines elements of different metrical systems within a single strophe. Occasionally Swinburne has a direct approximation of a Greek line, with stress accent replacing quantitative length. For example, Swinburne's line 'Fleeter of foot than the fleet-foot kid' (line 106) may be seen as a metrical equivalent to Aeschylus, *Seven Against Thebes*, line 229, κριμναμεναν νεφαλαν ορθοι. However, Swinburne is not attempting to imitate Greek metres but rather to bring into English poetry new rhythmical inventions inspired by Greek choral odes. See D. S. Carne-Ross, 'Jocasta's Divine Head', *Arion*, 3rd. ser. Winter 1990, pp. 138-9.

A manuscript of an early draft of the chorus is reproduced in Wise's 1919 *Bibliography*. See also Cecil Y. Lang, 'The First Chorus of Swinburne's *Atalanta*', *Yale University Library Gazette* 27 (1953), pp. 119-22.

First Episode (lines 121-313)

Chorus, Althaea.

For recollections of Greek poetry, compare 'Look you, I speak not as one light of wit' (line 201) with Aeschylus, *Agamemnon*, lines 590-3, where Clytemnestra rejects the rebuke that she had wandered in her wits. Compare the description of the destructive power of love at lines 209-10 with the choral ode on Eros in Sophocles, *Antigone*, lines 781-800. Lines 222-3 ('seeing I see not, hear / And hearing am not holpen') recall both *Prometheus Bound*, lines 447-8, and Matthew 13:13. Althaea's dream is reminiscent of Clytemnestra's dream in Aeschylus, *The Libation-Bearers*, lines 523-50; as Praz puts it, both mothers give birth to symbols of their sons' destinies.

For echoes of English literature, consider Shelley's description of hours that chase the day like a bleeding deer (*Prometheus Unbound*, 1820, Act 4, lines 73-4) in relation to 'Night, a black hound, follows the white fawn day' (line 125). 'Gall for milk' (line 155) recalls *Macbeth*, Act I, Scene 5. Praz compares lines 217-22 with Job 7:14, 'thou scarest me with dreams, and terrifiest me through visions'. 'Standing corn' (line 166) is an Old Testament phrase. 'Sweet grass' (line 168) occurs three times in William Morris, *Earthly Paradise* (1868-70; 'The Man Born to Be King', line 1503, 'The Watching of the Falcon', line 57, and 'The Land East of the Sun and West of the Moon', line 131). 'Touch of love' is from Shakespeare, *Two Gentlemen of Verona*, Act II, Scene 7, line 18. For the beaks of ships drinking death (line 271), compare the ships that 'drank death' in Shelley, 'Lines Written Among the Euganean Hills' (1824), lines 14-15.

The visit of the three Fates to Althaea in lines 242-6 is recounted in the

Fables of Hyginus, 171. Eurythemis (line 299), Althaea's mother, is the husband of Thestius and also the mother of Leda; thus the children of Leda (Castor and Pollux, Helen, Clytemnestra) are the nieces and nephews of Althaea.

Bruno Herlet suggests that there are two meanings combined in lines 135-6: first, that the least god is more than we are, asleep or awake, and second, that the least god is more than waking or even sleep (which itself is enough to destroy us in our dreams). The members of the chorus 'say well' according to Althaea (line 145) because they have just (line 144) unknowingly introduced the subject of her dream, fire.

'Ruined' (line 131) has the sense of calamity or disaster. 'North' in line 188 is the north wind (a poetic usage; see *OED* 4a, which cites Shakespeare and Shelley); 'sets', applied to a wind or current, means to have or take a direction or course (see *OED* 107a). 'Presage' (line 216) is a trochee, not an iamb. 'Salter' (line 231) is the comparative from the older adjective 'salt', now common only in phrases like 'salt water'. 'These' at line 300 refers to the gods; at line 303, 'these' may refer instead to 'such gifts'.

First Stasimon (lines 314-61)

There are several echoes of biblical passages. 'They breathed upon his mouth' (line 344) recalls the creation of Adam, Genesis 2:7. Lines 348-9 ('time for . . . a time for') resemble the parallel structure of Ecclesiastes 3:1-8. 'His speech is a burning fire' (line 354) recalls Proverbs 16:27 ('An ungodly man diggeth up evil: and in his lips there is as a burning fire'). 'Clothed with' (line 358, 'clothed with derision') is a biblical locution; compare, e.g., Ezekiel 7:27, 'clothed with desolation'.

Lines 316-17 reverses the expected description: time brings grief, but grief fades in time. Line 337 ('death beneath and above') may recall Shelley's lines from 'Death' (1824), lines 3-4, 'All around, within, beneath, / Above, is death.'

The three stanzas are of unequal length, but all rhyme *ababcdcd* . . . Each line is iambo-anapestic trimeter.

Second Episode (lines 362-718)

Meleager, Althaea, Chorus, Oeneus.

The first part of the episode is modelled on Homer, *Iliad*, Book 3, lines 161-244, where Helen identifies for Priam the Greek leaders before the walls of Troy; here, Meleager identifies for Althaea the assembled hunters (including Althaea's brothers). The comparison of the assembled fighters to rain-flakes (line 374) is the inverse of Pindar, *Pythian* 6.10–14, where he compares winter rain to an army.

Peleus (lines 390–5) is the father of Achilles and the husband of Thetis, the silver-shod (ἀργυρόπεζα in Homer) sea-nymph; Larissa is the chief city of Thessaly, where he rules.

Castor and Pollux (lines 396–425) are nephews of Althaea by her sister Leda, mother also of Helen and Clytemnestra. In the scene from the *Iliad*, Helen likewise shows particular interest in Castor and Pollux. They are Spartan; Eurotas (line 410) is a river in Sparta.

Telamon (lines 426–34) is the king of Salamis (an island in the Saronic Gulf) and a brother of Peleus. 'Twice-washed' (line 431) may have been suggested by ἀμφίρυτος, the epithet of Salamis in Sophocles, *Ajax*, line 134. He is 'vine-chapleted' (line 433) because he wore clusters of grapes around his head in honour of Salamis, rich in vines, according to a fragment surviving from Euripides' *Meleager* (Dindorf fragment 531).

Ancaeus (lines 435–9) and Cepheus (lines 439–40) are sons of Lycurgus from Tegea in Arcadia. Ancaeus may be 'girt round . . . roughly' because he was clothed in bear skin; he is 'two-edged' for fight because he fights with a two-edge battleaxe (see Apollonius Rhodius, *Argonautica* Book 1, lines 168–9).

Toxeus and Plexippus (lines 443–8), Althaea's brothers, have their left feet unsandalled; perhaps the description in Euripides' *Meleager* of the Aetolian custom to wear a sandal rather than a boot on the left foot is behind Swinburne's description. 'Unsandalled' occurs in Shelley, *Prometheus Unbound* (1820) Act 3, Scene 1, line 15 and *Prometheus Bound*, line 135; see also line 2043.

Althaea's speech (lines 466–568) begins with a warning about the just destruction (lines 471–3) of one who suffers infatuation (Atê in Greek); the furies are suggested. The 'twin-born fate' (line 471) has a particular application to Meleager: the firebrand that measures the span of his life (the δαλὸς ἥ κιξ of Aeschylus, *The Libation-Bearers*, line 608) is in his mother's control. 'Be man at one' (line 474) may be glossed 'If [or when, or should] a man be at one.' For the phrase 'use and wont' (line 478), see *OED* 'use' 8a(b), where Tennyson, *In Memoriam* XXIX.11, is cited. Althaea describes the Elysian fields as the destination of the just in lines 510–16 (see Homer, *Odyssey*, Book 4, lines 563–8); Swinburne intended her depiction of the aged just man as an allusion to Landor (Lang, 1, 115). 'Timeless' (line 532) means untimely or premature. 'Light and might communicable' (line 541) are embodied by the stars, and stars 'above the hours' (line 542) are those near the North Star which do not set. The raid of the Thessalians against the Aetolians (lines 549–58) seems to be Swinburne's invention; instead of hostile Thessalians, ancient tradition records a battle with a local tribe called the Curetes. (Herlet suggests that the Thessalians are called the mad people (line 550) because they are conflated with the Curetes of Crete, themselves associated with the Corybantes, who participate in orgiastic cults of Dionysus and Cybele.) Swinburne makes this battle the motive for Artemis's anger and her sending the boar. In lines 565–8, Althaea refers to Meleager's participation in the voyage of the Argonauts.

Meleager's speech (lines 571–621) further recounts the story of the Argonauts. To set one's mouth against something (line 572) is a biblical phrase; see Psalms 73:9. 'Reverencing' (line 578 and also line 1686), like other forms of that verb, is common in Tennyson. A Nereid (line 593) is a sea-nymph. The Symplegades are the clashing rocks that guarded the entrance at the Bosporus to the Euxine (line 613, the Black Sea). Jason succeeded in passing through by first sending ahead a dove, whose tail-feathers were nipped by the clashing of the rocks as it emerged; he then hurried through while the rocks were rebounding. 'Irremeable' (line 599) means admitting of no return, from the Latin *irremeabilis*. In English, the word was used in Dryden's *Aeneid* Book 6, line 575 and Pope's *Iliad*, Book 19, line 312. The Argonauts were on their way to Colchis (line 601) to recover the Golden Fleece. Once there, Medea (line 616), the daughter of Aeetes, the king of the region, fell in love with Jason.

'Overmuch', in Oeneus's speech (line 628), was frequently used by Browning and Morris as well as by Swinburne. The transitive use of 'abstain' (line 640) is 'rare, and probably a literary imitation of the transitive use of Latin *abstinere*', according to the *OED* (or we might hear Greek ἀπέχω).

In Althaea's response to Oeneus, she sees Meleager as 'three suns old' (line 667). This may mean either three days old or three years old (*OED*, 5), but perhaps 'blind' (line 676) suggests the former. The *OED* indicates that 'stabile' (line 687) is 'used by a few writers to express more unequivocally the etymological sense of stable' and cites this passage. Meleager's reference to 'time and the fruitful hour' recalls Shakespeare, *Macbeth* Act I, Scene 3, line 147, 'Time and the hour runs through the roughest day.'

Second Stasimon (lines 719–866)

For the description of the wings of Love (line 720) compare lines 696–7 of the cosmogony in Aristophanes's *Birds*, which Swinburne translates in 1880:

> Whence timely with season revolving again sweet Love burst out as a
> blossom,
> Gold wings glittering forth of his back, like whirlwinds gustily turning.

The 'wings of a dove' (line 720; also line 796) recall Psalms 55:6 and 68:13. In Homer's *Iliad*, Iris has feet like the wind (line 721).

'Sea-foam and the frothing of blood' (line 730) indicate Aphrodite Anadyomene, that is, Aphrodite rising from sea, having been born of the severed genitals of Uranus; see Hesiod, *Theogony*, lines 178–200. In Swinburne's 1887 *Selections*, this chorus is entitled 'Anadyomene'. She is the 'perilous goddess' of line 742.

The 'Sweet articulate words / Sweetly divided apart' (lines 751–2) that men hear are inspired by two Greek epithets: μέροψ, 'dividing the voice' or 'articulate', used of mankind in general; and ἡδυεπής, 'sweet-speaking', of particular speakers. 'Mere' (line 753) is the sea, where the 'footless herds' (*sc.* of fish) dwell.

'Shipwrecking reefs' (line 813) may be indebted to the 'shipwracking storms' of *Macbeth* Act 1, Scene 2, line 26. Compare the 'shipwrecking roar' of Tennyson, *Maud* Part 1, line 98.

The last stanza gives the story of Tyro, who loved the river Enipeus in Thessaly. She is taken in love by Poseidon in the form of Enipeus. The twins she conceived grow to kill the stepmother who abused and humiliated her. In a lost play by Sophocles on the subject, Tyro laments her hair shamefully hacked off; compare the 'rent hair' of line 855. Lines 860–1 imply that she was no longer a virginal worshipper of Artemis. 'Being mixed' (line 863) follows the Greek use of μείγνυμι for sexual intercourse (see also *OED* 4b).

The chorus consists of ten stanzas:

lines 719–28: The lines are pentameter, combining anapests and iambs, and rhyming *aabbccddee*. There is an internal rhyme after the third foot.

lines 729–36: The lines are trimeter, combining anapests and iambs, and rhyming *abcdabcd*.

lines 737–48: The lines are trimeter, combining anapests and iambs, and rhyming *abbabacdecde*.

lines 749–55: The lines are trimeter, combining anapests and iambs, and rhyming *abacbac*. In the first edition of 1865, these lines are not separated from the preceding stanza.

lines 756–61: The lines are trimeter, combining anapests and iambs, and rhyming *abcabc*.

lines 762–85: The lines are trimeter, combining anapests and iambs, and rhyming *ababcdcedfedgfbgfbagabaa*. The end of the first and last lines is 'born', which also occurs as the rhyme at lines 729 and 742.

lines 786–99: The lines are trimeter, combining anapests and iambs, and rhyming *abbabacbcbabca*. Note that lines 787–90 have the same scansion: / x x / xx / (the initial foot is a trochaic substitution for an iamb) although each of them has the caesura in a different position.

lines 800–26: The lines are trimeter, combining anapests and iambs, and rhyming *abcdabcdefdgefhghbijkjibkaa*. The end of the first and last lines is 'born'. *e* is a feminine rhyme.

lines 827–42: The lines are trimeter, combining anapests and iambs, except for the last line which is iambic dimeter (with a feminine rhyme). The rhyme scheme is *ababcdbecdfegfgf*. *e* and *f* are feminine rhymes.

lines 843–66: The lines are trimeter, combining anapests and iambs, and rhyming *abcdabcdefghefghijklijkl*. *c*, *g*, and *l* are feminine rhymes.

Third Episode (lines 867–1037)

Atalanta, Meleager, Toxeus, Plexippus, Althaea, Oeneus.

Atalanta's address to the sun, gods and the moon (Artemis, line 870) has a precedent in Prometheus's invocation of the natural elements in *Prometheus Bound*, lines 88–91. 'Just gods' is a Shakespearean phrase used by Alexander Pope in his Homeric translations (*Iliad*, Book 7, line 425, Book 23, line 750; *Odyssey*, Book 18, line 261, Book 23, line 275) and also by William Morris (*The Earthly Paradise*, 1868–70, 'The Doom of King Acrisius', lines 2180 and 2366). 'Extreme' (line 886, and also line 1072) is pronounced as a trochee, not an iamb. The golden day (line 890) is white (line 891) in the sense of bright or fortunate; see *OED* 8 and Greek λευκός. Elis (line 899) is a plain in the northwestern Peloponnesus, and the Acheloian horn (line 899) refers metonymically to Aetolia (see line 35 and the map in the appendix). Iasius (line 902), Atalanta's father, is spelled thus in Hyginus, *Fables* 70; it is also spelled 'Iasus'.

Meleager's immoderate praise of Atalanta (lines 906–16) may evoke Hippolytus's too exclusive praise of Artemis in Euripides' *Hippolytus*. The 'habit' of Atalanta's eyes is perhaps both their bearing (*OED* 4) and their outward appearance (*OED* 5c).

The contempt for manly work done by women and womanly work done by men (lines 920–2) is present in a fragment from Euripides' *Meleager*. 'What profit' (line 933) is a biblical phrase. Plexippus's lines 934–8 may recall the sacrifice of Iphigenia. Lines 941–2 are influenced by Cassandra's vision of Clytemnestra's murdering her husband Agamemnon: 'Ah, ah, keep the bull from the cow! Catching him in the cloths, with a black-horned thing she strikes!' (Aeschylus, *Agamemnon*, lines 1125–8).

Atalanta's reference to Artemis's sudden seven shafts (line 959) invokes Niobe, daughter of Tantalus (line 962), who (according to Ovid) bore seven sons and seven daughters. She boasts that she is more fertile than Leto, who bore only Artemis and Apollo. Artemis kills her daughters and Apollo her sons. The shafts are sudden because death is rapid (*OED* 6). The seven children are 'holy born' (line 962) since Tantalus was descended from Zeus.

'Loosening knees' (line 962) is a Homeric expression for dying. Herlet takes the back-blowing torch (line 973) to be part of a wedding procession; he also infers that the snows that face the first of the morning (lines 975–6) are those on mountaintops. 'Fill the dance' (line 1015) is also an imperative in Shelley, *Prometheus Unbound* (1820) Act 4, line 132. 'And no man see me more' quotes Wolsey in Shakespeare, *King Henry VIII*, Act III, Scene 2, line 227. The reinless mouths (line 1028) resemble the ἀχάλινα στόματα of Euripides, *Bacchae*, line 386. Atalanta is associated with Tegea (line 1031), a city in southeastern Arcadia, in Ovid, *Metamorphoses*, Book 8, line 317.

Oeneus's address to the head of Atalanta (line 1032) is a usage found in Greek tragedy; see also lines 2182 and 2270 (Meleager's farewell to his father and mother) and compare with lines 399, 650, 906 and 2076. 'Strike, cease not' (line 1036) resembles Tennyson, 'St. Simeon Stylites' (1842), line 178, 'Smite, shrink not.'

Third Stasimon (lines 1038–1204)

Contrast the opening lines ('Who hath given man speech?,' etc.) with Asia's words about Prometheus in Shelley, *Prometheus Unbound* (1820), Act 2, Scene 4, line 71: 'He gave man speech, and speech created thought, Which is the measure of the universe.'

Line 1062 may recall Jeremiah 51:36, 'and I will dry up her sea, and make her springs dry'. The 'weeping Seven' of line 1077 refers to the Pleiades, often represented as weeping (as in 'Anactoria', line 169) or rainy. Perhaps with Herlet we should understand the raiment (line 1077) as a cloud; see, for example, Horace, *Odes* IV 14, lines 21–2. The 'sad gods' (line 1081) indicate Hades. 'Iron heaven' (line 1086) recalls the 'brazen heaven' of Homer and Pindar. 'Fulfilled with' (line 1104) includes the archaic sense 'filled full with'. 'None' (line 1111) is perhaps to be understood as 'a nothing, a nobody': that heaven bow down to that which is insignificant in comparison to itself. The *OED* gives line 1194 as its first instance of 'over-speech', loquacity or indiscretion. The Lord's hands in Job 5:18 and Jesus Christ in Acts 9:34 are that which make whole, rather than fear (line 1198). For 'gathering thorns' (line 1202) see Matthew 7:16 and Luke 6:44.

There are seven stanzas in this choral ode, each irregularly rhymed. However, Paull F. Baum writes that 'the rhyme scheme of the stasimon is less complex or irregular than it might at first seem. The stanzas [excluding the coda, lines 1193–1204] are of unequal length: 17, 18, 29, 13, 15, 22, 41 lines respectively; within them couplets are frequent, next the *abab* pattern and *ababab*. Other simple patterns occur, mingled with these but in no set order or arrangement' ('The Fitzwilliam Manuscript of Swinburne's "Atalanta", Verses 1038–1204', *Modern Language Review* 54, 1959, p. 176). Note that the stanza breaks have been determined by reference to the 1865 text, and so the two stanzas which Baum describes as consisting of 17 and 18 lines respectively are here printed as one stanza. Because of the length of some of the stanzas, the rhyme schemes are not provided.

lines 1038–72: Lines 1038–54 are iambic pentameter, interspersed with iambic trimeter lines. Lines 1055–72 are iambic tetrameter, except for the iambic pentameter couplet at the end. There are several feminine rhymes.

lines 1073–1101: Most of the lines are iambic pentameter. Lines 1080, 1083 and 1087 are iambic tetrameter. The last line is trimeter. Two rhymes are feminine.

lines 1102–14: The lines are iambic pentameter except for the last, which is iambic hexameter.

lines 1115–29: The lines are iambic pentameter. One rhyme ('places', line 1119 and 'faces', line 1123) is feminine.

line 1130–51: Most of the lines are iambic pentameter. Lines 1135 and 1151 are iambic trimeter.

lines 1152–92: The lines are iambic pentameter, interspersed with two iambic dimeter lines and one iambic trimeter line. More often than usual, some of the feet are formed by the elision of consecutive syllables (when the first ends with a vowel and the second begins with a vowel or 'h').

lines 1193–1204: Iambic pentameter lines are interspersed with iambic trimeter lines.

Fourth Episode (lines 1205–1373)

Althaea, Herald, Chorus.

The 'warder gods' (line 1207) are represented by statues in front of the royal house, which faces east; see Aeschylus, *Agamemnon*, line 519. 'Frequent flames' (line 1211) are numerous or abundant (*OED*: somewhat archaic).

The herald's speech adapts the story of the hunt mainly from Ovid (*Metamorphoses* Book 8, lines 260–444), but with some details taken from Apollodorus (1.8.2). Acarnania (line 1233) is west of Aetolia, divided from it by the river Achelous. He mentions the participants in the following order:

Laertes (line 1235), king of the island Ithaca (and father of Odysseus).

Nestor (line 1236), king of Pylos, later the wise older statesman of the *Iliad*. Gerenian is a Homeric epithet of Nestor, derived from a city in Messenia.

Panopeus (line 1236) is named in Ovid but not elsewhere (Nestor and Toxeus are similarly included only in Ovid's account).

Cepheus and Ancaeus (line 1237) are first introduced in lines 436-9. Cepheus and Iphicles (line 1246) are not included in Ovid's narrative.

Atalanta (line 1239).

Meleager (line 1244).

Iphicles (line 1246), also called Iphiclus, is the twin brother of Heracles.

Theseus is he 'that slew the biform bull' (line 1247), the Minotaur, half-bull and half-man. See note to 'Phædra'.

Pirithous (line 1248), king of the Lapiths in Thessaly, is the close friend of Theseus.

Eurytion (line 1248), son of Actor, purified Peleus (Aeacides, line 1249) after the latter was banished with his brother Telamon for killing their half-brother Phocus. During the hunt, he is killed accidentally by Peleus (lines 1298–1304), as in Apollodorus but not in Ovid.

'Aeacides' (line 1249) means 'son of Aeacus', namely Peleus, husband of the sea nymph Thetis (and father of Achilles). He is first introduced at line 391.

Telamon (line 1250), brother of Peleus, is first introduced at line 429.

Amphiaraus (line 1252) is a seer and resident at Argos (and participant in the expedition of the seven against Thebes). His is the prophet's hand at line 1220.

'Thy mother's sons' (line 1253) are Althaea's brothers, Toxeus and Plexippus.

'Thy sister's sons' (line 1253) are Leda's sons Castor and Pollux, introduced at line 397.

Jason (line 1255) is the leader of the Argonauts; see Meleager's speech starting at line 571 for details of the expedition.

Dryas (line 1255) is the son of Ares.

Idas (line 1257) is the brother of Lynceus (line 1258).

Lynceus (line 1258), brother of Idas, 'excelled in sharpness of sight, so that he could even see things under ground', according to Apollodorus (3.10.3).

Admetus (line 1258), king of Pherae in Thessaly, is the husband of Alcestis, who sacrifices her own life for his, but is brought back to life by Heracles.

Hippasus (line 1259) is gored by the boar in Ovid, but not here.

Hyleus (line 1259) is killed by the boar in Apollodorus and here (line 1296).

Swinburne departs from Ovid mainly in order to develop the characters of his drama. Plexippus boasts that he has no need of Artemis's help at line 1266 (although seeing the boar, he does not finish saying that which he would say, line 1268); in Ovid, Ancaeus makes the boast, and it is Echio, not Plexippus, who shoots at but misses the boar. Atalanta prays to Artemis at line 1284; in Ovid, Mopsus prays for Apollo's help. Some of the description is Homeric: night coming over the eyes in death (line 1297; Homer, *Iliad*, Book 5, line 310) or the boar crashing like a tower when struck (line 1313; Homer, *Iliad*, Book 4, line 462).

'Wound' (line 1334) is perhaps the archaic form of the participle (*pace* OED 'missile', A.c.), as 'dedicate' is in line 1356. A faun (line 1355) is a rural deity like the satyr; a dryad (line 1355) is a wood-nymph. 'Melilote' (line 1350) means, literally, honey-clover. 'Laud ye the gods' (line 1362) resembles 'Laud we the gods' in Shakespeare, *Cymbeline*, Act V, Scene 5, line 475.

Fourth Stasimon (lines 1374–1468)

The opening of this choral ode resembles the Euripidean escape prayer, as at *Bacchae*, lines 402–16 or *Hippolytus*, lines 732–51, which may have little relevance to the plot.

The chorus first invokes Bacchus (whose 'yellow hair', line 1381, Shelley mentions in line 66 of his translation of Euripides' *Cyclops*, line 1840). Then Artemis is invoked in line 1400; Iamus, her 'brother's seed' (line 1425) is the son of Apollo and Euadne. In distress Euadne abandoned him among violets (line 1417); later, he became a prophet and the founder of a people; see Pindar, *Olympian* 6.28–73. Orion (line 1465), in one story (Homer, *Odyssey*, Book 5, lines 121–4), is killed by Artemis because he was loved by Eos.

'Reluctant' (line 1402) includes the sense of struggling and entangling. The 'indissoluble zone' (line 1467) is the maiden girdle, ζώνη, which is not to be loosened before marriage (cf. Homer, *Odyssey*, Book 11, line 245).

The metre is trochaic tetrameter, interspersed with a few lines of trochaic trimeter. The rhyme is irregular. As is common in English poetry, the trochaic lines are catalectic, that is, they lack the final unstressed syllable.

Fifth Episode (lines 1469–1808)

Messenger, Chorus, Althaea.

Several passages are reminiscent of Greek tragedy. Lines 1589–92 and 1674–5 on the irreplaceability of brothers (as opposed to sons) strongly recalls Antigone's assertion in Sophocles, *Antigone*, lines 905–12. The gnomic sentiment of line 1728 is similar to Sophocles, *Electra*, line 860, 'Death is the common lot.' Althaea's dark, visionary language at lines 1786–90 resembles Cassandra's in Aeschylus's *Agamemnon* (lines 1256, 1309, etc.). Finally, the expression of the chorus at line 1806 over the destruction of the royal house may recall Aeschylus, *The Libation-Bearers*, line 50, 'O destruction of the house.' Virgil is the source of another classical reminiscence: line 1754 recalls the famous simile in *Aeneid* Book 6, lines 309–10 about the throng of the dead, 'thick as the leaves of the forest that at autumn's first frost falls' (cf. Milton, *Paradise Lost* Book 1, lines 301–3). The pun of Meleager and grievous huntsman (lines 1498–9) is found in a fragment of Euripides' *Meleager* (Dindorf fragment 525: μελέα ἄγρα = unhappy hunt).

'It is here' occurs in Shakespeare, *Hamlet* Act V, Scene 2, line 302: 'It is here, Hamlet. Hamlet, thou art slain.' Althaea's desire not to be in sight of the sun may draw on Shakespeare, *Macbeth* Act V, Scene 5, line 49, 'I 'gin to be aweary of the sun', or Sophocles, *Oedipus the King*, lines 1425–31, where Oedipus cannot be suffered to remain in the presence of the sun. To shoot out lips in scorn (line 1537) recalls Psalms 22:7. 'Relume' (line 1584), to relight or rekindle, is used by Shakespeare, *Othello* Act V, Scene 2, line 13. 'Facile feet' (line 1635) are unconstrained, running freely (*OED*, 'facile' 3). For the son to eat and drink his mother as one who breaks bread (line 1679) recalls and distorts the Christian eucharist. 'Sect' (line 1680) is a cutting from a plant, used figuratively here and in Shakespeare, *Othello*, Act I, Scene 3. 'Creeping things, / Abominable' (lines 1730–1) echoes the language of Ezekiel 8:10 and elsewhere.

Lines 1524–31 might be glossed as follows: when dawn touches night, the sky sees three things happen: lips and eyelids laugh, redden, and divide; breasts heave; and undulation of hair colours the clouds. 'He' in line 1593 is Plexippus; in line 1595 'this man' is Toxeus. Herlet expands line 1655: '[stains that are] no festal stains [of delightful wine but stains] of undelightful wine.' Lines 1714–15 would have the more natural order 'beasts that slay, divide, and feed, [and so] cheer themselves'. Eurythemis (line 1740) is Althaea's mother; see line 299. 'Put back' in Althaea's question at line 1803, 'shall I put back my day?' may mean either 'to set back to an earlier position' (and thus pretend not to know what she must do) or 'to defer, put off' (and so delay the day that will destroy her as well as her son).

Fifth Stasimon (lines 1809–1855)

The choral ode consists of two stanzas, mostly rhymed irregularly. The first is composed of iambic tetrameter lines (with occasional elisions or anapaestic substitutions). The second consists of eight lines of iambo-anapaestic trimeter followed by ten lines of iambo-anapestic pentameter in rhyming couplets with an internal rhyme after the third foot.

Exodus (lines 1856–2317)

Althaea, Chorus, Second Messenger, Meleager, Atalanta, Oeneus.

A variety of Greek idioms is present in this scene. Line 1897, 'what word has flown out at thy mouth?', recalls the Homeric expression, 'What word has escaped the barrier of thy teeth?' The address to the head, 'O holy head of Œneus' (line 2182), is a form of address common in Greek tragedy; see also line 1032. The metaphor of the ploughed field for the womb (lines 2215–17) is Greek (see, for example, Sophocles, *Oedipus the King*, lines 1211–12 and 1256–7). For 'the doorway of thy lips' (line 1899), compare both Euripides, *Hippolytus*, line 882 ('the gates of my mouth') and Psalms 141:3 ('door of my lips').

Althaea's line 1893 may ironically recall the New Testament pronouncement 'This is my beloved Son, in whom I am well pleased' (Matthew 3:17, etc.). Althaea's name was 'a healing' (line 1944) because Swinburne, like Greek poets, freely puns with names and invokes here the verb ἀλθαίνω, to heal. Her final words (line 1947) are similar to Jocasta's in *Oedipus the King* (lines 1071–2) as she goes to her death.

The kommos begins at line 1948 and continues to line 2181. A kommos is a lament which takes the form of a lyric, or semi-lyric, dialogue between the chorus and one or more actors. (For more information, see the appendix 'Kommos, Threnos, Amoibaion' in H. D. Broadhead, *The Persae of Aeschylus*, Cambridge, 1960.) Swinburne adapts this Greek dramatic convention. His kommos consists of three parts:

1) lines 1948–83. The chorus splits into two companies, as in the kommos of Aeschylus, *Seven Against Thebes*, lines 875–960. Each semichorus delivers a stanza of six rhyming (*abccab*) lines of iambo-anapestic trimeter.

2) lines 1984–2026. The second messenger's lines are not lyric. He

speaks in sets of three unrhymed iambic lines, dividing the semichorus's rhymed (*abab*) four-line stanza into two sections. Their lines are also iambo–anapestic trimeter. This is perhaps modelled on the *amoibaion* in Aeschylus, *Agamemnon*, lines 1072–1177, the scene in which Cassandra's passionate lyrical utterances alternate with the iambic lines of the chorus, until they are caught up by her excitement and adopt her lyrical metre.

3) lines 2027–181. The lyrical exchange between the semichorus, Meleager, Atalanta and Oeneus occurs in five-line stanzas rhyming *ababb* and consisting of four iambo–anapestic dimeters followed by an iambo–anapestic hexameter (the stanza of Swinburne's 'Hertha', 1871). This four-part kommos was probably influenced by the three-part kommos of Aeschylus, *The Libation-Bearers*, lines 306–478. In particular, Oeneus's wish that Meleager had died more nobly (lines 2112–16) echoes Orestes' wish for a more noble death for Agamemnon at lines 345–53.

Mario Praz compares the third part of the kommos and the rest of the play to the end of Euripides' *Hippolytus*. Here Meleager is brought dying on the scene, is comforted by Atalanta, and forgives his mother who has killed him. In Euripides' play, Hippolytus is brought dying on the scene, is comforted by Artemis, and forgives his father who has killed him.

The language of the kommos is elevated. The 'blast of . . . God' (line 2046) recalls Job 4:9 ('by the blast of God they perish'). 'Without lyre' (line 2070) recalls the dirge described in Aeschylus, *Agamemnon*, line 990. The 'dreamer of dreams' (line 2078) is a phrase from Deuteronomy 13:1, 3, 5. 'Winter's wan daughter' (line 2104) is a kenning for snow. The Pontic sea (line 2126) and the Hellespont (line 2121) occur in Shakespeare, *Othello*, Act III, Scene 3, line 453. 'Pine' is used metonymically for a ship at line 2155 (and earlier at line 590), as *pinus* can be used for ship (or mast or oar) in Latin poetry.

Meleager's battle with the men of Thrace (lines 2107–12) is presumably a battle fought by the Argonauts on the way to Colchis. The enmity of the Thracians and the Lemnian women (who receive the Argonauts) is recorded in Apollonius Rhodius, *Argonautica*, Book 1, line 678.

The place-names can be located on the map in the appendix. 'Acroceraunian snow' (line 2121) refers to the mountains on the west shore of Epirus. The phrase occurs in Shelley's 'Prologue to Hellas' (1822) line 173, and his 'Arethusa' (1824) opens with a couch of snows in the Acroceraunian mountains. These mountains are the western limit of the Greek world, and the Hellespont (line 2121, 'the ford of the fleece of gold', now the Dardanelles) is the eastern limit. The Hellespont derives its name from Helle (line 2151), who fled with her brother Phrixos through it on a ram with golden fleece. Helle fell and was drowned in the sea (*pontos*); Phrixos reached Colchis on the golden ram. The Chersonese (line 2125) is the peninsula forming the northern side of the Hellespont, which connects the Aegean with the Propontis (line 2141, the Sea of Marmara), and thus is in fact south of the Bosporus (cf. line 2126). Swinburne, like most English poets except for Milton, uses the spelling 'Bosphorus' (βόσπορος in Greek).

Meleager's last words (line 2309) may be indebted to John 9:4, 'the night cometh, when no man can work'.

The six-line stanza at the end of the play rhymes *ababab*. The lines are iambo-anapestic trimeter. Lines 2314–15 may recall these lines from Blake's *Europe* (Plate 2, lines 28–9):

> And who shall bind the infinite with an eternal band,
> To compass it with swaddling bands?

Swinburne quotes these lines in his study *William Blake* (1868, but written earlier).

APPENDIX 1:

Notes on Poems and Reviews

Swinburne responded to hostile reviews of *Poems and Ballads* with this pamphlet, published in 1866 by Hotten. See Lang, 1, 192–8 for a full discussion.

The text was edited by Clyde Kenneth Hyder in *Swinburne Replies* (Syracuse University Press, 1966); he also annotated it. The text and notes are reprinted with the kind permission of the Syracuse University Press.

Notes on Poems and Reviews

'Je pense sur ces satires comme Épictète: 'Si l'on dit du mal de toi, et qu'il soit véritable, corrige-toi; si ce sont des mensonges, ris-en.' J'ai appris avec l'âge à devenir bon cheval de poste; je fais ma station, et ne m'embarrasse pas des roquets qui aboient en chemin.' – *Frédéric le Grand.*

'Ignorance by herself is an awkward lumpish wench; not yet fallen into vicious courses, nor to be uncharitably treated: but Ignorance and Insolence, these are, for certain, an unlovely Mother and Bastard!' – *Carlyle.*

It is by no wish of my own that I accept the task now proposed to me. To vindicate or defend myself from the assault or the charge of men whom, but for their attacks, I might never have heard of, is an office which I, or any writer who respects his work, cannot without reluctance stoop to undertake. As long as the attacks on my book – I have seen a few, I am told there are many – were confined within the usual limits of the anonymous press, I let them pass without the notice to which they appeared to aspire. Sincere or insincere, insolent or respectful, I let my assailants say out their say unheeded.

I have now undertaken to write a few words on this affair, not by way of apology or vindication, of answer or appeal. I have none such to offer. Much of the criticism I have seen is as usual, in the words of Shakspeare's greatest follower,

> As if a man should spit against the wind;
> The filth returns in's face.[1]

In recognition of his fair dealing with me in this matter, I am bound by my own sense of right to accede to the wish of my present publisher, and to the wishes of friends whose advice I value, that on his account, if not on mine, I should make some reply to the charges brought against me – as far as I understand them. The work is not fruitful of pleasure, of honour, or of profit; but, like other such tasks, it may be none the less useful and necessary. I am aware that it cannot be accomplished without some show of egotism; and I am perforce prepared to incur the consequent charge of arrogance. The office of commentator on my own works has been forced upon me by circumstances connected with the issue and re-issue of my last book. I am compelled to look sharply into it, and inquire what passage, what allusion, or what phrase can have drawn down such sudden thunder from the serene heavens of public virtue. A mere libeller I have no wish to encounter; I leave it to saints to fight with beasts at Ephesus or nearer.[2] 'For in these strifes, and on such persons, it were as wretched to affect a victory, as it is unhappy to be committed with them.'[3]

Certain poems of mine, it appears, have been impugned by judges, with or without a name, as indecent or as blasphemous. To me, as I have intimated, their verdict is a matter of infinite indifference: it is of equally small moment to me whether in such eyes as theirs I appear moral or immoral, Christian or pagan. But, remembering that science must not scorn to investigate animalcules and infusoria,[4] I am ready for once to play the anatomist.

With regard to any opinion implied or expressed throughout my book, I desire that one thing should be remembered: the book is dramatic, many-faced, multifarious; and no utterance of enjoyment or despair, belief or unbelief, can properly be assumed as the assertion of its author's personal feeling or faith. Were each poem to be accepted as the deliberate outcome and result of the writer's conviction, not mine alone but most other men's verses would leave nothing behind them but a sense of cloudy chaos and suicidal contradiction. Byron and Shelley, speaking in their own persons, and with what sublime effect we know, openly and insultingly mocked and reviled what the English of their day held most sacred. I have not done this. I do not say that, if I chose, I would not do so to the best of my power; I do say that hitherto I have seen fit to do nothing of the kind.

It remains then to inquire what in that book can be reasonably offensive to the English reader. In order to resolve this problem, I will not fish up any of the ephemeral scurrilities born only to sting if they can, and sink as they must. I will take the one article that lies before me; the work (I admit) of an enemy, but the work (I acknowledge) of a gentleman. I cannot accept it as accurate; but I readily and gladly allow that it neither contains nor suggests anything false or filthy. To him therefore, rather than to another,

I address my reclamation. Two among my poems, it appears, are in his opinion 'especially horrible'.[5] Good. Though the phrase be somewhat 'inexpressive', I am content to meet him on this ground. It is something – nay, it is much – to find an antagonist who has a sufficient sense of honesty and honour to mark out the lists in which he, the challenger, is desirous to encounter the challenged.

The first, it appears, of these especially horrible poems is *Anactoria*. I am informed, and have not cared to verify the assertion, that this poem has excited, among the chaste and candid critics of the day or hour or minute, a more vehement reprobation, a more virtuous horror, a more passionate appeal, than any other of my writing. Proud and glad as I must be of this distinction, I must yet, however reluctantly, inquire what merit or demerit has incurred such unexpected honour. I was not ambitious of it; I am not ashamed of it; but I am overcome by it. I have never lusted after the praise of reviewers; I have never feared their abuse; but I would fain know why the vultures should gather here of all places; what congenial carrion they smell, who can discern such (it is alleged) in any rose-bed. And after a little reflection I do know, or conjecture. Virtue, as she appears incarnate in British journalism and voluble through that unsavoury organ, is something of a compound creature –

> A lump neither alive nor dead,
> Dog-headed, bosom-eyed, and bird-footed;[6]

nor have any dragon's jaws been known to emit on occasion stronger and stranger sounds and odours. But having, not without astonishment and disgust, inhaled these odours, I find myself at last able to analyse their component parts. What my poem means, if any reader should want that explained, I am ready to explain, though perplexed by the hint that explanation may be required. What certain reviewers have imagined it to imply, I am incompetent to explain, and unwilling to imagine. I am evidently not virtuous enough to understand them. I thank Heaven that I am not. *Ma corruption rougirait de leur pudeur.*[7] I have not studied in those schools whence that full-fledged phœnix, the 'virtue' of professional pressmen, rises chuckling and crowing from the dunghill, its birthplace and its death-bed. But there are birds of alien feather, if not of higher flight; and these I would now recall into no hencoop or preserve of mine, but into the open and general field where all may find pasture and sunshine and fresh air: into places whither the prurient prudery and the virulent virtue of pressmen and prostitutes cannot follow; into an atmosphere where calumny cannot speak, and fatuity cannot breathe; in a word, where backbiters and imbeciles become impossible. I neither hope nor wish to change the unchangeable, to purify the impure. To conciliate them, to vindicate myself in their eyes, is a task which I should not condescend to attempt, even were I sure to accomplish.

In this poem I have simply expressed, or tried to express, that violence of affection between one and another which hardens into rage and deepens into despair. The key-note which I have here touched was struck long since by Sappho. We in England are taught, are compelled under penalties to learn, to construe, and to repeat, as schoolboys, the imperishable and incomparable verses of that supreme poet; and I at least am grateful for the training. I have wished, and I have even ventured to hope, that I might be in time competent to translate into a baser and later language the divine words which even when a boy I could not but recognise as divine. That hope, if indeed I dared ever entertain such a hope, I soon found fallacious. To translate the two odes and the remaining fragments of Sappho is the one impossible task; and as witness of this I will call up one of the greatest among poets. Catullus 'translated'[8] – or as his countrymen would now say 'traduced' – the Ode to Anactoria – Εἰς Ἐρωμέναν: a more beautiful translation there never was and will never be; but compared with the Greek, it is colourless and bloodless, puffed out by additions and enfeebled by alterations. Let any one set against each other the two first stanzas, Latin and Greek, and pronounce. (This would be too much to ask of all of my critics; but some among the journalists of England may be capable of achieving the not exorbitant task.) Where Catullus failed I could not hope to succeed; I tried instead to reproduce in a diluted and dilated form the spirit of a poem which could not be reproduced in the body.

Now, the ode Εἰς Ἐρωμέναν – the 'Ode to Anactoria' (as it is named by tradition) – the poem which English boys have to get by heart – the poem (and this is more important) which has in the whole world of verse no companion and no rival but the Ode to Aphrodite, has been twice at least translated or 'traduced'. I am not aware that Mr. Ambrose Phillips,[9] or M. Nicolas Boileau-Despréaux, was ever impeached before any jury of moralists for his sufficiently grievous offence. By any jury of poets both would assuredly have been convicted. Now, what they did I have not done. To the best (and bad is the best) of their ability, they have 'done into' bad French and bad English the very words of Sappho. Feeling that although I might do it better I could not do it well, I abandoned the idea of translation – ἔκων ἀέκοντί γε θυμῷ.[10] I tried, then, to write some paraphrase of the fragment which the Fates and the Christians have spared us. I have not said, as Boileau and Phillips have, that the speaker sweats and swoons at sight of her favourite by the side[11] of a man. I have abstained from touching on such details, for this reason: that I felt myself incompetent to give adequate expression in English to the literal and absolute words of Sappho; and would not debase and degrade them into a viler form. No one can feel more deeply than I do the inadequacy of my work. 'That is not Sappho,' a friend said once to me. I could only reply, 'It is as near as I can come; and no man can come close to her.' Her remaining verses are the supreme success, the final achievement, of the poetic art.

But this, it may be, is not to the point. I will try to draw thither; though the descent is immeasurable from Sappho's verse to mine, or to any man's. I have striven to cast my spirit into the mould of hers, to express and represent not the poem but the poet. I did not think it requisite to disfigure the page with a foot-note wherever I had fallen back upon the original text. Here and there, I need not say, I have rendered into English the very words of Sappho. I have tried also to work into words of my own some expression of their effect: to bear witness how, more than any other's, her verses strike and sting the memory in lonely places, or at sea, among all loftier sights and sounds – how they seem akin to fire and air, being themselves 'all air and fire';[12] other element there is none in them. As to the angry appeal against the supreme mystery of oppressive heaven, which I have ventured to put into her mouth at that point only where pleasure culminates in pain, affection in anger, and desire in despair – as to the 'blasphemies'* against God or Gods of which here and elsewhere I stand accused, – they are to be taken as the first outcome or outburst of foiled and fruitless passion recoiling on itself. After this, the spirit finds time to breathe and repose above all vexed senses of the weary body, all bitter labours of the revolted soul; the poet's pride of place is resumed, the lofty conscience of invincible immortality in the memories and the mouths of men.

What is there now of horrible in this? the expressions of fierce fondness, the ardours of passionate despair? Are these so unnatural as to affright or disgust? Where is there an unclean detail? where an obscene allusion? A writer as impure as my critics might of course have written, on this or on any subject, an impure poem; I have not. And if to translate or paraphrase Sappho be an offence, indict the heavier offenders who have handled and rehandled this matter in their wretched versions of the ode. Is my poem more passionate in detail, more unmistakable in subject? I affirm that it is less; and what I affirm I have proved.

---

* As I shall not return to this charge of 'blasphemy', I will here cite a notable instance of what does seem permissible in that line to the English reader. (I need not say that I do not question the right, which hypocrisy and servility would deny, of author and publisher to express and produce what they please. I do not deprecate, but demand for all men freedom to speak and freedom to hear. It is the line of demarcation which admits, if offence there be, the greater offender and rejects the less – it is this that I do not understand.) After many alternate curses and denials of God, a great poet talks of Christ 'veiling his horrible Godhead', of his 'malignant soul', his 'godlike malice'.[13] Shelley outlived all this and much more; but Shelley wrote all this and much more. Will no Society for the Suppression of Common Sense – no Committee for the Propagation of Cant – see to it a little? or have they not already tried their hands at it and broken down? For the poem which contains the words above quoted continues at this day to bring credit and profit to its publishers – Messrs. Moxon and Co.

Next on the list of accusation stands the poem of *Dolores*. The gist and bearing of this I should have thought evident enough, viewed by the light of others which precede and follow it. I have striven here to express that transient state of spirit through which a man may be supposed to pass, foiled in love and weary of loving, but not yet in sight of rest; seeking refuge in those 'violent delights' which 'have violent ends',[14] in fierce and frank sensualities which at least profess to be no more than they are. This poem, like *Faustine*, is so distinctly symbolic and fanciful that it cannot justly be amenable to judgement as a study in the school of realism. The spirit, bowed and discoloured by suffering and by passion (which are indeed the same thing and the same word), plays for a while with its pleasures and its pains, mixes and distorts them with a sense half-humorous and half-mournful, exults in bitter and doubtful emotions –

Moods of fantastic sadness, nothing worth.[15]

It sports with sorrow, and jests against itself; cries out for freedom and confesses the chain; decorates with the name of goddess, crowns anew as the mystical Cotytto,[16] some woman, real or ideal, in whom the pride of life with its companion lusts is incarnate. In her lover's half-shut eyes, her fierce unchaste beauty is transfigured, her cruel sensual eyes have a meaning and a message; there are memories and secrets in the kisses of her lips. She is the darker Venus, fed with burnt-offering and blood-sacrifice; the veiled image of that pleasure which men impelled by satiety and perverted by power have sought through ways as strange as Nero's before and since his time; the daughter of lust and death, and holding of both her parents; Our Lady of Pain, antagonist alike of trivial sins and virtues; no Virgin, and unblessed of men; no mother of the Gods or God; no Cybele, served by sexless priests or monks, adored of Origen or of Atys[17]; no likeness of her in Dindymus or Loreto[18].

The next act in this lyrical monodrame of passion represents a new stage and scene. The worship of desire has ceased; the mad commotion of sense has stormed itself out; the spirit, clear of the old regret that drove it upon such violent ways for a respite, healed of the fever that wasted it in the search for relief among fierce fancies and tempestuous pleasures, dreams now of truth discovered and repose attained. Not the martyr's ardour of selfless love, an unprofitable flame that burnt out and did no service – not the rapid rage of pleasure that seemed for a little to make the flesh divine, to clothe the naked senses with the fiery raiment of faith; but a stingless love, an innocuous desire. 'Hesperia', the tenderest type of woman or of dream, born in the westward 'islands of the blest',[19] where the shadows of all happy and holy things live beyond the sunset a sacred and a sleepless life, dawns upon his eyes a western dawn, risen as the fiery day of passion goes down, and risen where it sank. Here, between moonrise and sunset, lives the love that is gentle and faithful, neither giving too much nor asking – a bride rather than a mistress, a sister rather than a bride. But not at once, or not for ever, can the past be killed and buried; hither also the temptress follows her flying prey, wounded and weakened, still fresh from the fangs of passion; the cruel hands, the amorous eyes, still glitter and allure. *Qui a bu boira*:[20] the feet are drawn back towards the ancient ways. Only by lifelong flight, side by side with the goddess that redeems, shall her slave of old escape from the goddess that consumes: if even thus one may be saved, even thus distance the bloodhounds.

This is the myth or fable of my poem; and it is not without design that I have slipped in, between the first and the second part, the verses called *The Garden of Proserpine*, expressive, as I meant they should be, of that brief total pause of passion and of thought, when the spirit, without fear or hope of good things or evil, hungers and thirsts only after the perfect sleep. Now, what there is in all this unfit to be written – what there is here indecent in manner or repulsive in matter – I at least do not yet see; and before I can see it, my eyes must be purged with the euphrasy and rue[21] which keep clear the purer eyes of professional virtue. The insight into evil of chaste and critical pressmen, their sharp scent for possible or impossible impurities, their delicate ear for a sound or a whisper of wrong – all this knowledge 'is too wonderful and excellent for me; I cannot attain unto it.'[22] In one thing, indeed, it seems I have erred: I have forgotten to prefix to my work the timely warning of a great poet and humorist:–

> J'en préviens les mères des familles,
> Ce que j'écris n'est pas pour les petites filles
> Dont on coupe le pain en tartines; mes vers
> Sont des vers de jeune homme.[23]

I have overlooked the evidence which every day makes clearer, that our time has room only for such as are content to write for children and girls. But this oversight is the sum of my offence.

It would seem indeed as though to publish a book were equivalent to thrusting it with violence into the hands of every mother and nurse in the kingdom as fit and necessary food for female infancy. Happily there is no fear that the supply of milk for babes will fall short of the demand for some time yet. There are moral milkmen enough, in all conscience, crying their ware about the streets and by-ways; fresh or stale, sour or sweet, the requisite fluid runs from a sufficiently copious issue. In due time, perhaps, the critical doctors may prescribe a stronger diet for their hypochondriac patient, the reading world; or that gigantic *malade imaginaire* called the public may rebel against the weekly draught or the daily drug of MM.

Purgon and Diafoirus.[24] We, meanwhile, who profess to deal neither in poison nor in pap, may not unwillingly stand aside. Let those read who will, and let those who will abstain from reading. *Caveat emptor*. No one wishes to force men's food down the throats of babes and sucklings. The verses last analysed were assuredly written with no moral or immoral design; but the upshot seems to me moral rather than immoral, if it must needs be one or the other, and if (which I cannot be sure of) I construe aright those somewhat misty and changeable terms.

These poems thus disposed of are (I am told) those which have given most offence and scandal to the venal virtue of journalism. As I have not to review my reviewers, I need not be at pains to refute at length every wilful error or unconscious lie which a workman that way inclined might drag into light. To me, as to all others who may read what I write, the whole matter must continue to seem too pitiable and trivial to waste a word or thought on it which we can help wasting. But having begun this task, I will add yet a word or two of annotation. I have heard that even the little poem of *Faustine* has been to some readers a thing to make the scalp creep and the blood freeze. It was issued with no such intent. Nor do I remember that any man's voice or heel was lifted against it when it first appeared, a new-born and virgin poem, in the *Spectator* newspaper for 1862. Virtue, it would seem, has shot up surprisingly in the space of four years or less – a rank and rapid growth, barren of blossom and rotten at root. *Faustine* is the reverie of a man gazing on the bitter and vicious loveliness of a face as common and as cheap as the morality of reviewers, and dreaming of past lives in which this fair face may have held a nobler or fitter station; the imperial profile may have been Faustina's, the thirsty lips a Mænad's, when first she learnt to drink blood or wine, to waste the loves and ruin the lives of men; through Greece and again through Rome she may have passed with the same face which now comes before us dishonoured and discrowned. Whatever of merit or demerit there may be in the verses, the idea that gives them such life as they have is simple enough: the transmigration of a single soul, doomed as though by accident from the first to all evil and no good, through many ages and forms, but clad always in the same type of fleshly beauty. The chance which suggested to me this poem was one which may happen any day to any man – the sudden sight of a living face which recalled the well-known likeness of another dead for centuries: in this instance, the noble and faultless type of the elder Faustina,[25] as seen in coin and bust. Out of that casual glimpse and sudden recollection these verses sprang and grew.

Of the poem in which I have attempted once more to embody the legend of Venus and her knight, I need say only that my first aim was to rehandle the old story in a new fashion. To me it seemed that the tragedy began with the knight's return to Venus – began at the point where hitherto it had seemed to leave off. The immortal agony of a man lost after all repentance – cast down from fearful hope into fearless despair – believing in Christ and bound to Venus – desirous of penitential pain, and damned to joyless pleasure – this, in my eyes, was the kernel and nucleus of a myth comparable only to that of the foolish virgins,[26] and bearing the same burden. The tragic touch of the story is this: that the knight who has renounced Christ believes in him; the lover who has embraced Venus disbelieves in her. Vainly and in despair would he make the best of that which is the worst – vainly remonstrate with God, and argue on the side he would fain desert. Once accept or admit the least admixture of pagan worship, or of modern thought, and the whole story collapses into froth and smoke. It was not till my poem was completed that I received from the hands of its author the admirable pamphlet of Charles Baudelaire on Wagner's *Tannhäuser*. If any one desires to see, expressed in better words than I can command, the conception of the mediæval Venus which it was my aim to put into verse, let him turn to the magnificent passage in which M. Baudelaire describes the fallen goddess,[27] grown diabolic among ages that would not accept her as divine. In another point, as I then found, I concur with the great musician and his great panegyrist. I have made Venus the one love of her knight's whole life, as Mary Stuart of Chastelard's; I have sent him, poet and soldier, fresh to her fierce embrace. Thus only both legend and symbol appear to me noble and significant. Light loves and harmless errors must not touch the elect of heaven or of hell. The queen of evil, the lady of lust, will endure no rival but God; and when the vicar of God rejects him, to her only can he return to abide the day of his judgment in weariness and sorrow and fear.

These poems do not seem to me condemnable, unless it be on the ground of bad verse; and to any charge of that kind I should of course be as unable as reluctant to reply. But I certainly was even less prepared to hear the batteries of virtue open fire in another quarter. Sculpture I knew was a dead art, buried centuries deep out of sight, with no angel keeping watch over the sepulchre; its very grave-clothes divided by wrangling and impotent sectaries, and no chance anywhere visible of a resurrection. I knew that belief in the body was the secret of sculpture, and that a past age of ascetics could no more attempt or attain it than the present age of hypocrites; I knew that modern moralities and recent religions were, if possible, more averse and alien to this purely physical and pagan art than to the others; but how far averse I did not know. There is nothing lovelier, as there is nothing more famous, in later Hellenic art, than the statue of Hermaphroditus. No one would compare it with the greatest works of Greek sculpture. No one would lift Keats on a level with Shakespeare. But the Fates have allowed us to possess at once Othello and Hyperion, Theseus and Hermaphroditus. At Paris, at Florence, at Naples, the delicate divinity of this work has always drawn towards it the eyes of artists and poets.* A creature at once foul and dull enough to extract from a sight so lovely, from a thing so noble, the faintest, the most fleeting idea of impurity, must be, and must remain, below comprehension and below remark. It is incredible that the meanest of men should derive from it any other than the sense of high and grateful pleasure. Odour and colour and music are not more tender or more pure. How favourite and frequent a vision among the Greeks was this of the union of sexes in one body of perfect beauty, none need be told. In Plato the legend has fallen into a form coarse, hard, and absurd.[28] The theory of God splitting in two the double archetype of man and woman, the original hermaphrodite which had to get itself bisected into female and male, is repulsive and ridiculous enough. But the idea thus incarnate, literal or symbolic, is merely beautiful. I am not the first who has translated into written verse this sculptured poem: another before me, as he says, has more than once 'caressed it with a sculptor's love'.[29] It is, indeed, among statues as a lyric among tragedies; it stands below the Niobe as Simonides below Æschylus, as Correggio beneath Titian. The sad and subtle moral of this myth, which I have desired to indicate in verse, is that perfection once attained on all sides is a thing thenceforward barren of use or fruit; whereas the divided beauty of separate woman and man – a thing inferior and imperfect – can serve all turns of life. Ideal beauty, like ideal genius, dwells apart, as though by compulsion; supremacy is solitude. But leaving this symbolic side of the matter, I cannot see why this statue should not be the text for yet another poem. Treated in the grave and chaste manner as a serious 'thing of beauty',[30] to be for ever applauded and enjoyed, it can give no offence but to the purblind and the prurient. For neither of these classes have I ever written or will I ever write. 'Loathsome and abominable' and full of 'unspeakable foulnesses'[31] must be that man's mind who could here discern evil; unclean and inhuman the animal which could suck from this mystical rose of ancient loveliness the foul and rancid juices

---

* Witness Shelley's version:–

> 'A sexless thing it was, and in its growth
> It seemed to have developed no defect
> Of either sex, yet all the grace of both;
> In gentleness and strength its limbs were decked;
> The bosom lightly swelled with its full youth,
> The countenance was such as might select
> Some artist, that his skill should never die,
> Imaging forth such perfect purity.'

Witch of Atlas, st. xxxvi.

But Shelley had not studied purity in the school of reviewers. It is well for us that we have teachers able to enlighten our darkness, or Heaven knows into what error such as he, or such as I, might not fall. We might even, in time, come to think it possible to enjoy the naked beauty of a statue or a picture without any virtuous vision behind it of a filthy fancy: which would be immoral.

of an obscene fancy. It were a scavenger's office to descend with torch or
spade into such depths of mental sewerage, to plunge or peer into subter-
ranean sloughs of mind impossible alike to enlighten or to cleanse.

I have now gone over the poems which, as I hear, have incurred most
blame; whether deservedly or not, I have shown. For the terms in which
certain critics have clothed their sentiments I bear them no ill-will: they
are welcome for me to write unmolested, as long as they keep to simple
ribaldry. I hope it gives them amusement; I presume it brings them profit;
I know it does not affect me. Absolute falsehood may, if it be worth while,
draw down contradiction and disproof; but the mere calling of bad names
is a child's trick, for which the small fry of the press should have a child's
correction at the hands of able editors; standing as these gentlemen ought
to do in a parental or pedagogic relation to their tender charges. They have,
by all I see and hear, been sufficiently scurrilous – one or two in particular.

> However, from one crime they are exempt;
> They do not strike a brother, striking *me*.[32]

I will only throw them one crumb of advice in return; I fear the alms will
be of no avail, but it shall not be withheld:–

> Why grudge them lotus-leaf and laurel,
>   O toothless mouth or swinish maw,
> Who never grudged you bells and coral,
>   Who never grudged you troughs and straw?
>
> Lie still in kennel, sleek in stable,
>   Good creatures of the stall or sty;
> Shove snouts for crumbs below the table;
>   Lie still; and rise not up to lie.[33]

To all this, however, there is a grave side. The question at issue is wider
than any between a single writer and his critics, or it might well be allowed
to drop. It is this: whether or not the first and last requisite of art is to give
no offence; whether or not all that cannot be lisped in the nursery or
fingered in the schoolroom is therefore to be cast out of the library; whether
or not the domestic circle is to be for all men and writers the outer limit
and extreme horizon of their world of work. For to this we have come; and
all students of art must face the matter as it stands. Who has not heard it
asked, in a final and triumphant tone, whether this book or that can be read
aloud by her mother to a young girl? whether such and such a picture can
properly be exposed to the eyes of young persons? If you reply that this is
nothing to the point, you fall at once into the ranks of the immoral. Never

till now, and nowhere but in England, could so monstrous an absurdity rear for one moment its deformed and eyeless head. In no past century were artists ever bidden to work on these terms; nor are they now, except among us. The disease, of course, afflicts the meanest members of the body with most virulence. Nowhere is cant at once so foul-mouthed and so tight-laced as in the penny, twopenny, threepenny, or sixpenny press. Nothing is so favourable to the undergrowth of real indecency as this overshadowing foliage of fictions, this artificial network of proprieties. *L'Arioste rit au soleil, l'Arétin ricane à l'ombre.*[34] The whiter the sepulchre without, the ranker the rottenness within.[35] Every touch of plaster is a sign of advancing decay. The virtue of our critical journals is a dowager of somewhat dubious antecedents: every day that thins and shrivels her cheek thickens and hardens the paint on it; she consumes more chalk and ceruse than would serve a whole courtful of crones. 'It is to be presumed,' certainly, that in her case 'all is not sweet, all is not sound.'[36] The taint on her fly-blown reputation is hard to overcome by patches and perfumery. Literature, to be worthy of men, must be large, liberal, sincere; and cannot be chaste if it be prudish. Purity and prudery cannot keep house together. Where free speech and fair play are interdicted, foul hints and vile suggestions are hatched into fetid life. And if literature indeed is not to deal with the full life of man and the whole nature of things, let it be cast aside with the rods and rattles of childhood. Whether it affect to teach or to amuse, it is equally trivial and contemptible to us; only less so than the charge of immorality. Against how few really great names has not this small and dirt-encrusted pebble been thrown! A reputation seems imperfect without this tribute also: one jewel is wanting to the crown. It is good to be praised by those whom all men should praise; it is better to be reviled by those whom all men should scorn.

Various chances and causes must have combined to produce a state of faith or feeling which would turn all art and literature 'into the line of children'.[37] One among others may be this: where the heaven of invention holds many stars at once, there is no fear that the highest and largest will either efface or draw aside into its orbit all lesser lights. Each of these takes its own way and sheds its proper lustre. But where one alone is dominant in heaven, it is encircled by a pale procession of satellite moons, filled with shallow and stolen radiance. Thus, with English versifiers now, the idyllic form is alone in favour. The one great and prosperous poet of the time has given out the tune, and the hoarser choir takes it up. His highest lyrical work remains unimitated, being in the main inimitable. But the trick of tone which suits an idyl is easier to assume; and the note has been struck so often that the shrillest songsters can affect to catch it up. We have idyls good and bad, ugly and pretty; idyls of farm and the mill; idyls of the dining-room and the deanery; idyls of the gutter and the gibbet. If the

Muse of the minute will not feast with 'gig-men'[38] and their wives, she must mourn with costermongers and their trulls. I fear the more ancient Muses are guests at neither house of mourning nor house of feasting.[39]

For myself, I begrudge no man his taste or his success; I can enjoy and applaud all good work, and would always, when possible, have the workman paid in full. There is much excellent and some admirable verse among the poems of the day: to none has it given more pleasure than to me, and from none, had I been a man of letters to whom the ways were open, would it have won heartier applause. I have never been able to see what should attract men to the profession of criticism but the noble pleasure of praising. But I have no right to claim a place in the silver flock of idyllic swans. I have never worked for praise or pay, but simply by impulse, and to please myself; I must therefore, it is to be feared, remain where I am, shut out from the communion of these. At all events, I shall not be hounded into emulation of other men's work by the baying of unleashed beagles. There are those with whom I do not wish to share the praise of their praisers. I am content to abide a far different judgment:–

> I write as others wrote
> On Sunium's height.[40]

I need not be over-careful to justify my ways in other men's eyes; it is enough for me that they also work after their kind, and earn the suffrage, as they labour after the law, of their own people. The idyllic form is best for domestic and pastoral poetry. It is naturally on a lower level than that of tragic or lyric verse. Its gentle and maidenly lips are somewhat narrow for the stream and somewhat cold for the fire of song. It is very fit for the sole diet of girls; not very fit for the sole sustenance of men.

When England has again such a school of poetry, so headed and so followed, as she has had at least twice before, or as France has now; when all higher forms of the various art are included within the larger limits of a stronger race; then, if such a day should ever rise or return upon us, it will be once more remembered that the office of adult art is neither puerile nor feminine, but virile; that its purity is not that of the cloister or the harem; that all things are good in its sight, out of which good work may be produced. Then the press will be as impotent as the pulpit to dictate the laws and remove the landmarks of art; and those will be laughed at who demand from one thing the qualities of another – who seek for sermons in sonnets and morality in music. Then all accepted work will be noble and chaste in the wider masculine sense, not truncated and curtailed, but outspoken and full-grown; art will be pure by instinct and fruitful by nature, no clipped and forced growth of unhealthy heat and unnatural air; all baseness and all triviality will fall off from it, and be forgotten; and no one will then need to assert, in defence of work done for the work's sake, the simple laws of his art which no one will then be permitted to impugn.

A. C. SWINBURNE.

Explanatory Notes (Clyde Hyder)

[bold numbers refer to note numbers inserted in Swinburne's text]

1. As . . . face. John Webster, *The White Devil*, III. 2. 149–50.

2. Beasts at Ephesus. I Cor. 15:32.

3. 'For . . . them.' In Ben Jonson's 'To the Reader', at the conclusion of *The Poetaster*.

4. Infusoria. The passage anticipates the stance of *Under the Microscope*.

5. 'Especially horrible.' Quoted from the *London Review*, XIII (4 August 1866), 130.

6. A lump . . . bird-footed. Shelley's *The Witch of Atlas*, XI. 7–8.

7. *Ma corruption . . . pudeur*. The statement that 'my depravity would blush at their modesty' neatly fits the context. If the French is a quotation, the source is undiscovered.

8. Catullus 'translated'. In Catullus, LI. Latin *traducere*, 'to translate', also means 'to misrepresent'. Swinburne was fond of recalling the Italian equation of *traduttóre* and *traditóre*.

9. Ambrose Philips, as the name is usually written (*c.* 1675–1749), in 'A Fragment from Sappho', and Nicolas Boileau-Despréaux (1636–1711) in *Traité du sublime*, chap. VIII, a translation of Longinus's treatise, are referred to here.

10. The Greek quotation is from the *Iliad*, IV. 43: 'Of mine own will, yet with reluctant mind,' cited by Swinburne himself as the equivalent of the Homeric phrase (Lang, IV, 230).

11. By the side. Swinburne's letter to W. M. Rossetti of 13 October 1866 mentions his wish to change to this reading (Lang, I, 200).

12. 'All air and fire.' Michael Drayton's phrase in regard to Marlowe, in his 'To My Most Dearly-Loved Friend Henry Reynolds, Esquire, of Poets and Poesy'.

13. The quotations are from Shelley's *Queen Mab*, VII. 164, 172, 180. Moxon and Co., the publishers of *Queen Mab*, published *Poems and Ballads* before it was transferred to Hotten.

14. 'Violent . . . ends.' *Romeo and Juliet*, Act II, Scene 6, line 9.

15. Moods . . . worth. Matthew Arnold, 'To a Gypsy Child by the Seashore', line 18.

16. Cotytto. A Thracian goddess the nature of whose rites suggests identification with the originally Phrygian Cybele.

17. Origen (185–254), important Christian theologian, is mentioned as a type of the religious eunuch along with the mythical Atys, who, driven mad by the mother-goddess Cybele, emasculated himself (Swinburne knew the account in Catullus, LXIII). The corybantes and priests of Cybele also became eunuchs.

18. On Dindymus, a mountain in Phrygia, stood an early sanctuary of Cybele. In Loreto, in central Italy, was a church reputed to contain the Virgin's house, originally in Nazareth but said to have been brought thence by angels. At one time Loreto was regarded as 'the Christian Mecca'.

19. 'Islands of the blest' was used by Byron (*Don Juan*, III, line 700), in the poem beginning, 'The isles of Greece . . .' Byron's editors cite the Greek for 'the blessed isles' (Hesiod's *Works and Days*, line 171), interpreted as the Cape Verde islands or the Canaries. The name Hesperia was of course used for the western land, Italy, in Vergil's *Aeneid*, III, line 163.

20. The French for 'Who has drunk will drink' is apparently proverbial. [Balzac, *Le Père Goriot*, Part III, and *La Cousine Bette*, chapters 30 and 98.]

21. Euphrasy and rue. Cf. *Paradise Lost*, XI, line 414.

22. 'Is . . . it.' *The Book of Common Prayer* gives this reading for Psalm 139:6.

23. Théophile Gautier, *Albertus*, XCVIII: 'I warn the mothers of families that I am not writing for little girls, for whom one makes bread and butter; my verses are a young man's verses.'

24. MM. Purgon and Diafoirus are characters in Molière's *Le Malade imaginaire*.

25. The elder Faustina was the wife of the Emperor Antoninus Pius and the mother of the younger Faustina, who married her cousin Marcus Aurelius. Legend is less kind to the characters of the two women than sober history.

26. Foolish virgins. Matt. 25:1 ff.

27. The fallen goddess . . . divine. See, for instance, *Œuvres complètes de Charles Baudelaire*, ed. M. Jacques Crepet (Paris, 1925), II, pp. 215–16, 220, 226.

28. In Plato . . . absurd. In the *Symposium*.

29. More than once '. . . sculptor's love'. Though the phrasing quoted by Swinburne has not been found in Shelley, both *The Witch of Atlas* and 'Lines Connected with Epipsychidion' refer to 'that sweet marble monster of both sexes'. Chapter IX of Gautier's *Mademoiselle de Maupin*, a work Swinburne greatly admired, has much to say of the ancient piece of sculpture. [The quotation has been traced to Gautier's review of a play entitled *Fragoletta* in his *Histoire de l'art dramatique en France depuis vingt-cinq ans* (1859). See Catherine Maxwell, 'Swinburne, Gautier, and the Louvre Hermaphrodite', *Notes and Queries* 40:1 (March 1993), pp. 49–50.]

30. The words quoted are, of course, from the first line of Keats's *Endymion*; the following words sound like a reminiscence from the 'Ode on a Grecian Urn', line 26: 'For ever warm and still to be enjoy'd.'

31. The phrases 'loathsome and horrible', 'nameless and abominable', and 'unspeakable foulnesses' were used in John Morley's unsigned critique of *Poems and Ballads* in the *Saturday Review*, XXII (4 August 1866), pp. 145–47.

32. 'However . . . me.' From Landor's 'Appendix to the *Hellenics*', *Poems*, ed. Stephen Wheeler (London, 1935), III (*Complete Works*, XV), 236, lines 47–8.

33. In *A Swinburne Library*, p. 32, Wise quotes 'the lines as Swinburne first wrote them':

> A Query
>
> Why should you grudge me lyre and laurel,
>   O toothless mouth, O soundless maw?
> I never grudged you bell and coral,
>   I never grudged you troughs and straw.
>
> Lie still in kennel, snug in stable,
>   Good creatures of the stall or sty;
> Shove snouts for crumbs beneath the table;
>   Lie still; and rise not up to lie.

34. Ariosto (1474–1533), the great Italian poet most renowned for *Orlando Furioso*, 'laughs in the sun'; Aretino (1492–1556), some of whose works are obscene, 'sniggers in the shade'. Though the antithesis seems characteristic of Hugo's style, the lines have not been found in Hugo or other French authors.

35. The whiter . . . within. Cf. Matt. 23:27.

36. 'It . . . sound.' From Ben Jonson's song from *Epicæne, or The Silent Woman* (Act I, scene 1) beginning, 'Still to be neat, still to be dressed.'

37. 'Line' refers to standard of life or course of conduct.

38. The *OED* cites Carlyle's *Miscellanies* as using 'gig-man' in the sense of 'one whose respectability is measured by his keeping a gig; . . . a "Philistine".'

Swinburne's description fitted poems like Buchanan's 'Liz' and 'Nell', and Buchanan considered the passage aimed at him. But was it? One might with equal plausibility suppose that in referring to 'idyls of the . . . deanery' Swinburne was thinking of Patmore's *Angel in the House*. Since other poems, now forgotten, may have fitted descriptions like this or 'idyls of the gutter and the gibbet', one must distinguish between suspicion and certainty.

39. House . . . feasting. Cf. Eccl. 7:2.

40. I . . . height. From Landor's *Poems*, ed. Wheeler, III (*Collected Works*, XV), p. 277, in 'Poems on Books and Writers'.

APPENDIX 2:

Map of places in Atalanta in Calydon

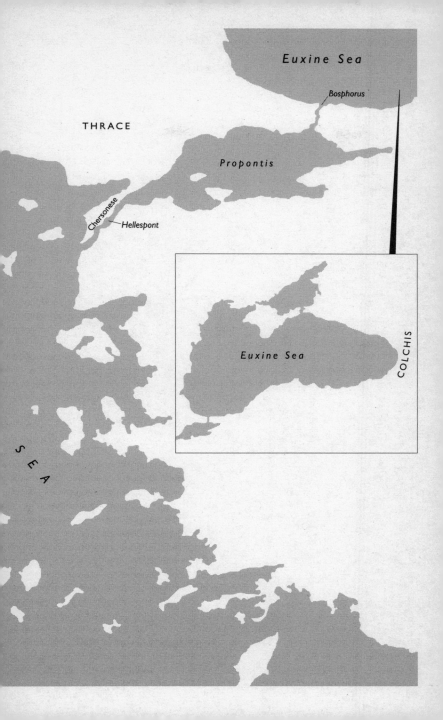

INDEX OF TITLES AND FIRST LINES

READ MORE IN PENGUIN

In every corner of the world, on every subject under the sun, Penguin represents quality and variety – the very best in publishing today.

For complete information about books available from Penguin – including Puffins, Penguin Classics and Arkana – and how to order them, write to us at the appropriate address below. Please note that for copyright reasons the selection of books varies from country to country.

In the United Kingdom: Please write to *Dept. EP, Penguin Books Ltd, Bath Road, Harmondsworth, West Drayton, Middlesex UB7 ODA*

In the United States: Please write to *Consumer Sales, Penguin Putnam Inc., P.O. Box 12289 Dept. B, Newark, New Jersey 07101-5289.* VISA and MasterCard holders call 1-800-788-6262 to order Penguin titles

In Canada: Please write to *Penguin Books Canada Ltd, 10 Alcorn Avenue, Suite 300, Toronto, Ontario M4V 3B2*

In Australia: Please write to *Penguin Books Australia Ltd, P.O. Box 257, Ringwood, Victoria 3134*

In New Zealand: Please write to *Penguin Books (NZ) Ltd, Private Bag 102902, North Shore Mail Centre, Auckland 10*

In India: Please write to *Penguin Books India Pvt Ltd, 11 Community Centre, Panchsheel Park, New Delhi 110017*

In the Netherlands: Please write to *Penguin Books Netherlands bv, Postbus 3507; NL-1001 AH Amsterdam*

In Germany: Please write to *Penguin Books Deutschland GmbH, Metzlerstrasse 26, 60594 Frankfurt am Main*

In Spain: Please write to *Penguin Books S. A., Bravo Murillo 19, 1° B, 28015 Madrid*

In Italy: Please write to *Penguin Italia s.r.l., Via Benedetto Croce 2, 20094 Corsico, Milano*

In France: Please write to *Penguin France, Le Carré Wilson, 62 rue Benjamin Baillaud, 31500 Toulouse*

In Japan: Please write to *Penguin Books Japan Ltd, Kaneko Building, 2-3-25 Koraku, Bunkyo-Ku, Tokyo 112*

In South Africa: Please write to *Penguin Books South Africa (Pty) Ltd, Private Bag X14, Parkview, 2122 Johannesburg*

READ MORE IN PENGUIN

POETRY LIBRARY

Blake	Selected by W. H. Stevenson
Browning	Selected by Daniel Karlin
Burns	Selected by Angus Calder and William Donnelly
Byron	Selected by A. S. B. Glover
Clare	Selected by Geoffrey Summerfield
Coleridge	Selected by Richard Holmes
Donne	Selected by John Hayward
Hardy	Selected by David Wright
Housman	Introduced by John Sparrow
Keats	Selected by John Barnard
Kipling	Selected by Craig Raine
Lawrence	Selected by Keith Sagar
Pope	Selected by Douglas Grant
Shelley	Selected by Isabel Quigly
Tennyson	Selected by W. E. Williams
Wordsworth	Selected by Nicholas Roe
Yeats	Selected by Timothy Webb

READ MORE IN PENGUIN

A CHOICE OF CLASSICS

Francis Bacon	**The Essays**
Aphra Behn	**Love-Letters between a Nobleman and His Sister**
	Oroonoko, The Rover and Other Works
George Berkeley	**Principles of Human Knowledge/Three Dialogues between Hylas and Philonous**
James Boswell	**The Life of Samuel Johnson**
Sir Thomas Browne	**The Major Works**
John Bunyan	**Grace Abounding to The Chief of Sinners**
	The Pilgrim's Progress
Edmund Burke	**A Philosophical Enquiry into the Origin of our Ideas of the Sublime and Beautiful**
	Reflections on the Revolution in France
Frances Burney	**Evelina**
Margaret Cavendish	**The Blazing World and Other Writings**
William Cobbett	**Rural Rides**
William Congreve	**Comedies**
Cowley/Waller/Oldham	**Selected Poems**
Thomas de Quincey	**Confessions of an English Opium Eater**
	Recollections of the Lakes
Daniel Defoe	**A Journal of the Plague Year**
	Moll Flanders
	Robinson Crusoe
	Roxana
	A Tour Through the Whole Island of Great Britain
	The True-Born Englishman
John Donne	**Complete English Poems**
	Selected Prose
Henry Fielding	**Amelia**
	Jonathan Wild
	Joseph Andrews
	The Journal of a Voyage to Lisbon
	Tom Jones
George Fox	**The Journal**
John Gay	**The Beggar's Opera**

READ MORE IN PENGUIN

A CHOICE OF CLASSICS

Oliver Goldsmith	**The Vicar of Wakefield**
Gray/Churchill/Cowper	**Selected Poems**
William Hazlitt	**Selected Writings**
George Herbert	**The Complete English Poems**
Thomas Hobbes	**Leviathan**
Samuel Johnson	**Gabriel's Ladder**
	History of Rasselas, Prince of Abissinia
	Selected Writings

Samuel Johnson/
  James Boswell
	**A Journey to the Western Islands of
	  Scotland and The Journal of a Tour of
	  the Hebrides**

Matthew Lewis	**The Monk**
John Locke	**An Essay Concerning Human Understanding**
Andrew Marvell	**Complete Poems**
Thomas Middleton	**Five Plays**
John Milton	**Complete Poems**
	Paradise Lost
Samuel Richardson	**Clarissa**
	Pamela
Earl of Rochester	**Complete Works**
Richard Brinsley Sheridan	**The School for Scandal and Other Plays**
Sir Philip Sidney	**Arcadia**
Christopher Smart	**Selected Poems**
Adam Smith	**The Wealth of Nations (Books I–III)**
Tobias Smollett	**Humphrey Clinker**
	Roderick Random
Edmund Spenser	**The Faerie Queene**
Laurence Sterne	**The Life and Opinions of Tristram Shandy**
	A Sentimental Journey Through France and Italy
Jonathan Swift	**Complete Poems**
	Gulliver's Travels
Thomas Traherne	**Selected Poems and Prose**
Henry Vaughan	**Complete Poems**

READ MORE IN PENGUIN

A CHOICE OF CLASSICS

READ MORE IN PENGUIN

A CHOICE OF CLASSICS

READ MORE IN PENGUIN

A CHOICE OF CLASSICS

READ MORE IN PENGUIN

A CHOICE OF CLASSICS